CALVIN AND THE BIBLE

During the past several decades a growing number of scholars have come to appreciate the importance of studying John Calvin's interpretive work as a commentator on Scripture in addition to his better-known writings on theology. In this volume ten essays by scholars specializing in Calvin's exegetical methods examine the approaches and themes Calvin emphasized when he interpreted major portions of Scripture. These essays focus on Calvin's work in his biblical commentaries with appropriate cross-referencing to his other writings, including his sermons. A concluding essay synthesizes the main features of what has gone before to present an overall view of John Calvin as an interpreter and commentator on Holy Scripture. An appreciation of Calvin's exegetical labors and his work as a biblical commentator is now recognized as a key element in Calvin scholarship.

DONALD K. MCKIM is Academic and Reference editor for Westminster John Knox Press. He is author and editor of over twenty-five books including the *Cambridge Companion*s to *Martin Luther* (2003) and *John Calvin* (2004).

D0863396

CALVIN AND THE BIBLE

EDITED BY

DONALD K. MCKIM

CAMBRIDGE
UNIVERSITY PRESS

CAMBRIDGE UNIVERSITY PRESS

Cambridge, New York, Melbourne, Madrid, Cape Town, Singapore, São Paulo

Cambridge University Press
The Edinburgh Building, Cambridge CB2 2RU, UK

Published in the United States of America by Cambridge University Press, New York

www.cambridge.org
Information on this title: www.cambridge.org/9780521547123

First published 2006

Printed in the United Kingdom at the University Press, Cambridge

A catalogue record for this book is available from the British Library

Library of Congress Cataloguing in Publication data

Calvin and the Bible / Donald K. McKim, editor.
p. cm.
Includes bibliographical references and index.
ISBN-13: 978-0-521-83827-6 (hardback)
ISBN-10: 0-521-83827-4 (pbk.)
ISBN-13: 978-0-521-54712-3 (hardback)
ISBN-10: 0-521-54712-1 (pbk.)
1. Bible – Criticism, interpretation, etc. – History – 16th century.
2. Calvin, Jean, 1509–1564. I. McKim, Donald K. II. Title.
BS500.C27   2006
220.6092–dc22
2005026194
ISBN-13 978-0-521-83827-6 hardback
ISBN-10 0-521-83827-4 hardback
ISBN-13 978-0-521-54712-3 paperback
ISBN-10 0-521-54712-1 paperback

Dedicated to
I. John Hesselink
Superb Calvin scholar and valued friend

Contents

Notes on contributors

RAYMOND A. BLACKETER is senior pastor of the Neerlandia Christian Reformed Church, Neerlandia, Alberta, Canada. He is the author of *The School of God: Pedagogy and Rhetoric in Calvin's Interpretation of Deuteronomy.*

WULFERT DE GREEF heads an organization promoting Reformation studies in the Netherlands. He is the author of *The Writings of John Calvin: An Introductory Guide* and is working on a study of Calvin as an interpreter of the Psalms.

DARLENE K. FLAMING is Associate Professor of Christianity at Mercer University, Macon, Georgia.

GARY NEAL HANSEN is Assistant Professor of Church History at the University of Dubuque Theological Seminary.

R. WARD HOLDER is Assistant Professor of Theology at St. Anselm College, Manchester, New Hampshire. He is the author of *John Calvin and the Grounding of Interpretation: Calvin's First Commentaries* (Leiden: E. J. Brill, forthcoming).

WILHELMUS H. TH. MOEHN is a pastor in the Netherlands and author of *God Calls Us to His Service: The Relation Between God and His Audience in Calvin's Sermons on Acts.*

BARBARA PITKIN is Acting Assistant Professor in the Department of Religious Studies at Stanford University. She is the author of *What Pure Eyes Could See: Calvin's Doctrine of Faith in Its Exegetical Context.*

SUSAN SCHREINER is Associate Professor of the History of Christianity and Theology at the University of Chicago Divinity School. She is the author of *Where Shall Wisdom Be Found? Interpretations of Job Against the Perspectives of Medieval and Modern Joban Interpretations.*

DAVID C. STEINMETZ is Amos Ragan Kearns Professor of the History of Christianity at Duke University Divinity School. Among his many books is *Calvin in Context*.

PETE WILCOX is Rector of St. Paul's Church at The Crossing, Walsall, West Midlands, United Kingdom and a member of the International Congress for Calvin Research.

RANDALL C. ZACHMAN is Associate Professor of Reformation Studies in the Department of Theology at the University of Notre Dame. He is the author of *John Calvin as Teacher, Pastor, and Theologian: The Shape of His Writings and Thought*.

Preface

A common perception of John Calvin (1509–1564) is that he was a rigid logician and systematic theologian of the Reformation period. While it is true that Calvin presented Christian theology in a more organized or "systematic" form than Luther, it is also true that there is much more to his theological understandings than is found within the pages of his *magnum opus*, the *Institutes of the Christian Religion*.

The past several decades have focused more attention on Calvin's biblical interpretation as found in his commentaries. A growing number of scholars have now contributed to the increasing recognition of the importance of studying Calvin's interpretive work as a commentator on Scripture. To recognize the issues, conversations, questions, and conclusions Calvin drew from his exegetical work on virtually all biblical books is to gain a much wider and deeper appreciation for the nature of his biblical and theological understandings than has been possible before. Scholars will continue to reflect on the relation of Calvin's interpretation of biblical texts to the development of his theology as a whole. But an appreciation of his exegetical labors and his work as a biblical commentator is now recognized as a key element in Calvin scholarship.

This book provides a study of Calvin as a biblical interpreter and commentator on Scripture. The following chapters are written by Calvin specialists who have studied Calvin as an interpreter of the major portions of Scriptures represented here. It struck me a few years ago while participating in the International Congress on Calvin Research that while it is now axiomatic in Calvin studies to recognize the importance of his exegesis, we did not have a scholarly resource where we could turn to understand the ways he functioned as a biblical interpreter on major segments of the Bible. This book seeks to fill this need and provide such a resource.

I would like to thank the international array of Calvin scholars who have participated in this project and those who have translated essays. They have contributed their expertise to help us gain a clearer understanding of Calvin and the Bible. This book supplements other studies but is unique in its format and gains its significance from the generosity of these colleagues who have shared their scholarship and insights. I would like to thank all of them and especially David Steinmetz for undertaking the challenging task of writing the concluding essay.

This book owes much at its inception to the interest and facilitation of Kevin Taylor of Cambridge University Press. He listened to the idea and encouraged me to shape an understanding of the project that made it more viable. I am grateful to him for valuable help and support.

Kate Brett, Senior Commissioning Editor for Religious Studies at the Press, took over Kevin's duties and has been unfailingly helpful, patient, and kind as the project took shape and as the manuscript was completed. It has been a great pleasure and delight to work with her again. I also greatly appreciate the competence of Joanne Hill in her copy-editing work on this volume.

The love and support of my wonderful family means even more as the years go by. I am grateful beyond words to my wife LindaJo and to our sons Stephen and Karl McKim. Their lives bring joys to mine and their love nurtures me in every way.

This book is dedicated to I. John Hesselink, former President and Albertus C. Van Raalte Professor of Systematic Theology, Emeritus at Western Theological Seminary in Holland, Michigan. John is a superb Calvin scholar who has contributed much to Calvin studies and to the Reformed tradition through the years. For his friendship, I am most grateful.

DONALD K. MCKIM

Abbreviations

BC   *Bibliotheca Calviniana: les oeuvres de Jean Calvin publiées au xvie siècle.* Ed. Rodophe Peter and Jean-François Gilmont. Travaux d'humanisme et Renaissance, no. 255, etc. *I. Écrits théologiques, littéraires et juridiques 1532–1554.* Geneva: Librairie Droz, 1991. *II. Écrits théologiques, littéraires et juridiques 1555–1564.* Geneva: Librairie Droz, 1994. *III. Écrits théologiques, littéraires et juridiques 1565–1600.* Geneva: Librairie Droz, 2000.

CCSL   *Corpus Christianorum, series Latina.*

CNTC   *Calvin's New Testament Commentaries.* Ed. David W. Torrance and Thomas F. Torrance (various translators). 12 vols. Edinburgh: Saint Andrew Press; Grand Rapids: Erdmans, 1959–1972.

CO   *Ioannis Calvini opera quae supersunt omnia.* Ed. G. [Wilhelm] Baum, E. Cunitz, and E. Reuss. 59 vols. bound in 31. *Corpus Reformatorum*, vols. 29–87. Brunswick: C. A. Schwetschke and Son, 1863–1900.

CR   Philip Melanchthon, *Philippi Melanchthonis opera quae supersunt omnia.* Ed. C. G. Bretschneider. Vols. 1–28 of *Corpus Reformatorum.* Halle: C. A. Schwetschke and Son, 1834–1860.

CSEL   *Corpus Scriptorum Ecclesiasticorum Latinorum.*

CSW   *Selected Works of John Calvin: Tracts and Letters.* Ed. Jules Bonnet, trans. Marcus Robert Gilchrist. Grand Rapids: Baker Books, 1983.

CTS   *Calvin's Commentaries.* 45 vols. Edinburgh: Calvin Translation Society, 1844–1856. Reprinted in 22 vols. Grand Rapids: Baker Books, 1981.

Inst.	John Calvin, *Institutes of the Christian Religion*. Ed. John T. McNeill, trans. Ford Lewis Battles. 2 vols. Library of Christian Classics. Philadelphia: Westminster Press, 1960.
LW	Martin Luther, *Luther's Works*. American Edition. 55 vols. St. Louis and Philadelphia: Concordia and Fortress Press, 1958–1986.
MW	Philip Melanchthon, *Melanchthons Werke in Auswahl* (Studienausgabe). Gen. ed. Robert Stupperich. Vol. IV, ed. Peter F. Barton. Gütersloh: Gütersloher Verlagshaus Gerd Mohn, 1980.
NPNF	A Select Library of the Nicene and Post-Nicene Fathers of the Christian Church. Ed. Phillip Schaff et al. 2 series of 14 vols. each. New York: Christian Literature, 1887–1894; reprint, Peabody, MA: Hendrickson, 1994.
OC	*Ioannis Calvini opera omnia*. Series 2: *Opera exegetica veteris et novi testamenti*. Geneva: Librairie Droz, 1992–. Series 3: *Scripta ecclesiastica*. Geneva: Librairie Droz, 1991–.
OE	John Calvin, *Opera exegetica veteris et novi testamenti*. Series 2 of *Ioannis Calvini opera omnia*. Geneva: Librairie Droz, 1992–.
OS	*Ioannis Calvini opera selecta*. Ed. Peter Barth, Wilhelm Niesel, and Dora Scheuner. 5 vols. Munich: C. Kaiser, 1926–1952.
PL	*Patrologiae Cursus Completus, Series Latina*. Ed. J. P. Migne. Paris, 1844–1864.
SC	*Supplementa Calviniana. Sermons inédits*. Ed. Erwin Mulhaupt et al. Neukirchen: Neukirchener Verlag, 1936–1961.
T&T	John Calvin, *Tracts and Treatises*. Trans. Henry Beveridge. 3 vols. Grand Rapids: Eerdmans, 1959.
TT	*Calvin: Theological Treatises*. Trans. with Introduction and notes by John K. S. Reid. Library of Christian Classics. Philadelphia: Westminster Press, 1954.
WA	Martin Luther, *D. Martin Luthers Werke: Kritische Gesamtausgabe* [*Schriften*]. 65 vols. in 127. H. Bohlau, 1883–1993.

CHAPTER I

Calvin as commentator on Genesis

Randall C. Zachman

Calvin first published his commentary on Genesis in 1554, and published it again with revisions with his Harmony on the Last Four Books of Moses in 1563. The commentary continued Calvin's interpretation of the Hebrew Scriptures that began with his Commentary on Isaiah of 1551, which was itself to be republished in a revised and enlarged edition in 1559.[1] Calvin likely began work on the commentary on Genesis in 1550, when he gave a two-year cycle of lectures on the book.[2] However, at the same time that Calvin was preparing the commentary on Genesis, he was also finishing his commentary on the epistles of the New Testament (1551), as well as the first part of the book of Acts (1552) and the Gospel of John (1553). In the same year that the Genesis commentary appeared Calvin also published the second part of his Acts commentary, and a year later he published his harmony of Matthew, Mark, and Luke (1555), along with a completely revised edition of all the other New Testament commentaries. Thus the Genesis commentary is but one part of a massive publication effort of Calvin during this period, in which he sought to finish his interpretation of the New Testament (excluding 2 and 3 John and Revelation), and to begin his interpretation of the Hebrew Bible.

Calvin was embroiled in several controversies during the preparation and production of the commentary on Genesis, all of which leave their mark on the commentary. The *Consensus Tigurinus* was published in 1551, and represented the agreement reached between Zurich and Geneva concerning the holy Supper of the Lord, which had badly divided the evangelical community. However, the publication of the *Consensus* led to a bitter polemic between Calvin and the Lutheran theologians in Germany. Joachim Westphal, a Lutheran minister in Hamburg, wrote against the

---

1 Wulfert de Greef, *The Writings of John Calvin: An Introductory Guide*, trans. Lyle D. Bierma (Grand Rapids: Baker Books, 1993), pp. 100–106.
2 T. H. L. Parker, *Calvin's Old Testament Commentaries* (Edinburgh: T. & T. Clark, 1986), p. 29.

Consensus Tigurinus in 1552 and 1553, and in 1554 Calvin wrote his first response to Westphal in his *Defense of the Sane and Orthodox Doctrine of the Sacraments*, which was published in January of 1555. Calvin dedicated the 1554 edition of the Genesis commentary to the three sons of John Frederick, Elector of Saxony, but the Lutheran theologians who were opposed to the *Consensus* convinced their rulers to refuse the dedication, noting Calvin's problematic views on the Supper, as well as his negative evaluation of Luther's interpretation of Genesis in his commentary. The controversy with Jerome Bolsec in 1551 over the eternal predestination and providence of God led Calvin to finish his response to Albertus Pighius in his treatise *Concerning the Eternal Predestination of God* of 1552, to which Calvin refers the reader in the Genesis commentary.[3] The trial and execution of Michael Servetus in Geneva in 1553 led to the publication in 1554 of Calvin's *Defense of the Orthodox Faith on the Trinity, against Prodigious Errors of Michael Servetus*, and Calvin makes direct reference to Servetus' position on the Trinity in his Genesis commentary.[4] Finally, the period between 1550 and 1554 saw a dramatic increase in the number of evangelical refugees coming to Geneva, many of whom left after having been cared for, while others stayed and even became citizens.[5] Calvin's awareness of the persecution of the small bands of evangelicals in France, and his own experience as a religious exile in Geneva, made him especially attuned to the picture of the small, afflicted, and exiled community of the fathers in Genesis. Thus, the controversies over the holy Supper of the Lord, the eternal election and providence of God, the doctrine of the Trinity, and the plight of the evangelical communities in France, all influenced Calvin's interpretation of Genesis.

THE AUTHORS OF GENESIS

Calvin thought that Moses wrote the book of Genesis, along with the four other books of the Pentateuch, by the inspiration of the Holy Spirit, while he was alone on Mount Sinai (Exod. 24:12–18; 31:18). "Hence we

---

3 *Comm. Gen.* 3:1, *CO* XXIII:56A; CTS 1:145.
4 "God, however, did not put forth his Word until he proceeded to originate light; because in the act of distinguishing his wisdom begins to be conspicuous. Which thing alone is sufficient to confute the blasphemy of Servetus. This impure caviler asserts, that the first beginning of the Word was when God commanded the light to be; as if the cause, truly, were not prior to its effect" (*Comm. Gen.* 1:3, *CO* XXIII:16C; CTS 1:74–75).
5 William G. Naphy, *Calvin and the Consolidation of the Genevan Reformation* (Manchester and New York: Manchester University Press, 1994), pp. 121–143.

gather that he wrote his five books not only under the guidance of the Spirit of God, but as God himself had suggested them, speaking them out of his own mouth."[6] Calvin can therefore speak of two authors of Genesis: Moses and the Holy Spirit. "I return now to the design of Moses, or rather of the Holy Spirit, who has spoken by his mouth."[7] As is widely acknowledged, Calvin can at times speak of the Scriptures being dictated to its human authors by the Holy Spirit. "At the same time, histories were added to these, also the labor of the prophets, but composed under the Holy Spirit's dictation."[8]

However, Calvin often refers to a previous oral tradition, stretching from Adam to Moses, to account for the content of the book of Genesis. "What the patriarchs received they handed on to their descendants. For the Lord left it with them on this condition, that they should so propagate it."[9] Thus, when scoffers ask how Moses, who lived during the exodus, could have known anything about the creation of the world, Calvin responds by appealing to the oral tradition of the fathers. "For he does not transmit to memory things before unheard of, but for the first time consigns to writing facts which the fathers had delivered as from hand to hand, through a long succession of years, to their children."[10] Moses does not, therefore, reveal things by the dictation of the Spirit that would otherwise remain unknown, but rather places into writing the oral tradition of the fathers, so that it might be more accurately preserved.

Therefore, we ought not to doubt that the creation of the world, as here described, was already known through the perpetual tradition of the fathers. Yet, since nothing is more easy than that the truth of God should be so corrupted by men, that, in a long succession of time, it should, as it were, degenerate from itself, it pleased the Lord to commit the history to writing, for the purpose of preserving its purity.[11]

Calvin is especially interested in vindicating the reliability of Moses as a historian over against the attacks of the "Lucianists" on his integrity and credibility. "Those Lucianist dogs, who carp at the doctrine of Moses, pretend that he was a vain man who wished to acquire for himself the command over the rude common people."[12] Calvin appeals to the way

---

6 *Comm. Exod.* 31:18, *CO* XXV:79C; CTS V:328.
7 *Comm. Gen. Argumentum*, *CO* XXIII:7–8; CTS I:59.
8 *Inst.* IV.8.6, *OS* V.138.11–13; (II:1154).
9 *Inst.* IV.8.5, *OS* V.137.17–21; (II:1153).
10 *Comm. Gen. Argumentum*, *CO* XXIII:5–6; CTS I:58.
11 *Comm. Gen. Argumentum*, *CO* XXIII:7–8; CTS I:59.
12 *Comm. Gen.* 49:5, *CO* XXIII:594–595; CTS II:446.

Moses dispossesses his own tribe of Levites of an inheritance of the land, as well as to the disgrace the Levites bring on themselves in his report of the slaughter of Shechem, to establish the reliability of Moses.[13] By acting against the interests of his tribe in his narrative, Moses shows that he is indeed an instrument of the Holy Spirit, according to Calvin. "We may perceive that, by censuring his whole tribe in the person of Levi, he acted not as a man, but as an angel speaking under the impulse of the Holy Spirit, and free from all carnal affection."[14]

Calvin also thinks that Satan had a hand in trying to convince people that Moses wrote fables, by having the poets invent stories that sound similar to the events narrated by Moses. For instance, the *Metamorphoses* of Ovid appears to undermine the credibility of Moses' account of Lot's wife turning into a pillar of salt.

But under the pretext of this narrative, captious and perverse men ridicule Moses; for since this metamorphosis has no more appearance of truth, than those of which Ovid has feigned, they boast that it is undeserving of credit. But I rather suppose it to have happened through the artifice of Satan, that Ovid, by fabulously trifling, has indirectly thrown discredit on this most signal proof of Divine vengeance.[15]

Ovid also echoes Moses' account of the re-creation of the world after a deluge. "By the poets, Deucalion with his wife, is feigned to have sown the race of men after the deluge, by throwing stones behind him."[16] According to Calvin, Satan influenced the pagan poets in this way not only to undermine the authority of Moses, but also to obscure the oral tradition about the restoration of the world handed on by Noah. "For since the memory of the deluge, and the unwonted propagation of a new world, could not be speedily obliterated, he scattered abroad new clouds and smoke; introducing puerile conceits, in order that what had before been held for certain truth, might now be regarded as a fable."[17]

The fables of the poets, representing the attempts of Satan to undermine the truth of the oral tradition of the fathers, may therefore be seen as one of the reasons Moses committed this tradition to writing. "Many ages afterwards, seeing that the wicked forgetfulness of men had rendered them callous to the judgment and mercy of God, the door was opened

---

13 *Comm. Gen.* 34:25, *CO* XXIII:461C; CTS II:226.
14 *Comm. Gen.* 49:5, *CO* XXIII:594–595; CTS II:446.
15 *Comm. Gen.* 19:26, *CO* XXIII:278B; CTS I:513.
16 *Comm. Gen.* 14:1, *CO* XXIII:196–197; CTS I:381.
17 Ibid.

to the lies of Satan, by whose artifice it came to pass, that heathen poets scattered abroad futile and even noxious fables, by which the truth respecting God's works was adulterated."[18] However, Calvin also sees in the poets accurate reflections of the tradition of the fathers, as when both Horace and Moses teach that the disorders of the natural world are the fruits of sin.

This has been celebrated in poetical fables, and was doubtless handed down, by tradition, from the fathers. Hence that passage in Horace: "When from heaven's fane the furtive hand / Of man the sacred fire withdrew, / A countless host – at God's command – / To earth of fierce diseases flew; / And death – till now kept far away – / Hastened his step to seize his prey."[19]

The tradition of the patriarchs is therefore known by the Gentiles, according to Calvin, though often in a corrupted form.

THE AUDIENCE FOR WHOM GENESIS WAS WRITTEN

Calvin understands Moses to be writing primarily for the Jews of his own day. "Whereas Moses was ordained the Teacher of the Israelites, there is no doubt that he had especial reference to them, in order that they might acknowledge themselves to be a people elected and chosen by God."[20] Hence, when Moses speaks of the location of the Garden of Eden, the reader must keep in mind that he is speaking to the Jews of his time. "Moreover, it is to be observed, that when he describes paradise as in the east, he speaks with reference to the Jews, for he directs his discourse to his own people."[21] According to Calvin, the capacities of the Israelites developed progressively over time, so that they began as young children and progressed to adolescence. At the time of the narrative of Genesis the Jews were at their most untrained and immature level, something that readers of Genesis need to keep in mind. "We have elsewhere said, that Moses, by a homely and uncultivated style, accommodates what he delivers to the capacity of the people; and for the best reason; for not only had he to instruct an untaught race of men, but the existing age of the Church was so puerile, that it was unable to receive any higher instruction."[22] Moses himself was not untrained or unlearned, for Calvin

18 *Comm. Gen.* 10:1, *CO* XXIII:157B; CTS 1:313.
19 *Comm. Gen.* 3:19, *CO* XXIII:75B; CTS 1:177.
20 *Comm. Gen. Argumentum, CO* XXIII:11–12; CTS 1:65.
21 *Comm. Gen.* 2:8, *CO* XXIII:36C; CTS 1:113.
22 *Comm. Gen.* 3:1, *CO* XXIII:53C; CTS 1:141.

insists that he had learned all the arts of the Egyptians. However, he did
not write as a learned person, but, rather, accommodated himself to the
capacities of his unlearned people. "I grant what they allege, that Moses,
who had been educated in all the science of the Egyptians, was not
ignorant of geometry; but . . . we know that Moses everywhere spoke in
a homely style, to suit the capacity of his people, and that he purposely
abstained from acute disputations, which might savor of the schools and
of deeper learning."[23]

Calvin appeals to the accommodated style of Moses to reconcile the
apparent conflict between the description of the world given in Genesis
and that found in the writings of the learned philosophers. When Moses
describes the waters as existing above the heavens (Gen. 1:6), he is not
speaking with scientific precision, but is, rather, speaking according to the
understanding of the world among the unlearned of his day. "He who
would learn astronomy, and other recondite arts, let him go elsewhere.
Here the Spirit of God would teach all men without exception; and
therefore what Gregory declares falsely and in vain respecting statues
and pictures is truly applicable to the history of the creation, namely,
that it is the book of the unlearned."[24] Astronomers also claim that the
stars such as Saturn are actually larger than the moon, over against Moses'
description of the moon as being the second largest heavenly body. "Here
lies the difference; Moses wrote in a popular style things which, without
instruction, all ordinary persons, endued with common sense, are able to
understand; but astronomers investigate with great labor whatever the
sagacity of the human mind can comprehend."[25] By keeping this distinction in mind, the learned will not scoff at the unlearned style of Moses,
nor will the unlearned condemn the labors of those who seek to study the
world with more acuteness and precision. "For astronomy is not only
pleasant, but also very useful to be known; it cannot be denied that this art
unfolds the admirable wisdom of God."[26]

Calvin is also concerned to adhere to the economy of divine self-
manifestation that God used during the time of Genesis. Calvin thinks
that the primary form of divine self-manifestation at this time was
through dreams and visions, the contents of which were then to be handed
on by oral tradition.[27] Calvin explicitly develops his understanding of this

23 *Comm. Gen.* 6:14, *CO* XXIII:123A; CTS 1:256.
24 *Comm. Gen.* 1:6, *CO* XXIII:18C; CTS 1:79–80.
25 *Comm. Gen.* 1:16, *CO* XXIII:22B; CTS 1:86.
26 *Comm. Gen.* 1:16, *CO* XXIII:22C; CTS 1:86–87.
27 *Comm. Gen.* 20:7, *CO* XXIII:289C; CTS 1:526.

economy of divine self-revelation in his commentary on Acts of 1552, in light of the passage of Joel quoted by Peter in his first sermon. "The sentence immediately following is to the same effect, 'Your young men shall see visions, and your old men shall dream dreams.' These were the two means by which the Lord usually revealed himself to the prophets, as we learn from Numbers 12:6."[28] Calvin is acutely aware that Luther was highly suspicious of dreams and visions, given his criticism of "the heavenly prophets" such as Karlstadt and insistance that the Spirit never works within a person apart from the external preaching of the Word. In his lectures on Genesis, Luther often notes that when a revelation by dream or vision is mentioned, we are to understand that a prophet was actually sent to preach to the father in question. Calvin thinks that Luther's position does not do justice to the economy of divine self-manifestation peculiar to the time of the fathers. Thus, when Moses says that God spoke to Cain, Calvin notes:

Moses does not state in what manner God spoke. Whether a vision was presented to him, or he heard an oracle from heaven, or was admonished by secret inspiration, he certainly felt himself bound by a divine judgment. To apply this to the person of Adam, as being the prophet and interpreter of God in censuring his son, is constrained and even frigid.[29]

Calvin expresses sympathy with Luther's desire to exalt the external ministry of the Word, but insists that the foundation of that ministry lies in the oracles delivered to the fathers in dreams and visions. "But we may observe, that the word of God was delivered from the beginning by oracles, in order that afterwards, when administered by the hands of men, it might receive the greater reverence."[30] The deliverance of oracles to the fathers in visions and dreams is as essential to the economy of divine self-manifestation at the time of the fathers as is the accommodation of Moses to the childish and unlearned capacity of the people. "They who have an aversion to this simplicity, must of necessity condemn the whole economy of God in governing the Church."[31]

28 *Comm. Acts* 2:17, *CO* XLVIII:33B; *CNTC* VI:58.

29 *Comm. Gen.* 4:6, *CO* XXIII:87C; *CTS* I:198. "I believe that these words were spoken by Adam himself. Moses says that these words were spoken by the Lord, because Adam had now been accounted just and had been endowed with the Holy Spirit. What he now says in accordance with the Word of God and through the Holy Spirit is correctly declared to have been said by God" (WA XXXXII:194; *LW* I:262).

30 Ibid.   31 *Comm. Gen.* 3:1, *CO* XXIII:53C; *CTS* I:141.

THE LANGUAGE IN WHICH GENESIS WAS WRITTEN

Since Moses wrote for the Jews, he must have written in their own language, which is Hebrew. Calvin therefore insists that the teaching of Moses simply cannot be understood unless one is skilled in Hebrew.[32] However, he claims that the church of his day had inherited a Latin translation of the Greek Septuagint that had become severely corrupted over time, helped in large part by the ignorance of Hebrew during long stretches of the church's history. "I suspect also that this happened from the following cause, that those who had to deal with the Scripture were generally ignorant of the Hebrew language."[33] Calvin therefore makes common cause with Valla, Stapulensis, Erasmus, Reuchlin, Vatable, Budé, and Münster, in seeking to restore the genuine meaning of Scripture by returning to the original languages in which it was written, over against the Council of Trent, which held the Old Vulgate to be authoritative in all matters of doctrine and morals.[34] "In condemning all translations except the Vulgate, as the error is more gross, so the edict is more barbarous. The sacred oracles of God were delivered by Moses and the Prophets in Hebrew, and by the Apostles in Greek. That no corner of the world might be left destitute of so great a treasure, the gift of interpretation was added."[35] Calvin clearly assumes that the readers of his commentary are trained in Hebrew. When he points to an error in the Greek translation, he says, "However, as any one, moderately versed in the Hebrew language, will easily judge of their error, I will not pause to refute it."[36] When he defends his own rendering of the phrase, he again says, "They who are skilled in the Hebrew language know that there is nothing forced, or remote from the genuine signification of the word."[37]

If one is rightly to understand Moses, therefore, one must know the language in which he wrote, and must establish the most reliable version of the Hebrew text available. Calvin contrasts his method with the one he claims the Roman Church follows, by which it draws false doctrine from corrupt and inaccurate translations of Scripture. For instance, Calvin

---

32 Max Engemarre, "*Johannes Calvinus trium linguarum peritus?* La question de l'Hebreu," *Bibliothèque d'Humanisme et Renaissance* 58 (1996): 35–60; Darryl Phillips, "An Inquiry into the Extent of the Abilities of John Calvin as a Hebraist" (D.Phil. thesis, University of Oxford, 1998).

33 *Comm. Gen.* 46:8, *CO* XXIII:562A; CTS II:391.

34 Jerome Friedman, *The Most Ancient Testimony: Sixteenth-Century Christian-Hebraica in the Age of Renaissance Nostalgia* (Athens, OH: Ohio University Press, 1983).

35 *Acta Synodi Tridentinae cum Antidoto*, *CO* VII:414A; *T & T* III:71.

36 *Comm. Gen.* 4:7, *CO* XXIII:88B; CTS I:199.

37 *Comm. Gen.* 4:7, *CO* XXIII:89A; CTS I:200–201.

thinks that Rome falsely attributes to Mary what he clearly thinks is attributed to Christ, that he shall crush the head of the serpent (Gen. 3:15). "There has been none among them who would consult the Hebrew or Greek codices, or who would even compare the Latin copies with each other. Therefore, by a common error, this most corrupt reading has been received. Then, a profane exposition of it has been invented, by applying to the mother of Christ what is said concerning her seed."[38] By contrast, Calvin will consult the best Hebrew codices, as well as the Greek and Latin translations, in order to arrive at the genuine translation and interpretation of a passage. For instance, he appeals to the Hebrew codices to correct the translation of Genesis 3:17 given in the Vulgate. "The ancient interpreter has translated it, 'In thy work'; but the reading is to be retained, in which all the Hebrew copies agree, namely, the earth was cursed on account of Adam."[39]

Calvin often makes it sound as though he has done a prodigious amount of research into the proper rendering of a passage, by comparing for himself the various Hebrew, Greek, and Latin versions. However, if we keep in mind the tremendous amount of writing Calvin was doing during the preparation of the commentary on Genesis, and his own acknowledgment that he often had little more than an hour to prepare for his lectures on Scripture, we will see that he must have been using the work of others to aid him in the task of interpretation.[40] Anthony Lane has carefully traced the various sources used by Calvin in the preparation of his Genesis commentary.[41] He made extensive use of the 1529 edition of the *Recognitio Veteris Testamenti ad Hebraicam Veritatem* by Augustinus Steuchus, the 1534–1535 edition of Münster's *Hebraica Biblia Latina*, and the Stephanus Bible of 1545, which included the Vulgate and Zurich translations as well as Vatable's notes. He also consulted two works by Fagius, his *Exegesis* and *Thargum*, from which he derived many of his references to Jewish exegesis. He also referred to Servetus' revisions of the Pagninus translation of Genesis, which was likely fresh in his mind after the trial of Servetus in 1553, and may have used Pagninus' *Thesaurus linguae sanctae*.[42] Finally, Calvin refers explicitly to Jerome's *Hebraicae*

---

38 *Comm. Gen.* 3:15, *CO* XXIII:71A; CTS 1:170.
39 *Comm. Gen.* 3:17, *CO* XXIII:72C; CTS 1:173.
40 Parker, *Calvin's Old Testament Commentaries*, p. 21.
41 See also H. F. van Rooy, "Calvin's Genesis Commentary – Which Bible Text Did He Use?" in *Our Reformational Tradition. A Rich Heritage and Lasting Vocation*, ed. B. J. van der Walt (Potchefstroom: Potchefstroom University for Christian Higher Education, 1984), pp. 203–216.
42 Max Engemarre concurs with this description of the sources used by Calvin, though he observes that the references to Steuchus could come from Münster, who makes constant reference to his

questiones in Genesim, and to the Vulgate translation of the Septuagint, which he refers to as "the old interpreter." Even though he refers to the Septuagint, which he calls "the Greek interpreters," he does not appear to have consulted it himself.[43]

Calvin thought that knowledge of the Hebrew way of speaking could correct the misunderstanding of different passages presented by those who did not know Hebrew. For instance, when Moses says that humans were created in the image and likeness of God, Calvin does not think that this is meant to distinguish between image and likeness, as many in the Christian tradition have claimed, but was, rather, a form of explanatory repetition that is common in Hebrew. "We know that it was customary with the Hebrews to repeat the same thing in different words. Besides, the phrase itself shows that the second term was added for the sake of explanation."[44] When Moses says that Noah found grace in the eyes of God, he again describes this as a Hebrew form of speaking that does not imply merit, over against the interpretation of Roman theologians. "This is a Hebrew phrase, which signifies that God was propitious to him and favored him. For so the Hebrews are accustomed to speak . . . Which phrase requires to be noticed, because certain unlearned men infer with great subtlety, that if men find grace in God's sight, it is because they seek it by their own industry and merits."[45] Thus attention to the Hebraic form of speaking can keep the interpreter from drawing false conclusions about the meaning of a given passage.

THE ARGUMENT OR SUBJECT MATTER OF GENESIS

Given the fact that Moses wrote in Hebrew for his own people, in a homely style accommodated to their unlearned capacities, the most important question to ask is, what did Moses have in mind when he wrote Genesis? What was it that he meant to communicate to his people? Calvin shared with others of his day the view that every author has a goal or target (*scopus*) toward which they steadily aim in a given text. Before one can interpret any chapter or verse of a book, one must first discover the goal the author had in mind in writing the entire book. Calvin sets

work. Jean Calvin, *Sermons sur la Genèse, Chapitres 1:1–11:4*, ed. Max Engemarre (Neukirchen-Vluyn: Neukirchener Verlag, 2000), p. lii.

43 Anthony N. S. Lane, *John Calvin: Student of the Church Fathers* (Grand Rapids: Baker Books, 1999), pp. 205–259.

44 *Comm. Gen.* 1:26, *CO* XXIII:26B; CTS 1:94.

45 *Comm. Gen.* 6:8, *CO* XXIII:119B; CTS 1:250–251.

forth this goal at the beginning of his commentary in what he calls the *Argumentum*, which might best be translated as, "The matter which lies at the basis of any written or artistic representation," following its use by Quintilian.[46] According to Calvin, the narrative of Genesis is written with five connected points in view, which form its argument or subject matter. First, humanity was placed in the world after its creation to behold the works of God and adore their author. Second, all things were created for the use of humanity so that we might be bound to God in gratitude. Third, humanity was created with understanding and reason to meditate on eternal life, and to tend directly towards God, having been created in the image of God. Fourth, humanity fell into sin in Adam and lost every good thing that would have united us to God in eternal life, subjecting us instead to eternal death. Fifth, God promises humanity its restoration in Christ the Mediator, and governs and preserves the church by God's providence, so that there might always be a community on earth that worships God, even as it suffers under the cross. "The end to which the whole scope (*totius contextus*) of the history tends is to this point, that the human race has been preserved by God in such a manner as to manifest his special care for his Church."[47] These five topics, all interconnected in one narrative, form the argument or principal subjects that Moses addresses in Genesis. "Whoever, therefore, desires to make suitable proficiency in this book, let him employ his mind on these main topics (*capita*)."[48]

The mind or intention of Moses, which is revealed in the whole context of the narrative that he wrote, should therefore govern the correct interpretation of Genesis. The proper task of the interpreter is to reveal the mind of the author, and the mind of the author is disclosed by the context.[49] Calvin makes this point explicitly in his commentary on Genesis, in his discussion of circumcision. Were he writing a summary of the teaching of Scripture, as in the *Institutes*, Calvin would gather all that Scripture says under the topic of circumcision. However, since he is acting in the office of interpreter, he will follow the order of the context. "Moreover, although it would, perhaps, be more suitable for the purpose

46 Charlton T. Lewis and Charles Short, *A Latin Dictionary* (Oxford: Oxford University Press, 1975), p. 159.
47 *Comm. Gen. Argumentum*, *CO* xxiii:11–12; CTS 1:64–65.
48 Ibid.
49 Randall C. Zachman, "Gathering Meaning from the Context: Calvin's Exegetical Method," *The Journal of Religion* 82/1 (2002): 1–26; David L. Puckett, *John Calvin's Exegesis of the Old Testament* (Louisville: Westminster John Knox Press, 1995), pp. 52–81.

of instruction (*docendi methodum*), were we to give a summary of those things which are to be said concerning circumcision; I will follow the order of the context (*ordinem contextus*), which I think is more appropriate to the office of an interpreter."[50] Following the order of the context is especially necessary when translating the text from Hebrew to Latin, which for Calvin forms one of the major tasks of the interpreter of Scripture. One must keep in mind the difference between the Hebrew and Latin ways of speaking, and must also attend to the immediate context of a passage, as well as its place in the overall context of the narrative. For instance, Calvin defends his translation of Genesis 16:12, which is a description of Ishmael, in terms of the context of the passage. "Some expound the word *pereh* to mean a forester, and one addicted to the hunting of wild beasts. But the explanation must not, it seems, be sought elsewhere than in the context; for it follows immediately after, 'His hand shall be against all men, and the hand of all men against him.' "[51] The context can also reveal the difference between a genealogy and a record of events, even though the same Hebrew word may be taken in either way. "By the word *toledoth* we are not so much to understand a genealogy, as a record of events, which appears more clearly from the context."[52] When Calvin disagrees with the translations of others, even if they have their own merit, he defends his decision on the basis of the context. "Others translate the passage, 'If they have done this, their final destruction is at hand: but if not, I will see how far they are to be punished.' But the former sense is most accordant with the context."[53]

CALVIN'S COMMENTS ON THE CHAPTERS AND
VERSES OF GENESIS

In distinction from his commentaries on the New Testament, in which he translates three or four verses before commenting on them, in the Genesis commentary Calvin translates the entire chapter into Latin before commenting. Given the fact that Calvin often equates translation with interpretation, this is a major aspect of his work as an interpreter, even if he never explicitly comments on the verse subsequently. He will then proceed to locate the place of the chapter in the overall argument or narrative

---

50 *Comm. Gen.* 17:9, *CO* xxiii:239C; CTS 1:451.
51 *Comm. Gen.* 16:12, *CO* xxiii:229C; CTS 1:434.
52 *Comm. Gen.* 37:2, *CO* xxiii:480C; CTS ii:258.
53 *Comm. Gen.* 18:21, *CO* xxiii:261B; CTS 1:485.

context of Moses. For instance, at the beginning of Genesis 16, Calvin says that "Moses here recites a new history, namely, that Sarai, through the impatience of long delay, resorted to a method of obtaining seed by her husband, at variance with the word of God."[54] At other times, Calvin will reconnect the chapter with the main thread of the narrative, as he does after the description of Sodom and Gomorrah. "What Moses related respecting the destruction of Sodom, was a digression. He now returns to a continuation of his history, and proceeds to show what happened to Abraham."[55] Calvin will also set forth the goal or *scopus* of a given chapter, within the context of the end toward which the whole book is written, as in Genesis 21. "In this chapter, not only is the nativity of Isaac related, but because, in his very birth, God has set before us a lively picture of his Church, Moses also gives a particular account of this matter."[56] Thus each chapter is placed within the context of the argument and narrative of the whole book, while also being given its own goal and subject matter.

Calvin will also weight the importance of a given chapter in the overall development of the narrative. Some chapters are highlighted as being especially noteworthy, such as the trial of Abraham created by the divine commandment to sacrifice his son Isaac. "This chapter contains a most memorable narrative. For although Abraham, through the whole course of his life, gave astonishing proofs of faith and obedience, yet none more excellent can be imagined than the immolation of his son."[57] Calvin makes a similar remark with regard to the narrative regarding the tower of Babel. "For this is a truly memorable history, in which we may perceive the greatness of men's obstinacy against God, and the little profit they receive from his judgments."[58] Other chapters appear to be of less gravity or import, but Calvin defends their usefulness nonetheless, as in the deception of Isaac by Jacob.

It seems even like child's play to present to his father a kid instead of venison, to feign himself to be hairy by putting on skins, and, under the name of his brother, to get the blessing by a lie. But in order to learn that Moses did not in vain pause over this narrative as a most serious matter, we must first observe, that when Jacob received the blessing from his father, this token confirmed to him the oracle by which the Lord had preferred him to his brother.[59]

---

54 *Comm. Gen.* 16:1, *CO* XXIII:222C; CTS 1:422.
55 *Comm. Gen.* 20:1, *CO* XXIII:286A; CTS 1:520.
56 *Comm. Gen.* 21:1, *CO* XXIII:296C; CTS 1:537.
57 *Comm. Gen.* 22:1, *CO* XXIII:310C; CTS 1:559.
58 *Comm. Gen.* 11:1, *CO* XXIII:162C; CTS 1:323.
59 *Comm. Gen.* 27:1, *CO* XXIII:372B; CTS II:81–82.

However, there are some chapters, such as genealogies, that Calvin does not seem to take all that seriously, although he does not forbid others to examine their meaning in more detail. "It shall, however, suffice for me briefly to allude to those things which I deem more useful to be noticed, and for the sake of which I suppose these genealogies to have been written by Moses."[60]

After Calvin sets the chapter in the context of the overall history, and discusses the scope and weight of the chapter, he proceeds to comment on roughly half of the verses of each chapter, although this varies from chapter to chapter. In some, such as the fall narrative and the discussion of Hagar, Calvin comments on nine out of ten verses. In others, such as the genealogies, he comments on one in ten verses. Moreover, the number of verses on which he comments in each chapter diminishes as one proceeds through the commentary, from six in ten in Genesis 1–24, to five in ten from Genesis 25–36, dropping to four in ten in Genesis 37–50. Either Calvin thought that the difficulties of translation and interpretation diminish as one gets further into Genesis, or he began to feel the press of time as he got deeper into the commentary. In either case, he falls far short of a line-by-line exposition of Genesis in this commentary.

The nature of Calvin's comments on verses also varies. Some comments seek to relate a section of Scripture to the overall argument of Genesis and the thread of its historical narrative. "Because what Moses has said concerning the Ishmaelites was incidental, he now returns to the principal subject of the history, for the purpose of describing the progress of the Church."[61] Others highlight the drama of a particular event, such as the plan of Joseph's brothers to kill him.

If, at any time, among heathens, a brother murdered his brother, such impiety was treated with the utmost severity in tragedies, that it might not pass into example for imitation. But in profane history no such thing is found, as that nine brethren should conspire together for the destruction of an innocent youth, and, like wild beasts, should pounce upon him with bloody hands.[62]

At other times, Calvin will detail his reasons for giving a different translation of a passage than that given by others. A good example of this is found in Genesis 15:2, when Abram speaks of his only heir as the son of a foreigner.

---

60 *Comm. Gen.* 10:1, *CO* XXIII:157A; CTS 1:312–313.
61 *Comm. Gen.* 25:19, *CO* XXIII:347A; CTS II:40.
62 *Comm. Gen.* 37:18, *CO* XXIII:485A; CTS II:265.

He also calls him the son of *mesek*, concerning the meaning of which the grammarians are not agreed. Some derive it from *shakak*, which means to run to and fro, and translate it, steward or superintendent, because he who sustains the care of a large house, runs hither and thither in attending to his business. Others derive it from *shook*, and render it cupbearer, which seems to me incongruous. I rather adopt a different translation, namely, that he was called the son of a deserted house because *mesek* sometimes signifies to leave.[63]

Calvin may also seek to identify the rhetorical form of the verse, as in the description of the tower of Babel as reaching unto heaven. "This is an hyperbolical form of speech, in which they boastingly extol the loftiness of the structure they are attempting to raise."[64] When God is said to have repented of creating humanity, Calvin describes this form of speech as *anthropopatheia*, by which human affections are ascribed to God, "because he could not otherwise express what was very important to be known; namely, that God was not induced hastily, or for a slight cause, to destroy the world."[65] Calvin will also consider whether a given passage is an allegory. At times, he categorically rejects such an option, suggesting that it distorts the genuine meaning of Scripture. "We must, however, entirely reject the allegories of Origen, and of others like him, which Satan, with the deepest subtlety, has endeavored to introduce into the Church, for the purpose of rendering the doctrine of Scripture ambiguous and destitute of all certainty and firmness."[66] On the other hand, Calvin will endorse the interpretation of Paul in Galatians 4, according to whom the narrative concerning Sarah and Hagar "was written allegorically," even though he is at pains to distinguish Paul from the interpretation of Origen, "who, by hunting everywhere for allegories, corrupts the whole Scripture."[67]

The ultimate goal of Calvin's comments, however, is to reveal the mind of Moses, which is gathered from the context. For instance, over against those like Origen who wish to understand the Garden of Eden allegorically, Calvin says that they "speculate in vain, and to no purpose, by departing from the literal sense. For Moses has no other design than to teach man that he was formed by God, with this condition, that he should have dominion over the earth, from which he might gather fruit, and thus learn by daily experience that the world was subject unto him."[68] Calvin will also reject various interpretations of a passage by claiming that "not

63 *Comm. Gen.* 15:2, *CO* XXIII:210A; CTS 1:402.
64 *Comm. Gen.* 11:4, *CO* XXIII:165A; CTS 1:327.
65 *Comm. Gen.* 6:5, *CO* XXIII:116C; CTS 1:247.
66 *Comm. Gen.* 2:8, *CO* XXIII:37A; CTS 1:114.
67 *Comm. Gen.* 21:12, *CO* XXIII:302B; CTS 1:545.
68 *Comm. Gen.* 2:8, *CO* XXIII:37B; CTS 1:114.

one of these interpreters has apprehended the mind of Moses (*Mosis mentem*)."[69] He can even agree with the thrust of a given interpretation, such as the idea that we were created in the image of God in order to arrive at perfection, without agreeing that the idea reveals the mind of Moses. "The thing indeed is true; but I do not think that anything of the kind entered the mind of Moses."[70]

CALVIN'S ENGAGEMENT WITH OTHER
INTERPRETERS OF GENESIS

Since the goal of interpretation is to set forth the mind and meaning of Moses as it emerges from the context of his history, Calvin will often appear to take little interest in the interpretations of Genesis given by his predecessors and contemporaries, at times suggesting that they were delirious. "It is not my intention to relate the ravings or the dreams of every writer, nor would I have the reader to expect this from me; here and there I allude to them, though sparingly, especially if there be any color of deception; that readers, being often admonished, may learn to take heed unto themselves."[71] Calvin follows this method in his interpretation of the promise of God that Abraham's seed will be as numerous as the dust. "Omitting those subtleties, by means of which others argue about nothing, I simply explain the words to signify, that the seed of Abram is compared to the dust, because of its immense multitude; and truly the sense of the term is to be sought for only in Moses' own words."[72]

However, Calvin is well aware of the interpretations of others, even when he does not directly allude to them. He makes a significant division between the Jewish and Christian interpreters of Genesis, placing himself clearly in the second camp. In the debate with the Jews over the meaning of the prophecy of Jacob that the scepter will not depart from Judah (Gen. 49:10), Calvin refers to himself as one of many Christian commentators, even though he does not completely agree with their interpretation of this passage. "Our commentators (*nostri*), therefore, conclude that, although the royal majesty did not shine brightly from David until Christ, yet some preeminence remained in the tribe of Judah, and thus the oracle was

---

69 *Comm. Gen.* 16:13, *CO* XXIII:231B; CTS 1:437.
70 *Comm. Gen.* 1:26, *CO* XXIII:27A; CTS 1:95.
71 *Comm. Gen.* 4:24, *CO* XXIII:102A; CTS 1:221–222.
72 *Comm. Gen.* 13:16, *CO* XXIII:194A; CTS 1:375–376.

fulfilled."[73] One of Calvin's major objectives in the commentary, therefore, is to show that the book of Genesis, originally written by Moses for the Jews of his day, is no longer properly understood by the Jews, but only by the Christians.

Even though Calvin knew that the recovery of Hebrew in his day came from Christian engagement with the synagogue, he was convinced that the Jews did not understand their own Hebrew texts, having been misled by the trifling fables of rabbinic exegesis. When Moses says that God rested from work on the seventh day, Calvin immediately rejects the interpretation of this passage by the Jews.

Here the Jews, in their usual method, foolishly trifle, saying, that God being anticipated in his work by the last evening, left certain animals imperfect, of which kind are fauns and satyrs, as though he had been one of the ordinary artificers who have need of time. Ravings so monstrous prove the authors of them to have been delivered over to a reprobate mind, as a dreadful example of the wrath of God.[74]

So serious is the delirium of the Jews, and their desire to trifle with the genuine meaning of Scripture, that Calvin will at times suggest that they do not understand their own language, as in their elaborate explanation of the beauty of Sarah based on the repetition of the word "years" in the description of her age (Gen. 23:1). "This is their custom; while they wish to prove themselves skilful in doing honor to their nation, they invent frivolous trifles, which betray a shameful ignorance; as, for instance, in this place, who would not say that they were entirely ignorant of their own language, in which this kind of repetition is usual?"[75] Calvin thinks that the "trifles and fables" of the Jews only further confuse the meaning of obscure passages, making it even more difficult to gather the genuine sense, as in the prophecy of Jacob in Genesis 49:10. "Though this passage is obscure, it would not have been very difficult to elicit its genuine sense, if the Jews, with their accustomed malignity, had not endeavored to envelop it in clouds."[76] Calvin thinks that the Jews trifle with Scripture in this way because of their over-arching desire to glorify their own race.

73 *Comm. Gen.* 49:10, *CO* xxiii:600B; CTS ii:455.
74 *Comm. Gen.* 2:3, *CO* xxiii:34A; CTS i:107. See Heiko Oberman, "Discovery of Hebrew and Discrimination against the Jews: The *Veritas Hebraica* as Double-edged Sword in Renaissance and Reformation," in *Germania Illustrata. Essays on Early Modern Germany Presented to Gerald Strauss*, ed. Andrew C. Fix and Susan C. Karant-Nunn, Sixteenth Century Studies 18 (Kirksville, MO: Sixteenth Century Journal Publishers, Inc., 1992), pp. 19–34.
75 *Comm. Gen.* 23:1, *CO* xxiii:321B; CTS i:576.
76 *Comm. Gen.* 49:10, *CO* xxiii:598A; CTS ii:452.

"The ambition of the Jews often compels them to trifle; seeing that they apply their whole study to boasting of the glory of their race."[77]

However, Calvin's evaluation of the Jewish interpretation of Genesis is not uniformly negative.[78] For instance, while he rejects David Kimchi's interpretation of the serpent's interrogation of Eve, he is more approving of the Chaldean paraphrast.[79] Calvin will at times approve of the interpretation of the Hebrews, even as he extends its meaning more fully than they do.

The word *moadim*, which they translate "certain times," is variously understood among the Hebrews: for it signifies both time and place, and also assemblies of persons. The Rabbis commonly explain the passage as referring to their festivals. But I extend it further to mean, in the first place, the opportunities of time, which in French are called *saisons*; and then all fairs and forensic assemblies.[80]

At other times Calvin will endorse the Jewish interpretation without qualification. "Under the names of heaven and earth, the whole is, by the figure of synecdoche, included. Some of the Hebrews think, that the essential name of God is here at length expressed by Moses, because his majesty shines forth more clearly in the completed world."[81] Calvin will at times even agree with the Jews when they criticize Christian interpretation, as in his agreement with the Jews that the scepter of rule did not always appear in Judah even before the coming of Christ. "I shall, perhaps, seem to grant too much to the Jews, because I do not assign what they call a real dominion, in uninterrupted succession, to the tribe of Judah."[82] He explicitly agrees with the Jewish interpreters, against his fellow Christian interpreters, that the right of dominion remained in Judah, but that its glory was often absent. "Whereas some of the Jews explain, that the right of government was given to the tribe of Judah, because it was unlawful for it to be transferred elsewhere, but that it was not necessary that the glory of the crown once given should be perpetuated, I deem it right to subscribe in part to this opinion."[83] Thus, even though Calvin's evaluation of Jewish exegesis is predominantly negative,

---

77 *Comm. Gen.* 16:13, *CO* XXIII:230–231; CTS 1:436.
78 See Stephen G. Burnett, "Calvin's Jewish Interlocutor: Christian Hebraism and Anti-Jewish Polemics During the Reformation," *Bibliothèque d'Humanisme et Renaissance* 55 (1993): 113–123.
79 *Comm. Gen.* 3:1, *CO* XXIII:57A; CTS 1:147.
80 *Comm. Gen.* 1:14, *CO* XXIII:21C; CTS 1:85.
81 *Comm. Gen.* 2:4, *CO* XXIII:34B; CTS 1:109.
82 *Comm. Gen.* 49:10, *CO* XXIII:601C; CTS II:457.
83 *Comm. Gen.* 49:10, *CO* XXIII:601–602; CTS II:458.

he does in fact at times agree with them, even in a passage as sensitive as the messianic prophecy of Jacob.

At the head of the Christian interpreters of Genesis stand the apostles, especially Paul. Calvin clearly expresses his indebtedness to Paul's interpretation of Genesis 15:6, "And he believed the Lord; and the Lord reckoned it to him as righteousness." According to Calvin, "None of us would be able to conceive the rich and hidden doctrine which this passage contains, unless Paul had borne his torch before us (Rom. 4:3)."[84] However, he expresses his surprise and dismay that so few Christian interpreters follow Paul in their interpretation of this passage. "I omit the Jews, whose blindness is well known. But it is (as I have said) monstrous, that they who have had Paul as their luminous expositor, should so foolishly have depraved this place."[85] Calvin understands Paul's allegory of Sarah and Hagar in Galatians 4 to be the definitive interpretation of Genesis 21:12. "But because I have before declared, that this history is more profoundly considered by Paul, the sum of it is here briefly to be collected."[86] Calvin even refers his readers to his own commentary on Galatians 4 to find a fuller account of Paul's interpretation of Genesis 21. "And although I here allude in few words to those things, which my readers will find copiously expounded by me, in the fourth chapter to the Galatians; yet, in this short explanation, it is made perfectly clear what Paul designs to teach."[87]

Among the subsequent Christian interpreters of Genesis, Calvin is the most indebted to Luther, whose lectures on Genesis were published between 1544 and 1554.[88] Anthony Lane has shown that all of Calvin's explicit or implicit references to Luther's lectures end at Genesis 25:10, which is also the close of the second volume of published lectures.[89] Calvin is clearly indebted to Luther in his interpretation of crucial passages, such as his claim that the primary sin of Eve and Adam lay in doubting the truth of the Word of God. "Therefore, unbelief was the root

---

84 *Comm. Gen.* 15:6, *CO* XXIII:211B; CTS 1:404.
85 Ibid.
86 *Comm. Gen.* 21:12, *CO* XXIII:302B; CTS 1:545.
87 *Comm. Gen.* 21:12, *CO* XXIII:302C; CTS 1:546.
88 For a comparison of Luther's and Calvin's exegesis of Genesis, see David Steinmetz, "Calvin as an Interpreter of Genesis," in *Calvin as Protector of the Purer Religion*, ed. Wilhelm Neuser and Brian Armstrong (Kirksville, MO: Sixteenth Century Journal Publishers, 1997), pp. 53–66.
89 Lane, *John Calvin*, p. 211. A complete evaluation of the patristic and contemporary interpreters to whom Calvin refers in his Genesis commentary may be found in this work. See also R. C. Gamble, "The Sources of Calvin's Genesis Commentary: A Preliminary Report," *Archiv für Reformationsgeschichte* 84 (1993): 206–221.

of their defection; just as faith alone unites us to God."[90] Calvin will also specifically endorse the interpretation of Luther, as in his understanding of the suffering of the patriarchs. "Luther very properly compares the incredible torments, by which they were necessarily afflicted, to many martyrdoms."[91] Calvin's interpretation of the binding of Isaac also significantly echoes Luther's lectures on Genesis 22. However, Calvin can also be sharply dismissive of Luther's interpretation, as in his evaluation of Luther's explanation of the missing years in Abraham's genealogy. "The conjecture of Luther, that God buried that time in oblivion, in order to hide from us the end of the world, in the first place is frivolous, and in the next, may be refuted by solid and convincing arguments."[92] He is critical of Luther's understanding of the righteousness of faith as reckoning God to be true in God's Word. "They also, no less unskillfully, corrupt the text, who say that Abram is here ascribing to God the glory of righteousness, seeing that he ventures to acquiesce surely in his promises, acknowledging him to be faithful and true."[93] Calvin is especially critical of Luther's insistence that every oracle delivered to the patriarchs came through the ministry of a prophet. "The speculation of Luther here (as in other places) has no solidity; namely, that God spoke through some prophet."[94] Calvin seems to have intentionally distanced himself from Luther in this way, in order to show that the interpretation of Scripture should never be bound to one person. As he comments a year later, "If I was not permitted at any point to depart from the opinion of Luther, it was utterly ridiculous of me to undertake the office of interpretation (*munus interpretandi*)."[95]

Calvin seems to take a similar approach with another influential Latin interpreter of Genesis, Augustine of Hippo.[96] He usually accuses Augustine of overly refined and speculative interpretations, as in his interpretation of the image and likeness of God. "But Augustine, beyond all others, speculates with excessive refinement, for the purpose of fabricating a Trinity in man."[97] He makes a similar observation regarding Augustine's

90 *Comm. Gen.* 3:6, *CO* XXIII:60–61; CTS 1:152.
91 *Comm. Gen.* 11:10, *CO* XXIII:169A; CTS 1:334.
92 *Comm. Gen.* 11:27, *CO* XXIII:170A; CTS 1:335–336.
93 *Comm. Gen.* 15:6, *CO* XXIII:212A; CTS 1:406.
94 *Comm. Gen.* 13:14, *CO* XXIII:193C; CTS 1:375.
95 Calvin to Francis Burkhardt, 27 February 1555, *CO* XV:454.
96 Anthony Lane finds that Calvin worked primarily with Augustine's *Quaestiones in Heptateuchum*, though he also referred to *De Genesi ad litteram*, as well as *De Genesi contra Manichaeos* and *De civitate Dei*. Lane, *John Calvin*, pp. 218–220.
97 *Comm. Gen.* 1:26, *CO* XXIII:25–26; CTS 1:93.

interpretation of the names "Jacob" and "Israel." "What Augustine adduces is specious rather than solid; namely, that he was called Jacob in reference to his present life, but Israel in reference to his future life."[98] Calvin is also critical of Augustine's use of allegory, as in his discussion of the ark. "I purposely pass over the allegorical application which Augustine makes of the figure of the ark to the body of Christ, both in his fifteenth book of 'The City of God,' and his twelfth book against Faustus; because I find there scarcely anything solid."[99] However, he willingly embraces Augustine's understanding of the meaning of the restoration of Abraham's strength in his old age.[100] Calvin also appeals to Augustine frequently in order to accentuate the grace of God, even when he disagrees with his interpretation of a specific passage. For example, even though Calvin does not think it is possible to say that the fall happened six hours after the creation of Adam, as Augustine thought, he still agrees with Augustine's description of the weakness of free choice. "I therefore readily subscribe to the exclamation of Augustine, 'O wretched free-will, which, while yet entire, had so little stability!' "[101]

THE GOAL OF THE INTERPRETATION OF GENESIS

The goal of interpretation, as we have seen, is to reveal the mind and intention of the author, which is to be drawn from the genuine meaning of the text. One may get a vivid sense of the kind of exegesis Calvin favored by examining the contrasting terms he uses to describe various exegetical options. He prefers the "simple sense" to the "refined speculations" and "philosophical subtleties" of others; the "genuine meaning" as opposed to the "fables, dreams, and trifles" of others; the "natural meaning" in contrast to the "violent, forced, harsh, and tortured" interpretations of others; the "solid and certain sense" as opposed to the "futile and baseless conjectures" of others; the "sober meaning" in contrast to the "ravings" of others; and the "edifying sense" as opposed to the "frigid interpretation" of others. Since Calvin is convinced that all Scripture is given to us in order to build up and edify the faith and piety of the church, the goal of all interpretation is edification.

---

98 *Comm. Gen.* 35:10, *CO* XXIII:470C; CTS II:241.
99 *Comm. Gen.* 6:14, *CO* XXIII:123C; CTS I:257.
100 *Comm. Gen.* 25:1, *CO* XXIII:343B; CTS II:34.
101 *Comm. Gen.* 3:6, *CO* XXIII:63A; CTS I:156.

Calvin is aware that many passages in Genesis do not appear to have any edifying meaning, and have often been held up to ridicule by the opponents of the Christian faith. For instance, he refers to those who claim that the ark built by Noah was far too small to contain all the animals that Moses claims it held. "Porphyry, or some other caviler, may object, that this is fabulous, because the reason of it does not appear; or because it is unusual; or because it is repugnant to the common order of nature. But I make the rejoinder; that this entire narration of Moses, unless it were replete with miracles, would be cold, and trifling, and ridiculous."[102] The same might be said about the formation of the woman out of the rib of the man while he slept. "Although to profane persons this method of forming woman may seem ridiculous, and some of these may say that Moses is dealing in fables, yet to us the wonderful providence of God here shines forth."[103] Other passages may seem to be superfluously repetitive, as in the three ways that God commands Abram to leave his home. "But the case is quite otherwise. For since exile is in itself sorrowful, and the sweetness of their native soil holds nearly all men bound to itself, God strenuously persists in his command to leave the country, for the purpose of thoroughly penetrating the mind of Abram."[104] Calvin even makes an effort to link the genealogies to the central themes of Genesis, even though he does not investigate their meaning in detail.

Further, the design with which this catalogue was made, was, to inform us, that in the great, or rather, we might say, prodigious multitude of men, there was always a number, though small, who worshipped God; and that this number was wonderfully preserved by celestial guardianship, lest the name of God should be entirely obliterated, and the seed of the Church should fail.[105]

On the other hand, Calvin claims that there are in fact passages of Scripture that contain no edifying message. For example, he expresses little interest in the eating customs followed by Joseph with his brothers in Egypt. "But because these things are trivial, and are not conducive to piety, I only slightly touch upon them; and would even omit them entirely, except that, to remove a scruple from the minds of the unskillful, is sometimes useful, if it be but done sparingly and with brevity."[106] Calvin makes a similar observation about the problem of calculating the

102 *Comm. Gen.* 6:14, *CO* XXIII:123A; CTS I:257.
103 *Comm. Gen.* 2:21, *CO* XXIII:48C; CTS I:132.
104 *Comm. Gen.* 12:1, *CO* XXIII:174B; CTS I:343.
105 *Comm. Gen.* 5:1, *CO* XXIII:105A; CTS I:227.
106 *Comm. Gen.* 43:25, *CO* XXIII:543C; CTS II:360.

time needed to manifest the sterility of the people of Gerar. "Yet, since the correct notation of time does little for the confirmation of our faith, I leave both opinions undecided."[107] Calvin does not see any meaning in the names given to Joseph's children in Egypt, other than that they are foreign names. "I prefer following the Greek interpreters who, by leaving both words untouched, sufficiently prove that they thought them to be of a foreign language."[108] There are other issues on which he refuses to take a position, as in the method by which Joseph removed the people from the land during the famine. "Yet, since the matter is not of great moment, and the signification of the word is ambiguous, I leave the question undecided."[109]

In other instances, edification is to be found not in the words of Moses themselves, but in the probable conjectures Calvin offers with regard to the things Moses left unspoken. According to Calvin, "Moses has not expressed all that ought to come freely into the mind of the reader."[110] When this happens, he thinks it is perfectly legitimate for the interpreter to offer the most probable conjecture regarding the omissions of Moses. For instance, even though Moses does not say why the Lord made the woman out of the rib of the man, Calvin states, "Yet I am more in favor of a different conjecture, namely, that something was taken from Adam, in order that he might embrace, with greater benevolence, a part of himself."[111] On the basis of this conjecture, Calvin goes on to draw doctrine that is edifying for faith. "And in this we see a true resemblance of our union with the Son of God; for he became weak that he might have members of his body endued with strength."[112] When Moses mentions that two years of Joseph's captivity passed before Pharaoh had his dreams, Calvin opens his discussion of the chapter with a conjecture based on experience: "What anxiety oppressed the mind of the holy man during this time, each of us may conjecture from his own feeling; for we are so tender and effeminate, that we can scarcely bear to be put off for a short time."[113] Thus, even though Calvin can be dismissive of the "futile conjectures" of others, he will frequently offer conjectures on those matters which he thinks lead to edification, seeing that "Moses passes

---

107 *Comm. Gen.* 20:17, *CO* xxiii:295B; CTS i:534.
108 *Comm. Gen.* 41:40, *CO* xxiii:525B; CTS ii:330.
109 *Comm. Gen.* 47:21, *CO* xxiii:574A; CTS ii:412.
110 *Comm. Gen.* 33:17, *CO* xxiii:453B; CTS ii:213.
111 *Comm. Gen.* 2:21, *CO* xxiii:49A; CTS i:133.
112 Ibid.   113 *Comm. Gen.* 41:1, *CO* xxiii:518A; CTS ii:317–318.

over many things in silence which may come unsought into the reader's mind."[114]

Other passages raise difficulties for faith and piety on the basis of what they explicitly say. One of the major tasks Calvin sets for himself as an interpreter is to address these questions, so that obstacles are removed that might otherwise cause the pious reader to stumble. This is especially the case in the narrative of the temptation and fall of humanity in the garden. "He then declares, that the whole world, which had been created for the sake of man, fell together with [Satan] from its primary original; and that, in this way, much of its native excellence was destroyed. But here many and arduous questions arise."[115] Calvin then goes on to pose and answer a series of difficult questions, including whether the serpent could of itself have tempted Adam and Eve without Satan; why Moses makes no mention of Satan in this narrative; why there is no narrative detailing the prior fall of Satan; and why God permitted Satan to tempt Adam and Eve when God knew they would fall. He concludes this series of questions by referring the reader to others of his writings. "Whether he sinned by necessity, or by contingency, is another question; respecting which see the *Institutes* and the treatise on *Predestination*."[116]

Calvin raises other questions that would naturally arise in the pious as they read the narrative of Moses. He encourages this kind of questioning, for he wants his readers to inquire into the meaning of Scripture. For instance, when Moses says that God rested on the seventh day, Calvin says, "The question may not improperly be put, what kind of rest this was." He responds by saying that this expression was meant to represent the completion of God's work of creation.[117] When God threatens Adam and Eve with death if they eat of the tree of the knowledge of good and evil, Calvin remarks, "But it is asked, what kind of death God means in this place?"[118] When Moses describes Adam and Eve eating the forbidden fruit, Calvin says, "It is now asked, What was the sin of both of them?"[119] Calvin even asks whether the angels who appeared to Abraham had real bodies, so that they could eat the food that was served to them. Far from forbidding such questions, he thinks that they are edifying. "But, as it is profitable briefly to touch upon such questions; and, as religion in no way

---

114 *Comm. Gen.* 19:4, *CO* XXIII:268B; CTS 1:497.
115 *Comm. Gen.* 3:1, *CO* XXIII:52C; CTS 1:139.
116 *Comm. Gen.* 3:1, *CO* XXIII:56A; CTS 1:145.
117 *Comm. Gen.* 2:2, *CO* XXIII:31–32; CTS 1:103–104.
118 *Comm. Gen.* 2:16, *CO* XXIII:45B; CTS 1:127.
119 *Comm. Gen.* 3:6, *CO* XXIII:60B; CTS 1:152.

forbids us to do so; there is, on the other hand, nothing better than that we should content ourselves with a sober solution of them."[120] Calvin seems to think that such questions will arise naturally in the mind of the reader, even as his conjectures seem to suggest themselves from the silence of Moses.

The two major objectives of interpretation for Calvin are to gather general doctrine from a passage, and to set forth good examples to imitate, as well as bad examples to avoid. By "general doctrine," he means the teaching of Moses that is not bound to the Jews of his day, but may properly be extended to the pious of all ages, including those in Calvin's day. In some passages, Calvin turns immediately to the general doctrine to be gathered from the verse. When Moses says that God reckoned Abram's faith to be righteousness, Calvin speaks of "the rich and hidden doctrine which this passage contains," and proceeds to give a lengthy discussion of justification by faith.[121] When God goes up from Abraham after speaking to him in a vision, Calvin says, "This expression contains a profitable doctrine, namely, that Abraham certainly knew this vision to be from God; for the ascent here spoken implies as much. And it is necessary for the pious to be fully assured that what they hear proceeds from God."[122] In other passages, Calvin gathers the doctrine only after the genuine meaning of the passage has been established. When Moses ascribes the destruction of the world in the deluge to the fact that every imagination of the human heart was evil, Calvin claims that the doctrine of original sin is properly gathered from this passage. "Nevertheless, though Moses here speaks of the wickedness which at that time prevailed in the world, the general doctrine is properly and consistently here elicited. Nor do they rashly distort the passage who extend it to the whole human race."[123] When God tells Abraham that his covenant is with him, Calvin draws the doctrine that faith has reference to God. "Whence a useful doctrine is deduced, that faith necessarily has reference to God: because, although angels and men should speak to us, never would their authority appear sufficiently great to confirm our minds."[124]

Calvin will frequently contrast the general doctrine drawn from the genuine meaning of Genesis to what he takes to be the false doctrine of

---

120 *Comm. Gen.* 18:6, *CO* XXIII:253A; CTS 1:472.
121 *Comm. Gen.* 15:6, *CO* XXIII:211B; CTS 1:404.
122 *Comm. Gen.* 17:22, *CO* XXIII:247B; CTS 1:463.
123 *Comm. Gen.* 6:5, *CO* XXIII:117C; CTS 1:248.
124 *Comm. Gen.* 17:4, *CO* XXIII:236A; CTS 1:446.

the Roman Church. For example, after he elicits the general doctrine of the way faith refers to God alone, he remarks, "Whence also it appears what kind of religion is that of the Papacy: where, instead of the word of God, the fictions of men are alone the subject of boast."[125] When Calvin draws the conclusion from Moses' discussion of circumcision that the word should never be divorced from the sign, he claims "that sacraments are abolished by the Papists; because, the voice of God having become extinct, nothing remains with them, except the residuum of mute figures."[126] Calvin concludes that Sarah laughs at the promise that she shall have a child because she divorces the power of God from God's word, whereas the two ought always to be held together. "In this way the Papists plunge themselves into a profound labyrinth, when they dispute concerning the absolute power of God."[127]

Calvin will also reject the general doctrine that Roman theologians draw from a particular passage, even if it sounds like a plausible interpretation. For instance, when God warns Cain that he should avoid the sin that is tempting him, Calvin claims:

They, however, foolishly trifle, who distort this passage to prove the freedom of the will (*liberum arbitrium*); for if we grant that Cain was admonished of his duty in order that he might apply himself to the subjugation of sin, yet no inherent power of man is hence to be inferred; because it is certain that only by the grace of the Holy Spirit can the affections of the flesh be so mortified that they shall not prevail.[128]

When God punishes Adam and Eve even after having appeared to have forgiven them, Calvin rejects the solution proposed by Roman theologians. "To untie this knot, some have invented a twofold remission, namely a remission of fault and a remission of the punishment, to which the figment of satisfactions was afterwards annexed."[129] Over against this inference, he claims that "this general axiom is to be maintained," that the sufferings of the present life are meant to lead to repentance, humility, and care for the future.[130] When the angel seems to make the blessing of Abraham contingent on his willingness to sacrifice Isaac, Calvin notes that "the Papists boldly seize upon this, and similar passages, in order to

---

125 Ibid.
126 *Comm. Gen.* 17:9, *CO* xxiii:240B; CTS 1:452.
127 *Comm. Gen.* 18:13, *CO* xxiii:255B; CTS 1:476.
128 *Comm. Gen.* 4:7, *CO* xxiii:90C; CTS 1:204.
129 *Comm. Gen.* 3:19, *CO* xxiii:75C; CTS 1:178.
130 *Comm. Gen.* 3:19, *CO* xxiii:76B; CTS 1:179.

prove that works are deserving of all the good things which God confers upon us."[131] He replies by observing that, in order to stimulate us to a holy life, God "transfers to our works what properly belongs to his pure beneficence."[132]

The other way Calvin seeks to edify the faith and piety of the church is by highlighting good examples for the godly to follow, and bad examples which they are warned to avoid. For instance, when God protects Sarai from harm after Abram exposes her to Pharaoh's advances, Calvin offers consolation to the small and endangered evangelical community of his own day. "Instructed by such examples, we may also learn, that however the world may hold us in contempt, on account of the smallness of our number, and our weakness; we are yet so precious in the sight of God, that he will, for our sake, declare himself an enemy to kings, and even to the whole world."[133] If the help of God appears to be absent, we ought to follow the example of Noah, who was delivered from the tomb of the ark when God appeared to be absent. "Let us therefore learn, by this example, to repose on the providence of God, even while he seems to be most forgetful of us; for at length, by affording us help, he will testify that he has been mindful of us."[134] When God confronts us in our trials, as though God were our enemy, we ought to remember the example of Jacob. "Therefore, what was once exhibited under a visible form to our father Jacob, is daily fulfilled in the individual members of the Church; namely, that in their temptations, it is necessary for them to wrestle with God."[135]

On the other hand, Calvin will highlight what he takes to be the sins of the patriarchs in order to refute the Roman teaching that the example of the fathers is always to be followed. When Jacob sins by loving Rachel more than Leah, Calvin says, "At the same time, it appears how dangerous it is to imitate the fathers while we neglect the law of the Lord. And yet the foolish Papists so greatly delight themselves in this imitation, that they do not scruple to observe, as a law, whatever they find to have been practiced by the fathers."[136] This problem was especially acute at the time of Noah, when only examples of impiety could be seen. "Whence it appears, how foolishly the Papists clamor that we ought to follow the fathers; when the Spirit expressly recalls us from the imitation of men,

---

131 *Comm. Gen.* 22:15, *CO* XXIII:318C; CTS I:572.
132 *Comm. Gen.* 22:15, *CO* XXIII:319A; CTS I:572.
133 *Comm. Gen.* 12:17, *CO* XXIII:186C; CTS I:364.
134 *Comm. Gen.* 8:1, *CO* XXIII:135C; CTS I:276.
135 *Comm. Gen.* 32:24, *CO* XXIII:442B; CTS II:196.
136 *Comm. Gen.* 29:30, *CO* XXIII:404C; CTS II:134.

except so far as they lead us to God."[137] Calvin is also concerned lest the evangelicals of his own day appeal to the examples in Genesis in order to excuse their own behavior. When the servant of Abraham adorns Rebekah with a gold earring, Calvin expresses his own aversion to luxury and pomp, in contrast to this example. "Whatever the Lord commands in general terms is to be accounted as an inflexible rule of conduct; but to rely on particular examples is not only dangerous, but even foolish and absurd. Now we know how highly displeasing to God is not only pomp and ambition in adorning the body, but all kind of luxury."[138]

Calvin also highlights the way that the fathers were permitted to do certain things in their own time and situation that would be culpable in another time and place. For instance, when Abraham bows before the Hittites, Calvin interprets this apparently excessive gesture of reverence in light of the customs of eastern peoples.

For it is well known that the Orientals were immoderate in their use of ceremonies. If we compare the Greeks or Italians with ourselves, we are more sparing in our use of them than they. But Aristotle, in speaking of the Asiatics and other barbarians, notes this fault, that they abound too much in adorations. Therefore we must not measure the honor which Abraham paid to the princes of the land by our customs.[139]

The fathers may also have acted by the special impulse of God in ways that should not be held up for emulation, such as the severity and deception exercised by Joseph towards his brothers in Egypt.

Whether God governed his servant by some special movement, to depart without fault, from the common rule of action, I know not; seeing that the faithful may sometimes piously do things which cannot lawfully be drawn into a precedent. Of this, however, in considering the acts of the holy fathers, we must always beware; lest they should lead us away from that law which the Lord prescribes to all in common.[140]

CONCLUSION

Calvin's interpretation of Genesis is marked by an impressive awareness of the historical and cultural distance that separates him from the events being narrated by Moses. He is aware that Moses is writing for the Jews of

137 *Comm. Gen.* 6:9, *CO* xxiii:120C; CTS 1:253.
138 *Comm. Gen.* 24:22, *CO* xxiii:335C; CTS ii:21.
139 *Comm. Gen.* 23:7, *CO* xxiii:325A; CTS 1:582.
140 *Comm. Gen.* 42:7, *CO* xxiii:530C; CTS ii:339.

his day, in a form accommodated to their capacities, under an economy of divine self-disclosure distinct from that of the gospel, in a language with a different dynamic than either Latin or French. He is also aware of the cultural differences separating him from the world of Abraham and Sarah. Calvin tries to interpret Genesis in its own historical, cultural, linguistic, and religious context, and also attempts to place the history of the early Israelites in the context of the wider Gentile world. However, he is also convinced that the fathers and mothers in Genesis are part of the same church of which he is a member, and worship the same God as he. His interpretation is shaped in particular by his own experience of exile for the sake of the right worship of God. It is this experience that draws Calvin close to the narrative of the patriarchs and matriarchs in Genesis, in spite of his awareness of the distance that separates them.

And the condition of the pious, at this day, is not dissimilar: for since they are hated by all, are exposed to contempt and reproach, wander without a home, are sometimes driven hither and thither, and suffer from nakedness and poverty, it is nevertheless their duty to lay hold on the inheritance which is promised. Let us therefore walk through the world, as persons debarred from all repose, who have no other resource than the mirror of the word.[141]

---

141 *Comm. Gen.* 13:16, *CO* xxiii:194B; CTS 1:376.

CHAPTER 2

Calvin as commentator on the Mosaic Harmony and Joshua

Raymond A. Blacketer

CALVIN'S FINAL COMMENTARIES

The final two expositions of Scripture that John Calvin produced before his death were the *Commentary on the Last Four Books of Moses, Arranged in the Form of a Harmony* (referred to as the *Mosaic Harmony*) and his commentary on Joshua.[1] The *Mosaic Harmony* appeared in Latin, along with Calvin's second edition of his Genesis commentary, in 1563. The next year Calvin published the French version, which he himself had translated, with minor revisions.[2] Calvin died on May 27, 1564, but not

---

1 Representative general studies of Calvin's Old Testament expositions include T. H. L. Parker, *Calvin's Old Testament Commentaries* (Edinburgh: T. & T. Clark, 1986; Louisville: Westminster John Knox Press, 1993); David L. Puckett, *John Calvin's Exegesis of the Old Testament* (Louisville: Westminster John Knox Press, 1995); and Wulfert de Greef, *Calvijn en het Oude Testament* (Amsterdam: Ton Bolland, 1984). On the *Mosaic Harmony*, see Raymond A. Blacketer, *The School of God: Pedagogy and Rhetoric in Calvin's Interpretation of Deuteronomy*, Studies in Early Modern Religious Reforms 3 (Dordrecht: Springer, 1995); David F. Wright, "Calvin's Pentateuchal Criticism: Equity, Hardness of Heart, and Divine Accommodation in the Mosaic Harmony Commentary," *Calvin Theological Journal* 21/1 (1986): 33–50; David F. Wright, "Accommodation and Barbarity in John Calvin's Old Testament Commentaries," in *Understanding Poets and Prophets*, ed. A. Graeme Auld (Sheffield: JSOT Press, 1993), pp. 413–427; Marten Woudstra, "Calvin Interprets What 'Moses Reports.' Observations on Calvin's Commentary on Exodus 1–19," *Calvin Theological Journal* 21 (1986): 151–174; and on Joshua see Marten Woudstra, *Calvin's Dying Bequest to the Church: A Critical Evaluation of the Commentary on Joshua* (Grand Rapids: Calvin Theological Seminary, 1960).

2 *Mosis Libri* v, *cum Iohannis Caluini Commentariis. Genesis seorsum: reliqui quatuor in formam harmoniae digesti* (Geneva: Henr. Stephanus, 1563). Calvin's French version appeared the next year: *Commentaires de M. Iean Calvin, sur les cinq liures de Moyse. Genesis est mis à part, les autre quatre liures sont disposez en forme d'Harmonie* (Geneva: François Estienne, 1564), cited as *Commentaires sur les cinq liures de Moyse*. For the chronology of Calvin's publications see Wulfert de Greef, *The Writings of John Calvin: An Introductory Guide*, trans. Lyle Bierma (Grand Rapids: Baker, 1993). Whether Calvin wrote the commentary in French or Latin, the reason for its initial appearance in French may very well have to do with the precarious political situation of Calvin's coreligionists in France. See my article, "The Moribund Moralist: Ethical Lessons in Calvin's Commentary on Joshua," in *The Formation of Clerical and Confessional Identities in Early Modern Europe*, ed. Wim Janse and Barbara Pitkin [= *Nederlands Archief voor Kerkgeschiedenis* 85] (Leiden: Brill, 2005): 149–168.

before he had completed his commentary on Joshua. The French version appeared first, for unknown and debated reasons,[3] followed by the Latin edition. To both of these editions Theodore Beza had added his *Life of Calvin*.[4]

Thus the *Mosaic Harmony* and *Joshua* represent Calvin's exegetical work at its most mature. Calvin had consolidated his position and his program of reform in Geneva, but he was never complacent about the stability of those reforms. He continued to defend his positions to the end. His health, which had always been a problem for Calvin, was quickly declining in these last years. But there is no evidence of diminished capacity or energy in either of these final commentaries that he produced.

While most of Calvin's published interpretations of the Old Testament had originated as academic lectures, his expositions of the latter Pentateuch and Joshua were among his *commentarii* proper; he wrote and intended these works for publication and a wide readership. Both of these commentaries likely had their genesis in *congrégations* that Calvin had led. These Friday morning sessions were devoted to the study of Scripture. The ministers of Geneva were required to participate, while other interested parties could also attend. Apparently Calvin often dominated, or at least directed, these meetings. By late 1559 Calvin had already planned out his innovative rearrangement of the material of the latter Pentateuch, and he was testing it out in the Friday *congrégations*.[5] One of the *congrégations* on Joshua was recently discovered and published.[6]

Calvin had also preached through the book of Deuteronomy from March 1555 through July 1556, producing 200 weekday sermons on the last book of the Pentateuch. The existence of these sermons provides an excellent opportunity to compare Calvin's exegesis of Deuteronomy in the mid-1550s with his expositions in the *Mosaic Harmony* from 1563.[7] His

---

3 While Parker argues that Calvin wrote the commentary in French, more evidence would be required before one could conclude that Calvin deviated from his lifelong practice of writing his commentaries in Latin. Cf. Parker, *Calvin's Old Testament Commentaries*, p. 33.

4 *Commentaires de M. Iean Calvin sur le livre de Iosué* (Geneva, F. Perrin, 1564); *Ioannis Calvini In librum Iosue brevis commentarius* (Geneva, F. Perrin, 1564).

5 See Colladon's *Vie de Calvin*, *CO* xxi:90: "Ceste annee-la sur la fin on commença à exposer en la Congregation les Vendredis les quatre derniers livres de Moyse par forme d'harmonie, ainsi que Calvin l'a comprinse en son Commentaire qu'il fit imprimer depuis." Cf. Parker, *Calvin's Old Testament Commentaries*, p. 31.

6 Danielle Fischer, ed. "Congrégation sur Josué 1, 1–5 (4 Juin 1563): Première édition du manuscrit original," *Freiburger Zeitschrift für Philosophie und Theologie* 35 (1988): 201–221.

7 See Blacketer, *The School of God*, for comparisons between the Deuteronomy sermons and the *Mosaic Harmony*. On Calvin's rhetoric, see Olivier Millet, *Calvin et la dynamique de la parole. Etude de rhétorique réformée* (Paris: Librairie Honoré Champion, 1992); Olivier Millet, "*Docere/*

treatment of a pericope can differ significantly from the sermon to
the commentary. But most of these differences result from the diverse
methods Calvin employed in the genres of sermon and commentary. The
greatest contrast between the two forms of exposition is found in his
rhetorical style. In the commentaries he sought to maintain a style marked
by brevity. Calvin believed that, when it comes to commentaries, less is
more. He diverged from this principle somewhat in the *Mosaic Harmony*,
as we shall observe. But in the sermons Calvin had few qualms about
repetition or prolixity. He believed that copious oratory has a place,
particularly when one is trying to teach students who are slow to learn
and quick to forget.

Calvin does not pepper his *Mosaic Harmony* with references to classical
authors, but this commentary is lightly seasoned with references to
Xenophon, Plato, Aristotle, Pythagoras, Cicero, Cato, Strabo, Tacitus,
and the poets Horace and Ovid. The legal material of the Pentateuch
affords an opportunity for Calvin to dust off his skills as a Renaissance
lawyer; he will occasionally cite classical authorities while interpreting the
legal portions of the Pentateuch.[8] In this respect the *Mosaic Harmony* is
somewhat reminiscent of his first work, the commentary on Seneca's *De
Clementia*.[9]

CALVIN'S SOURCES

Contrary to the impression one might receive from older studies of
Calvin's exegesis, he did not interpret Scripture in isolation from the
interpretive tradition or other commentators of his day. Calvin is in
constant dialogue with the exegetical tradition. In the case of the latter
Pentateuch and Joshua, there are a number of possible sources that he
could have used.[10]

Movere: Les catégories rhétoriques et leurs sources humanistes dans la doctrine calvinienne de la
foi," in *Calvinus sincerioris religionis vindex*, ed. W. H. Neuser and B. G. Armstrong (Kirksville,
MO: Sixteenth Century Journal Publishers, 1997): 35–51.

8 Calvin's one reference to Cicero in *Joshua* also pertains to a legal question; see below, n. 69.

9 *Commentary on Seneca's* De Clementia, ed. and trans. Ford Lewis Battles and André Malan Hugo
(Leiden: E. J. Brill/The Renaissance Society of America, 1969), cited as *Comm. Sen. De Clem.*,
followed by the 1532 pagination/Battles-Hugo pagination.

10 There was an inventory taken of the books in the Genevan Academy in 1572, but this was eight
years after Calvin's death, and most of these volumes did not belong to him. Nonetheless, this
inventory provides an interesting glimpse into some of the resources that could have been
available to Calvin. See Alexandre Ganoczy, *La Bibliothèque de l'Académie de Calvin* (Geneva:
Librairie Droz, 1969); hereafter cited as *BAC*.

Among patristic sources, there was Augustine's *Quaestiones in Hepta-teuchum libri VII*, and *Locutionum in Heptateuchum libri VII*,[11] as well as the *Quaestiones veteris et novi testamenti* once attributed to Augustine but now identified with Ambrosiaster.[12] Origen produced homilies on Exodus, Leviticus, Numbers, and Joshua.[13] Isidore of Seville also commented on the Pentateuch and numerous other Old Testament books.[14]

Most commentators in Calvin's day would have been familiar with the medieval *Glossa ordinaria* and Nicholas of Lyra's comprehensive *postillae*.[15] Calvin's knowledge of this medieval interpretive tradition, however, may have been mediated through Luther and other commentators.[16] Another possible source is Denis the Carthusian's commentary on the Pentateuch, which was printed twice in Cologne during Calvin's lifetime.[17] Calvin's knowledge of rabbinic interpretations may be derived from these medieval students of the Jewish exegetical tradition; but it is even more certain that he regularly consulted Sebastian Münster's *Hebraica Biblia*.[18]

11 The texts of these works can be found in *CCSL*, vol. XXXIII (Turnholt: Brepols, 1958).

12 Pseudo-Augustine (Ambrosiaster), *Quaestiones veteris et novi testamenti* CXXVII, ed. Alexander Souter, in *CSEL*, vol. L (Leipzig: G. Freytag, 1907). See Johannes Quasten and Angelo DiBerardino, eds., *Patrology*, 4 vols. (Westminster, MD: Christian Classics, 1992), IV:180.

13 Some of these works by Origen have been translated into English or French: *Homélies sur l'Exode*, trans. P. Fortier, ed. H. de Lubac (Paris: Éditions du Cerf, [1947]); *Homilies on Leviticus: 1–16*, trans. and ed. Gary Wayne Barkley (Washington: Catholic University of America Press, 1990); *Homélies sur Josué*, trans. and ed. Annie Jaubert (Paris: Éditions du Cerf, 1960).

14 *Isidori Hispalensis episcopi, theologi peruetusti, enarrationes doctissimae breuissimae in Genesim, Exodum, Leuiticum, Numeros, Deuteronomiu, Iosue, Iudicum, Regu IIII, Esdram, Machabae* (Cologne: Petrus Quentel, 1530). Reprinted in *PL* LXXXIII:207–424.

15 In 1572 the library of the Genevan Academy possessed an edition of Lyra's literal and moral *postillae* which included the *Glossa ordinaria* and the *Additiones* of Paul of Burgos and Matthias Döring: Nicholas of Lyra, *Biblia Sacra cum glossis interlineari et ordinaria, Nicolai Lyrani Postilla & Moralitatibus, Burgensis Additionibus, & Thoringi Replicis*, 6 vols. (Lyon, 1545), *BAC* #73, cited as "Lyra" followed by the volume and folio.

16 See A. N. S. Lane, *John Calvin: Student of the Church Fathers* (Grand Rapids: Baker Books, 1999), p. 227 and n. 159.

17 The 1572 Genevan Library Catalogue lists the Carthusian's commentary on the *Sentences*, as well as a three-volume *Opera*, which is not identified (see *BAC* #88, #89, p. 189). His Pentateuch commentary was printed in 1534, 1548, and 1566.

18 Münster, one of the leading Hebraists of the sixteenth century, produced an edition of the Hebrew text with Latin translation and notes entitled . . . מִקְרַשׁ יְעֶשְׂרִים וְאַרְפַּ ע / *Hebraica Biblia, latina planeque nova Sebast. Munsteri translatione* . . . 2nd edn (Basel, 1546), cited as *Hebraica Biblia*. The editor of the CTS edition of the *Mosaic Harmony* makes 112 references to this work in his notes. It is also likely that Calvin obtained much of his knowledge of rabbinic exegesis through other commentators. See Max Engammare, "*Joannes Calvinus trium linguarum peritus?* La question de l'Hébreu," *Bibliothèque d'Humanisme et Renaissance* 58 (1996): 35–60 (esp. p. 47). There was also Paul Fabius' Latin translation of the *Targum Onkelos* to the Pentateuch; *BAC* lists a 1546 edition printed in Strasbourg: #20(1), p. 165.

There were also more recent expositions of the Pentateuch and Joshua that Calvin may have studied. These included Luther's lectures on Deuteronomy,[19] Conrad Pellikan's comprehensive *Commentaria Bibliorum*,[20] and Johannes Bugenhagen's commentary on Deuteronomy and the books of Samuel.[21] Martin Borrhaus, also known as Cellarius, had flirted with the radical wing of the Reformation, but later rehabilitated himself as a more mainstream reformer. He published his Pentateuch commentary in 1555.[22] Johannes Brenz commented on the Pentateuch and Joshua.[23] The learned exegete Thomas Cardinal de Vio (Cajetan) authored commentaries on the Pentateuch and Joshua that emphasized the literal sense and exhibited humanistic influences.[24] Wolfgang Musculus wrote a rather prolix exposition of the Decalogue, published in 1553.[25] In addition, as T. H. L. Parker observes, not all of Calvin's sources were printed books. Twice in his lectures on Daniel Calvin reveals that his exposition was informed by discussions with his colleague at the Academy, professor of Hebrew Antoine Chevallier.[26]

---

19 Note the edition of Luther's *Opera omnia* listed in *BAC*, #93 (p. 191), printed at Wittenberg, 1551–1561. The edition used in this work is *Deuteronomion Mosi cum annotationibus* (1525), in *D. Martin Luthers Werke, Kritische Gesamtausgabe*, 60 vols. to date (Weimar: Hermann Böhlhaus Nachfolger, 1883–), vol. xiv, cited as WA. ET in *Luther's Works*, American Edition, vol. ix, ed. Jaroslav Pelikan and Daniel Poellot (Saint Louis: Concordia, 1960), cited as *LW*.

20 Conrad Pellikan, *Commentaria Bibliorum*, 5 vols. (Zurich: Christopher Froschauer, 1532); *BAC* #105, p. 195. On Pellikan, see Christoph Zürcher, *Konrad Pellikans Wirken in Zürich 1526–1556* (Zurich: Theologischer Verlag, 1975).

21 *Ioannis Bvgenhagii Pomerani Annotationes ab ipso iam emissae. In Deuteronomium. In Samuelem prophetam, id est duos libros Regum* (Basel: Adam Petri, 1524), *BAC* #113(1), p. 198.

22 Martin Borrhaus, *In Mosem, diuinum legislatorem, paedagogum ad Messiam Seruatorem mundi, Commentarii* (Basel: Ioannis Oporinus, 1555); *BAC* #201, p. 228. Cited as *In Mosem*. On Borrhaus, see R. L. Williams, "Martin Cellarius and the Reformation in Strasburg," *Journal of Ecclesiastical History* 32/4 (1981): 477–497; Abraham Friesen, "Martin Borrhaus: On the Borders of Heresy," in *Profiles of Radical Reformers*, ed. Hans-Jürgen Goertz and Walter Klaasen (Kitchener, ON and Scottdale, PA: Herald Press, 1982), pp. 234–246.

23 Johannes Brenz, *In Exodum Mosis commentarii* (Halle: Brubachius, 1544); *In Leviticum librum Mosis commentarius* (Frankfurt: Brubachius, 1552), see *BAC* #162A, B (p. 215); *Brevis et pia explicatio in Librum Iosuae* (Frankfurt: Petrus Brubacchius, 1553), cited as *In Librum Iosuae*. His commentaries on Numbers and Deuteronomy seem to have appeared only in his collected works, published after Calvin's death: *Operum reverendi et clarissimi theologi D. Joannis Brentii*, 8 vols. (Tübingen: G. Gruppenbach, 1576–1594), vol. i.

24 Ganoczy lists the Paris, 1539 edn, *BAC* #77, p. 184; the edition used in this study is the *Opera omnia quotquot in sacrae scriptura* (Lyon: Iacobus and Petrus Prost, 1639), cited as *Opera Omnia*.

25 Wolfgang Musculus, *In Decalogum praeceptorum Dei explanatio* (Basel: Ioan. Hervagius, 1553), cited as *In Decalogum*. On Musculus, see Craig S. Farmer, "Wolfgang Musculus and the Allegory of Malchus's Ear," *Westminster Theological Journal* 56 (1994): 285–301; Craig S. Farmer, *The Gospel of John in the Sixteenth Century: The Johannine Exegesis of Wolfgang Musculus*, Oxford Studies in Historical Theology (New York: Oxford University Press, 1997).

26 Parker, *Calvin's Old Testament Commentaries*, p. 23. The references occur at Dan. 2:1 and 2:44 (*CO* XL:557, 604).

Calvin's dialogue with the exegetical tradition and with contemporary biblical expositors is typically subtle and oblique. He mentions primarily those interpretations with which he disagrees, and he only infrequently mentions another interpreter by name.[27] Exceptional is Calvin's explicit reference to Hesychius (or Isychius) of Jerusalem in his *Mosaic Harmony.* Hesychius, a fifth-century monk and cleric, produced a commentary on Leviticus that was decidedly allegorical in nature.[28] Commenting on Leviticus 3:16 (the Lord's claim to the fat of the burnt offerings), Calvin derides allegorical interpretations "suitable only for tickling people's ears" and mentions those of Hesychius, who "pretended that the fat represented spiritual affections" and then "metamorphoses it into gross appetites."[29] Calvin prefers the "simple" interpretation, namely that the choicest part of the sacrifice should be reserved for God in order to restrain the priests' natural inclination to gluttony. He again makes explicit mention of Hesychius' allegories at Leviticus 11:9, which categorizes fish with fins and scales as clean foods. Calvin dismisses Hesychius' speculations about the spiritual significance of scales and fins as mere triflings that he will not stoop to discuss. Similarly foolish, Calvin says, is his theory that the names of the fish are not mentioned because the church, which is signified by the fish, does not seek a name on earth. Those who love allegories such as those dreamed up by Hesychius, as far as Calvin is concerned, can be left to "wander in their labyrinth."[30]

Calvin is typically silent about authors with whom he agrees, especially if he happens to concur with an allegorizer like Hesychius, as is the case when Calvin takes up Leviticus 18:5 (those who keep God's decrees and laws will live). Contrary to those who interpret the passage as pertaining to temporal existence, Calvin asserts that the reference is to eternal life. In this he agrees with Hesychius, but this is not something Calvin would be quick to reveal.[31]

---

27 See Lane, *John Calvin,* p. 3.

28 A sixteenth-century edition is *Isychii Presbyteri Hierosolymorum, In Leviticum Libri Septem* (Basel: A. Cratandrus, 1527). The authenticity of this work has long been disputed, but the current consensus is that it is authentic; see Quasten and DiBerardino, *Patrology,* III:488–491.

29 Lev. 3:16 is categorized in the *Mosaic Harmony* under the second commandment, *CO* XXIV:514; ET in CTS *Mosaic Harmony,* II:335. CTS references in this chapter are to the original Edinburgh edition. See Hesychius, *In Leviticum,* fol. 18^r–18^v.

30 See Hesychius, *In Leviticum,* fol. 59^r–59^v; Calvin on Lev. 11:9, categorized under the first commandment, *CO* XXIV:349, CTS *Mosaic Harmony,* II:65. Calvin, on occasion, is less hostile to allegories that he finds particularly suitable; see Blacketer, *The School of God,* ch. 6.

31 *CO* XXV:7; CTS *Mosaic Harmony,* III:204 and n. 1, where the editor cites the comments of Andrew Willet on various interpretations of the passage. Cf. Hesychius, *In Leviticum,* fol. 105^r, where he speaks of the "*iudicia & praecepta . . . per quas aeterna vita hominibus praestant.*"

THE METHOD OF THE 'MOSAIC HARMONY'

Certainly the most significant feature of Calvin's final commentaries is his unusual method of interpreting the latter books of the Pentateuch.[32] It was his most ambitious and innovative exegetical venture, and for that reason it also held the greatest risk. In the *Mosaic Harmony* Calvin borrows a method commonly used to exposit the first three gospels and applies it to the books of Exodus through Deuteronomy. He arranges all of the historical narrative into a chronological harmony and organizes all of the doctrinal and legislative material into a topical harmony.

These two main divisions, history and doctrine, constitute the most basic hermeneutical distinction that Calvin employs in the *Mosaic Harmony*. For Calvin, biblical history is simply an alternate mode of teaching doctrine. In his commentary on Seneca's *De Clementia*, he had observed that "for Cicero, *History is life's schoolmistress*; in her, as in a mirror, we see our own life. We discern with our eyes what we are to avoid, what to follow."[33] Thus the Old Testament narrative serves as a mirror in which the people of God see themselves, and, if they are wise, profit from what they see in this historical reflection.[34] This perspective on biblical history as a mode of teaching doctrine is reminiscent of what Luther, in his own lectures on Deuteronomy, calls "proper allegories," which he carefully distinguishes from irresponsible allegories (*inepta studia in allegoriis*) such as those perpetrated by Jerome and Origen. A proper allegory, according to Luther, is one that draws doctrine from history by describing the ministry of the Word or the progress of the gospel and of faith.[35]

In the middle of this narrative history, at Exodus 20, Calvin switches to the topical section. He organizes this section according to various *loci communes*. The doctrinal section of the *Mosaic Harmony*, then, is reminiscent of Melanchthon's commentary method, with the exception that Calvin treats every verse of the text. The Decalogue provides the ten major *loci* or topics that give order and meaning to all of the legal and didactic material of the Pentateuch. After all, one of the primary purposes of such *loci*, according to both Melanchthon and Calvin, is to point out to the student what major subjects must be sought in Scripture.[36]

---

32 See Blacketer, *The School of God*, ch. 4.   33 *Comm. Sen. De Clem.*, 14/50–51.
34 Cf. Sermon 1 on Deuteronomy, *CO* xxv:606.   35 WA xiv:500 (*praef.*), *LW* ix:7–8.
36 See Melanchthon, *Loci Communes* (1521), dedicatory letter: "Porro, quod ad argumenti summam attinet, indicantur hic Christianae disciplinae praecipui loci, ut intelligat iuventus, et quae sint in scripturis potissimum requirenda . . ." (*CR* xiii:81–82), and cf. with Calvin, *Institutes* (1539), *Epistola ad lectorem*, fol. *1ᵛ: "Porro hoc mihi in isto labore propositum fuit, sacrae Theologiae

These *loci*, Melanchthon says, help one to determine the *scopus* of a study.[37]

The Decalogue constitutes the main set of *loci*, which Calvin supplements with other categories such as the Preface to the Law and the Sanctions of the Law. Calvin then categorizes all of the legal and didactic material found dispersed through the latter Pentateuch according to one of these headings. He interprets all of the laws and teachings of the Pentateuch as elaborations on, or explications of, one of the Ten Commandments or the other *loci* related to the Decalogue. In rhetorical terms, moreover, the expository passages of the law function as a *repetitio* of the main topic or *locus*, and the supplements serve as *amplificationes*.[38]

For example, under the seventh commandment Calvin categorizes not only legislation pertaining to adultery, but also the prohibition against bestiality. Under each of the commandments Calvin includes subcategories that he calls appendices or supplements to the commandment. Under the political supplements to the seventh commandment he includes prohibitions against incest and regulations pertaining to sexual matters such as consanguinity, dowries, betrothal, divorce, prostitution, homosexuality, and the seduction of a virgin. Calvin even has to deal with the sensitive matter of a woman who fights dirty and attacks a man below the belt (Deut. 25:11–12), as well as the prohibition against cross-dressing (Deut. 22:5). Both of these precepts, according to Calvin, serve to teach the virtue of modesty. In the former case, the penalty for a woman who attacks a man's genitals is severe (her hand is to be cut off) because, as Calvin explains, any chaste woman would naturally recoil from the sight or touch of that part of a man's body.[39]

IMPROVING ON PERFECTION

Calvin begins his *Praefatio* to the *Mosaic Harmony* with a defense of his atypical method. He recognizes that no previous interpreter has attempted

candidatos ad divini verbi lectionem ita praeparare et instruere, ut et facilem ad eam aditum habere, et inoffenso omnibus partibus sic mihi complexus esse videor, et eo quoquo ordine digessisse, ut siquis eam recte tenuerit, ei non sit difficile statuere et quid potissimum quaerere in Scriptura, et quem in scopum quicquid in ea continetur referre debeat" (*OS* III:6). Calvin's purpose in his *Institutes* is virtually identical to that of Melanchthon's *Loci Communes*. Calvin's *Institutes* is in fact his own repository of *loci communes*.

37 *Loci Communes* (1521): "Requiri solent in singulis artibus loci quidam, quibus artis cuiusque summa comprehenditur, qui scopi vice, ad quem omnia studia dirigamus." *CR* XIII:83.

38 Cf. Millet, *Calvin et la dynamique de la parole*, ch. 24: "L'Abondance (répétition, variation, *expolitio*) et la brièveté calviniennes: formes codifiées," 733–762.

39 *CO* XXIV:667–668; CTS *Mosaic Harmony*, III:108–110.

to harmonize the latter four books of the Pentateuch, at least not in the manner or scale that he has undertaken. He anticipates that his enemies will accuse him of novelty and innovation, which are tantamount to heresy. But he also worries that some of his fellow Protestants might think him presumptuous for attempting to improve on the teaching of Moses, who wrote under the inspiration of the Holy Spirit. Calvin takes pains to affirm the flawlessness of the inspired text; it is *"optimum"* and *"in omni utilitatis genere perfectissimum."*[40]

Nevertheless, Calvin needs to make a number of improvements on this perfect text. The substance of the teaching is flawless and divine in origin; but the method that Moses employs to teach this doctrine is not what Calvin would consider optimal. Moses taught the people whenever the opportunity would arise. Calvin implies – but does not dare state – that the resulting texts lack clarity and organization. They require an expert to sort them out; otherwise an untrained reader would "wander around" in the text, and fail to discern the themes and purpose (*scopus*) of the work. Fortunately, Calvin is just such an expert.

One of Calvin's primary concerns in all of his work is that of proper pedagogy, what he calls the "right order of teaching." It is that concern that drives his unusual method in the *Mosaic Harmony*. His intention is to provide order and clarity to the material, so that a pastor or teacher with limited time or training can more easily navigate this vast textual terrain. A person with less training, or a busy pastor, could easily get lost among the numerous precepts of the Pentateuch; thus Calvin provides such persons with the big picture. Calvin explicitly compares his method in the *Mosaic Harmony* to Moses' procedure in Deuteronomy. Just as Moses provided the people with a compendium and summary of forty years' worth of teaching, so Calvin will provide his readers with a compendium of the latter Pentateuch, organized in such a way as to bring out the meaning of its frequently obscure and arcane passages.

The interpretive key to most of the doctrinal and legal material of the latter Pentateuch, according to Calvin, is the Decalogue. But not everyone will be able to figure out which of the Ten Commandments has to do with prescriptions such as the prohibition against boiling a kid in its mother's milk (Exod. 23:19, 34:26; Deut. 14:21). Calvin's commentary remedies this situation by clarifying that this strange piece of legislation pertains to the sacrifices, and by placing this prescription under the

40 *CO* xxiv:5–6, CTS *Mosaic Harmony*, 1:xiv.

second commandment, which prescribes how God's people should worship him properly and purely. There the reader will find Calvin's opinion that this prescription also teaches the people a lesson about cruelty.[41] In this way Calvin seeks to set before his readers the "intention and design of the holy Prophet they may be enabled to profit more from his writings."[42]

At the beginning of his exegetical career Calvin had declared his unrelenting adherence to the principle of brief and clear expositions in his commentaries.[43] He would leave his extended polemical discussions and *loci communes* out of his commentaries and put them into his *Institutes*. In this he differed from the approach of Martin Bucer, who would digress into discussions of theological topics as they arose in the text. The result was that Bucer's commentaries were bulkier and more prone to repetition. Calvin judged this method to be tedious for the average reader; he preferred the Laconic rhetorical style, that of perspicuous brevity. Calvin continues to declare his allegiance to the principle of brevity in the *Mosaic Harmony*.[44] How consistently he actually practiced it, however, is another matter.

In fact, while Calvin does not engage in excessively long discussions of the biblical text in his *Mosaic Harmony*, he does deviate somewhat from his principle of leaving *loci communes* out of his commentaries.[45] The ten *loci* of the Decalogue function as an organizational and interpretive structure, and so this in itself would not qualify as digressing into commonplaces, that is, creating excursuses in which to debate theological questions. But there are other instances in which Calvin does digress. For example, he precedes his treatment of the fifth commandment with a discussion of how the commandments should be numbered and distributed between the two tables of the law.[46] Calvin disagrees with the

---

41 *CO* XXIV:543–544.   42 *CO* XXIV:5–6; cf. CTS *Mosaic Harmony* I: xv, alt.

43 He does so in the often cited dedicatory letter from his Romans commentary, addressed to Simon Grynaeus, *CO* X:402–406.

44 Calvin makes this claim of brevity in his dedicatory letter to the French version of the complete Pentateuch commentary of 1564, addressed to Henry, Duke of Vendôme, later Henry IV of France. *Comm. Gen.* I, *CO* XX:121; CTS 1:3.

45 Richard Muller observes that this deviation from Calvin's earlier method can be observed particularly in the Psalms commentary and the *Mosaic Harmony*. See his discussion in *The Unaccommodated Calvin: Studies in the Foundation of a Theological Tradition* (New York: Oxford University Press, 1998), pp. 113, 155–156, 182–183.

46 *CO* XXIV:601–602.

traditional Roman Catholic enumeration of the commandments, which Luther had adopted. His treatment of the matter is not so much an exposition of the text as a digression into a disputed theological topic, something which Calvin ordinarily seeks to avoid in his commentaries. His comments here are a summary of what he says about the matter in his *Institutes,* where, significantly, he refers to the question of the division of the commandments as a *locus,* and, in this case, a disputed topic of discussion.[47]

Two more examples are to be found in the sections that Calvin adds following his exposition of the Decalogue and all of its related precepts. The first section is a discussion of the end and use of the law; the second considers texts that confirm and ratify the law by means of promises or threats. In the latter section, Calvin precedes his exposition of the biblical text with what appears to be a brief *locus communis.* He makes it clear that God is not inherently indebted to humanity. Nonetheless, by making a covenant with sinners, God voluntarily obligates himself to us. "And this has been pointed out by the common theologians, that the reward of good works does not depend on their dignity or merit, but upon his covenant (*ex pacto*)."[48] Calvin had previously rejected as useless speculation the traditional scholastic distinction between God's absolute and ordained power.[49] Now, however, he finds the distinction quite useful, despite the fact that he still disagrees with the "common theologians" over so-called congruent merits.[50] This mini-*locus* parallels a section in the *Institutes,* dating from the 1539 edition, where Calvin had also cited Leviticus 18:5, one of the texts that he categorizes under the sanctions of the law. In the *Institutes,* however, he had emphasized humanity's debt to God; there is no mention of God obligating himself to humanity.[51] Thus one must look

---

47 *Inst.* ii.8.12: "Nobis quidem hic locus necessario attingendus est, ne quam posituri sumus divisionem, ceu novam et nuper excogitatam lectores aut rideant aut mirentur." *OS* iii:353. This section of the text first appeared in the 1539 edition.

48 *CO* xxv:6.

49 See David C. Steinmetz, "Calvin and the Absolute Power of God," in his *Calvin in Context* (New York Oxford University Press, 1995), pp. 40–52.

50 For the late medieval theology of *pactum* and the related concepts of the *potentia Dei absoluta* and the *potentia Dei ordinata,* see Heiko Oberman, *The Harvest of Medieval Theology: Gabriel Biel and Late Medieval Nominalism,* 3rd edn (Durham, NC: Labyrinth, 1983); Francis Oakley, "Pierre d'Ailly and the Absolute Power of God: Another Note on the Theology of Nominalism," *Harvard Theological Review* 56/1 (1963): 59–73; Martin Greschat, "Der Bundgedanke in der Theologie des späten Mittelalters," *Zeitschrift für Kirchengeschichte* 81/1 (1970): 44–63; Berndt Hamm, *Promissio, Pactum, Ordinatio: Freiheit und Selbstbindung Gottes in der scholastischen Gnadenlehre,* Beiträge zur historischen Theologie 54 (Tübingen: J. C. B. Mohr [Paul Siebeck], 1977).

51 *Inst.* ii.8.4; *OS* iii:345–346.

to the *Mosaic Harmony* to find Calvin's most mature systematic reflection on the topic of God's contractual obligations.

The most obvious instance of a *locus communis* is Calvin's discussion of the "End and Use of the Law." This section of the commentary is unmistakably a digression into commonplaces.[52] Here Calvin discusses the first and third uses of the law, the *usus theologicus* (whereby persons are convicted of their sin and helplessness before God) and the *usus in renatis* or *usus normativus* (the law as a moral guide). Calvin asserts that the law in general is not abrogated, and thus still pertains to the Christian life.[53] There are three senses, however, in which the law is abrogated. Those elements which pertain exclusively to the era of Moses, and not to that of Christ (this is "the letter" of which Paul speaks in 2 Cor. 3:6) are no longer in force. Secondly, with respect to the threats and promises of the law, perfect obedience is no longer demanded as a condition of salvation. Finally, the ceremonial provisions of the law, the elementary rudiments by which God educated his people in preparation for the gospel (French: "an ABC for little children") have been rendered obsolete by the coming of Christ and his advanced curriculum for a more mature people of God. Calvin concludes this section by referring his readers to his *Institutes* (II. vii), where they may find a more ample and extended discussion of this theological *locus*.[54]

When Calvin takes up these theological topics that are related to the text, but not directly derived from a particular passage, his method begins to mirror that of Bucer, if only for a few fleeting pages. One likely reason for this loosening up of Calvin's self-imposed strictures is the fact that he no longer anticipated any new editions of his *Institutes* after 1560. Since he would not be augmenting or adding *loci* to that work, he occasionally exempts himself from the rule that he will not discuss theological *loci* in his biblical commentaries. One more example of this digression into commonplaces occurs at Calvin's exposition of Exodus 3:14. Here he

---

52 Cf. Bucer's comments on this topic: *Enarratio in Evangelion Iohannis*, ed. Irena Backus, Martini Buceri Opera Latina 2 (Leiden: E. J. Brill, 1988), pp. 386–389.

53 Cf. *Inst.* II.7.14–16. Calvin here significantly differs from Melanchthon in the 1521 *Loci Communes*. Melanchthon concedes that most writers consider only the ceremonial and political aspects of the law to have been abrogated by the New Testament: "*Et consensus scriptorum obtinuit iudicialia et cerimonialia exolevisse. Moralia novata esse.*" Nevertheless, he asserts that even the moral law, i.e. the Decalogue, has been "antiquated" by the New Testament: "*Esse antiquata novo testamento partem legis, quam decalogum, seu praecepta moralia vocant . . . Necesse est itaque fateri decalogum etiam antiquatum esse.*" *CR* XXI:193–194.

54 *CO* 24:728. In the French, Calvin refers his readers to the "*plus ample declaration*" of the topic found in his *Institutes*. Cf. *Commentaires sur les cinq liures de Moyse*, p. 457.

engages in an extended discussion of God's essence and attributes, a topic that he had, for the most part, passed over in the *Institutes*.[55] While Calvin had stopped revising the *Institutes*, he had not stopped reflecting on theological topics. The results of his most mature theological reflections, then, are as likely to appear in his later commentaries as in his *Institutes*.

POSSIBLE SOURCES OF INSPIRATION

No previous commentator had attempted to interpret the Pentateuch in precisely the same way that Calvin does in the *Mosaic Harmony*. Calvin himself had expressed anxiety about how his method would be received. The fact that his approach was novel and innovative was not necessarily a selling point. These qualities could be indicators of doctrinal deviation or excessive pride on the part of the author.

Yet Calvin's method is not entirely without precedent. Latent within the exegetical and theological tradition was the idea that the Ten Commandments are a summary of all conceivable laws. Every moral, religious, or political prescription stems from one of these ten basic principles. Thomas Aquinas, for example, affirms that "all the moral precepts of the Old Law are reducible to the ten precepts of the Decalogue."[56]

Moreover, there had been similar, but less ambitious, attempts at categorizing the pentateuchal legislation. In the rabbinic tradition there were interpreters who speculated that between the Ten Commandments were inscribed all of the supplementary precepts, so that all of the 613 commandments of the Torah appeared on the original stone tablets. The result would look something like a medieval interlinear gloss. The tenth-century rabbi Saadiah Gaon had even classified all of the biblical precepts according to the Decalogue in his *Sefer ham-Mizwoth*.[57] Calvin actually refers to Saadiah in his comments on Isaiah 40:31.[58] But he certainly never studied Saadiah's writings; he almost certainly derives this reference from Oecolampadius.[59] Most of his rabbinic knowledge is secondhand in

---

55 As Muller observes in *The Unaccommodated Calvin*, pp. 153–154; see *CO* xxiv:43–44; CTS *Mosaic Harmony*, 1:73–74. Cf. Pellikan's discussion of the Tetragrammaton, *Commentaria Bibliorum*, 1:70ʳ.

56 *Summa Theologiae* Ia IIae Q. 100, art. 3, ET from Blackfriars edn, 60 vols. (London and New York: Blackfriars, 1964–1981), xxix:64–67.

57 See Isadore Twersky, *Introduction to the Code of Maimonides* (Mishneh Torah), Yale Judaica Series 22 (New Haven: Yale University Press, 1980), p. 248.

58 Calvin refers to him as Zaadias. *Comm. Isa.* 40:31, *CO* xxxvii: 30; CTS iii:239–240.

59 The reference to Saadiah likely originates from Johannes Oecolampadius' commentary on Isaiah, *ad loc., In Iesaiam prophetam . . . Commentariorum* (Basel: 1525): 215ᵛ.

origin, derived from other commentators or sources such as Münster's *Hebraica Biblia.*

Another possible source of inspiration is the work of Philo of Alexandria. While Calvin would have no sympathy for Philo's allegorical proclivities, he did share his concern for proper method. Philo also used the Decalogue as an organizing principle and interpretive key to the legal material in the Pentateuch. The Ten Commandments, he says, "are the generic heads (γενικὰ κεφάλαια), and roots (ῥίζαι), and principles (ἀρχαί) of the infinite multitude of particular laws; being the everlasting source of all commands, and containing every imaginable injunction and prohibition to the great advantage of those who use them.[60] Philo's treatise on the Decalogue was entitled *On the Ten Words, Which are Headings of Laws.*[61] Had Calvin simply perused the table of contents from a collection of Philo's works, this title alone could have helped give birth to the plan that lay behind his *Mosaic Harmony.*

Nonetheless, Philo did not attempt to classify every piece of Mosaic legislation. Nor did he employ the same criteria for categorizing the laws. For example, Philo treats the dietary restrictions under the tenth commandment, explaining them as restraints on the appetites in the Stoic sense.[62] Calvin's criteria, by contrast, are more theological than philosophical. He treats the clean and unclean foods under the first commandment, interpreting them as a symbol of the moral and religious distinction between the sanctified Israelites and the unclean Gentiles. These dietary restrictions symbolize God's requirement that he be worshipped purely and exclusively, without any superstitious contaminants; thus Calvin places them under the first commandment, which for him covers all regulations pertaining to proper worship.

There is another possible source of inspiration – one that is closer to Calvin in time, in theological proclivity, and in methodological spirit. But this source is neither a treatise on the Decalogue nor a commentary on the Pentateuch. It is the Proverbs commentary of Philip Melanchthon. The first authorized edition of this work appeared in 1529, followed by

---

60 *De congressu eruditionis gratia* 21, §120. *Philonis Alexandrinus Opera quae supersunt,* ed. Leopold Cohn and Paul Wendland, 7 vols. in 8 (Berlin: Georgius Reimerus, 1896–1930), III:96; ET in *The Works of Philo,* trans. C. D. Yonge (Peabody, MA: Hendrickson, 1993), p. 314.

61 Περὶ τῶν δέκα λόγων, οἵ κεφάλαια νόμων εἰσί, in *Opera,* IV:267.

62 See Yehoshua Amir, "The Decalogue According to Philo," trans. Yvonne Glikson, in *The Ten Commandments in History and Tradition,* ed. Ben-Zion Segal and Gershon Levi (Jerusalem: Magnes Press, Hebrew University of Jerusalem, 1990), pp. 121–160.

revised versions in 1550 and 1555.[63] Melanchthon uses the Decalogue as an interpretive device in his exposition of the Proverbs, albeit in various ways through the successive editions.

In the first edition of this work, Melanchthon makes the traditional observation that the Decalogue is the source of all moral and legal precepts.[64] Melanchthon's experience of the sad moral state of the parishes in the Visitations (the initiative of Luther and Elector Johann to investigate, report on, and reform the parishes of Saxony) moved him to put more emphasis on the ethical implications of the law. In his Proverbs commentary he seeks to provide a means of reforming and maintaining the moral condition of the churches. Since all wisdom flows from the Decalogue, he attempts to use the Ten Commandments as an interpretive guide to the Proverbs – or at least to a portion of the Proverbs – and he seeks to use the Proverbs to bring out the practical application of God's law for Christian faith and life.[65]

Both Calvin and Melanchthon were preoccupied with proper method. Despite their difference over the optimal method of writing a biblical commentary, they both sought out main themes or *loci* that would help readers to understand the meaning and intention of the biblical texts. Both worked to improve and maintain a higher moral standard in their respective Protestant communities. And both recognized the Decalogue as the foundation for Christian ethics and morality. Thus, if one may be allowed to speculate on possible sources of inspiration for Calvin's audacious project, Melanchthon's Proverbs commentary is a likely candidate.

MAKING SENSE OF THE PENTATEUCHAL LAWS

Eduard Reuss, one of the editors of the *Corpus Reformatorum* edition of Calvin's works, identifies him as the first exegete to attempt such a doctrinal and historical harmony of the Pentateuch. But Reuss, judging Calvin by nineteenth-century critical standards, characterizes this endeavor

---

63 The 1529 edition is entitled *Nova Scholia in Proverbia Salomonis ad iusta paene commentarii modum conscripta* and can be found in *Melanchthons Werke in Auswahl* (Studienausgabe), gen. ed. Robert Stupperich, vol. IV, ed. Peter F. Barton (Gütersloh: Gütersloher Verlagshaus Gerd Mohn, 1980), pp. 305–464, hereafter cited as *MW*. The 1555 edition is in *CR* XIV:1–88. Robert Stupperich examines this commentary in his article, "Melanchtons Proverbien-Kommentare," in *Der Kommentar in der Renaissance*, ed. August Buck and Otto Herding (Boppard: Harald Boldt Verlag, 1975), pp. 21–34.

64 ". . . decalogus fons est omnium praeceptorum." *MW* IV:310.

65 See especially the excellent examination of this subject in Nicole Kuropka, *Philipp Melanchthon: Wissenschaft und Gesellschaft* (Tübingen: Mohr Siebeck, 2002), pp. 90–133.

as "in many respects unsuccessful and hardly useful today."[66] Despite these disparaging remarks, the *Mosaic Harmony* is arguably the crowning achievement of Calvin's exegetical work. It is his attempt to make the often obscure and arcane legal and cultic material of the Pentateuch understandable and practical for preachers and students of theology.

Traditionally, interpreters had exposited much of this material in allegorical fashion, according to the spiritual senses, most often categorized as allegory, anagogy, and tropology. These senses corresponded to what the literal sense of the Scripture taught about doctrine, Christian expectations for the future, and Christian morals (faith, hope, and love). Calvin, for the most part, shies away from allegorical interpretation, but he still manages to derive Christian doctrines, anticipations of the future life, and moral lessons from the text. When Calvin does resort to allegory, he usually does not admit that he is doing so. Rather, he professes to adhere only to what he calls the natural or simple meaning of a passage. Whereas many expositors had tried to make sense of the Pentateuch through spiritualizing forms of interpretation, Calvin prefers to categorize rather than allegorize.

DIVINE ACCOMMODATION IN THE 'MOSAIC HARMONY' AND 'JOSHUA'

David F. Wright has noted an important hermeneutical strategy that Calvin employs in both the *Mosaic Harmony* and *Joshua*, namely, that God accommodates himself to human beings in the revelation of himself and his will. Unlike other examinations of Calvin's principle of divine accommodation, however, Wright observes that in the commentaries Calvin is not merely speaking of an epistemological accommodation, translating divine thoughts into words that mere mortals can understand. Rather, Calvin recognizes that the very laws and commands that God delivered to his people – the laws recorded in the inspired biblical record – were not always the perfect or optimal expression of the divine will.[67] Sometimes God's laws or commands were concessions to the spiritually primitive state of the Hebrew people. At other times, God accommodated these laws to the people's hardness of heart. A further

---

66 ". . . übrigens in vieler Hinsicht misslungenen und heute kaum brauchbaren . . ." Eduard Reuss, *Die Geschichte der Heiligen Schriften Alten Testaments*, 2nd edn (Braunschweig: Schwetschke, 1890), p. 504.
67 Wright, "Calvin's Pentateuchal Criticism," p. 36.

ingredient in this hermeneutic of accommodation is Calvin's criterion for judging the pentateuchal legislation, namely, "the principle of natural equity (*aequitas*), which from time to time he observes to be breached in the laws and deeds of the Israelites." Wright identifies this idea as "a compound of natural law, moral law, and the law written on the conscience."[68] In his Joshua commentary, Calvin cites Cicero's opinion that the concept of *aequitas* must temper the application of the law.[69]

Calvin provides a window into his own hermeneutical practice when he considers the meaning of זוֹנָה in Joshua 2:1. He confidently interprets the meaning as *harlot*, not *innkeeper*, as suggested by some Jewish interpreters.[70] While the rabbis (in Calvin's estimation) might be willing to twist the text in an attempt to preserve the honor of their nation, Calvin does not see any need to euphemize the text. In fact, the offensive elements of the text often serve as lessons in themselves; in this case, we learn about the graciousness of God who can use even a prostitute to accomplish his purposes, and who can even transform that prostitute into a perpetual example of faith.[71]

CALVIN'S "DYING BEQUEST TO THE CHURCH"

Henry Beveridge characterized Calvin's *Joshua* commentary as the reformer's "dying bequest to the church." Like all of Calvin's commentaries, he intends this final biblical exposition as a guide for readers to find their way through the Scriptures, ensuring that the reader can easily discern the theme and goal of the book, and easily identify the main teachings and practical applications throughout the course of the narrative. Calvin exhibits no diminished capacity in this regard, even as his health was failing.

The purpose of the book of Joshua, in Calvin's estimation, is to bear perpetual witness to the faithfulness of God, despite the predictable

---

68 Ibid., p. 38.
69 At Joshua 2:14ff., *CO* xxv:444–445, CTS *Joshua*, 54. Here Calvin defends the action of the spies who surreptitiously escape from the city by going over the wall – an act that in previous ages would have been widely condemned as unlawful. Calvin cites Cicero, who observes that a person who scales the city wall to defend the city would be received as a hero, not condemned as a criminal.
70 Cf. Lyra, II, fol. 5ᵛ; Pellikan, *Commentaria Bibliorum*, II, fol. 3ʳ; Münster, *Hebraica Biblia*, p. 419; Cajetan, *Opera Omnia*, II:3. Denis argues for *meretrix* on the basis of the Septuagint, which renders the term γυνὴ πόρνη, and on the basis of James 2:25; *Enarrationes piae et eruditae in libros Iosue* . . . (Cologne: Quentel, 1535), fol. IIIIʳ, cited as *Enarrationes*.
71 *CO* xxv:437; CTS *Joshua*, 43–44.

unfaithfulness of his people.[72] God renews his covenant promises to each succeeding generation, and ultimately makes good on those promises. But Calvin admits that there is a serious problem raised by the fact that the Hebrews never come into the full possession of the land promised by the LORD. The sloth of the people seems to have eclipsed God's covenant promise.[73] And yet this is merely another occasion for God to display his mercy. The LORD moderates the chastisements of his people, and the incomplete conquest of the land moves them to hope for a fuller possession of God's blessings, which would ultimately come in Jesus Christ.

JUSTICE AND CRUELTY IN JOSHUA

The narrative of Israel's conquest of the Promised Land, with the concomitant annihilation of its inhabitants, raises numerous issues relating to the generally accepted rules of conducting war. Much of what God commands, as well as the way in which Israel carries out those commands, seems to contradict the principles of martial justice. At numerous points the text relates acts of apparent cruelty, inhumanity, and even barbarism.

It is not that Calvin has any problem with the command to utterly annihilate the inhabitants of Canaan. In his understanding, the Hebrews are merely God's instrument of judgment upon a particularly wicked people; they are the agents of his wrath.[74] The Canaanite peoples are the spiritual equivalent of the reprobate, and Calvin uses their fate to illustrate what happens to the reprobate.[75] But Calvin is very careful to point out that the methods employed in the conquest of Canaan would be considered cruel, barbaric, and unlawful, were the conquest not an exceptional case. The indiscriminate slaughter of women and children would have been an act of "detestable cruelty," worse than crimes committed by "savage tribes scarcely raised above the level of brutes." But because Joshua and his army are carrying out the express command of God, and are merely agents of his judgment, this massacre is really an act of reverence. Even the principle of clemency in war, in which Calvin was well versed, is suspended in the exceptional case of the conquest.[76]

---

72 Calvin says in the *argumentum*, "the faithfulness of God never fails." *CO* xxv:421–422; CTS *Joshua*, xix.

73 *CO* xxv:423–424; CTS *Joshua*, xxii.

74 See Calvin's comments on Josh. 6:20: *CO* xxv:469; CTS *Joshua*, 97.

75 E.g. at Josh. 10:29: *CO* xxv:505; CTS *Joshua*, 162.

76 Calvin on Joshua 10:40: *CO* xxv: 505–506; CTS *Joshua*, 163.

At Joshua 7:24 Calvin is troubled by the case of Achen, who is put to death along with his children and livestock for pilfering valuables from Jericho. The punishment of children and dumb animals for the sin of their father seems "harsh, barbaric, and inhumane" to Calvin.[77] Not only that, but the punishment of children for the sins of the father is contrary to what the LORD says in Ezekiel 18. This one stumps Calvin completely; he concludes that we must simply trust that God's justice was served, even if we cannot discern how.

At other times, apparently cruel acts serve as warnings to the people of Israel. The cruel treatment of the five Amorite kings (Josh. 10:24–27) appears to be an act of "barbarous atrocity and monstrous pride," except that God commands it. He does so in order to strike terror in the hearts of his people, so that they would never dare imitate the wicked behavior of the Canaanites.[78] Similarly, the cruel treatment of the king of Ai served to teach God's people how much the LORD detests evil, and how those who are the source of that evil are even more culpable.[79]

Despite the exceptional nature of the wars of conquest, Calvin does apply the rules of just war whenever possible. He emphasizes the fact that Joshua had to hold out the offer of peace to the various Canaanite peoples. This exercise provided the Hebrews with just cause for waging war upon the Canaanites when they inevitably refused the offer of peace.[80] This is an analogue to how preachers are required to address the promise of forgiveness in Christ to all people indiscriminately, even while God has ordained that some will refuse his gospel.

Calvin also justifies the tactics of the Hebrews wherever possible. He thinks it inane to ask whether it is just to employ deception and ambush in war,[81] and he demonstrates that such tactics were no violation of the principles of just war.[82] Calvin becomes positively lawyer-like in his extended discussion of whether the Hebrews were bound to their covenant with the Gibeonites, given that it was made under false pretenses.

---

77 *CO* xxv:479; CTS *Joshua*, 116–117.
78 "Alioqui barbara fuisset atrocitas et immanis superbia . . ." *CO* xxv:502–503; CTS *Joshua*, 158–159.
79 Calvin on Josh. 8:29: *CO* xxv:486–487; CTS *Joshua*, 129.
80 Calvin on Josh. 9:3: *CO* xxv:492; CTS *Joshua*, 138.
81 Denis the Carthusian asks precisely this question; cf. *Enarrationes*, fols. xvᵛ–xvıʳ.
82 Calvin on Josh. 8:15: *CO* xxv:484; CTS *Joshua*, 125.

MORAL LESSONS FROM JOSHUA

A notable feature of Calvin's *Joshua* is his ongoing wrestling with moral issues that arise in the text. Calvin is very concerned about drawing the correct moral lessons from the events and actions narrated in Joshua. He often (though not always) refers to Joshua as a model and example of faith.[83] But he is not to be imitated in his role as the agent of God's wrath and retribution against the Canaanites. Anyone who would presume to do so would be guilty of unbridled zealotry, cruelty, and bloodthirstiness.[84]

The story of Rahab's blatant deceit of the king's messengers (Josh. 2:4–5) brings up two moral problems for Calvin. The first is Rahab's treason against her countrymen; the second is the fact that she told a lie in order to save the Hebrew spies. In the first case, Calvin justifies Rahab's transfer of allegiance by appeal to the extraordinary spiritual insight that God had somehow communicated to her.[85] This insight exempts her from the natural requirement of loyalty to one's nation. Otherwise, her act would be contrary to nature, and even "a detestable act of inhumanity."[86] As it is, Rahab simply acquiesces in God's judgment on her city.

The second case – that of Rahab's lie – is more problematic, and engages Calvin in a longstanding theological dispute. Certainly Rahab employed her falsehood for a noble end: to preserve the lives of the Hebrew spies. But for Calvin, a lie is a lie. Here he finds himself in a traditional argument about whether deception is ever justifiable. On the one side of this debate stands Augustine, who wrote two treatises on the subject of lying.[87] Augustine argues that lying is always a sin, even in Rahab's case. God rewarded the goodness of her intention, not the iniquity of her invention.[88] He overlooked her sin of deception for numerous reasons, such as the fact that Rahab could not be expected to unravel moral quandaries that vex even the most learned. On the other side of the debate are those such as Jerome and John Cassian, who assert that there is such a thing as a dutiful lie (*mendacium officiosum*).[89] Cassian,

---

83 An exception is Calvin's criticism of Joshua's "foolish credulity" in allowing himself to be taken in by the ruse of the Gibeonites, at Josh. 9:3: *CO* xxv:491; CTS *Joshua*, 137.

84 Calvin on Josh. 11:12: *CO* xxv:509; CTS *Joshua*, 176–177.

85 Cf. Brenz, *In Librum Iosuae*, p. 17. Brenz explains that Rahab believed the prophetic words of the spies, and this faith "renewed her mind."

86 Calvin on Josh. 2:4: *CO* xxv:440, CTS *Joshua*, 46. Cf. Brenz, *In Librum Iosuae*, p. 12: "Non potuit Raab totam civitatem liberare, igitur conatur liberare cognationem suam."

87 *De Mendacio*, *PL* xl:487–518; and *Contra Mendacium, PL* xl:517–547.

88 "benignitas mentis, non iniquitas mentientis," *Contra Mendacium* 15.32, *PL* xl:540.

89 The debate began as an epistolary argument between Jerome and Augustine, after Jerome (Letter 48) suggested that Paul's harsh rebuke of Peter was more rhetorical and pastoral than truthful.

for example, points out that Rahab obeyed God by lying about the spies, while Samson committed a sin by telling Delilah the truth about his source of strength.[90]

Calvin sides unequivocally with Augustine on this point. As a result, he ends up with the rather messy conclusion that Rahab was wrong to lie, but right to preserve the spies. Her act was praiseworthy and virtuous, yet not free from fault or sin.[91] Calvin had provided a similar interpretation of one of the other *loci classici* in this dispute, the lie of the midwives in Exodus 1:18; there he again rejects the concept of a dutiful lie.[92] He seems to have avoided commenting on 1 Samuel 16:2, where the LORD explicitly instructs Samuel to lie (or at least dissemble) about his intention to anoint David as king.

Like most of his fellow reformers, Calvin had a deep distaste for those voices within the Christian tradition that approved of mental reservation and other forms of deception. Well known are his vehement exhortations against those who disguised their evangelical sentiments, whom he labeled "Nicodemites." He was also a man of considerable moral rigor; nonetheless, he was the same man who affixed the pseudonym "Alcuin" to his early writings, and addressed letters to European nobility with the nom de plume "Charles d'Espeville" – a name under which he first fled his native France. Calvin rejected the use of deception to protect oneself or to protect others, but he used pseudonyms for precisely that end. Were these deceptions dutiful lies? Or were they justified stratagems in a spiritual battle? This apparent inconsistency between Calvin's principles and his practice warrants further investigation.[93]

The religious and political turmoil in France in the last years of Calvin's life sheds some light on the reformer's moral rigor in this commentary. Calvin wants to portray Reformed Christians and their leaders as law-abiding citizens who respect the governing authorities. They are not the kind to foment rebellion or instigate treason against the government. And when certain rash persons act seditiously, such as

---

90 See John Cassian, *Conferences*, II.17–18, *PL* II:1062–1066. Proponents of this position include Denis, *Enarrationes*, fol. IIII^r; Lyra, II, fol. 5^v; Cajetan, *Opera Omnia*, II:3. Pellikan thinks it useless to speculate whether she could have achieved the same ends without lying, because God can achieve his ends by any means he pleases; see *Commentaria Bibliorum*, II, fol. 3^r.

91 *CO* xxv:440–441; CTS Joshua, 47–48.

92 *CO* xxiv:18–19; CTS *Mosaic Harmony* 1:34–35. Cf. the more sophisticated presentation of the same perspective in Peter Martyr Vermigli, *Loci Communes* (London, Thomas Vautrollerius, 1583), II.13.28–33, pp. 368–370.

93 See Blacketer, "The Moribund Moralist."

happened in the ill-fated conspiracy of Amboise, they do not represent the principles of Reformed believers. Calvin particularly wants to portray the Huguenots in this light, and in his commentary he also wants the Reformed leaders in France to adopt this law-abiding, loyal, identity as their own.[94]

CALVIN AS GUIDE THROUGH DIFFICULT TERRAIN

In both the *Mosaic Harmony* and *Joshua* Calvin's purpose and goal as a commentator is clear. The biblical text is often quite difficult to navigate, particularly for pastors who lack time or extensive training. In the sixteenth century there were undoubtedly many such leaders in the newly reformed churches. Calvin recognizes the importance of proper pedagogy, the right order of teaching, as he plans out and writes his commentaries. In the latter Pentateuch Calvin does not only clarify the chronological flow of the narrative. He also provides an ingenious method of ordering and making sense out of the diverse and diffuse mass of Mosaic legislation – some of which is rather obscure and difficult to apply to the life of the church. With Calvin's commentary in hand, the pastor can preach meaningfully and practically from relatively inaccessible books such as Leviticus, without recourse to excessive or fanciful allegory.

Joshua presents its own problems, particularly because of the ambiguous moral character of figures such as Rahab, and because of issues relating to the rules of war and the apparent harshness of God's judgment. In this commentary Calvin has to vindicate the integrity of the biblical text. He seeks to demonstrate that while the book of Joshua narrates events that often are often offensive to the reader's moral sensibilities, these troubling passages continue to speak to the life of the believer and the mission of the church. Such difficult texts may be reflections of God's inscrutable counsel, and thus to be accepted reverently and without question. They may be instances of God accommodating himself to limited, sinful, human capacity, in which case the fault lies not in God, but in human beings, who are limited by their stage of moral and spiritual development, as well as their lack of docility and just plain stubbornness. In any case, Calvin's dying bequest to the church is a guide for discerning which persons are models, which acts are exemplary, and which are not.

---

94 Ibid.

In his final two commentaries, we see Calvin pursuing what he considered some of his most important work. He acts as a guide and mentor to pastors and teachers in the church, helping them to navigate a textual terrain that is often treacherous, and in which one can easily get lost. Calvin conducts his readers through this often unfamiliar or challenging literary landscape so that they will always return to their pulpits and classrooms with practical lessons for the faith and life of the Christian church.

CHAPTER 3

Calvin as an interpreter of Job

Susan Schreiner

Calvin never wrote a commentary on the book of Job. His interpretation of this classic biblical story is found in his 159 *Sermons sur le livre de Job.*[1] Because his exegesis of Job occurs only in this sermonic material, it is useful to begin with a few introductory remarks about his preaching activity.

No one needs to stress the importance of preaching for Calvin.[2] The number of sermons alone shows how significant he believed preaching to be to his reforming mission. Rodolphe Peter has estimated that Calvin preached over 4,000 sermons in Geneva.[3] From 1549 to 1563, his general pattern of preaching consisted of two sermons on Sunday and a sermon every day of the week in alternate weeks. The Sunday morning sermon was on a New Testament book. The sermons on Sunday afternoons were devoted also to a New Testament book or, occasionally, to a Psalm. The

---

1 The Sermons on Job are in *CO*, vols. XXXIII–XXXV.

2 On Calvin's preaching see: B. G. Armstrong, "Exegetical and Theological Principles in Calvin's Preaching with Special Attention to his Sermons on the Psalms," in *Ordentlich und Fruchtbar: Festschrift für Willem van't Spijker*, ed. Wilhelm Herman Neuser and Herman Selderhuis (Leiden: J. J. Groen en Zoon, 1997), pp. 191–203; Jean-François Gilmont, "Les sermons de Calvin: de l'oral à l'imprimé," *Bulletin de la Société de l'Histoire du Protestantisme Français* 141 (1995): 146–162; Paul Lobstein, "Calvin considéré comme prédicateur," in his *Études sur la pensée et oeuvre de Calvin* (Neuilly: Editions de "La Cause,"), pp. 15–49; Paul Lobstein, "Les sermons de Calvin sur le livre de Job," in ibid., pp. 51–67; Erwin Müllhaupt, *Die Predigt Calvins: ihre Geschichte, ihre Form und ihre religiösen Grundgedanken* (Berlin and Leipzig: DeGruyter, 1931); T. H. L. Parker, *Oracles of God: An Introduction to the Preaching of John Calvin* (London: Lutterworth Press, 1947); T. H. L. Parker *Calvin's Preaching* (Louisville: Westminster John Knox Press, 1992); Rodolphe Peter, "Jean Calvin prédicateur, notice bibliographique à propos d'un ouvrage récent," in *Revue de l'Histoire et de la Philosophie Religieuses* 52 (1972): 111–117; Richard Stauffer, "Un Calvin méconnu: Le prédicateur de Genève," *Bulletin de la Société de l'Histoire du Protestantisme Français* 123 (1977): 184–203; Richard Stauffer *Dieu, la création et la providence dans le prédication de Calvin* (Berne, Frankfurt, Las Vegas: Peter Lang, 1978); Richard Stauffer, "L'homilétique de Calvin," in his *Interprètes de la Bible* (Paris: Éditions Beauchesne, 1980), pp. 167–181.

3 Rodolphe Peter, "Genève dans la prédication de Calvin," in *Calvinus Ecclesiae Genevensis Custos*, ed. W. H. Neuser (New York and Frankfurt: Peter Lang: 1984), pp. 23–48.

weekday sermons were an exposition of an Old Testament book. Calvin always preached through an entire biblical book, verse by verse, from beginning to end. The book of Job was the subject of the weekday sermons preached from February 26, 1554 to March 15 or 16, 1555.[4] Calvin preached in French and extemporaneously. We possess these sermons because of a committee called *la compagnie des étrangers*. This "Immigrants' Society" of fellow exiles was dedicated to helping refugees who had fled to Geneva, chiefly, but not exclusively, from France. They employed a French refugee named Raguenier as a secretary to Calvin. Beginning in 1549, Raguenier took down 2,042 of Calvin's sermons in shorthand. He then transcribed his shorthand into a longhand manuscript by dictating to a scribe. When the series was completed the manuscript was bound as a volume and entrusted to the Deacons. By the time of Calvin's death about twenty–one volumes of his sermons had been published. *Sermons on Job* were published twice in their first year and then again at five-year intervals for the next decade. Calvin's sermons were highly prized outside of Geneva. Arthur Golding's translation of these sermons went through five editions in just ten years. Moreover, Golding said of the Job sermons in his 1573 dedication to the Earl of Leicester that "this work is the first of any greate weight that ever I translated out of the French toong to be published."[5]

Calvin's own words also tell us the importance he attached to preaching. For Calvin preaching was God himself speaking with the preacher as the instrument of the Holy Spirit.[6] As Parker and other scholars have shown, Calvin considered preaching to be the handing on of the Word of God and to possess the authority of God himself. Since Scripture is the "Word of God," the preacher bore the heavy responsibility of being a humble servant of that Word. He must, therefore, preach the "pure teaching" of the "pure Word" without intruding his own opinions into the text.[7] When listening to a sermon, the congregation was entering the "school of God (*l'escole de Dieu*) where it was to hear the Word and be "taught by God (*enseignez de Dieu*)."[8] Scholars have now rejected the argument of Paul Henry who asserted in 1851 that because Calvin spoke extemporaneously, he preached without preparation. Calvin insisted to Lord Protector Somerset:

---

4 Parker, *Calvin's Preaching*, p. 169.   5 Cited by Parker, *Calvin's Preaching*, p. 169.
6 *CO* xxxv:43–44.   7 Cited by Parker, *Calvin's Preaching*, pp. 1–56.
8 *CO* xxxv:43–44.

If I should step into the pulpit, without vouchsafing to look at any book, and fondly imagine that . . . God will give one enough whereof to speak, at the same time that I scorn to study or read beforehand what I shall say, and come hither without minding how to apply the holy Scripture to the edification of the people . . . I should play the presumptuous fool, and God would put me to shame for my overboldness.[9]

Calvin's delivery was grounded in the tools of rhetoric, knowledge of the Bible, as well as the philological, historical, and theological tools necessary to expound the text.

The principles of Calvin's exegesis are well known, particularly his emphasis on *perspicua brevitas* and *facilitas* that characterized his commentaries.[10] He paid close attention to grammar, philology, and history and sought to expound the literal sense of the text. This "literal," "historical," "natural," "simple," or "genuine" sense was more than the historical-grammatical meaning of the narrative. Calvin's purpose was to explain the "mind of the author," by which he meant the human writer as guided by the Holy Spirit. Genre, however, is important when we attempt to determine Calvin's exegetical style and principles.[11] There were four occasions on which Calvin interpreted Scripture. In his academic lectures (*praelectiones*) to students and other listeners he spoke in Latin. His commentaries were published in both Latin and French. The intended audience for the commentaries was the clergy and educated laity. Here the elements of *perspicua brevitas* and *facilitas* were paramount. Calvin also led weekly discussions of the Bible (*congrégations*) in French for ministers and educated laity. The sermons, delivered in French, were aimed at the

---

9 Cited by Richard Muller, *The Unaccommodated Calvin* (New York and Oxford, 2000), p. 144.
10 Peter De Klerk, ed. *Calvin as Exegete*, Papers and responses at the Ninth Colloquium on Calvin and Calvin Studies, April 22–23, 1993 (Grand Rapids: Calvin Studies Society, 1995); Benjamin W. Farley, "Recurring Hermeneutical Principles," in ibid. pp. 69–87; Alexandre Ganoczy and Stefan Scheld, *Die Hermeneutik Calvins: Geistesgeschichtliche Voraussetzungen und Grundzüge* (Wiesbaden: F. Steiner, 1983); Richard Gamble, "*Brevitas et facilitas*: Toward an Understanding of Calvin's Hermeneutic," *Westminster Theological Journal* 47 (1985): 1–17; Hans Joachim Kraus, "Calvin's Exegetical Principles," *Interpretation* 31 (1977): 8–18; Richard A. Muller, "The Hermeneutic of Promise and Fulfillment in Calvin's Exegesis of the Old Testament Prophecies of the Kingdom," in *The Bible in the Sixteenth Century*, ed. David C. Steinmetz (Durham, NC: Duke University Press, 1990), pp. 68–82; Barbara Pitkin, "Biblical Interpretation in the Work of John Calvin," in *History of Biblical Interpretation*, ed. Alan J. Hauser and Duane F. Watson, vol. II (Grand Rapids: Eerdmans; E. Reuss, forthcoming); "Calvin considéré comme exégète," *Revue de Théologie et de Philosophie Chrétienne* 6 (1853): 223–248; Henri Strohl, "La méthode exégétique des Réformateurs," in *Le problème biblique dans le Protestantisme*, ed. J. Boisset (Paris: Presses Universitaires de France, 1955), pp. 87–104; Thomas Torrance, *The Hermeneutics of John Calvin* (Edinburgh: Scottish Academic Press, 1988).
11 On the "division of labor" in Calvin's work and the importance of genre see, Muller, *The Unaccommodated Calvin*, pp. 140–158.

general audience. In the sermons the exegetical ideal of *brevitas* yielded to more polemic and expansiveness.[12] In his preaching Calvin used the rhetorical technique of *amplificatio* or *copia*.[13] As Muller has argued, the sermons show that "the 'oratorical' style has fully replaced the 'scholastic' and the task of edification in the 'school of God' has led to considerable theological, polemical, and pastoral amplification."[14] In order to elaborate on a theme more freely, Calvin made use of historical, philosophical, poetic, and scientific allusions and images. He was carefully attuned to biblical tropes and the various figures of speech he found in Scripture. He was convinced that the speaker or commentator must be aware of biblical rhetoric in order to deepen theological understanding. Such a technique had as its purpose edification, not merely eloquence that might distract or delight the listener. As Bouwsma has explained, Calvin was always mindful of decorum as a central rhetorical virtue. "A wise teacher," Calvin explained, "accommodates himself to the understanding of those who must be taught."[15] Teachers must carefully consider the "needs of the times and what is appropriate to the people."[16] Just as God accommodated himself to humanity at various places and times in Scripture, so, too, the preacher had to accommodate himself to his congregation. Those who have compared Calvin's sermons with his respective commentaries have concluded that this *amplificatio* and edification took the form of more frequent applications to the present situation and circumstances as well as a more pronounced pastoral concern.[17] We will see that these latter elements also characterize the Job sermons.

---

12 See, for example, Brian G. Armstrong, "Exegetical and Theological Principles in Calvin's Preaching," in *Ordentlich und Fruchtbar*, ed. Neuser and Selderhuis, pp. 191–203.

13 Olivier Millet, *Calvin et la dynamique de la parole. Étude de rhétorique réformée* (Paris: Librairie Honoré Champion, 1992). See also William J. Bouwsma, "Calvinism as *Theologia Rhetorica*," in *Calvinism as Theologia Rhetorica*, ed. William Wuellner (Berkeley: Center for Hermeneutical Studies, 1986), pp. 1–2; Muller, *The Unaccommodated Calvin*, p. 145 and compare Cornelius Augustijn, "Calvin und der Humanismus," in *Calvinus Servus Christi*, ed. Wilhelm H. Neuser (Budapest: Presseabteilung des Ráday-Kollegiums, 1998), pp. 127–142; Rodophe Peter, "Rhétorique et prédication selon Calvin," *Revue d'Histoire et de la Philosophie Religieuses* 55 (1975): 249–272.

14 Muller, *The Unaccommodated Calvin*, p. 145.

15 *Comm. 1 Cor.* 3:2, cited by Bouwsma, "Calvinism as *Theologia Rhetorica*," p. 2.

16 Comm. on Matt. 3:7, cited in ibid.

17 Max Engammare, "Le paradis á Genève. Comment Calvin prêchait-il la chute aux Genevois?" *Études Théologiques et Religieuses* 69 (1994): 329–47; Max Engammare "Introduction," in Jean Calvin, *Sermons sur Genèse* in vol. XI, pp. vii–lvii; Wulfert de Greef, "Das Verhältnis von Predigt und Kommentar bei Calvin, dargestellt an den Deuteronomium Kommentar und den Predigten," in *Calvinus Servus Christi*, ed. Neuser, pp. 195–204.

As noted above, Calvin's sermons treated entire biblical books, proceeding passage by passage or verse by verse. The *Sermons on Job* were no exception. This expository method produced a connected series that viewed the biblical book as a coherent whole. In recent years we have benefited from path-breaking studies on the history of sixteenth-century exegesis. These studies have used various methods and have asked a variety of questions in order to determine the nature of exegesis during this important era. Some scholars have studied Calvin's exegesis by comparing his sermons to his corresponding biblical commentary.[18] Others have analyzed a passage, verse, or biblical figure in light of the preceding exegetical tradition or in terms of various themes in Calvin's theology.[19] The book of Job, however, does not lend itself to these methods. The former is obviously impossible since there is no corresponding commentary. The latter method is unsuitable because it would obscure the fact that Calvin had to interpret the story of Job as a whole. Rarely did an isolated passage from Job serve to illustrate a central doctrine such as justification, sanctification, or the sacraments. Nor did the figures of the Job story ever take on the status of Abraham, David, Isaac, or Paul. The *Sermons on Job*, however, demonstrate the way in which Calvin saw his interpretation of Job's story as constantly having to move forward and confront the problems posed by the upcoming portions in the text. He expounded each passage in light of what he had already preached on the

18 See n. 15 and John L. Thompson, *Writing the Wrongs: Women of the Old Testament Among Biblical Commentators from Philo through the Reformation*, Oxford Studies in Historical Theology (New York and Oxford: Oxford University Press, 2001); P.-D. Nicole and C. Rapin, "De l'exégèse á l'homilétique. Évolution entre le commentaire de 1551, les sermons de 1558 et le commentaire de 1559 sur le prophète Esaïe," in *Calvinus Ecclesiae Genevensis Custos*, ed. Neuser pp. 159–162.
19 Richard A. Muller and John L. Thompson, eds., *Biblical Interpretation in the Era of the Reformation: Essays Presented to David C. Steinmetz in Honor of His Sixtieth Birthday* (Grand Rapids: Eerdmans, 1996); Barbara Pitkin, *What Pure Eyes Could See: Calvin's Doctrine of Faith in Its Exegetical Context*, Oxford Studies in Historical Theology (New York: Oxford University Press, 1999); Barbara Pitkin, "Imitation of David: David as a Paradigm for Faith in Calvin's Exegesis of the Psalms," *Sixteenth Century Journal* 24/4 (1993): 843–863; David C. Steinmetz, *Calvin in Context* (New York: Oxford University Press, 1995); John I. Thompson, *John Calvin and the Daughters of Sarah: Women in Regular and Exceptional Roles in the Exegesis of Calvin, His Predecessors, and His Contemporaries* (Geneva: Librairie Droz, 1992); John L. Thompson, "Hagar: Victim or Villain? Three Sixteenth-Century Views," *Catholic Biblical Quarterly* 59 (1997): 213–233; David F. Wright, "Calvin's Pentateuchal Criticism: Equity, Hardness of Heart, and Divine Accommodation in the Mosaic Harmony Commentary," *Calvin Theological Journal* 21/1 (1986): 33–50; Derek Thomas, *Calvin's Teaching on Job: Proclaiming the Incomprehensible God* (Geanies House, Ross-shire, Scotland: Christian Focus Publications, 2004); Marten H. Woudstra, "The Use of 'Example' in Calvin's Sermons on Job," in *Bezield Verband: Opstellen aangeboden aan Prof. J. Kamphius*, ed. M. Arntzen (Kampen: J. H. Kok, 1984), pp. 344–51, 456–58.

text as well as in terms of the ongoing movement of the story. His expository method was particularly well suited to the book of Job since he knew that his interpretation had to respect various viewpoints, different speakers, a prologue, epilogue, and the fact that the earthly speakers did not know the whole story. In short, Calvin had to respect the integrity of the complete text.

In the following essay I shall attempt to give an overall view of Calvin's exegesis of Job. That exegesis was a difficult one because Job was not a character that Calvin found particularly easy to like. Job's constant complaints and challenges to God made Calvin continually uneasy. Nor was he ever completely comfortable with the God depicted in this book of Scripture. Why was God willing to let Job suffer just in order to prove something to Satan? And why did the text say that God acted "without cause"? Could this possibly mean that God acted arbitrarily, irrationally, or tyrannically? We see Calvin constantly worried that Job's God seemed to act according to an "absolute" or tyrannical power. In short, the sovereignty of Job's God scared even Calvin. We will find that there were other crucial elements of the book that troubled him. But we shall also discover that for all of its difficulties, the book of Job demonstrated to Calvin profound truths that it was necessary to know and to apply to his congregation.

Calvin began each sermon with a brief recapitulation of his exposition of the previous passage. This allowed him to keep the stream of exegesis intact and to place the current passage in the context of the book as a whole. He then read (or translated) the biblical passage for the day, at times clarifying words and difficulties in the text.[20] Following these introductory remarks he would explain the meaning of the text. In so doing he would include its application to his hearers so that they might "profit" or be "edified" by the passage. He concluded by summarizing the message and its usefulness and ended with a prayer.

The application of the text encompassed many themes ranging from warnings about rebelling against God, exhortations to frame our lives according to Scripture, reminders that we are to praise God in all his creatures, and calls for patience in suffering. All of these "applications," however, revolved around what Calvin perceived to be the main message

20 For a summary of the present state of research on Calvin's biblical text and his translations, see Parker, *Calvin's Preaching*, pp. 172–178. See also Max Engammare, "Calvin connaissait-il la Bible? Les citations de l'Écriture dans ses sermons sur la Genèse," *Bulletin de la Société d'Histoire du Protestantisme Français* 141 (1995): 163–184; Max Engammare, "*Johannes Calvinus trium linguarum peritus*? La question de l'Hébreu," *Bibliothèque d'Humanisme et Renaissance* 58 (1996): 35–60.

of the book of Job; namely, to trust in the often incomprehensible providence of God. The book was written in order to show that we "are in God's hands and that it is for God to ordain matters concerning our life and to dispose of it according to his good pleasure."[21] Job's life, like all human life, was under the just and wise rule of divine providence.

Calvin was certainly not unique in seeing providence as the message of Job's story. Pre-critical exegetes had long interpreted this text in terms of God's governance over history, evil, and suffering.[22] Calvin's famous references to "*aucuns*" do not always allow us to identify exactly which interpreters he had consulted when preaching on Job. Clearly, however, he knew the general themes of both the allegorical tradition stemming from Gregory the Great and the literal tradition formulated most decisively by Thomas Aquinas. While Calvin did not know Aquinas' *Expositio super Iob ad litteram*, he may have known the literal interpretation through the commentary on Job by Nicholas of Lyra. He may also have known the allegorical tradition through the *Glossa ordinaria* or through comments made by Lyra. In any event, Calvin stood in a long line of interpreters who undertook the exposition of this difficult book in order to explain the issues of suffering, theodicy and providence.

We will have a fuller understanding of these sermons if we reflect briefly on the issue of providence in the sixteenth century. I have argued elsewhere that Calvin saw the true doctrine of providence as under attack.[23] I should like to elaborate on this somewhat in order to provide a more comprehensive context for Calvin's Job sermons. In his book *King Lear and the Gods*, William R. Elton has explained that in the latter half of the sixteenth century two attitudes toward providence gained ground. The first view was that if providence existed at all, it had little to no relationship to the particular affairs of individual people. The second belief held that providence operated in ways "bafflingly inscrutable and hidden to human reason"[24]

21 *CO* xxxiii:21.
22 The following sections are adapted in part from my book, *Where Shall Wisdom Be Found? Calvin's Exegesis of Job from Medieval and Modern Perspectives* (Chicago: University of Chicago Press, 1994). The references to Gregory the Great are from Gregory the Great, *Moralia in Iob*, cura et studio Marci Adriaen, *CCSL* cxxxxiii, cxxxxiiia, cxxxxiiib. The references to Thomas Aquinas are from Thomas Aquinas, *Expositio super Iob ad litteram*, in *Opera Omnia*, iussu Leonis xiii P. M. edita, cura et studio Fratrum Praedicatorum, vol. xxvi (Rome, 1965).
23 Susan E. Schreiner, *The Theater of His Glory* (Durham, NC: Labyrinth Press, 1991; repr. Grand Rapids : Baker Book House, 1995).
24 William R. Elton, *King Lear and the Gods* (San Marino, CA: The Huntington Library, 1968), p. 9. For the following section see pp. 9–33.

The first view, which doubted the reality of providence, coincided with an "Epicurean revival." This is not to say that there was a religious sect of Epicureans. As Lucian Febvre has argued, the term "atheist," which sometimes included the "Epicureans," was a common one of abuse, much like the term "communist" during the Cold War.[25] In 1978 a colloquium was held in Strasbourg that revisited the issues posed by Febvre regarding the Epicureans.[26] In that study the research pointed to a kind of popular irreligion associated with the term "Epicurean." This lay movement criticized sermons, worship services and ritual, and had a generally critical attitude toward the church. Some apparently claimed that Christian doctrines were false. Mar Lienhard noted the existence of several modern editions of Epicurean and anti-Epicurean works, the first appearing in 1469. Some argued that Epicureanism at Strasbourg left its mark on ethics, law, and theology. Nonetheless, the meaning of the term, and the true nature of such Epicureanism, are still hard to determine. As Lienhard argued in the preface, Epicureanism was not strictly speaking a heterodox movement but an intellectual means to distance oneself from the ecclesiastical and doctrinal system. Certainly, for Calvin, Epicureanism signaled a dangerous intellectual ferment that included, among other things, a doubt about the providence of God.

Among the texts that interested the "Epicureans" were those by Lucretius and Lucian. The Renaissance had reintroduced Epicureanism into the religious discourse of early modernity. This revival included the return of the pleasure doctrine as well as the eliminating of superstitious fears that would destroy happiness. While the gods might have existed, they were absolutely indifferent to human concerns and need not be placated or feared. Fortune or Chance ruled human affairs. The belief in miracles came under attack. Some skeptics argued that the idea of God was nothing more than the imaginings of the human mind. These *epicuriens et atheists* laughed at prayer, scoffed and mocked divine providence, and attributed the events of history and nature to the arbitrary and blind operations of fortune. In his treatise of 1595, *La constance et consolation ès calamitez publiques,* Guillaume Du Vair explained that while few people would deny providence outright, nonetheless, "There are a number indeed, whose opinions I have heard . . . which acknowledging divine

---

25 Lucien Febvre, *The Problem of Unbelief in the Sixteenth Century: The Religion of Rabelais,* trans. Beatrice Gottlieb (Cambridge, MA: Harvard University Press, 1982), p. 131.

26 Marc Lienhard, ed., *Croyants et sceptiques au XVIe siècle.* Actes du colloque organizé par le GRENEP, Strasbourg, 9–10 juin 1978 (Strasbourg: Librairie ISTRA, 1981).

wisedome, and power in the first creation of the world, have taken the government thereof from it . . . some attributing it unto that order, which they call Nature; some to a fatall necessitie, some others unto Chance and Fortune . . ."[27] The controversy caused by "Epicureanism" is also reflected in Theodore Beza's *Job Expounded*. In that commentary Beza wrote, "Who knoweth not the wicked opinion of the *Epicures* attributing all things to the concourse or meeting of their small motes which they call Atomi?"[28] The treatise *Propositions and Principles of Divinitie* (Edinburgh, 1591) gives us evidence of what was considered to be the "Epicurean" or "atheistic" questioning of providence. Among the beliefs that are rejected we find:

Wherefore we do condemne all ungodlie Epicures, who dreame of a certaine idle and daintie God, that neither regardeth his owne, nor yet other mens affaires: who also thinke, that all things are turned and rolled by the blind power of Fortune . . . who make a subalternall or second providence, that is; do attribute unto the true God a generall kinde of providence, whereas they ascribe unto Saints or false Gods, a more speciall . . . who faine a linking together of causes, & that there is a fatall destenie of things . . . that affirme heavenlie affaires, to be governed by God; and earthly things to be disposed, by the vertue, influence, and constellations of the Stars . . . who make Gods providence, to bee onely a bare knowledge of things . . . men and their affaires to bee guided by the power, but not by the appointment of God. (Pp. 18–19)[29]

Busson noted that by 1596 numerous apologies had been written to defend the orthodox doctrine of providence and to beat back the rising tide of Epicurean and atheistic speculations.[30] Certainly Calvin was among those who, long before 1596, combated such notions of God's providence. Early in the *Institutes* (1.2.2.) he asked rhetorically, "What good is it to profess with Epicurus some sort of God who has cast aside the care of the world only to amuse himself in idleness? What help is it, in short, to know a God with whom we have nothing to do?" He repeatedly dismissed Lucretius as a "filthy dog" (1.5.5). In his treatise *Concerning Scandals* (1550), Calvin railed against those who were filling the world with "atheism." These "filthy dogs" wanted "to abolish all fear of God from the minds of men. For they finally break through to the point that all religions have their origins in men's minds saying that God exists because

---

27 Cited by Elton, *King Lear and the Gods*, p. 16 (translation by Andrew Court, 1622).
28 Cited in ibid., p. 20.
29 Ibid., p. 21.
30 Henri Busson, *Le rationalisme dans la littérature française de la Renaissance (1533–1601)* (Paris: J. Vrin, 1957), pp. 514–515.

it pleases men to believe so and that the hope of eternal life has been invented in order to deceive the simple and that the fear of judgment is a childish terror." Such "atheism," he said, "is rampant everywhere throughout the world and particularly reigns in the courts of kings and princes, in courts of justice and other distinguished walks of life."[31] These "Siren voices" included Agrippa, Villanovanus, Dolet, Rabelais, Des Périers, and Gouvea. In the final edition of the *Institutes* Calvin devoted Book 1.16 to the correct doctrine of providence against those who would make God into a "momentary Creator," an "empty, idle, and almost unconscious" deity. He proceeds to argue, "I say nothing of the Epicureans (a pestilence that has always filled the world) who imagine that God is idle and indolent." (1.16.1, 3).

The *Sermons on Job* were not an anti-Epicurean document. They were, however, preached in the midst of the intellectual ferment caused by doubts regarding divine providence. Throughout the sermons Calvin was anxious to make it clear that God was not idle or indolent, despite appearances that sometimes indicated the contrary. These sermons were a strong defense of the doctrine of individual providence; a sovereign God created and continually cares for every event, including those events that seem unjust, evil, and chaotic. These sermons belong to the second view delineated by Elton: namely, that providence was "bafflingly inscrutable and hidden to human reason." Moreover, the Job sermons constitute a defense of providence against those who might conclude that God has "turned away," a defense on the basis of the most challenging book of the Bible.

In this challenging book, Calvin, like those who went before him, saw that there was a tension between the notion of revelation with its promise of God's just rule over history and the reality of human experience within that history. In his interpretation Calvin also saw the complexity of the text in terms of the different speakers, points of view, and arguments about justice. Calvin was always aware that the text of Job was an inherently perspectival text with speakers who argued from different positions within the story. Job spoke as the sufferer who demanded an answer from God. Job's friends spoke as pious men who were not experiencing suffering but were defending the justice of God. Both God and Satan spoke from a higher perspective altogether, a perspective unknown to both Job and his friends. This shifting perspectival nature of the text

---

31 Calvin, *De scandalis*, *OS* II:202–203; *CR* VIII:44ff. Also see Charles Trinkaus, "Renaissance Problems in Calvin's Theology," *Studies in the Renaissance* I (1954): 59–80.

allowed Calvin to explore the varying degrees of perception or under-standing of each speaker in terms of their presuppositions about suf-fering providence, spiritual growth, the nature of God, and the rule of providence.

The crucial verse for interpreting the book of Job and being true to its coherence was always 42:7 where it says, "After the LORD had spoken these words to Job, the LORD said to Eliphaz the Temanite: My wrath is kindled against you and your two friends; for you have not spoken of me what is right as my servant Job has." This verse loomed over the entire exposition of the preceding forty-one chapters and raised the pivotal question that every exegete had to answer: Why did Job speak rightly when it was the friends who had consistently defended and praised the justice of God? In the pre-critical Christian tradition this question had been resolved in significantly different ways. Gregory the Great accounted for the lack of insight by Job's friends in terms of their pride and failure to turn inward. For Gregory, Job's wisdom came through the ascent attained by suffering and interiority.[32] Thomas Aquinas concluded that Job "spoke rightly" about God because his belief in the immortality of the soul afforded him a perceptual superiority over his friends. The existence of the afterlife functioned as an extension of history where God would exercise his justice after death. Aquinas' Job showed that only the belief in immortality enabled one to trust that there was a just order to human affairs. Without a belief in immortality, Job's friends had to conclude either that there was no just providence or that history gave evidence of already being justly ordered. Neither of these propositions was true. By making the debate between Job and his friends center on the question of immortality, Aquinas actually focused the book of Job on the nature of history.[33]

Calvin also struggled to understand why Job, who so frequently com-plained and challenged God, was said to have "spoken rightly" while the friends were rebuked. The friends, after all, had justified the transcend-ence and righteousness of God, the sinfulness of man, the just order of history, and the reality of providence. To defend the justice of divine providence, Eliphaz, Bildad, and Zophar claimed to see within history an equitable order whereby the wicked were always punished and the good were rewarded. They could defend God's justice only by insisting on the visibility of providence and thereby associating all suffering with

32 Schreiner, *Where Shall Wisdom Be Found?*, pp. 22–54.   33 Ibid., pp. 70–90.

punishment for sin. Calvin had to wonder how these men, who voiced all his favorite themes and convictions, could have been rebuked in the end.

Calvin explained this dilemma by arguing that Job had a "good cause" but argued it poorly. The friends, however, voiced correct doctrine but applied it wrongly to Job.

Job maintained a good cause although he proceeded poorly . . . On the contrary, Job's friends had beautiful reasons from which we have received holy doctrine. But the fact remains that their foundation was wrong. They take a general argument and apply it wrongly; that is; that Job was being punished because of his crimes and they considered him an evil and abominable man . . . They, therefore, have a false and perverse doctrine in saying that God treats people in this world as they have deserved. But that doctrine would take away hope of eternal life and would enclose all of God's grace within this fallen and fragile life. This, then, is to pervert everything.[34]

With this explanation Calvin focused on the alleged perception of order within human events, an order that was supposed to be unchanging, consistent, visible, and knowable throughout history. He continually identified the "beautiful reasoning" of the friends with the doctrine of the law. By making this identification Calvin wrestled openly with the danger that the book of Job contradicted the theory of God's just punishment for disobeying the law. He attempted to reconcile the doctrine of the law with the more troubling Joban view of history. Zophar had promised Job that, if he were pure, his life would be "brighter than noonday." The wicked, however, would "fail and all way of escape would be lost to them." Calvin's interpretation of Job's refusal to accept this seemingly orthodox statement revealed his recurring ambivalence toward Job. Job, Calvin thought, spoke "too passionately" and irreverently but was fundamentally right. According to Calvin, "Job responds contrary to that which has been said in order to show that although this doctrine is taken from the Law, nevertheless, it is poorly applied." Calvin then proceeded both to defend Zophar's doctrine of punishing justice and at the same time to explain how Zophar had misinterpreted the Law.

When, therefore, it is said in the Law that we will be at peace and rest when we have followed the Law of God, why are we tormented and troubled by men except that we have made war on God? . . . If we are persecuted by men, let us see if we have been at peace with God. Let us see if we have provoked his wrath . . . Let us note, then, that it is not without cause that this benediction is given in the Law, i.e., that we will be at peace if we adhere to God without contradiction . . .

34 CO xxxv:494.

This promise is not frustrated but sometimes God will permit men to hurt and molest us in order to test our constancy . . . We see, therefore, how he chastises people in this world, some more and some less, and at the same time he reserves many punishments for the last day. We must not then pronounce such a general sentence as Zophar has done . . . By this Job shows that it is great folly to pronounce in general and without exception that God punishes in this life all those who have offended him and that as soon as man does evil, God rebukes him . . . We see the opposite.[35]

Calvin defended Job not only because of his belief in immortality and the afterlife but also because of the issue of perception. In Calvin's interpretation, there was one central problem in the book of Job: who *saw* things correctly. The doctrine of the law, as espoused by Job's friends, was a view of providence that exulted in visibility and rationality. However, because this view so clearly defended divine justice, Calvin wanted to defend the argument of the friends. He was clearly uneasy when he had to criticize Eliphaz's words at 4:7–9 ("Think, I pray you, who that was innocent ever perished or when have the righteous been cut off?"). He obviously approved of Eliphaz's view but warned that this principle had been poorly applied in order to conclude that Job was not righteous. Calvin was true to the Joban text and knew that an honest perception of history did not support the arguments of the friends. Hence Calvin insisted that the believer must not make a universal rule about how God governed the world or limit the divine judgments "to that which we see in the present."[36] According to Calvin, Eliphaz was right to defend God's justice but wrong to have said that we could always visibly perceive God's providential rule. So, too, against Bildad, Calvin had to argue that we "see" that things are confused in this world and that our life is "hidden" until Christ appears.[37] Commenting on Zophar's statement at 20:10–11 that the children of the wicked "will give back his wealth," Calvin again reminded his listeners that they had to contemplate by faith that which at the present time they could not yet "see with the eye."[38]

As Calvin proceeded through the text, the perceptual issues became more and more pronounced in all those themes that dominated the book of Job; namely, creation, providence, divine justice, and human suffering. His exegesis also took on a disquieting turn. Because he was continually aware of the problem of perception, Calvin's preaching on Job was characterized by a recurring tension between visibility and inscrutability, knowability and unknowability. In Job's story Calvin saw a God who held

35 *CO* XXXIII:556–559.   36 *CO* XXXIII:196.
37 *CO* XXXIII:402–406.   38 *CO* XXXIV:163.

sovereign sway over nature, history, and Satan. But he also found evidence that the wisdom, providence, goodness, and justice of God were often inscrutable and far beyond the judgments of human beings. It is in the Job sermons that we find Calvin's most extended discussions about the hiddenness of God. Calvin's Job confronted a God who repeatedly "hides his face." This hiddenness of God is a hiddenness that darkened history, threatened faith, and tempted the believer to despair. As Calvin progressed through his passage-by-passage interpretation, he struggled more and more intensely with the hidden and darker side of the divine nature. In so doing he also became increasingly aware of the true nature of Job's suffering. For Calvin, Job's real torment was his spiritual suffering, his doubt, and his noetic agony, all of which was evident in his relentless calling upon an inscrutable and silent God. Calvin saw that the Joban story required him to deal with the doctrine of providence in such a way that he also had to probe the frightening reality of spiritual despair. Job exemplified the believer who experienced the anguish caused by the fear that "God was his enemy," who had "turned away" and "hidden his face."[39]

The tension between visibility and inscrutability was a tension that pointed to human limits and the inscrutable transcendence of God. While Calvin was eager to state that providence was at times visible to the faithful during this earthly life, he saw that the text of Job presented the full reality of the opposite view. Job finally "spoke rightly" about God because he alone "saw" or perceived the reality of history. Job acknowledged that history appeared to be disordered and unjust. Job also knew that those who honestly observed the visibility of history would have to conclude that God did not care about earthly events. They would be the "atheists" or "Epicureans" of their time. Calvin's Job recognized that God's rule was not always evident and that divine justice could not always be used to judge the cause of human suffering. Even the belief in immortality, which was of crucial importance, could not completely mitigate the horrors of history. In Calvin's interpretation, Job confronted the dark and inscrutable nature of divine providence, a darkness which even the eyes of the just could not always penetrate.[40] Thus, for Calvin,

---

39 *CO* XXXIII:120, 123, 190, 223, 302, 434–435, 439, 451–452; *CO* XXXIV:52–53, 57, 65, 100–101, 224, 258–259, 263, 347, 370–374, 539, 624.

40 On the issue of how much the faithful believer could discern divine providence, see Pitkin, *What Pure Eyes Could See*. Pitkin analyzes the various editions of the *Institutes*, the New Testament commentaries, and the 1557 commentary on the Psalms. She concludes that in these texts Calvin allows for more "vision" on the part of the faithful that I have found in the Job sermons.

Job personified the difficulty of trusting God in the midst of highly ambiguous historical reality.

Calvin turned to many arguments and exegetical devices in order to expound the book of Job in such a way that he defended divine justice, explained Job's vindication, accounted for the rebuke of the friends, and fully treated the reality of inexplicable suffering. He insisted that although Job was not being punished for past sins, nonetheless, he was not sinless. Eliphaz "spoke poorly" by applying his views to Job but was right when he declared at 4:18, "those who serve him are not stable and in his angels he has found wickedness." Relying on the Vulgate translation, Gregory and Aquinas had argued that the reference to "instability" showed that because the angelic nature was mutable, some angels had fallen and become wicked while others adhered to God through grace.[41]

Calvin disagreed with this interpretation and read the verse as "Voici il ne trouve point fermeté en ses serviteurs, et a mis vanité en ses Anges." Moreover, he interpreted this verse in conjunction with Eliphaz's words at 15:15 ("Behold he finds no stability in his holy ones and the heavens are not clean before Him"). Calvin refused to interpret these verses as references to the fallen angels or devils; Eliphaz was charging the angels with "vanity," not apostasy or rebellion.[42] Calvin concluded that even the unfallen angels were full of "folly" or "vanity" and were incapable of withstanding the severity of God's higher justice.[43] If God willed, he could judge even the unfallen angels "with rigor" and find them guilty, for "what comparison is there between the infinite and the finite?"[44] Arguing that there was "no proportion" between the infinite and the finite, Calvin said that the unfallen angels and the just shared in a common creaturely justice embodied in the law. However, that creaturely justice was "like smoke when one comes before the infinite majesty of God."[45] On the basis of Eliphaz's words, Calvin defended the doctrine of a twofold or double justice in God. According to this view, God possessed a righteousness or standard of a hidden and secret justice that transcended the law. According to this higher justice, even the unfallen angels were impure in his sight. Thus Calvin chose to stress the transcendence of God by insisting that these verses meant the unfallen angels could be condemned if God exercised the extreme rigor of his "secret justice." For Calvin, the book of Job demonstrated that all creaturely perfection,

---

41 *Moralia*, IV.38.68; *Expositio*, IV:18.   42 *CO* XXXIII:206–208.
43 *CO* XXXIII:206.   44 *CO* XXXIII:726; XXXIV:96–97.
45 *CO* XXXIII: 495–496.

even that of the angels, was only accepted by God insofar as God "contents himself with the lower, median, or created justice revealed in the Law."[46] When Job himself cried that even if he were just God would still "throw him into the mud," Calvin believed that Job acknowledged that God's secret justice could condemn even the purity of the law.[47] Before this higher justice, no one, not even the angels, could be found to be righteous. In Calvin's view, Job's relentless search for justice led him to acknowledge that God was not so bound to the law that he was "subjected to it."[48] God could judge both the angels and Job according to the "extreme rigor" of his hidden justice, before which they all would perish. We can see how important verse 4:18 was to Calvin's understanding of Job's knowledge by observing a striking hermeneutical device: Although 4:18 was originally uttered by Eliphaz, in the later sermons Calvin came to attribute this insight and these words to Job.[49]

Nonetheless, as the Prologue had demonstrated, God was not punishing Job for sinning against either the law or his higher secret justice. Job was, indeed, correct in saying that his suffering was not due to sin. The friends were wrong in applying this retributive principle to Job in order to defend God. Calvin returned to this point at 42:7 where he saw a unique opportunity in this verse. He absolutely pounced on the phrase, "My wrath is kindled against you and your two friends." Why did God rebuke only *two* friends when there were four people who spoke to Job? Calvin concluded that Elihu was not included in the divine rebuke. Instead of having to interpret this verse by relying solely on Job's often unruly and suspect words, Calvin could turn to Elihu.

The reader can almost hear Calvin breathe a sigh of relief. There were few people in the Bible, especially in the book of Job, that Calvin loved more than Elihu. Former exegetes had criticized Elihu for vainglory and pride by making him the object of God's reproval at 38:2, "Who is that man wrapping his opinions in ignorant speeches?" Calvin would have none of this criticism. According to Calvin, the rebuke at 38:2 applied to *Job*, not Elihu. In Calvin's view, Elihu was not speaking vainly or proudly

---

46 *CO* XXXIII:205–207, 457–459, 496, 633, 643, 726; XXXIV:496–497.

47 *CO* XXXIII:455–456.

48 *CO* XXXIII:633; cf. *CO* XXXIV:341, 496–497. In the opening sermon Calvin made clear that this story was true, not fictional, and that Job was from the land of Uz. The pagan setting also explains why these sermons are not particularly Christocentric.

49 *CO* XXXIV:35. For a more detailed discussion of Calvin's teaching on the twofold or double justice of God see my article "Exegesis and Double Justice in Calvin's Sermons on Job," *Church History* 58/3 (September 1988): 322–338 and *Where Shall Wisdom Be Found?*, pp. 105–120.

but as a true doctor of the church. Elihu taught "the true doctrine perfectly as he received it from God."[50] For Calvin, Elihu stood as proof that from ancient times the "seed of religion" survived in the midst of darkness. Moreover, this "seed" apparently led not to idolatry but to "some good and holy doctrine."[51] Calvin was careful to state that although Elihu was not like one of the prophets or the children of Israel, nonetheless, "we see that God has imprinted such a mark on the doctrine of Elihu that the celestial spirit has appeared in his mouth so that we ought to be moved to receive what he says."[52] Elihu even represented a model for the Reformed church; he was an example of one who defended and upheld the truth of God in much the same way as the church must do against the "Papists."[53] When commenting on Elihu, Calvin did not have to apply the usual caveats by saying that he argued well but "spoke poorly" or that he was "overcome by his passions" or that he "had a good cause but applied it wrongly." Calvin made it very clear that "God has not condemned Elihu . . . He condemned Job. He condemned Job's friends, and showed that they all erred in one way or another. Elihu alone was justified."[54] Elihu became Calvin's mouthpiece and chapters 32–37 offer a straightforward presentation of Calvin's unqualified attitude toward Job and his friends.

In Calvin's interpretation, Elihu's anger at Job was perfectly justified. Unlike Eliphaz, Bildad, and Zophar, Elihu did not think that Job was being punished for his sins. Nonetheless, Elihu rightly charged Job with being impatient, excessively passionate, and wrongly thinking himself to be just before God.[55] Job's many complaints and impatient accusations against God always troubled Calvin. Throughout the sermons he valiantly tried to defend Job's statements by explaining that Job argued correctly but spoke excessively or too passionately because of his grief. In Elihu's speeches Calvin was relieved to find evidence that Job had not glorified God as he ought to have done.[56]

However, Elihu did more than grant Calvin permission to criticize Job. Chapters 32–37 provided a summary of Calvin's own theology. Calvin's Elihu understood the grave sinfulness of human nature, the impossibility of merit, the justice of all suffering, the inability of anyone to plead against God, and the duty to render praise to the Lord.[57] Elihu even

---

50 *CO* xxxv:259.   51 *CO* xxxiii:633.

52 *CO* xxxv:35–36; cf. *CO* xxxv:38.   53 *CO* xxxv:13, 37–38, 41–42.

54 *CO* xxxv:34.   55 *CO* xxxv:7–8, 131, 135, 215, 217–220.

56 *CO* xxxv:135.   57 *CO* xxxv:9–10, 145, 174–175.

appeared to have known the correct doctrine of imputation![58] Elihu
properly understood the transcendence and purity of God's justice. Like
Calvin, Elihu knew that God's will was the rule of justice. The many
verses in Elihu's speeches about divine transcendence meant that he
understood the importance of that infinite distance between God and
his creatures as well as the vast gulf between divine and human righteousness.[59] In Calvin's preaching, Elihu also talked about the inseparability of
the divine attributes, a principle that allowed him to perceive that God's
justice and power were inseparable from his goodness.[60] Therefore, no
matter how incomprehensible or unfair God's judgments appeared to be,
one could always trust that God was acting justly. Moreover, because
Elihu grasped the inseparability of the divine attributes he rightly charged
Job with wrongfully accusing God of acting according to an absolute or
tyrannical power.[61]

However, by far the most important function of the Elihu chapters was
to provide the correct perspective on divine providence. In all its essen-
tials, Elihu's doctrine was the same as that of Calvin's Job. In Elihu's
words, he found affirmation of both divine justice and divine hiddenness,
of the occasional inexplicableness of human suffering as well as the
promised judgment of the wicked. Moreover, the design of chapters
32–37 provided Calvin with an argument that went beyond a mere
summary of Calvin's doctrine of providence as expounded by Elihu and
Job. In these chapters Calvin also found an extensive use of nature
imagery. He made use of this imagery in order to exploit what he saw
to be an important interplay between nature and history that was, in
reality, a dialectic between revelation and hiddenness. This dialectic
enabled Calvin to unite chapters 32–37 with the whirlwind speech. In
these chapters he found a way to draw together the themes of hiddenness,
inscrutability, and inexplicable suffering with a trust in the often-baffling
providence of God.

---

58 *CO* xxxv: 88.
59 *CO* xxxv:131, 174, 175, 178.   60 *CO* xxxv:58–60, 131, 151, 154, 206, 222, 315.
61 *CO* xxxv:54–55, 58–60, 136, 150. On the problem of the "absolute power" in the Job sermons,
    see Schreiner, *Where Shall Wisdom Be Found?*, pp. 110–120; Jelle Faber, "Nominalisme in
    Calvijns preken over Job," in *Een sprekend begin*, ed. R. ter Beek et al. (Kampen: Uitgeverij Van
    den Berg, 1993), pp. 68–85. It should be asked, however, whether the "nominalists" ever taught
    that the absolute power of God was tyrannical or arbitrary. On the history of this concept see
    William J. Courtenay, *Capacity and Volition: A History of the Distinction of the Absolute and
    Ordained Power* (Bergamo: P. Lubrina, 1990); William J. Courtenay, "Nominalism in Late
    Medieval Religion," in *The Pursuit of Holiness in Late Medieval Religion*, ed. C. Trinkaus and
    H. A. Oberman (Leiden: E. J. Brill, 1974), pp. 26–59.

On the basis of Elihu's words, Calvin affirmed that the purpose of affliction was usually to make us sense our sins and lead us to repentance. Earlier in the sermons Calvin had explained that it was a "special privilege" if God afflicted someone for any other purpose than sin. Calvin's Elihu, therefore, insisted on the thoroughly traditional view that suffering was pedagogical, medicinal, and instrumental to finding wisdom.[62] However, Elihu also reaffirmed the central message of the book; namely, that sometimes providence and the purpose of suffering were unclear, inscrutable, and hidden. Recognizing that Job was not being afflicted because of his past sins, Calvin's Elihu acknowledged the ambiguity and difficulty in discerning God's purposes. Providence was often inscrutable and justice was not always exercised in the present historical realm. The friends had argued wrongly for the constant visibility and knowability of divine providence.[63] The superiority of Elihu's perception was clear to Calvin at 34:10–12 where Elihu said, "Can there be injustice in God or iniquity in the Almighty? For God will render to man according to his work, according to the ways of each one, he will judge him." In the arguments of the friends, these words would have justified the erroneous belief that divine providence was visible and evident in earthly events. But Calvin's Elihu gave them the opposite meaning:

This is not to be understood as if God immediately punishes the transgressors of his Law and supports the good . . . He [God] can, indeed, act (as happens all the time) so that he will support the wicked for awhile. We see that he hides (*dissimule*) when men burst forth into evil and it does not seem to us as though he thinks about it or sees them . . . Thus God does not punish the wicked immediately and Elihu does not intend to say that he does so . . . God does not execute his judgments on the first day such that we can visibly perceive (*appercevoir á l'oeil*) that he renders to each according to his works . . . But when Elihu says, "God renders," he presupposes what is true; namely, that we must hold our spirits in suspense until God shows us that which is hidden for a time.[64]

Sometimes, therefore, God gave visible signs of his providence. But the book of Job dealt with different historical times, those times when "confusion" or "disorder" marked the historical sphere. But this disorder was not to cause doubt and unbelief about the providence of God. Rather, such times were a "trial" when believers had to endure divine hiddenness. According to Calvin, the Job story taught that things were "not yet put back in order." To claim a visible and discernible order in history was to

62 *CO* xxxv:9–10, 30, 117–118, 270, 285–286.   63 *CO* xxxv:34, 134–135.
64 *CO* xxxv:145–146.

confuse the present with the Last Judgment when God would, indeed, execute his judgments. Within human history, God left many things "unpunished" while he "hid his face."[65]

Calvin portrayed Elihu as facing history with the same realism as Job. He told his auditors that, as in the present situation, the honest observer had to admit that history seemed disordered and God appeared to have abandoned human events.[66] Commenting on verse 34:29 ("When he will have hidden his face, who will be able to see him?"), Calvin saw Elihu expressing the horrible "temptation" caused in the heart of the believer by the inscrutability of divine providence. It is, he said, a "hard" or "great temptation" to think that God acts "without reason."[67] In these times of temptation, "it seems that God has no regard for us; we see only darkness and the clarity which ought to guide us does not shine."[68] Experiencing the "confusion" of human history, it is truly "as if God had hidden his face."[69] The endurance, hope, and trust required during times of God's hiddenness was, for Calvin, the "edifying" message of the book of Job. In the person of Job, Calvin preached that believers had to "wait in patience" until God finally revealed that which was still hidden. During this present life, the believer could only "know in part."[70]

However, the "application" of Job's story was not limited to the call for patience. Calvin also believed that the story of Job was intended to instill trust in the God who was now hidden. Calvin developed the theme of trust by calling attention to both the hiddenness and the revelation of God. Juxtaposed to Calvin's descriptions of the hiddenness of God in history was his emphasis on the clarity and revelation of God in nature. In Elihu's words, particularly in chapter 37, Calvin found references to the wonders of creation. The heavens, thunder, lightning, snow, rain, the skies, and the animals were all "mirrors" in which the believer should "contemplate the majesty of God."[71] In fact, the Job sermons are the

---

65 *CO* xxxv:263.

66 *CO* xxxv:142. See also *CO* xxxv:139–142, 223, 231–232, 263–264, 269.

67 Calvin often made this referral back to Job 2:3, only in order to insist that God did not really act "without reason" or "without cause."

68 *CO* xxxv:192–194.

69 *CO* xxxv:193.

70 *CO* xxxv:28, 63, 141, 192.

71 *CO* xxxv:315–318. In the nature passages Calvin preached at length regarding the workings of nature. He did so by employing the traditional cosmology of his time. For further discussion of his portrayal of nature see Susan Schreiner, *The Theater of His Glory: Nature and the Natural Order in the Thought of John Calvin* (Durham, NC: Labyrinth Press, 1991; repr. Baker Book House, 1995).

clearest example of the way in which Calvin denied a natural theology but developed a "theology of nature."[72] Despite God's hiddenness, divine providence was still visible in the natural order. That order, which was due only to the immediacy of God's power and governance, should serve as the basis for trust in a providence we cannot yet fully see in history. Preaching on Elihu's words at 37:5 ("God does marvelous things which we cannot comprehend"), Calvin argued, "We see, then, that if we have our eyes open to contemplate the providence of God in the natural order which is placed before us, that order ought to serve as instruction so that we put our full trust in him."[73] According to Calvin, the visible creation taught Job that "we live here in the world as in a beautiful and spacious theater where God gives us a view of all his creatures."[74] Although God often "hides his face" in history, nevertheless, Calvin's Elihu knew that in this "theater" nature remained "as the face of God" and revealed divine wisdom, glory, goodness, and power.[75]

Calvin repeatedly explained that the key to understanding the Joban text was to distinguish between nature and the often-chaotic realm of history. He made this distinction between nature and history the key to interpreting the book of Job and the key to understanding providence correctly. He argued that Job's friends were rebuked precisely because they had failed to understand this distinction. Correcting Bildad in chapter 18, Calvin argued:

But it is also necessary that we know how to discern properly between the works of God . . . God wills that the sun rises and sets and by that we are shown that until the end of the world he will give us the things that are necessary to preserve us here . . . But with reference to his judgments there is another reason, for he wills only that we have some taste therein during this life and that we wait in patience so that [God's judgments] will appear on the last day. For at that time the things that are now confused will be put back into their proper condition. Until then, God will carry out his judgments only in part.[76]

The friends wrongly sought the visibility of providence equally in nature and history. Elihu explained their "misunderstanding" and thereby allowed Calvin to argue that the revelation visible in nature could not be imposed on the very real ambiguity that permeated human events. In the

---

72 For the "theology of nature" see David C. Steinmetz, "Calvin and the Natural Knowledge of God," in *Via Augustini: Augustine in the Later Middle Ages, Renaissance, and Reformation*, ed. Heiko A. Oberman and Frank A. James III, Studies in Medieval and Renaissance Thought 49 (Leiden: E. J. Brill, 1991), pp. 142–156.

73 *CO* xxxv:320.   74 *CO* xxxv:341.

75 Ibid.   76 *CO* xxxiv:68.

speeches of Elihu (and Job) Calvin found proof for both the revelatory character of the natural realm and the inscrutability of the historical realm. This juxtaposition between nature and history became Calvin's hermeneutical strategy by means of which he emphasized the dialectic, and often the discontinuity, between visibility and hiddenness, knowability and inscrutability, nature and history.

After preaching on Elihu, Calvin had to confront the whirlwind speech. By this time, however, he had created a problem for himself in the preceding sermons. Having insisted on the different revelatory capacity of nature and history, Calvin now had to explain why God spoke about nature. In the whirlwind speech it was God, not the friends, who argued against Job on the basis of the visible wonders of creation. Did God, too, fail to distinguish properly between nature and history? How could God answer Job's complaints about the confusion in history with appeals to the miracles of nature? Did the whirlwind speech threaten Calvin's carefully formulated argument about the proper distinction between the works of God?

Calvin admitted to his listeners that one could "find it strange that, wanting to maintain his justice and shut the mouth of men so that they do not slander him, God talks about the stars, the labor of the earth, speaks like a navigator, and refers to the nature of the beasts." Calvin concluded that it might seem as though God had resorted to rather "extravagant arguments."[77] Nevertheless, Calvin actually found the whirlwind speech to be the perfect answer to Job. His interpretation of these last chapters reveals that in Calvin's preaching on Job, nature had a twofold function, neither of which was the condemnation of man's drive toward idolatry. As read through the spectacles of Scripture, nature should arouse one to praise the beauty of creation and encourage the contemplation of God's glory in the cosmos. Nature also should humble human beings and render them inexcusable.[78] In the whirlwind speech Calvin discovered both purposes in the passages about the stars, waters, ostriches, snow, horses, and other beasts. He used these chapters to expound the wonders of creation. But he also saw that their exegetical purpose in the context of the story was to answer Job.

The key to the nature passages in the whirlwind speech was divine transcendence. This emphasis on transcendence allowed Calvin to sustain the importance of the dialectic between hiddenness and visibility that he

---

77 *CO* xxxv:435.   78 *CO* xxxv:367, 409, 419, 431–432. 435, 437–438.

had developed in the previous sermons. Calvin preached that the created realm could successfully humble Job's attempts at self-vindication because the functioning of the cosmos went far beyond both human power and human understanding. This human inability to control, restrain, or comprehend nature resolved the problem of providence by placing the difference between revelation and hiddenness within the heart of nature itself. Calvin linked the whirlwind speech to the problem of history by stressing human ignorance with respect to *all* the works of God, both natural and historical.

By describing the transcendent wisdom and power necessary to regulate the earth, stars, and animals, Calvin believed the whirlwind speech taught Job that creation was, as Elihu said, "the face of God." Calvin constantly stressed the tension between visibility and inscrutability by using the metaphor of God's "face." God "hid his face" in history but nature remained the "face of God." Nonetheless, while stressing this revelatory aspect of the cosmos, Calvin insisted that human beings could never fully comprehend the works of God. Even if Job – and Calvin's listeners – "opened their eyes" they would fail to understand the reasons behind the composition and functioning of nature. Even after contemplating the works of creation, "we must always conclude that the wisdom of God is hidden from us (in all of these clear things) and that there is some cause above us to which we cannot attain."[79] In the whirlwind speech we learn that 1 Corinthians 13:12 ("For now we see in a mirror dimly, but then face to face") finally applied to both nature and history; even in the contemplation of creation humans could know "only in part." In Calvin's exposition of the whirlwind speech the very majesty of nature infused it with a kind of hiddenness. By arguing that the wisdom and governance of creation transcended human understanding, Calvin placed within nature itself that dialectic between visibility and inscrutability. Now even the "theater" or "mirror" of nature left the believer with only a "glimpse" or "taste" of divine providence.

Calvin's unrelenting insistence on the literal exegesis extended also to the whirlwind speech and caused him to interpret it in a thoroughly naturalist manner. The consequence of this exegetical principle became most fully evident in his interpretation of Behemoth and Leviathan. In order to appreciate fully Calvin's interpretation of these passages it is important to summarize the traditional interpretation found in previous

79 *CO* xxxv:396.

Christian exegetes. The crucial texts were "Behold Behemoth" and "Can you draw out Leviathan with a hook?" Gregory the Great taught that the "mystical" sense of these verses referred to the Antichrist and Satan.[80] By reading these chapters in terms of Satan, Gregory was able to focus the book of Job, and the whirlwind speech in particular, on the great drama of salvation history. The great battle of that drama was between God and Behemoth or Leviathan; that is, between God and the "Ancient Enemy." This battle had raged since the beginning of time and now Job understood that he, too, was involved in that warfare. Thomas Aquinas tried to maintain both the literal and the "metaphorical" sense of these passages. He concluded that in the "metaphorical" sense, Behemoth and Leviathan referred to the devil "under the figures of the elephant and the whale."[81] Therefore, both Gregory and Aquinas found the whirlwind speech to be about Christ's victory over the devil. References to the "hook" by means of which God captured Leviathan depicted the way Christ overcame Satan with the "hook" of his seemingly mortal nature. Witnessing the slyness, power, and ferocity of the devil, Job confessed that he could never hope to win this warfare through human power. The whirlwind speech, therefore, became a description of that ancient battle that characterized all of human history. When God said to Job, "Remember the battle and speak no more," he was telling Job that only the deity could defeat the raging power of Satan through the "hook" of Christ. Job was in the midst of that momentous battle but it was not his to win.

Calvin utterly refused to find any mystical, metaphorical, or allegorical meanings in the whirlwind speech. To find Satan in the figures of Behemoth and Leviathan would turn Scripture into a "nose of wax" and would ignore the plain sense of the text.[82] Behemoth was simply an elephant and Leviathan was only a whale. Calvin's refusal to indulge in these "trashy details" could not have been based solely on his dislike of allegorically interpretation. In his commentary on Isaiah 27:1 he was willing to interpret Leviathan allegorically as Satan. So why was he so determined to be literalistic or naturalistic in the whirlwind speech?

The refusal to allegorize the great beasts served Calvin in several important ways. First, by retaining the "natural sense" of the text, Calvin reasserted his insistence on the role of nature. By "Beholding Behemoth," one could again contemplate the "admirable order" God instituted in the

---

80 For a fuller discussion of the history of the exegesis of the whirlwind speech see, Schreiner, *Where Shall Wisdom Be Found?*, pp. 48–52, 83–87, 138–146.
81 Ibid., p. 85.   82 *CO* xxxv:464–467.

world. In this awe-inspiring design a creature as small as the human being was able to be the "lord and master" over a huge beast such as the elephant.[83] Moreover, the fact that such huge beasts did not devour human beings demonstrated that God held back their fury with that all-important "secret bridle" of divine providence[84] Leviathan was called the "King over the sons of pride" not because he was Satan but because he taught the prideful that they could not subdue the whale by their own strength, thereby making them humble before their creator.[85]

Calvin's rejection of any "mystical" or "metaphorical" sense also lessened the role of Satan in the book of Job as a whole. If Behemoth and Leviathan remained only the elephant and the whale, there could be no re-entrance of Satan at the end of the story. Calvin's interest in diminishing Satan's role was clear from the very beginning of the sermons. Preaching on the Prologue, he explained that Satan's original appearance in the heavenly council demonstrated that God did not merely permit but ordered and controlled all of the devil's actions against Job. God had loosened the reins or bridle on Satan and allowed him to afflict Job.[86] The decision not to allegorize the great beasts, therefore, enabled Calvin to stress once again the sovereignty of God. Without the reintroduction of Satan, the power struggle depicted in chapters 40–41 was not between God and Satan but, rather, between God and Job. In comparison with previous exegetes, Calvin thereby shifted the balance of the book. In Calvin's interpretation there was no "third party" so that Job and God could be aligned against a common enemy. Calvin's Job did not have to withstand the power and cleverness of the devil so much as he had to find a way to stand before God, especially now that he had learned about "the master with whom he had to deal."[87]

By not interpreting the great beasts as Satan, Calvin gave up the opportunity to connect the whirlwind speech with the Prologue. He also bypassed the traditional way of connecting the whirlwind speech to the issues of salvation history. The power of God that Calvin stressed was not the victory of Christ over Satan. He was, in fact, uninterested in the formerly crucial verse, "Remember the battle and speak no more." Calvin's focus was on God's words to Job: "Will you overthrow my judgment? Will you condemn me to justify yourself?" and "Who is he that can stand in my presence?"

83 *CO* xxxv:460–461.   84 *CO* xxxv:462.
85 *CO* xxxv:465.   86 *CO* xxxiii:75, 91–92, 106–107.   87 *CO* xxxv:353.

Calvin did, however, interpret God's statements and questions by connecting the whirlwind speech to history. The appeal to the incomprehensibility of nature, seen in the elephant and the whale, tied the divine response to the question of historical providence. The whirlwind speech rebuked Job's questioning of God's power and justice. Most importantly, however, the divine response demonstrated that the governing of history required a wisdom and power far beyond that which was revealed even in nature. Therefore, Calvin argued, if nature astounds us, history will certainly be beyond our judgment. By placing the dialectic between hiddenness and revelation within the heart of nature itself, Calvin did blur his own distinction between the "works of God." But he did so for a very important reason. By merging the two spheres he formed a *continuity* between nature and history that would lead the believer to trust in God's providence. The wonders in nature should lead one to trust that God governed human history with the same power and goodness evident in creation.

All interpreters of the book of Job explained the whirlwind speech in terms of the wisdom they thought Job needed. For Gregory and Aquinas the whirlwind speed was about the "warfare" or "battle" that raged between God and Satan. For these exegetes Job needed protection and he received it though Christ's victory over the devil. Calvin's Job, however, needed a promise. He needed the promise that history was in some way an extension of nature. To provide that promise Calvin had to reconnect the realms of nature and history. He had to merge the powerful imagery of light and darkness, clarity and hiddenness, knowability and inscrutability. In Calvin's Job sermons the imagery of "nature" as "mirror," "light," "brightness," and "reflection" finally shaded off into darkness and incomprehensibility. The providential rule of human history was inexplicable, incomprehensible, and hidden to human reason. Nevertheless, Calvin offered faith and hope by arguing that nature pointed beyond itself and by promising that the same God who brought beauty and order out of creation was also wise and powerful enough to bring order out of the present historical "confusion." While Calvin insisted repeatedly that there was no continuity between God and Job or between divine and human justice, he held out the promise of a continuity between God's revelation in nature and God's governance of history. Calvin's Job had to rely on that promise offered by the "mirror" of nature and trust that the wisdom and power reflected in the cosmos were inherent and inseparable aspects of God's rule. Within the "disorder" of the historical present, Calvin's Job was left not with "knowledge" but with faith and hope. He had to trust that the wisdom reflected in the cosmos would someday be evident in God's rule of history. Job, therefore, "spoke rightly" because he perceived the necessity for that trust and faith in the midst of very dark and troubling times. God seemed to have abandoned human events but faith reached for trust in his justice, a faith that could presently see only "in part" and "through a glass dimly." Job may not have understood the justice and mercy of this providence but he could have faith or trust in the promise reflected in nature. This was Job's only hope until the Last Day when he could finally see God "face to face."

Calvin's sermons on Job were an exegetical exposition that was intended to edify the faithful. These 159 sermons are among his longest and most sustained treatments of divine providence. His preaching on Job taught his hearers that they did not need to fear to look at their own historical times with ruthless honesty. Like Job, Calvin's congregation learned that the "disorder," "confusion," and unjust suffering they saw was very real and should not piously be explained away by pretending that one understood or "perceived" God's judgments. While believers were never to challenge the judgments of God, nonetheless, they were not to presume that God's reasons were visible and comprehensible. Providence often required trust in a hidden God who appeared to have turned away and "hidden his face."

We can see the importance of a faithful trust in providence by returning to Calvin's definition of Job's "temptation." In Job, Calvin saw the greatest of spiritual trials; namely, the doubt that God cared for human events. Job feared that God had abandoned him to the apparently chaotic world of human events. Job fell into despair and came to doubt and distrust divine providence.[88] Thus in the person of Job Calvin portrayed the existential dimensions of doubt regarding providence. In his interpretation, Job fought despair about providence and the suspicion that God was cruel and unjust, "playing with men like balls." Job was not the model of patience and constancy. He was, however, an example of that spiritual temptation that must be endured when one "looks at present things and sees that the course of human events is confused, disordered, and mixed up."[89] When Job cried that "the earth is given into the hands of the wicked," Calvin respected the fact that he was just being honest;

---

88 *CO* XXXIII:120, 123, 190, 223, 302, 434–435, 439; XXXIV:52–53, 57, 65, 100–101, 224, 258–259, 263, 347, 370–374, 539, 624.

89 *CO* XXXIII: 123, 224–225, 444, 447; XXXLV:52, 64, 241, 246–247, 252–253, 255, 258–259, 262–266, 369, 535.

he spoke of things as they really appeared. Job's words reflected that horrible temptation caused by the inscrutability of providence. Preaching on Job's words in verse 24:1 ("Are not the times hidden from the Almighty and why do those who know him not see his days?") Calvin said:

It seems that God is hidden and that he withdraws from this world, that he separates himself in order to abandon it completely. Briefly, except when God makes us experience his providence and we are convinced that he governs high and low, we are as in the night, in an obscure time . . . We do not see [God's judgments] according to our understanding. There are some times that are hidden from men but known to God; that is, when God delays his judgments and does not execute them immediately . . . It is indeed an evil temptation for the faithful when things are confused in the world and it seems that God does not get involved but, instead, that fortune rules and dominates.[90]

For Calvin, the despair caused by the doubt regarding providence made the faithful believe that God had forsaken them. When the judgments of God were hidden, faith had to struggle to maintain trust in that which was not seen. Calvin's Job knew a central and crucial truth; to cling to that which was visible was to conclude that one had been abandoned by God. Calvin portrayed Job as engaged in a "spiritual combat" against the conclusion of his own reason and "natural sense." This sense depended only on reason or what he could actually see.[91] When Job spoke according to this sense he expressed the feeling that he had been forsaken by God. However, Calvin reminded his listeners that there was in the believer an apprehension that went beyond nature; namely, faith. Faith "ought to restrain the natural sense" and should "rise above" what one saw here below. Faced with the injustice of history, believers like Job were "elevated by faith" in order to trust that, despite everything they saw, God did bridle the wicked and maintain his justice.[92] Faith in providence had to cling not to that which the "eye sees," but to that which was real despite appearances. Job's spiritual remedy against despair was a trust in that which he could not perceive; i.e., the existence and justice of God's rule. Present situations were the "times hidden," or the times of darkness. In the future the believer would come to "that celestial clarity where there will be no more knowledge in part (*cognoissance in partie*) but where there will be total perfection when we contemplate our God face to face (*face á face*)."[93]

---

90 *CO* xxxiv:370–371.   91 *CO* xxxiv:538.
92 *CO* xxxiii:224, 434, 441–442, 585; *CO* xxxiv:163, 242, 259, 266, 368–369, 480, 538–539, 604; *CO* xxxv: 257, 487.
93 *CO* xxxiv:259, 263, 266.

Calvin never fell into the temptation to allegorize Job as a type of the suffering church. But clearly he saw Job's situation mirroring the state of God's elect in the midst of the world. He understood that the message of the book of Job had to be "applied" for "our profit." The main teaching that Job's story was meant to convey was the fight to trust in divine providence. Therefore in order to "*armez á l'exemple de Iob*," the congregation was to recognize that their situation was Job's situation.[94] "Today," Calvin preached, Job's story was like a "*miroir*" reflecting the suffering of the church at the hands of God's enemies.[95] The "poor church" was endangered and had to hope in God. The condition of the church "today" caused the same "temptation" as that suffered by Job.[96] The "*pire tentation*," worst temptation, was always that one would begin to suspect that God had abandoned his own when their prayers were not heard.[97] Calvin explained that, like Job, "we" are taunted that we trust in God in vain because all one sees is "disorder and confusion." Calvin admitted, "It seems as if God has no regard for this world . . . that he is asleep."[98] The same temptations which had assailed Job now assailed the church.

God has promised to be protector of his church . . . We see the horrible tyranny which dominates and yet where is the hand of God which ought to help his own? Does God show that he wants to uphold his purpose when we see the church oppressed and the enemies of all religion rule today in such fury, without pity and God does not repress them?[99]

According to Calvin, Job "shows us here that during this life things are so mixed up that one will not know either white or black. The earth will be delivered into the hands of the wicked; that is to say, the wicked will have here their own way."[100] Calvin's Job protested to his friends that this is indeed the reality of human history as it appears "here below." He also insisted that one must believe in providence with an unblinking realism, with the admission that providence was not visible and evident. A true belief in providence could not be an easy discernment of God's judgments but a trust that God was present at all – and true to the promise revealed in creation.

Even a cursory reading of Calvin's letters during the same period that he preached on Job demonstrate that the reformer believed he and his congregation lived in the "hidden times" of darkness. The letters from 1554 to his death in 1564 encompass that period when he was engaged in

94 *CO* xxxiii:323.   95 *CO* xxxiii:256.   96 Ibid.
97 *CO* xxxiv:124. See also *CO* xxxv:11–12, 101.   98 *CO* xxxiii:447.
99 *CO* xxxiii:614.   100 *CO* xxxiii:447.

struggles about the sacramental controversies, the Servetus affair, the various calumnies and slanders against him, the fight with the "Libertines," and the troubles of various churches. As the years wore on his letters became increasingly concerned with the grave dangers of the Reformed churches in France. He feared that civil war was inevitable. He knew the details of the tortures that the "martyrs for the faith" would have to endure. He expressed his anxiety and his encouragement to those who had to face persecution. He did not recommend Job as their example; David and St. Paul received that honor. Nevertheless, the lesson drawn from the book of Job was depicted clearly in these letters. In 1557 he wrote to the church in Paris that believers must not doubt that God had his eyes on them and was listening to their groaning and their tears.

For if we do not rely on his providence, the slightest distress will become an abyss and will swallow us up. We will be shaken to and fro at every breath of wind – we will be troubled by our perplexities and led astray in our counsels; in a word, our whole life will be a labyrinth, especially when the bridle on Satan is loosened (*la bride est laschee a Sathan*) and his agents in order to torment and disturb the poor church of God. Surely we must fly to this thought for our refuge; that if God cares for all his creatures, he will not abandon those who call upon him. No, if a single bird does not fall to the ground without his willing it, he will never be absent to his own children.

It is true that the temptation is great and difficult to withstand; that is, to see such extreme desolation and to see God so slow in raising his arm to remedy this situation . . . God desires to try our faith like gold in the furnace. Although he does not stretch forth his hand to help us as soon as we would wish, let us never abandon our conviction that the hairs on our head are numbered by him and that if he sometimes permits the blood of his people to be shed, yet he does not fail to treasure their precious tears . . . We pray you to practice the lesson that our great master has taught us; that is, to keep our souls patient. We know how difficult this is for the flesh but remember also that it is the moment to strive against ourselves and our passions when we are assailed by our enemies . . . It is certain that he has not permitted what has now happened, except in order to prepare the way for some great matter that surpasses our understanding (*noz sens*).[101]

---

101 Calvin to the church at Paris, September 16, 1557, *CO* xv:629–630; *Selected Works of John Calvin: Tracts and Letters*, ed. Henry Beveridge and Jules Bonnet, vol. vi (Grand Rapids : Baker Book House, 1983). In Calvin's letter to the Brethren of France, June, 1559, he wrote: "[W]e thought we could do nothing better than address to you a common letter to exhort you, in the name of God, that whatever alarms Satan may create, not to faint, or by withdrawing from the combat to deprive yourselves of the fruit of the victory which has been promised and assured to you. It is indeed certain that if God had not let loose the reins of Satan (*ne laschoit la bride a Satan*) and his

The last two decades of his life were a time when Calvin thought deeply about the nature of divine providence. As Barbara Pitkin has demonstrated, Calvin developed a twofold notion of faith; namely, saving faith, which was the focus of the *Institutes* and the commentaries on the New Testament, and providential faith, which dominated his commentary on the Psalms.[102] His struggle with the ambiguity of history and the difficulty of discerning providence governed his Job sermons. His 1557 Psalms commentary reflected his ever-deepening concern with the relationship between creation, providence, and faith. The 1559 *Institutes* further revealed his concern with the nature of providence, creation, and history. His letters increasingly contained messages about the necessity of relying on providence, even when it could not always be perceived. Throughout these discussions Calvin's imagery was that of "seeing," "perceiving," "not seeing," or merely "glimpsing," the reality of providence. Moreover, while faith in God's saving action required certain knowledge, Calvin admitted, at least in the Job sermons, that faith in providence required a mighty act of trust. The church, like Job, was being tested with the greatest of spiritual temptations: the fear that God had "turned away" and "hidden his face." Hiddenness added a darker dimension to Calvin's usual emphasis on the majesty, transcendence, and sovereignty of God. Throughout his letters to the persecuted Christians in France, he spoke of the necessity for trust in a God who seemed presently to be hidden. While composing many of those letters Calvin was preaching on the book of Job

---

henchmen, they would not have been able to trouble you. And for this reason you should come to this conclusion, that if your enemies plot your ruin it is because God on his part has granted them such license in order to prove your faith, having an infinite number of means at his disposal to check all their fury when he shall have glorified his name by your constancy . . . For it is but reasonable that we should allow ourselves to be governed by the hand of so good a father, although it may seem to us heavy and unfeeling. If we were exposed so as to the abandonment of God, then we might feel dismay. But since he who has taken us under his protection has himself willed to try us all by the combats into which we will be brought, it is for us to subdue our affections and not to think the condition to which we have been called is strange. We are perfectly aware what terrors you shall have to endure, when we reflect that you are not armed with insensibility, but, on the contrary, feeling much repugnance and many conflicts in your flesh. But, nevertheless, God must prevail . . . Not that the devil and his children are less hardened and bent upon doing evil more than ever, but because God, bearing with our weakness, keeps them chained up like so many wild beasts. For it is certain that if he had not until now intervened with his hand, we should have been destroyed a thousand times, and if he did not still continue in a secret way to watch over us, we should quickly be swallowed up. Knowing then by experience the pity and compassion that God feels for us, so much more should we, with a feeling of security, rest on his protection, trusting that he will prove how dear our lives are to him." *CO* XVII:571–572; *Selected Works of John Calvin, Tracts and Letters*, VII:50–51.

102 Pitkin, *What Pure Eyes Could See.*

where he found a God both hidden and revealed. He sought for a God whose "secret providence" still governed history. In Job's vindication he saw that when God "has unbridled the wicked" believers must go beyond what they see and cling to a trust in the just providence of God. To fight temptation was to fight giving in to the visible evidence of history and to insist that God would be true to the promise of his providential nature. That was the great trial – and triumph – of Job.

CHAPTER 4

Calvin as commentator on the Psalms

Wulfert de Greef
Translated by Raymond A. Blacketer

THE COMMENTARY ON THE PSALMS

Calvin's commentary on the Psalms (*In librum Psalmorum commentarius*) came off the press of Robert Estienne at Geneva in 1557. In the preface Calvin explains the circumstances that moved him to write this commentary. When he began giving lectures on the Psalms in 1552 he had not intended to follow his usual procedure by writing yet another commentary on the Psalms. Nonetheless, some of his friends had urged him to undertake this task, but he said he did not think this was necessary. There were already outstanding commentaries from the pens of both Bucer and Musculus.[1] But when his friends renewed their appeals to him to publish the content of these lectures, he conceded that he might consider writing something on the Psalms in French. Nevertheless, he began by way of experiment with the exposition of a single Psalm in Latin. When his friends saw this, they continued to press him to publish a complete commentary on the Psalms. Calvin finally gave in, partly because he was worried that someone might publish an unauthorized version of the lectures. A French translation of his commentary appeared in 1558, and a new, improved, and expanded version came out in 1561.[2]

The Psalms commentary was not the first commentary that Calvin had written. In 1540 his commentary on the epistle to the Romans had come off the press. Various other commentaries on the New Testament followed. His commentary on Isaiah was his first on an Old Testament book. The

---

1 At Strasbourg in 1529 the first edition of Bucer's Psalms commentary appeared, bearing the pseudonym Aretius Felinus: *Psalmorum libri quinque ad ebraicam veritatem versi, et familiari explanatione elucidati*. A second improved and expanded edition appeared in 1532, followed by further editions in 1547 and 1554. Musculus' Psalms commentary was published at Basel in 1551, entitled *In sacrosanctum Davidis Psalterium commentarii*.

2 *Le Livre des Pseaumes exposé par Jehan Calvin* ([Geneva], 1558); *Commentaires sur le livre des Pseaumes. Ceste traduction est tellement reveüe et si fidelement conferee sur le Latin, qu'on la peut juger estre nouvelle* (Geneva, 1561).

first edition appeared in 1551, and an expanded version came off the press in 1559. His Genesis commentary was published in 1554. His exposition of the Psalms is thus the third in his series of Old Testament commentaries. So by the time he began this work he had already acquired some experience in the writing of Old Testament commentaries.

Calvin never formally studied theology. After his initial university training in Paris, he went on to study law. His first scholarly publication appeared in 1532: his commentary on the Roman philosopher Seneca's *De Clementia*. In this work Calvin not only provided a critical edition of the text, but also wrote a linguistic and stylistic commentary on that text. His first publication provided him with an opportunity to put his humanist training into practice.[3] This experience was to be of great profit to him later when he undertook to write his various biblical commentaries. It is noticeable in his close attention to detail in the text. But also significant is the fact that he was thoroughly well versed in rhetoric and thus had an eye for various figures of speech.[4] In his commentary he is not out to focus his attention on each and every one of these figures. He only points out rhetorical figures if he considers them important for understanding the text.[5] And he restricts himself almost exclusively to the most significant figures of speech, such as metaphor, synecdoche, and hyperbole.

CALVIN'S LIBRARY

It is difficult to determine exactly which books Calvin had on hand when he wrote his commentary on the Psalms. Nonetheless, a few comments are necessary in order to shed some light on his exegetical method. Anyone who peruses his commentaries will soon encounter various

---

3 See, for example, Ford Lewis Battles on "Calvin's Rhetorical Sources" in the critical edition of this work: *Calvin's Commentary on Seneca's De Clementia*, ed. Ford Lewis Battles and André Malan Hugo (Leiden: E. J. Brill, 1969), pp. 81–84.

4 In his exposition of Ps. 18:5–6 and 8 Calvin comments on David's style in these verses. He observes that the Holy Spirit had instructed David in hyperbolic eloquence in order to move the world to consider God's benefits.

5 A conspicuous example of this is Calvin's interpretation of Ps. 22:16, where the psalmist laments, "they have pierced my hands and feet." The Jews contended that the Christians had deliberately altered the original literal text ("as a lion his hands and feet") in order to read "pierce." The Jews made this charge in connection with the fact that Christians related this piercing to the crucifixion of Christ. The Jews, accordingly, pointed out that David was never nailed to a cross. To this they added the claim that "pierce" was a bad translation. Calvin observes that the piercing of the hands and feet must be understood as a vividly symbolic (*metaphorice*) complaint from David, namely, that he was no less oppressed by his enemies than someone who was pierced through the hands and feet to be fastened to the wood of a cross.

Hebrew words. Calvin worked from the Hebrew text in his exposition of the Psalms. It is not easy to determine which edition of the Hebrew text he used. From 1539 on he had in his possession a Hebrew Bible, printed by Bomberghen, that he had inherited from his cousin Pierre Olivétan. Yet it is improbable that he would have used this rabbinic Bible, with its difficult to read, unpointed, text. It is probable that he made use of the *Hebraica Biblia* that Sebastian Münster published in Basel.[6] This work included the Hebrew text with Münster's own Latin translation side by side, along with notes from Jewish commentaries.

Calvin also consulted other biblical translations. He sometimes follows the Vulgate and, much more frequently, the Septuagint. On occasion he mentions the text of the Chaldean translation (the *Targum*). He must have had other translations at his disposal as well. He makes frequent reference to how others had translated a particular word or pericope; often these were references to sixteenth-century exegetes. They used the Hebrew text as the basis for their interpretations. They wrote their commentaries in Latin, and also provided their own Latin translations of the text. But those Latin translations differed from the Vulgate, which was based on the Greek Septuagint, and which had a variety of shortcomings. Thus, for example, Bucer in his Psalms commentary first provides his own Latin paraphrase of the particular Psalm under consideration, followed by his exegesis of the individual verses, with which he included a virtually literal Latin translation.

The sixteenth century also saw the publication of a few new Latin translations of the Bible. The best known were those of Sanctes Pagnini and Sebastian Münster.[7] Felix Pratensis had published a translation of the Psalms based on the Hebrew text. In the margins of this work he provided alternative translations if warranted by the text, and he added his own observations after many of the Psalms.[8] Johannes Campensis' paraphrasing translation of the Psalms was a work that many interpreters found

---

6 In 1534–1535 Münster published his *Hebraica Biblia latina planeque nova . . . adjectis insuper e Rabinorum commentariis annotationibus haud paenitendis, pulchre & voces ambiguas, & obscuriora quaeque elucidantibus* . . . This was a two-volume work comprising the Hebrew text from the first rabbinic Bible along with Münster's own precise Latin translation. In 1546 a second, revised, edition appeared.

7 The Dominican Sanctes Pagnini (1470–1541) produced the first complete Latin Bible translation since Jerome that was based on, and sought to remain as faithful as possible to, the Hebrew and Greek texts. His *Biblia* appeared in 1528 at Lyon.

8 Felix Pratensis (1470–1558) entitled his translation *Psalterium ex hebraeo diligentissime ad verbum fere translatum* (Venice, 1515; Hagenau, 1522; and, without Pratensis' comments, Basel, 1524).

useful.[9] Calvin would certainly have known and used these translations, yet in his commentary he provides his own Latin translation of the Psalms.

One book that Calvin possessed and undoubtedly used was Robert Estienne's Bible, published in 1545 at Paris.[10] This Bible was formatted with two columns. In the first column was the text of the Vulgate; the second column reproduced the text of the highly regarded *Biblia sacrosancta*. The latter translation came largely from the pen of Leo Jud and had come off the press at Zurich in 1543. Estienne's 1545 Paris Bible also included many annotations, not only from Vatable, but also from Jewish writings.[11] Calvin also consulted commentaries that others had written on the Psalms. He was convinced that an interpreter must listen to other exegetes, who have also been blessed by God with gifts for interpreting the Scriptures. No one person has been given perfect insight into the Bible. Nor is it necessary to agree on the interpretation of every single passage of Scripture. Interpreters should allow each other room for disagreement on particulars, and as brothers endeavor to preserve their unity.[12] One problem is that Calvin rarely mentions other exegetes by name; thus it is difficult to determine with precision which commentaries he consulted.

Calvin was well read in the church fathers.[13] Those few that he mentions by name in the Psalms commentary are Jerome, Eusebius, and Augustine. Calvin mentions Eusebius only once, in connection with a story about a monk.[14] Jerome makes three appearances in Calvin's commentary: once in

9 Johannes Campensis (1491–1538) was an instructor in Hebrew at the Collegium Trilingue in Louvain. Out of his teaching experiences came his *Psalmorum omnium iuxta Hebraicam veritatem parafrastica interpretatio*, published in 1532 at Nuremberg. This work went through over thirty printings and was also translated into Dutch, French, and English.

10 See Jean-François Gilmont, *Jean Calvin et le livre imprimé* (Geneva: Librairie Droz, 1997), pp. 189 (with reference to *CO* XII:231), and 197.

11 *Biblia. Quid in hac editione praestitum sit, vide in ea quam operi praeposuimus, ad lectorem epistola* (Paris, 1545).

12 See Calvin's letter to Grynaeus of October 18, 1539, *CO* XB:402–406. This letter appeared as the epistle dedicatory to Calvin's 1540 Romans commentary. See *Ioanis Calvini Opera exegetica* XIII, *Commentarius epistolam Pauli ad Romanos*, ed. T. H. L. Parker and D. C. Parker, (Geneva: Droz, 1999), pp. 3–6. In a March 15, 1551 letter to Bullinger, Calvin also indicated that biblical exegetes were mutually dependent on each other, *CO* XIV:74.

13 He mentions his estimation of the exegesis of various church fathers in the preface that he prepared for a proposed edition of several of Chrysostom's sermons. See *CO* IX:831–838; also W. Ian P. Hazlett, "Calvin's Latin Preface to his Proposed French Edition of Chrysostom's Homilies: Translation and Commentary," in *Humanism and Reform: The Church in Europe, England and Scotland, 1400–1643. Essays in Honour of James K. Cameron*, ed. J. Kirk (Oxford: Blackwell, 1992), pp. 129–150. See also Anthony N. S. Lane, *John Calvin: Student of the Church Fathers* (Grand Rapids: Baker Books, 1999).

14 See Calvin's commentary on Ps. 141:3. Eusebius (264–340) wrote a commentary on the Psalms that is almost entirely preserved.

the discussion of the meaning of a Hebrew word and twice in connection with place names.[15] He frequently cites Augustine – an indication of Augustine's weighty authority. Calvin cites him approvingly in connection with important theological concepts. But on more than one occasion Calvin is critical of Augustine's exegesis, because the reformer finds his interpretations fanciful or not in accord with the original intention of the author.[16] Calvin's observations make it unmistakably clear that his interpretations of the Psalms differ from the method employed in the early church, and particularly from those exegetes who could more or less be identified with the Alexandrian school of exegesis. In Calvin's perspective, the way that these exegetes filled the Psalms with Christological content did violence to their historical context, and thus nullified what the psalmists experienced in their relationship to God. To fail to take God's dealings with Israel seriously, Calvin warns, is to do an injustice not only to Israel, but much more so to God himself.[17] For this reason Calvin devotes plenty of attention to what the psalmists believed, experienced, and hoped.

Calvin was also well acquainted with Jewish exegesis of the Psalms. On one occasion he cites David Kimchi (1160–1235) by name and characterizes him as the most trustworthy of the Jewish exegetes.[18] From this observation we can infer that Calvin was knowledgeable about the interpretations of Kimchi and other Jewish exegetes, such as Rashi (1040–1105) and Ibn Ezra (1089–1165). But he would have rarely consulted their original writings, since the Bibles of Sebastian Münster and Robert Estienne provided him with numerous references to Jewish interpretations. Two very important sources of Calvin's knowledge of Jewish interpretations were the commentaries of Bucer and Musculus. He mentions their commentaries with praise in the preface to his own Psalms commentary, but he does not cite them by name in the main body of the commentary. But it is certain that he would have continually consulted their commentaries as he produced his own work. Unlike

---

15 See Calvin's commentary on Ps. 18:5–6, Ps. 19:10, and Ps. 132:6.

16 See, e.g., Calvin's comments on Ps. 88:6, Ps. 99:5, Ps. 101:1 and Ps. 118:25.

17 See Calvin's interpretation of 1 Cor. 10:11, where he with particular vehemence refutes those who fail to take God's dealings with Israel seriously. "This is a most damaging piece of nonsense, because it does serious injury to the holy fathers, and still more serious injury to God. For those people foreshadowed the Christian Church in such a way that they were at the same time a genuine Church." ET from John W. Fraser, *Calvin's Commentaries* (Grand Rapids: Eerdmans, 1979).

18 *CO* xxxii:174 (Ps. 112:5): ". . . qui fidellissimus est inter Rabbinos."

Calvin, Bucer and Musculus cited other exegetes by name. They often made approving reference to Abraham Ibn Ezra and David Kimchi. Musculus would begin his interpretation of a Psalm with a *lectio* in which he provided text-critical observations. He would then take note of other translations and other interpreters. Calvin must have made grateful use of these commentaries of Bucer and Musculus, because they provided a wealth of information about a variety of translations and interpreters. But a comparison of these commentaries with Calvin's work reveals that Calvin also found his own way through the text. He was an independent exegete who paid careful attention to the Hebrew text and who listened to other exegetes. In the end, however, he provided an independent judgment and his own distinctive interpretation on the Psalms.

CALVIN AS EXEGETE

The book of Psalms, with its 150 Psalms, forms a coherent unity. When Calvin summarizes the content of the first Psalm, he begins with the observation that Ezra or some other person collected all the Psalms into one book. Psalm 1 was probably placed at the front as a kind of preface, intended to encourage readers to meditate on God's law, and thus learn heavenly wisdom. The law of God, according to Calvin, comprises everything that pertains to the law. The whole of Scripture is an exposition of the law. Thus the exhortation to meditate on the law, according to Calvin, also implies that believers should read the Psalms. Just as the first Psalm functions as a kind of introduction (*praefatio*), so Psalm 150 sounds a powerful closing chord that calls everyone and everything to praise God.

While the Psalms were intentionally composed into a unified book, each Psalm nonetheless comprises an independent unit. In Calvin's case this comes out in the way that he treats each Psalm individually. He inquires about the identity of each Psalm's author – a matter that was often far from clear. David was the author of many Psalms; his name appears in the headings of seventy-three Psalms.[19] Yet David was, according to Calvin, the author of many more Psalms. But Calvin does not follow the lead of those church fathers and Jewish exegetes who had

---

19 Thus Calvin assigns the name of David to Ps. 2 and claims that most of Pss. 120–134 could be assigned to the authorship of either David or Solomon. When the "Sons of Korah" appear in the heading, the author can also be identified as David. This is also the case when the name of Asaph appears, for Calvin was of the opinion that Asaph was not the composer of these Psalms.

attributed all of the Psalms to David.[20] Calvin's opinion was that David could not have authored all of the Psalms, because some Psalms exhibit clear evidence of having been written at a later date, for example, during or after the time of the exile.[21] Calvin was aware that some interpreters did identify David as the author of these Psalms.[22] Their argument was that David spoke of the future through a spirit of prophecy.[23] But Calvin does not agree. While it is true that speech inspired by the spirit of prophecy could very well refer to the future, Calvin does not think that the prophetic psalmist would employ such concretely historical (*historice*) references to events that occurred after the time of David.[24]

In any case, Calvin is not overly concerned to identify precisely the author of each Psalm. More than once he writes, "David, or whoever the author of this Psalm may be . . ." More significant is Calvin's customary reference to a Psalm's author as "the prophet." He can even refer to the author of one and the same Psalm as, alternatively, David, the prophet, and the Holy Spirit.[25] This way of speaking derives from the manner in which the Psalms are cited in the New Testament. In Acts 2:30 David is referred to as a prophet. And according to Acts 1:15 the Holy Spirit spoke through the mouth of David. Hebrews 3:7–11 introduces a portion of Psalm 95 with these words: "Therefore, as the Holy Spirit says . . ." Calvin's identification of the Psalms as belonging to the prophetic writings also has its precedent in the New Testament. The word "prophetic" has to do with the content of the Psalm, which speaks prophetically about the kingdom of God as it takes shape in the New Testament context.

Calvin pays attention to the headings of the Psalms in his interpretations. In these headings are found numerous words, the meanings of which are not entirely clear. Calvin frequently reports what other interpreters say about these terms. It is notable that he often connects these terms with a familiar song, a musical instrument, or a melody. In any

---

20 Church fathers who held this view include Augustine, Cassiodorus (*PL* LXX:14) and Origen. Exceptions to this rule were Hilary (*CSEL* XXII.4.4.5 and 6) and Jerome. A Jewish exegete who held to universal Davidic authorship was David Kimchi (see the introduction to his Psalms commentary). Rashi, however, in his commentary on Ps. 1:1, challenged the assumption that David was the author of all the Psalms.

21 This is the case, for example, with Ps. 44. Calvin dates the laments in this Psalm from the time of Antiochus. He dates Pss. 85 and 87 from the period of the Babylonian exile.

22 E.g., Theodore of Mopsuestia.

23 See his exposition of Pss. 74, 79, and 137.

24 See *CO* XXXI:746 (Ps. 79:1).

25 See, e.g., his interpretation of Ps. 20.

case, he does not deduce too much from these terms, because they are of minor significance. He finds it much more important to pay heed to the content and meaning of the Psalm. Sometimes he observes that the heading consisted of a word that was connected with the content of the Psalm. This is the case with the term לְתוֹדָה (Latin: *ad laudandum*) from the heading of Psalm 100. Calvin also judges that the term לְהַזְכִּיר (Latin: *ad reminiscendum*) in the headings of Psalms 38 and 70 has to do with the content of these Psalms. David composed these Psalms as a reminder to himself and to others. Calvin connects the term מַשְׂכִּיל (Latin: *erudiens*) with the content of the Psalm as well. This word appears in the headings of many Psalms that deal with adversity. Times of adversity are to be understood in terms of God's discipline. The experience of adversity is actually intended for our profit, and it should humble us before God.

When the heading related the circumstances that occasioned David's composition of the Psalm, Calvin considers this a significant interpretive factor as well, since he seeks to interpret the Psalm in terms of its historical context. The information that the heading provided about the circumstances that gave rise to the Psalm made it easier for Calvin to provide the context for his interpretation of the Psalm.

It is typical of Calvin's exegesis that he pays significant attention to the precise meaning of the words. Often it is not all that easy to determine the meaning of the biblical vocabulary. Calvin often relates the explanations of other exegetes: some say it means this, others think it means that. Calvin makes his determination on the basis of the context or by comparison with other texts.

We may characterize Calvin's interpretation as *literal* and *historical*. In the history of exegesis these terms indicate the original meaning of the text, the *sensus literalis* or *sensus historicus*. In Calvin's case I would connect the term "literal" with the serious attention that he pays to the words of the text and their meaning. That his exegesis is "historical" is evidenced by the way he attempts to locate a Psalm in its historical context. But Calvin was not the only one who employed this method. Bucer had earlier interpreted the Psalms in the same way. He established what the words meant in their context, and he attached great value to the historical context (*historia*) for his interpretation of any given Psalm.

Nonetheless one must be cautious in characterizing Calvin's exegesis as literal and historical. The danger in using these terms is that one might connect his exegesis too closely with the medieval exegetical method of interpreting Scripture according to the four senses (the Quadriga). The fourfold method of interpretation had as its basis the old distinction between the literal and the spiritual meaning of the text. Beginning with Origen, this distinction played a major role in biblical interpretation.[26] The spiritual meaning was ultimately broken down into three categories: the allegorical meaning (*sensus allegoricus*), which pertained to what must be believed; the tropological or moral meaning (*sensus tropologicus*), in which behavior was emphasized; and the anagogical meaning (*sensus anagogicus*), which was concerned with what one should hope for. Throughout the history of exegesis interpreters had wrestled with the problem of how to determine the precise relationship between the literal and spiritual senses of the text.[27] In the first half of the sixteenth century there arose, under the influence of Jewish exegetes Abraham Ibn Ezra and David Kimchi, an exegetical school that focused on what the Hebrew text has to say to us in the framework of its historical context.[28] Capito and Bucer belonged to this school. They were also criticized, by Pellikan for example, for giving too much credence to Jewish exegesis.[29] The main thrust of this criticism was the contention that the Christian interpretation

26 The distinction between literal and spiritual has a biblical basis. See 2 Cor. 3:6, and in this connection Jer. 31. In the new covenant the Lord God would, by his Spirit, inscribe his law on his people's hearts. When Origen distinguished between the literal and spiritual meanings of Scripture, he rejected the literal understanding of the text. One must seek the deeper, spiritual, meaning that is hidden behind the literal meaning. Calvin wanted nothing to do with that kind of distinction made by Origen and others; see his comments on Gal. 4:22. It is notable that Calvin could also use the term *allegory* in a positive sense, as the term was used in its rhetorical significance. Quintilian had observed in his *Institutio oratoria* 8.14 and 44 that an allegory is an extended metaphor. In his interpretation of the Psalms Calvin frequently comments negatively on other expositors' allegorical interpretations of a word or text. See, e.g., his comments on Pss. 8:3, 19:4, 27:10 and 36:6.

27 I have in mind the exegetes who belonged to the "Antiochene school," e.g., Diodorus of Tarsus, Theodore of Mopsuestia, and Theodoret of Cyrus. In contrast to the "Alexandrian school," these interpreters focused on the literal-historical meaning of the text. Following Andrew of St. Victor and Herbert of Bosham, Nicholas of Lyra (1270–1349) held to the literal sense of the text, but he distinguished this meaning into two literal senses: the literal-historical and the literal-prophetic. Jacques Lefèvre d'Étaples (*c.* 1455–1536) rejected a double literal sense such as that suggested by Lyra. He advocated a single meaning that he referred to as the true, literal meaning; but what is characteristic about this sense is that it corresponds with what was meant by the literal-prophetic sense.

28 See Bernard Roussel, "De Strasbourg à Bâle et Zurich: Une 'école Rhénane' d'exégèse (ca. 1525 – ca. 1540)," *Revue d'Histoire et de Philosophie Religieuses* 68 (1988): 19–39.

29 Pellikan wrote a letter to Bucer on August 6, 1529, with his reaction to the latter's interpretation of Pss. 1–41. The letter is included as an appendix in the Gerald Hobbs article "Pellicanus and the Psalms. The Ambivalent Legacy of a Pioneer Hebraist," in *Reformation and Renaissance Review* 1 (1999): 72–99. Pellikan had previously (in 1528) been critical of the use that Capito had made of Jewish sources. See R. G. Hobbs, "Monitio amica: Pellican à Capiton sur le danger des lectures rabbiniques," in *Horizons Européens de la Réforme en Alsace. Das Elsass und die Reformation im Europa des XVI. Jahrhunderts.* Mélanges offerts à J. Rott, ed. M. de Kroon and M. Lienhard (Strasbourg: Librairie Istra, 1980), pp. 81–93. The text of the letter is found on p. 91.

of Old Testament passages is significantly different from a purely Jewish exposition of the texts.

In the case of Calvin's interpretive method, he cannot be strictly identified with any existing method. He completely abandoned the manner in which the fourfold method (Quadriga) dealt with the biblical text. Moreover, the basis for this method, the distinction between literal and spiritual meanings, was no longer a consideration for him. In fact, he does not use this terminology. In his interpretation of the Psalms he only rarely uses the term "literal." What David says in Psalm 22:18 about the dividing up of his clothes is a metaphor, according to Calvin; it is a vivid manner of speaking. The Evangelists, Calvin notes, cited this text in connection with Christ literally and non-figuratively (*literaliter – ut aiunt – et absque figura*). And Calvin, in his exposition of Psalm 45:6–7, starts out with the simple and natural sense of the text (*simplex et genuinus sensus*), which he also refers to as the literal meaning, in order to proceed further into the comparison of Solomon with Christ. What is conspicuous in Calvin's interpretation of the Psalms is that he has a definite preference for what he calls the simple and natural meaning of the text.[30] The designation "simple and natural" is typical of Calvin. Rather than choosing existing categories, such as those of the Quadriga, his use of the phrase "simple and natural" indicates his intention to remain fixed on what the words of the text signify. Thus he will have nothing to do with allegorical interpretations that do violence to the text, when the natural sense, in his view, so clearly emerges from the text and comes to the fore.[31]

The distinction that was made in the exegetical tradition between the literal and spiritual meanings pertained to more than just the various senses; it also had to do with what the Old Testament has to say to Christians. This is exhibited most clearly in the further distinction of the spiritual meanings. These senses have to do with the text's implications for our faith (*sensus allegoricus*), for our behavior (*sensus tropologicus*), or

---

30 See, e.g., his expositions of Pss. 48:7, 85:11 (in both cases he noted: "we must be content with the natural meaning of the text"), and 22:1 (where he expresses his preference for the interpretation that is simpler and more natural). Note also Calvin's interpretation of Ps. 16:10 ("because he will not abandon my soul to the grave"). In contrast to those Greek and Latin church fathers who interpreted the text in terms of Christ's soul being brought back from the underworld, Calvin contended that David here prophesied that God would liberate him from death. In his comments Calvin expressed his preference for the text's natural simplicity, in order to prevent Christians from making themselves look ridiculous in the eyes of the Jews.

31 See his comments on Ps. 8:3 and further, e.g., his exposition of Ps. 12:8 where, in contrast to some exegetes who interpreted the term סָבִיב allegorically, Calvin chose an explanation that he considered to be the simple meaning.

for our expectations for the future (*sensus anagogicus*). Because Calvin does not work with this schema of distinguishing different senses, but has a definite predilection for the simple and natural meaning of the text, the question remains of how he explains what the Psalms have to say to Christians.

INTERPRETATION IN THE BROADER CONTEXT OF
THE WHOLE SCRIPTURE

The Psalms do not stand alone in the Old Testament. They have a place in our Bible, comprising as it does the Old and New Testaments. They have a meaning that pertains to us as Christians as well. This is what stands out in Calvin's interpretation of the Psalms, as will become clear in the following.

First of all, in his interpretation of the Psalms Calvin makes frequent reference to the church (*ecclesia*), but he does not mean by this the New Testament situation in which the word "church" or "congregation" is used to indicate all those who belong to Christ. In his interpretation of the Psalms Calvin also uses the term "church" to designate Israel as the people of God. This may seem strange to the modern ear. Because of his customary reference to Israel as the church, one might get the impression that Calvin has lost sight of Israel's special position as the people of God. But that is not the case. Calvin is fully cognizant of the fact that Israel occupies a special place among the nations. In his exposition of the Psalms he accentuates Israel's position by his recurrent reference to her people as the descendants of Abraham. What is striking about this is that Abraham is mentioned only twice in the Psalms, in Psalms 47 and 105. By regularly referring to Israel as the offspring of Abraham, Calvin's intention is to emphasize that Israel is the nation God has chosen. The covenant that God made with Abraham and his descendants remains in force; and it continues to be valid after Jesus bridges the gulf between Israel and the nations. The God of Israel is now also the God of the nations; they may also share in God's blessings to Israel. The fact that the nations are also now included among God's people does not imply that Israel's import-ance is in any way diminished. Calvin observes that God's care for us as Gentiles implies that he has joined us together with the Jews. We have been united with the descendants of Abraham into one body. We are, together with Israel, the people of God. When Calvin bestows the title of "church" on Israel in his Psalms commentary, his intention is to emphasize the intimate bond that the church should have with Israel.

In any case, Calvin's use of the title "church" for Israel in no way detracts from Israel's unique significance as the people of God. In his exposition of 1 Corinthians 10:10–11 he vehemently attacks those exegetes who saw in Israel's history nothing but foreshadowings of God's promises that only became concrete realities after the advent of Christ. In their view Israel is merely a symbolic figure of the church. This is not only an insult to the Old Testament fathers, Calvin contends, but much more so to God. For Calvin, Israel is a figure of the church in such a way that she was at the same time also the true church. Originally, the church comprised only Israel. Later we, as Gentiles, came to be included in the church. Calvin is deeply aware of this temporal succession and this is quite evident in his exposition of the Psalms. We as Christians may share with Israel in God's blessings to his people. The Psalms are significant not only for Israel, but also for us.

Secondly, there are a few New Testament texts that play a particularly important role in the way in which Calvin brings out the significance of the Psalms for Christians. In 2 Timothy 3:16–17 Paul speaks of the importance of the Holy Scriptures. They have the power to give us wisdom concerning salvation through faith in Jesus Christ. Moreover, the purpose of each scriptural word is to provide instruction. In Romans 4:23–24 Paul writes that the words "it was credited to him" apply not only to Abraham, but also to us. What was written about Abraham is also important for New Testament believers. In Romans 15:4 the apostle cites Psalm 69:10, and then goes on to say that everything that had been written in the past was written for our instruction. We must strive, wrote Calvin in his Romans commentary, to allow ourselves to be taught by everything that is handed down in Scripture. In 1 Corinthians 10:11 Paul talks about God's judgment that befell the fathers on certain occasions; these events happened "as an example for us" and "were written down as a warning for us." A final example is found in 1 Corinthians 13:12, where Paul says that at present we see as through a mirror, in mysteries, but later we will see face to face. Calvin connects this text to the vision of God. We cannot see God directly as the angels do; we see his face, as it were, reflected in a mirror. Here Calvin has in mind the function of the Word and sacraments. They provide us with trustworthy knowledge of God. On the Last Day we will receive a clearer revelation of God that will enable us to see him face to face.

It is from these aforementioned texts that Calvin derives the terms "instruction," "mirror," and "example" that he uses with regular frequency to explain how the Psalms are meaningful for Christians. There are many ways in which he illustrates how the Psalms provide us with *instruction*. Sometimes in the brief summary (*argumentum*) that he provides preceding his exposition of a Psalm, he will tell the reader what this Psalm teaches us. During the exposition of the Psalm he may also mention what the Psalm teaches, or what kind of instruction David or the author is providing, or what the Holy Spirit is teaching us.

Calvin uses the image of the *mirror* in various ways. Often with reference to 1 Corinthians 13:12 he uses this image first of all in connection with the knowledge of God that was conveyed through the temple and the ancient system of worship. Through these earthly aids, Calvin says, God still continues to draw us to himself. He goes on to bring up the Word, the sacraments, and public prayer. Through these means God shows himself to us, as in a mirror. The Psalms themselves also function as a mirror through which we learn of God. Just as the Psalms provide us with insight into how God dealt with Israel, so we may learn through the Psalms how God will be with us. Calvin also uses the image of the mirror when the Psalms talk about the relationship of David and others to God. When, for example, in Psalm 18:6 David calls out to God in his distress, this is like a mirror held before us, so that we will not let adversity prevent us from praying to God. Through the Psalms, as in a mirror, we can learn how we as the children of God can live with God in all situations.

In his commentary on the Psalms Calvin also makes frequent use of the term *example*. When he does so he usually focuses on what David intends to teach us by his example. In this regard it is similar to how Calvin uses the term "mirror." When David is exemplary, he functions as a mirror that is held up before us. Calvin speaks of David as an example not only with regard to his interaction with God, but also in his dealings with other people. But he emphatically points out the fact that David is not always an example to be followed. This is particularly true with respect to what David says about his enemies.[32] That Calvin takes his cue from the New Testament in his use of the term "example" can be highlighted by reference to a few more texts. Speaking of the practice of patience, James (5:10) points to the example of the Old Testament prophets. And Paul, on more than one occasion, encourages his readers to set a good example (see, e.g., 1 Tim. 4:12, Titus 2:7, and 1 Thess. 1:6).

32 See Calvin's exposition of Pss. 40:14–16, 55:16, 59:5–6, 69:23 and 109:6.

CALVIN'S INTERPRETATION OF THE PSALMS IN RELATION TO
THE NEW TESTAMENT

We have seen that in Calvin's interpretation of the Psalms he begins with what is stated in the text and concentrates on the historical context. He is guided by various New Testament passages in his effort to bring out the meaning of the Psalms for Christians. But another subject that calls for our attention is how Calvin makes that connection with the New Testament. There are, of course, various citations of the Psalms in the New Testament. Often the text of the Psalm is connected with Jesus Christ. Does Calvin also devote attention to this phenomenon in his exposition of the Psalms? And what kind of influence does the New Testament treatment of the Psalm exert on Calvin's exegesis? How does Calvin connect the Psalms with the New Testament and, more particularly, with Jesus Christ?

When we examine how Calvin treats Psalms that are cited in the New Testament (both in his Psalms commentary and in the corresponding New Testament commentaries), it is notable that he does not always pay attention to their mutual relationship.[33] This indicates to the reader that he will concentrate on interpreting the text at hand, and that he does not always find it necessary to indicate the mutual relationship between the text of the Psalm and its citation in the New Testament. But when he does in fact consider this relationship it becomes clear how differently the New Testament handles Old Testament texts. He had already focused his attention on this topic in his comments on Hosea 13:14.[34] There he notes that Old Testament citations in the New Testament do not always have an identical function. A New Testament author may cite a text as a proof in his argument, or as an allusion. It might also serve as an analogy or comparison. For Calvin the function of the citation is a very important factor. When in a New Testament citation there is an allusion to a single word from an Old Testament text, then it is not necessary to delve deeply into the meaning of the text. When the New Testament cites a text as an analogy, one must consider that the meaning that the cited text has in the New Testament does not have to correspond in every respect to what the text means in its Old Testament context. One must be cognizant of what

---

33 In his comments on Ps. 35:19 Calvin makes no reference to John 15:25 where Christ says, "But this is to fulfill what is written in their Law: 'They hated me without reason.'" The same goes for his comments on Ps. 78:24, cited in John 6:31 ("He gave them bread from heaven to eat").
34 See *CO* XLII:493.

the point of comparison is. When the New Testament cites a text as a proof, the interpreter must pay attention to the Old Testament text and examine the original passage to discover its simple and natural sense.

Calvin's comments in his exposition of Hosea 13:14 about the various functions of such citations are mirrored in his exegesis of Psalms that are cited in the New Testament. A Psalm can serve as a proof, it can be used in an allusion, and it can also be employed as an analogy. The distinction that Calvin makes among a proof, an allusion, and an analogy clarifies the various ways that the New Testament uses the Psalms. But by making these distinctions Calvin most of all intends to show that our interpretation of a Psalm cannot simply be guided by its use in the New Testament. When the text of a Psalm is cited in order to prove a point, moreover, one must be attentive to the original context from which the text derives in order to determine its meaning. This perspective of Calvin underscores how much importance he attached to the interpretation of texts in their own context. When a passage from the Psalms is cited in the New Testament, that passage now stands in a new context. One must pay careful attention to this and determine what consequences it may have for the meaning of the text.

THE RELATIONSHIP OF THE PSALMS TO JESUS CHRIST AND HIS KINGDOM

It is notable in Calvin's interpretation of the Psalms that he is not intent on relating each and every Psalm to Jesus Christ. In his exposition of numerous Psalms he never mentions the name of Christ. Yet there are Psalms that he connects with Jesus Christ and his kingdom; but only when there is real justification will he do so.

When the New Testament cites a Psalm in connection with Jesus Christ, Calvin almost always comments on the meaning of the citation. But there are also Psalms that are not cited in the New Testament that Calvin nonetheless applies to Jesus Christ. When Calvin makes a connection between a Psalm and Christ and his kingdom, he will often remark that the Psalm in question speaks prophetically about Christ. An expression that we find more than once in his commentary is that the psalmist spoke "through the spirit of prophecy." It is an expression that is found regularly in the exegetical tradition, beginning with Justin Martyr. It is a manner of speaking that is closely linked with a few New Testament texts. In 2 Peter 1:20–21 the apostle directs attention to the fact that the prophets did not speak of their own accord or by their own understanding.

Through the leading of the Holy Spirit they spoke from God. In 1 Peter 1:11 Peter says that the prophets let themselves be guided by the Spirit of Christ when they testified about all the sufferings that would befall Christ and his consequent glory. What Peter says about the prophets applies just as well to the psalmists. In Acts 2:30–31 Peter calls David a prophet, thus David could speak of the resurrection of Christ. Perhaps under the influence of these texts, Calvin will sometimes observe that David or the Psalmist spoke through a spirit of prophecy, and he assigns the Psalms to the prophetic writings. Calvin contends that prophetic speech has reference to something that is presently hidden, but which will be brought to light in the future. Here he specifically has in mind the advent of Christ and his kingdom. Nonetheless it is evident in his Psalms commentary that he does not arbitrarily connect texts with Christ and his kingdom. When he talks about prophetic speech he means precisely that the text points in that direction.

It strikes me that in this regard Calvin lets himself be guided by two important themes. The first of these is that he continually has in mind the fact that the position of the nations has been changed since the crucifixion and resurrection of Jesus Christ. They are now included in the salvation that God bestows in Christ. In Romans 15:9–13 the apostle Paul talks about the nations who will glorify God because of God's mercy in Christ. In this connection he cites texts from the Psalms. When a Psalm refers to the nations or to the world praising God, Calvin emphasizes that the text is speaking prophetically of the kingdom of Christ.

In addition, the figure of the king plays a special role in Calvin's exposition of the Psalms. The LORD God has made a covenant with David and his house. His throne will be established forever. The kingship of David and his successors is of particular importance, because the king does not stand alone, but is, rather, a figure of the coming Messiah. Calvin identifies this as a basic principle that teaches us to understand texts prophetically with a view to Christ.[35] This means that Christ is the end and fulfillment of the Davidic kingship. Thus he often characterizes the kingdom of David as shadowy. The kingdom of Christ is portrayed under the shadow of David's kingdom. In comparison with David's temporal kingdom, he refers to Christ's kingdom as eternal and spiritual.

It is important that we observe how Calvin ascertains the relationship between David and Christ in his exposition of the Psalms. He does not do this in such a way that David never comes into the picture. It is a mistake,

---

35 For the implications for Calvin's exegesis see his comments on Pss. 2:1–2, 68:19.

Calvin contends, to interpret Psalm 72 as exclusively referring to Christ. To do so is to make ourselves look ludicrous in the eyes of the Jews. The Psalm refers in the first instance to Solomon and his successors, and then ultimately to Jesus Christ. In his comments on verses 10–11 Calvin claims that David was not only thinking of his son and the children of his son; rather, by a spirit of prophecy he ascended to the kingdom of Christ.[36] In his interpretation of the Psalm Calvin repeatedly draws a line from David to Christ, in whom the succession of David reaches its goal and complete fulfillment. David's kingdom, as the kingdom of shadows, receives its substance and solidity in Christ.

Calvin draws this line from the king to Christ not only in Psalm 72, but in other Psalms as well, for example, in Psalms 2, 45, and 89. Psalm 110 is an exceptional case. According to Calvin, what David says about a king also being a priest can only be applied to Christ. Thus David sings of both the eternal kingship and the eternal priesthood of Christ. Calvin applies the entirety of this Psalm to Christ.

In his Psalms commentary Calvin can also say that the psalmist speaks prophetically about the sufferings of Christ. But even then one need not apply the Psalm exclusively to Christ. In Psalm 22 David is speaking about himself. But the Psalm is also a prophecy about Christ, because David, in his own person, sets before us the image of Christ. That which was portrayed in a shadowy way in David is visibly fulfilled in Christ, so that we should understand that Christ is described for us in the Psalm by a prophetic spirit. Calvin's expositions of Psalms 60 and 109 exhibit strong affinities with his interpretation of Psalm 22.

It is noteworthy in Calvin's interpretation of these "suffering Psalms" that he points out that David is not just talking about himself. For example, he observes in connection with Psalm 69 that David composed this Psalm not so much in his own name (*privato nomine*) as in the person of the whole church, since he himself was an image of the Head of the church. More often Calvin makes a connection between David, Christ, and the church. Here his approach is reminiscent of Augustine's exegesis of the Psalms. According to Augustine, the Psalms are about Christ and the church. In the Psalms the whole Christ (*totus Christus*) is speaking. What Christ says in the Psalms pertains sometimes to himself as Head of the church, sometimes just to her members, and sometimes to both.[37]

---

36 Cf. Calvin's comments on Ps. 45:7–8.
37 See M. Fiedrowicz, *Psalmus vox totius Christi. Studien zu Augustins Enarrationes in Psalmos* (Freiburg: Herder, 1997).

Calvin differs from Augustine in that Calvin does not exclusively associate the text with Christ. When in a Psalm it is David who is speaking, Calvin explains the text with reference to David, and, if there is reason to (as in the case of the suffering Psalms), he will also indicate the broader connection among David, Christ, and the church. Calvin's interpretation of Psalm 16 exemplifies this very clearly. Psalm 16:8–11 is cited in Acts 2:25–28, where Peter connects these verses from the Psalms to the resurrection of Christ, just as Paul does in Acts 13:34, citing the latter part of Psalm 16:10. When Calvin exposits Psalm 16:10 he is aware of how Peter and Paul had used it. Calvin says that it is indeed correct to understand these words of David as a prophecy that is fulfilled in Christ. But what David says applies first of all to David himself; in Christ it acquires a deeper meaning. David does not fear death, and he is confident of eternal salvation.

Because of the special relationship that obtains between David and Christ, Calvin says on more than one occasion that David represents Christ. He can also say that David speaks in the person of Christ. The latter is a peculiar expression, given that it is reminiscent of the manner in which the Psalms were interpreted in the early church, and subsequently, under the influence of Augustine, through the medieval period. To speak in the person of someone else, what is called *prosopopoeia*, is a concept that goes back to classical rhetoric.[38] Students had to deliver addresses in which they had to put themselves in another person's place. And in classical drama, of course, actors had to practice such role playing.

We read in the New Testament that Christ prayed some of the texts of the Psalms.[39] Using the prosopopoeial method, this would imply that the entire Psalm should be read as a prayer of Christ, not just those verses that Christ used in his prayers. Athanasius assigned every Psalm a place in God's plan of salvation.[40] The exegete must then proceed to examine each Psalm to determine who is speaking in the Psalm, which could be one of a number of possibilities. The psalmist might speak in the person of Christ. But he can also speak in the person of the apostles, in the person of the

---

38 See, e.g., Quintilian, *Institutionis oratoriae*, IX 2, 29 (Darmstadt: Wissenschaftliche Buchge-sellschaft, 1988).

39 Ps. 22:2 ("My God, my God, why have you forsaken me?") in Matt. 27:46 and Mark 15:34; Ps. 31:6 ("Father, into your hands I commit my spirit") in Luke 23:46; Ps. 22:16 ("I thirst") in John 19:28.

40 See P. F. Bouter's study, *Athanasius van Alexandrië en zijn uitleg van de Psalmen. Een onderzoek naar de hermeneutiek en theologie van een psalmverklaring uit de vroege kerk* (Zoetermeer: Boeken-centrum, 2001).

church, in the person of Israel, and so forth. Athanasius not only distinguishes various possible persons in whose names the psalmist speaks, but also considers the question of whom the Psalm addresses.

To speak in the person of another is an expression that one also encounters in Calvin. In his interpretation of Psalm 109:8 (". . . may another take his office") Calvin indicates that Peter made use of this principle in Acts 1:20, where he has David speak in the person of Christ. According to Calvin, this is implied by Peter's fitting explanation of the Psalm in terms of Judas' apostleship. Calvin does not often explain the text in terms of the author speaking in the person of another; more frequently he speaks of the psalmist "who represents the person of Christ." I suspect that he preferred the latter expression because it comported better with his method of interpreting the text. The concept of speaking in the person of another could convey the impression that the psalmist himself no longer matters. Thus has Christ spoken, and so the whole Psalm comes to be understood as a prayer of Christ. This is a route that Calvin categorically avoids. This is exemplified in his interpretation of Psalm 41:9. In John 13:18 Jesus quotes this text in reference to Judas, who would betray him ("He who shares my bread has lifted up his heel against me"). In his exposition of Psalm 41 Calvin interprets the cited text first of all with reference to David. But because Christ quotes this text and applies it to Judas, Calvin says that we must remember that while David in fact speaks about himself in this text, he does not speak as "a common and private person." He represents the person of Christ. And thus Calvin points out the connection between David and Christ and so also the meaning that the text has for Christians. David is a universal example for the whole church. The suffering that began with David, in the form of betrayal by a friend, must be completely fulfilled in Christ, and we as members of Christ will experience the same. Once again it should be noted that Calvin, in his interpretation of Psalm 41, only refers to Christ in verse 9, and only there does he discuss the relationship among David, Christ, and Christians, because the text of the Psalm is cited in John 13. Calvin affirms that the Psalm as a whole is about David. More than once in his exposition of the Psalm Calvin shows what God seeks to teach believers through the example of David.

ASSESSMENT OF CALVIN'S EXEGESIS

How should one appraise Calvin's interpretation of the Psalms? It has struck me that scholars often have difficulty classifying Calvin when they compare his exegetical method with the work of other exegetes from the early church, the Middle Ages, and even from his own era. In his study on Calvin and the Old Testament, David Puckett observes that all scholars detect a certain tension in Calvin's exegetical method. The tension has to do with Calvin's interpretation of the Old Testament in relation to the New Testament. On the one hand there is the Jewish interpretation of the Old Testament which emphasizes the literal, historical, context, and the Christian interpretation of the Old Testament that is oriented toward Christ. According to Puckett, the tension arises when Calvin disagrees with Christian exegetes who often fail to pay attention to the historical context, and when, over against Jewish exegetes, Calvin holds firmly to the unity of the biblical witness. Puckett then concludes: "Calvin unquestionably would have placed himself on the Christian end of any Jewish–Christian exegetical continuum."[41] In the conclusion of his study on Calvin's preaching on Job, Derek Thomas considers Puckett's assessment of Calvin's exegesis, and makes this concluding observation: "As a result of our study, it might be more accurate to say that, here at least, Calvin locates himself almost entirely at the centre of this continuum."[42]

Seldom does Calvin mention an exegete by name. He frequently makes reference to "some," "others," and "still others" as he reports how other interpreters translate a word or exposit a passage. But sometimes he does talk about Jewish exegetes. He can agree with them; he can also maintain a different opinion than they do. But it is the same with his opinion of Christian exegetes. He rarely names names. That he frequently mentions Augustine is exceptional. I have already observed that Calvin can be quite critical of Augustine's interpretation of the Psalms. But he also criticizes other Christian exegetes. In his exposition of Psalm 72 Calvin observes that those who regard the Psalm as a simple prophecy concerning the royal dominion of Christ do violence to what is plainly stated in the Psalm. Calvin's comments are here directed against Christian exegetes. He goes on to bolster his argument by adding that we must always be careful not to give the Jews an opportunity to complain; in our expositions we must not appear as if we are out to deviously relate things to Christ that do not directly apply to him. With this observation in mind it is still extraordinary to see how Calvin attempts to bridge the gap between

---

41 David L. Puckett, *John Calvin's Exegesis of the Old Testament* (Louisville: Westminister John Knox Press, 1995), p. 140.

42 Derek Thomas, *Calvin's Teaching on Job: Proclaiming the Incomphrehensible God* (Geanies House, Ross-shire, Scotland: Christian Focus Publications, 2004), p. 333.

Jewish and Christian exegesis in his comments on Psalm 22:16, and particularly the final words of the verse ("they have pierced my hands and feet").[43]

I think that Calvin was well acquainted with the criticism that Jewish exegetes directed against Christian exegesis, despite rarely having met any Jews during his lifetime. He was acquainted with the commentary that David Kimchi had written on the Psalms. In that commentary there are passages in which Kimchi specifically opposes interpretations that Christians had provided for particular verses or for entire Psalms. By doing so, Kimchi seeks to offer Jews a helping hand in their discussions with Christians about how to interpret the Scriptures. Kimchi's criticism of the exegesis of Christians centered on how they related the text to Jesus. When we examine how Calvin exposits the text, we cannot avoid the conclusion that there is far less distance between Kimchi's method of interpreting the Psalms and Calvin's technique than the anti-Christian passages in Kimchi's commentary would suggest.

Where can we locate Calvin? Closer to the Christian exegetes than to the Jewish exegetes, as Puckett suggests? Or more in the middle, as Thomas would have it? I would rather point out that Calvin, in his method of interpreting the Psalms, seeks as much as possible to rise above the antithesis between Jewish and Christian exegetes. He pays ample attention to what the text means in its concrete historical context. Moreover, he constantly has in mind the fact that the Psalms are about the God of Israel, whom we, thanks to Jesus Christ, can now come to know as the God of our salvation.

In the *Institutes* Calvin paid significant attention to the relationship between the Old and New Testaments.[44] He emphasized the unity of the covenant. The covenant that God made with the fathers, he says, differs not at all in substance and reality from his covenant with us, but in fact they are one and the same. The only difference is in their administration. Calvin's vision of the relationship between the Old and New Testaments plays an important role in his interpretation of the Psalms. In the Psalms we have to do with the God of Abraham, who keeps his covenant in his relationship with Israel, and who ultimately includes us in his salvation. The emphasis in Calvin's exposition of the Psalms falls on the LORD God, who never changes the way he relates to humanity. The church is a unity. The Psalms are important for Christians as well. Calvin expresses this by

---

43 See my comments above, n. 5.
44 See *Inst.* II.9–11.

repeatedly emphasizing what a particular Psalm has to teach us. Nevertheless he also has an eye for what has changed with the advent of Christ. These changes pertain mostly to the worship of God. Calvin identifies various factors that are affected by the change. They have to do with the place of Jerusalem, the significance of the temple, and all those things that pertain to temple worship. In his exposition of Psalm 24 Calvin provides a thorough examination of the meaning of the tabernacle and temple. The temple and the ark, which can be taken as visible shadows that pointed to Christ, faded away when Christ himself came to dwell among us. But that does not diminish the fact that we find ourselves in the same situation as the fathers. We require aids, just as they did, to help lift us up to God. The fact that God provides these means is an inestimable grace. For the Jews, these means were the tabernacle, the temple, and the Ark of the Covenant. For us they are the preaching of the Word, the sacraments, public worship ("the holy assemblies"), and the whole external government of the church.

In his commentary Calvin allows the meaning of the Psalms for Christians to shine through. He accomplishes this by using the text to involve the reader in the relationship that God has sought with humanity from time immemorial. There are a number of reasons why Calvin's commentary on the Psalms has much to offer in the study of his biblical exegesis. The place that the Psalms occupy in the totality of Scripture is one reason. But the Psalms also play a major role in the lives of Jews and Christians. And exegetes through the centuries have paid considerable attention to the Psalms. What stands out in Calvin's commentary on the Psalms is that his concentration on the meaning of the Hebrew text also entails that he frequently listen to what Jewish exegetes had to say. In the history of exegesis, and particularly with the rise of Rashi, Kimchi, and Ibn Ezra, Christian interpreters were increasingly aware of Jewish exegesis. This was also the case in the sixteenth century. But at that time the amount of credence a Christian exegete should give to Jewish exegesis was a matter of dispute. Calvin was not concerned about this discussion. He listened to both Jewish and Christian exegetes in order that they might help him understand the Psalms. But in his expositions he made the final decision about what he thought the text had to say.[45]

---

45 I examine the topics covered in this article in more detail in my study *Calvijn en zijn uitleg van de Psalmen. Een onderzoek naar zijn exegetische methode* (Kampen: Uitgeverij Kok, 2005).

CHAPTER 5

Calvin as commentator on the Prophets

Pete Wilcox

COMMENTARY CONTEXTS

Calvin's "commentaries" on the prophetic books of the Old Testament were among the last of his expository publications. The series began with a *Commentary on Isaiah*, first published in 1550, but subsequently revised in 1559. Then (after Genesis in 1554 and the Psalms in 1557) followed expositions of Hosea published in 1557, of the Twelve Minor Prophets in 1559, of Daniel in 1561, of Jeremiah and Lamentations in 1563, and (published posthumously) of the first twenty chapters of Ezekiel in 1565. Of these only the exposition of Isaiah is a "commentary" in any modern sense of the term. The others were not written by Calvin, but were compiled by his friends from lectures he gave in the Academy in Geneva. They are transcriptions, published as *Praelectiones*, not *Commentarii*.[1] (Indeed, strictly speaking, not even the so-called *Commentary on Isaiah* was "written" by Calvin. It too was written up for him from his lectures by a friend,[2] although, unlike the later "Lectures," it was not intended to be a transcript of them and is evidently addressed to readers, rather than hearers.)

Calvin's "commentaries" on the Old Testament Prophets thus stand apart from his other published expositions of Scripture. With the possible

---

1 Most readers find easiest access in the relevant volumes of the *Calvini Opera* (XXXVII–XLIV), where their character as lectures is obscured, partly because the expositions have been published according to their biblical rather than their chronological sequence – thus the *Lectures on Jeremiah*, for example, delivered in 1560–1562, appear in volumes XXXVII–XXXIX, whereas those *on Malachi*, delivered in 1558, appear in volume XLIV – and partly because, with the peculiarly inconsistent exception of the first fourteen *Lectures on Jeremiah* (*CO* XXXVII:469–580), the prayers with which Calvin habitually concluded his lectures have been omitted. Quite apart from their own inherent theological interest, these extemporary prayers might have been included, as in the sixteenth-century editions, in order to assist the reader in following the transition from one lecture to the next. As it is, successive lectures are not clearly distinguished in the *CO*.
2 Nicholas Des Gallars; see *CO* XXI:70; *CO* XXXVI:11–17. See T. H. L. Parker, *Calvin's Old Testament Commentaries* (Edinburgh: T. & T. Clark, 1986), p. 24.

exception of the Isaiah commentary, their character as lectures (and the particular nature of the audience to whom they were addressed) must be allowed to inform the reading of them.

The transcription of Calvin's lectures[3]

The evolution of a method for the transcription of Calvin's lectures in Geneva took place during his exposition of the Psalms in 1552–1556. An account of the process was given by Jean Budé, one of the participants, in a preface to the 1557 *Lectures on Hosea*:

When, some years ago, Jean Calvin undertook to expound the Psalms of David, some of us who were hearers took notes for our own private study. At length, however . . . we began to consider what a great loss it would be . . . if the benefit of such Lectures should be confined to so few hearers. It seemed possible [to rectify this] if instead of our usual practice, we tried to take down the Lectures word for word . . . It came about, through God's kindness, that our labours were not entirely unsuccessful. For when the work of each one of us was compared, and the Lectures were written out, we found that so little had escaped us that the gaps could easily be filled.[4]

It is evident that Budé was satisfied with this first attempt. On the other hand, he also considered the recording of the *Lectures on Hosea* to be an improvement: "[That few things escaped us even] in the work which was simply a first trial of our abilities, Calvin himself will bear witness. That this has been far more fully the case with respect to the *Lectures on Hosea* (as by long use and exercise we became more skilful) even all the hearers will readily acknowledge."[5] Within another two years the system had developed some sophistication. In an additional preface to the omnibus edition of the *Lectures on the Twelve Minor Prophets,* Jean Crespin, the printer, declared himself confident that "[a]stonishing – indeed, incredible – as it might seem to some, these Lectures were compiled with such fidelity and diligence that M. Jean Calvin did not utter a single word in delivering them which was not immediately written down."[6] Crespin's preface seems intended chiefly to convince potential sceptics of the accuracy the recorders achieved, and he includes a detailed description of the "plan" which they followed:

---

3 See also Parker, *Calvin's Old Testament Commentaries,* pp. 26–28; D. L. Puckett, *John Calvin's Exegesis of the Old Testament,* Columbia Studies in Reformed Theology (Louisville: Westminster John Knox Press, 1995), Appendix, pp. 147–150.

4 *CO* XLII:183–184.   5 *CO* XLII:186.   6 *CO* XLII:189.

Each had his own paper prepared in the most convenient fashion, and each independently took notes with the greatest speed. If a word escaped one (which sometimes did happen, particularly on controversial matters and in passages which were delivered with some feeling), it was caught by another. When this happened, the author easily replaced it. Immediately after the end of the Lecture, Jonvillier took the papers of the other two, placed them before him, and collated them with one another, dictating to someone else a copy of what they had written down in haste. Finally, he read it all over for himself, in order to recite it the following day to M. Calvin, at home. Occasionally, when any little word was lacking, it was added in its place; or if anything seemed to have been explained insufficiently, it was easily clarified.[7]

These descriptions refer specifically to the *Lectures on Hosea* and *on the Minor Prophets*. However, it is clear that the system remained in place for the rest of Calvin's life. The title pages of the first editions of the *Lectures on Daniel, on Jeremiah and Lamentations,* and *on Ezekiel* all bear the inscription, "*Ioannis Budaei et Caroli Jonvilaeo labore et industria exerptae.*" In the case of the two former volumes, the printer's preface confirms that Budé and Jonvillier followed the same plan as before, with "care, fidelity and dilligence."[8] And in the case of the *Lectures on Ezekiel*, Jonvillier himself confirmed that "in editing these last Lectures [my beloved brother Jean Budé and I] have used the same industry, diligence and fidelity which we exercised in those which have already been published."[9]

There is a consistent emphasis in all these accounts upon the care which was taken to achieve a reliable transcript of the lectures. With regard to the *Lectures on Hosea*, Calvin himself endorsed the view that the result of these efforts was a verbatim record: "I would not have believed, unless I had seen it with my own eyes, how, when they read it all back to me on the following day, their transcripts did not differ in any respect from my spoken words."[10] It is true that Calvin had reservations about the project. He went as far as to say that "these Annotations would never have been disseminated at my initiative."[11] But it is important to note that, as T. H. L. Parker has put it, Calvin's "misgivings did not arise from doubts about the accuracy of the transcripts, but only from a mistrust of his own extemporary lecturing."[12] To Calvin, the material seemed

---

7 *CO* XLII:189–190.
8 *CO* XXXVII:13–14; cf. XL:23–24. While Budé and Jonvillier are universally acknowledged as the key figures in this project, they apparently worked with one or two other, anonymous, colleagues: see *CO* XLII:189–190; XLII: 183–184.
9 *CO* XL:7–8.   10 *CO* XLII:183–184.   11 Ibid.
12 Parker, *Calvin's Old Testament Commentaries*, p. 28.

"tolerable as lectures," but insufficiently polished for publication. "It might have been better," he conjectured,

if they had taken greater liberty to delete redundant expressions and to arrange other parts into a better order, and to make still other places clearer or more stylish. However, that is only my opinion. I simply want to testify with my own signature that they have recorded so faithfully what they heard me say, that I can perceive no change.[13]

His embarrassment stems precisely from the fact that his words have been accurately recorded. The point is, of course, that even if a scholar today publishes a commentary on a biblical book on which he or she has previously lectured, the lectures are usually invisible: the commentary is so thoroughly revised that there is no sense of the original lecture audience still being addressed. The commentary is fashioned anew for a reader, not a hearer. In the case of Calvin's lectures, even the published versions are still quite obviously addressed to hearers, not readers.

The sequence of Calvin's lectures[14]

When Calvin was detained by Farel in Geneva in 1536, his first official appointment was to be "Lecturer in Holy Scripture."[15] It is, however, difficult to shed much light on his activity in that post over the next twenty years. After 1556, the evidence is somewhat fuller; and after the founding of the Academy in 1559, it is comprehensive.

What information we do have suggests that Calvin first lectured on the epistles of St. Paul, and then on other parts of the New Testament.[16] His lectures on the Old Testament had begun by 1549, with Isaiah,[17] and continued uninterrupted (except by periods of illness) until his death fifteen years later.

Calvin began a series of lectures on Genesis in 1550, which concluded in 1552. This was followed by a series on the Psalms (which, importantly, he considered to be a prophetic work[18]), and then by the series starting with Hosea and finishing with Ezekiel, which found their way into print as *Praelectiones*. The lectures on the Minor Prophets were finished in

---

13 *CO* XLII:183–184.
14 See P. Wilcox, "The Lectures of John Calvin and the Nature of his Audience," *Archiv für Reformationsgeschichte* 87 (1996): 136–148.
15 Ep. 73, *CO* X/II:118.
16 See Wilcox, "The Lectures of John Calvin," pp. 137–138.
17 *CO* XXI:71.   18 *CO* XXI:75.

fall 1558, during one of Calvin's frequent periods of illness.[19] He was not able to resume lecturing until June 1559, when he began to expound Daniel. He completed that book in 1560, "in the month of April; and on the fifteenth, he began Jeremiah."[20] Apparently conscious of his failing health, Calvin expressed the view in his introduction to these lectures that although he hoped to live long enough to finish them, he expected the exposition of Ezekiel to be undertaken by "a more competent commentator."[21]

In the event the lectures on Jeremiah only gave way to those on Lamentations over two years later, in September 1562. Calvin delivered the last of the lectures on Jeremiah on Wednesday 9, and after the customary alternate week of preaching, he embarked on the interpretation of Lamentations on Monday 21.[22] This was concluded in early 1563. The following day, January 20, he began to lecture on the prophet Ezekiel.[23] This series was interrupted by his final illness, at the beginning of February, 1564, when he had reached the end of chapter twenty. "On Wednesday, the second of the said month, at two o'clock in the afternoon, he gave his last lecture in the school, that is to say, on Ezekiel."[24] Calvin died on 27 May.

The audience of Calvin's lectures[25]

To whom, then, did Calvin address these lectures? According to Calvin's first biographer, Nicolas Colladon (speaking of the lectures Calvin was delivering in 1549), they were addressed "to the scholars, the ministers and the other auditors."[26] It can be safely assumed that this description of Calvin's hearers held true throughout the time he was lecturing in Geneva. Further light can be shed on each of these three groups; "scholars," "ministers," and "other auditors," to show that (especially in the period during which Calvin was lecturing on the prophets – i.e., 1555– 1564) all three groups were closely associated with the efforts being made at that time to spread the reformed gospel in France.

Presumably "the scholars" were Calvin's primary audience; but who were they and what was the purpose of their study? It has been argued that

19 *CO* XXI:88.   20 *CO* XXI:90.   21 *CO* XXXVII:469.

22 Colladon (*CO* XXI:93) says that the series *on Lamentations* began on September 20, but, as Parker notes (*Calvin's Old Testament Commentaries*, p. 18), that date was a Sunday in 1562.

23 *CO* XXI:95.   24 *CO* XXI:96.

25 See Wilcox, "The Lectures of John Calvin."   26 *CO* XXI:71.

they "were Genevan schoolboys . . . [of] between twelve or thirteen, and sixteen."[27] This is, however, not so. Certainly for the period after the formal inauguration of the Academy in Geneva in 1559, it is clear that Calvin's students were, on the whole, adult men rather than boys.

Those who enrolled in the Academy in Geneva after 1559 signed a register, which has survived.[28] By the end of 1561, 159 students had entered their names, and in a minority of cases (twenty-five) it has been possible to establish their ages and later occupations.[29] Three were aged between 10 to 12; but they are exceptions, and it may be significant that all three came from noble families. Fifteen of the twenty-five students were aged 16–20. The other seven were still older: one was 31; another was at least 50.[30] Today they would be called "mature students." It is likely that this sample accurately reflects the student body as a whole.

Moreover, at least forty-three of these first students had left the Academy to serve as pastors in churches in France before the end of 1564.[31] It is true that these envoys may, in the extreme circumstances of the period, have taken on responsibilities for which, in another era, they might have been considered too young. Nevertheless, it is improbable that any were younger than eighteen, and the evidence we have suggests they were older.

The Academy of 1559–1564 (junior and senior schools together) was intended "to prepare children for the ministry as well as for civil government."[32] In reality, the senior school at least catered more for the future leaders of the church than for those of the state, and more for the church in France than for that in Geneva. The overwhelming majority of the first 250 students came to the Academy to be taught by Calvin with the intention of returning to France to put what they had learned at the service of the Reformed church there. As Émile Doumergue put it, "les progrès de l'Académie et les progrès de l'évangélisation allaient de pair."[33]

A concern for the evangelization of France was characteristic not only of the "scholars" to whom Colladon refers, but also of the "ministers and other auditors." It is well established that the Company of Pastors in Geneva was dominated by Frenchmen throughout Calvin's time in the

27 Parker, *Calvin's Old Testament Commentaries*, pp. 15–16.
28 S. Stelling-Michaud, *Le Livre du Recteur de l'Académie de Genève, 1559–1878* (Geneva: Librairie Droz, 1959).
29 Ibid. 1:81–84.
30 Ibid. v:451; 11:482.
31 See Wilcox, "The Lectures of John Calvin," p. 145.
32 *CO* x/1.21.
33 Émile Doumergue, *Jean Calvin: les hommes et les choses de son temps*, 7 vols. (Lausanne: G. Bridel, 1899–1927), VII:321.

city; this was the case above all during the period between 1555 and 1564. The increasingly rapid rate at which ministers in Geneva took on new responsibilities during these years (itself the result of the changing situation in France) makes it difficult to arrive at a comprehensive picture. Nevertheless it is perfectly clear that almost all the men who ministered in the three churches in Geneva either came from France, or went on assignments to France, or both.[34]

Moreover, there is ample evidence that the "other auditors" to whom Colladon refers were part of the same circle. Parker downplays the significance of this group. He says that these "others" who are mentioned were "restricted to those who had sufficient command of Latin, and enough free time."[35] This is true, but misleading. There was a massive influx of refugees into Geneva from France during the late 1550s – following Calvin's own example. Since it was undoubtedly the Reformed church which attracted most of these immigrants, it is highly probable that, although regular attendance at lectures was not compulsory in the way that attendance at sermons was, large numbers of those who arrived in Geneva from France after 1555 would have availed themselves occasionally, if not on a regular basis, of the opportunity to hear Calvin teach. The two men who took it on themselves to record Calvin's lectures, Jean Budé and Charles Jonvillier, are examples.

After 1555, and especially after 1559, reaching a climax in 1561 and 1562, there is a further consideration to be taken into account. By then, it was not just a question of refugees pouring into Geneva from France, but also of Geneva-trained ministers being sent to France, at the request of Reformed congregations there.[36]

It is absolutely clear from the archives of ecclesiastical correspondence in Geneva, as well as from the minutes of its Company of Pastors, that what began in a measured way in 1555 had grown by 1561 into a movement that overwhelmed the authorities in Geneva. Calvin wrote to Bullinger in that year to complain that:

---

34 In his preface to the *Lectures on Hosea*, Budé notes their value, not to schoolboys or students in general, but specifically to "ministers of the Word," *CO* XLII:187–188.

35 Parker: *Calvin's Old Testament Commentaries*, p. 16.

36 Few studies of Calvin have given his role in the evangelization of France the prominence it deserves. The notable exception is Robert Kingdon, *Geneva and the Coming of the Wars of Religion in France, 1555–1563* (Geneva: Librairie Droz, 1956) – an excellent study, in which the growth of the missionary movement from a trickle in 1555 to a flood in 1561 is documented with meticulous care.

From all sides, pastors are requested from us with no less avidity than that with which priests are normally solicited from the papacy . . . We certainly want to comply with [these] requests, as far as it is possible, but our resources are completely exhausted. Indeed, we have already been obliged to squeeze to the dregs the labourers' workshops, to find those who have even a smattering of learning and godly teaching.[37]

In late 1561 one of these envoys in Geneva, awaiting an assignment to a church in France, wrote a letter to Guillaume Farel in Neuchâtel. He begins with a report that there were currently people in Geneva "from a great many places in France, recruiting labourers for the harvest there." He goes on to draw particular attention to the spectacular growth of the church in Troyes, and concludes with news of the movements of specific envoys from Geneva, such as Farel's close friend, Pierre Viret. Midway through his letter, which is plainly focused from beginning to end upon the evangelization of France, he remarks, without any break in his train of thought, "It is wonderful to see so many auditors at M. Calvin's Lectures. I estimate that there are more than a thousand every day."[38] Even allowing for a degree of exaggeration, the comment strongly suggests that the "other auditors" of whom Colladon speaks were a large group, far outnumbering both the formally enrolled students at the Academy, and the members of the Company of Pastors. It also indicates that many of these other auditors were also directly involved in the evangelistic enterprise: they had come to Geneva from all over France "recruiting labourers" (that is, pastors), and were taking the opportunity to hear Calvin lecture during the time that it took them to accomplish their business. The same people, presumably, who, in a letter to Bullinger, Calvin described as "laying siege" to his house,[39] also laid siege to his lectures.

Not everyone who attended Calvin's lectures was a missionary in training; they were not all out of their teens; nor were they even all French: they included boys, and adults from elsewhere in Europe – from Italy, Germany, England, Scotland, and elsewhere; but the majority of his hearers were French men caught up with Calvin in the evangelization of his homeland. It was primarily for them that his lectures were intended, and this highly particular character of Calvin's audience must be allowed to inform our reading of them. To give just a single example, it is easy to imagine what an immediate application Calvin's hearers will have made to their own circumstances when, in the autumn of 1559, in his fifteenth

37 Ep. 3397, *CO* xviii:467.   38 Ep. 3545, *CO* xix:10.
39 Ep. 3397, *CO* xviii:467.

lecture on the book of Daniel, Calvin said, "Only he really profits in the Word of God who learns that his life is in God's care and that his guardianship suffices. Whoever has got to this stage will be able to face a thousand risks, for he will not hesitate to follow whither he has been called."[40]

The extemporary character of Calvin's lectures

The prefaces to the *Lectures on Hosea* and *on the Minor Prophets* also supply some details about Calvin's lecture style. The printer, Jean Crispin, recalls how Calvin habitually lectured "for a full hour without writing down a single word in his book to help his memory."[41] Parker suggests that this book was a Hebrew Old Testament,[42] since the preface to the *Lectures on Daniel* states: "[Calvin] is accustomed to read each verse in Hebrew first, and then to turn it into Latin."[43]

Budé's account is interesting in confirming the extemporary character of the lectures. He evidently feels some sort of explanation is necessary for their unpolished state.

The author thought first of the school (as was right) and to some extent departed from the accustomed grace of his other works and from the style of oratory. He preferred to consult the edification and profit of his hearers by drawing out and clarifying the true sense rather than by an empty display of words to gratify their ears or to study ostentation and his own glory. Yet I cannot deny that these lectures were delivered more in the scholastic than in the oratorical manner. The language here is bare and simple, very much like that which, as we know, used to be common in lectures. He was not like many we have heard of, who from a script read to their hearers digests they have made at home.[44]

Colladon adds that, when lecturing, Calvin had "only the bare text of Scripture." He marvels especially that, during his lectures on Daniel, "although at some places he had to narrate historical facts at length . . . he never had any paper before him to aid his memory." This seems all the more remarkable to Colladon, because Calvin had so little preparation time – perhaps only an hour for each lecture.[45] Jonvillier also refers to "Doctor Calvin's extemporaneous expositions."[46]

The extemporary nature of the lectures comes over clearly. It is, for example, clear that Calvin had no precise idea on any given day how far

---

40 *CO* XL:633.   41 *CO* XLII:189–190.
42 Parker, *Calvin's Old Testament Commentaries*, p. 20.   43 *CO* XL:23–24.
44 *CO* XLII:185–188.   45 *CO* XXI:108–109.   46 *CO* XL:7–8.

his exposition would proceed, so that the breaks between lectures often come at oddly inappropriate places, in terms of the flow of the biblical text. His expositions in the lectures are broken into much smaller sections than in his commentaries (often only a single verse, sometimes up to four or five verses). This was presumably intended to enable Calvin to close a lecture at the end of a section; and indeed many of his lectures do begin with a fresh portion of the biblical text. Often, however, Calvin misjudges this process and, with only a few moments left before the end of a lecture, embarks on an entirely new piece of exposition, only to abandon it with an apology almost as soon as he has begun.[47] On more than one occasion, apparently having lost all track of time, he can do no more than read out a verse, closing the lecture without any explanation of the text whatsoever.[48] Similarly, the lectures are littered with references to what was "said yesterday," and to what will be "left until tomorrow." Occasionally, Calvin will begin a lecture with an acknowledgment that something slipped his mind yesterday.[49] Occasionally also, Calvin abandons a lecture within the allotted hour, either because of his ill-health or because of other pressing business.[50]

The extemporary prayers with which Calvin closes his lectures are also worth noting. His lectures also began with a prayer; but this, to judge from its inclusion as a preface in the first printed editions, was according to a set form: "May the Lord grant us so to study the heavenly mysteries of his wisdom that we may progress in true godliness, to his glory and our edification."[51] The prayers with which Calvin concluded each lecture, however, were extemporary compositions, although usually following a fixed shape. Each prayer begins "*Da, Omnipotens Deus*" and then makes a petition arising (if sometimes tenuously) out of the content of the lecture he has just given, before concluding with an eschatological reference: "so that at last we may be gathered into your heavenly kingdom"; or "until at last you gather us into that glory which was won for us by the blood of your only begotten Son."[52] The emphasis on grace and eschatology in his prayers will not surprise readers of Calvin's writings.

---

47 E.g., *CO* xxxix:575, xl:684.   48 E.g., *CO* xliii:416.

49 E.g., *CO* xliii:50.   50 E.g., *CO* xxxvii:499, 665; xl:389.

51 Again, these are omitted in the *CO*, but are invariably included in the sixteenth-century editions. Presumably this prayer offers at least a preliminary answer to Parker's helpful question about the intention of Calvin's lectures: "were they for education or for edification?" (*Calvin's Old Testament Commentaries*, p. 14). It is difficult to imagine Calvin asserting that his lectures had no intent to edify.

52 Lecture 7 on Ezek. 2:10; Lecture 18 on Dan. 4:16.

The humanist style of Calvin's lectures

By virtue of the thoroughness of Colladon's biography of Calvin, and the detailed character of the *Leges Academiae Genevensis*, the pattern of Calvin's lectures in the last five years of his life can be reconstructed with reasonable precision. The Academy Laws indicate, for example, that Calvin lectured three times a week, in alternate weeks, on Mondays, Tuesdays, and Wednesdays, from two until three in the afternoon.[53] The Laws also contribute to an understanding of the style of Calvin's lectures: the Academy was established as a humanist institution, intended to be a centre of learning in Geneva along the lines of those already flourishing in other centres of Renaissance learning, such as Strasbourg. There can be little doubt that Calvin and others at the Academy aspired, and were expected, to lecture in this humanist tradition.

Calvin's humanist aspirations from a young age are well known. He was self-consciously part of a movement, in reaction to the philosophical and hermeneutical scholasticism of previous centuries. The hallmarks of this humanism were a preference for rhetoric over logic in communication, and a resurgence of interest in classical writers in their original languages. In the interpretation of texts, humanism exhibited a particular interest in context and authorial intention. Its watchwords were *claritas*, *brevitas*, and *facilitas*. It is clear that Calvin experienced some ambivalence about whether or not his lectures contributed to the humanist cause: "If I can hardly succeed in being slightly useful to the Church by compositions well worked over, how foolish I should be to claim a place for my spoken words among my published works." He compares his lectures to their disadvantage "with works which I write or dictate privately at home, when there is more leisure for thinking, and where I attain a definite brevity by care and diligence."[54] Nevertheless, it is plain that his lectures were delivered in the humanist style. The prefaces to the lectures frequently praise Calvin for typical humanist virtues: according to the printer, Crespin, for example, what distinguishes the *Lectures on Daniel* is their "clarity"; and to Theodore Beza, the *Lectures on Ezekiel* are "succinct in teaching and yet so solid."[55]

There is some debate about the extent of Calvin's facility in Hebrew.[56] But although his ability as a Hebraist is open to question, what is not in

---

53 *CO* x/1:87–88.   54 *CO* XLII:183–184.   55 *CO* XL:521–522; XXXIX:11–12.
56 M. Engammare, *"Johannes Calvinus trium linguarum peritus?* La question de l'Hébreu," *Bibliothèque d'Humanisme et Renaissance* 58 (1996):37–39.

doubt is his aspiration in his lectures to engage as far as possible with the original language. At each new section of biblical text, Calvin offers an extemporary translation, offering a justification for his own rendering and commenting on alternatives. Occasionally, he cites a particular Hebrew word and explores its etymology: he is not always accurate in this process, but in terms of his humanist ideals it is the attempt itself which is significant. He strives to establish the plain or simple sense of the text, as opposed to what is "*coactum,*" "*frigidum*" or "*durum.*" Where the meaning of a Hebrew word is uncertain to him, Calvin says so; and where the "sense" is clear, he is impatient with controversies about "words."

To a modern theologian or Christian reader, the frequency with which Calvin refers to classical authors, and the authority he is capable of attributing to them, are striking. It can be surprising to be confronted by an appeal to a secular poet or philosopher rather than a scriptural writer, or at least an ecclesiastical one. Perhaps the breadth of these references is all the more striking given the extemporary character of the lectures. There are references to Latin writers[57] and to Greek poets and historians[58] as well as more general references to Greek and Latin mythology,[59] and more critical references to philosophers such as Aristotle, Epicurus and Socrates, and the Jewish historian Josephus.[60] There is no suggestion that Calvin was personally immersed in all the classical literature he cites. But he was evidently keen to demonstrate some kind of familiarity with it. Similarly, Calvin's efforts to establish the chronology of biblical events in relation to classical history betray his humanist instincts. None of this is evidence of Calvin's scholarship – but it is evidence of his aspiration to sit at the humanist table.

The engagement with other commentators in Calvin's lectures

Where Calvin's engagement in these lectures with other expositors of Scripture is concerned, what is striking is not the frequency of references, but the paucity of them – especially to his own contemporaries.

---

57 Cicero (e.g., *CO* XL:255); Virgil (e.g., *CO* XL:621).
58 Herodotus (e.g., *CO* XL:692); Xenophon (e.g., *CO* XL:621), Sophocles (e.g., *CO* XL:564); Homer (e.g., *CO* XL:559).
59 E.g., the references to Acheron and the Furies in the *Salutation to the Reader* before the *Lectures on Daniel* (Ep. 3485, *CO* XVIII:618, 619).
60 E.g. *CO* XL:559; e.g., *CO* XL:577; e.g., *CO* XL:621; e.g., *CO* XL:126.

It is easy to understand why Calvin might wish to minimize criticisms of other reformers in these lectures, and this might account for the fact that the lectures contain relatively few references to other commentators whose expositions of the Prophets Calvin might well have known,[61] or to other more general theological works by Luther or Zwingli or Bucer. Indeed, Budé suggests that reverence for Bucer and a reluctance to take issue with him in print at first kept Calvin from contemplating the publication of his lectures on Hosea.[62] As has often been observed, it is much more common for Calvin's references to other Christian commentators to be vague and impersonal: he will refer to "some," and "others." Even when he is citing those of whom he is critical, his practice is usually to be general: when speaking of Roman Catholic authors, he tends to refer to Papists, scholastics, and Romanists; and when speaking of Anabaptists and other radical reformers, he will refer to "madmen" and "extremists" – although there are occasional personal references, such as those to Castellio and Servetus.[63]

Similarly, Calvin engages with Jewish expositors of the prophets, though seldom by name.[64] He tends to speak of them generally as "the Hebrews" or "the rabbis," though in his *Lectures on Daniel* he does cite "Barbinel" by name more than once.[65] Interestingly, however, in the first of these references, Calvin acknowledges that he owes his information to his colleague, the Hebraist Antoine Chevalier,[66] and there is little evidence of any first-hand familiarity with rabbinical writings on Calvin's part. Calvin is at his most appreciative of "the rabbis" in lexicological, etymological, and grammatical matters, upon which he frequently defers to them.[67] Occasionally, he also affirms their exegetical insights, especially when, in Calvin's view, "the rabbis" have grasped the original sense more fully than traditional, allegorical, Christian interpretations.[68] However, he can also be scathing in his criticism of "rabbinic fables" and of the refusal of the Jews to acknowledge what he regards as direct references in the Prophets to Christ Jesus. They are blind, obstinate, and ignorant. Infamously, in his lecture on Daniel 2:44–45, Calvin remarked: "I have spoken with many Jews. I never saw the least speck of holiness, never a crumb of truth or honesty, nor even discerned any common sense in any

---

61 Eg., by Pellikan, Münster, Oecolampadius, and Bucer.   62 *CO* XLII:185–186.

63 *CO* XL:649; XL:54.   64 see Puckett, *John Calvin's Exegesis*, esp. p. 78, n. 64.

65 *CO* XL:604, 658; XLI:85; i.e., Isaac ben Judah Abarbanel, whose commentary on Daniel was published in 1497.

66 *CO* XL:649.   67 *CO* XXXVII:473; XL:294; *CO* XLII:211.

68 E.g., *CO* XXXVIII:680.

Jew whatsoever."[69] This combination of generous approval and harsh criticism of rabbinical sources has led to Calvin himself being condemned from the outset as both judaizing and anti-semitic.

The situation is similar where the church fathers (primarily the Latin, but to a lesser extent also the Greek fathers) are concerned – although these Calvin cites by name more often. A. N. S. Lane's judicious and thorough study, *John Calvin: Student of the Church Fathers*, cautions readers against setting too much store by such citations, and argues that Calvin was perfectly capable of making maximum use of minimal reading, and of citing works he had not read. He observes that, in his writings as a whole, Calvin mostly cites the fathers as an appeal to authority, but that in his exegetical works he is more likely to engage with them "as dialogue partners." In fact, where Calvin's lectures on the Prophets are concerned, his citations of Augustine and Jerome, for example, seem to be casual and opportunist: they occur less because Calvin is wrestling with an exegetical problem and needs to engage with the fathers in that process, and more because, in the course of his exposition, he remembers a relevant patristic saying, and includes it. A typical example comes in his lecture on Daniel 3:18, where Calvin is making a distinction between martyrs and madmen. "As Augustine says," he concludes, "the cause makes the martyr, not the punishment."[70] On the other hand, Lane is right that Calvin was not afraid to contradict the exegetical conclusions of the fathers.[71] In one of his final lectures, on Ezekiel 20:18, Calvin sets out the view that because antiquity deserves some reverence, it would be barbarous to reject the fathers altogether – but that their traditions must be examined, and utterly rejected if they lead away from the true worship of God.[72]

COMMENTARY CONCERNS AND EXEGETICAL EMPHASES

Calvin's expositions of the Prophets have much in common with his other expository writings and with the *Institutes*. However, they also include some distinctive characteristics.[73] Some exegetical emphases prominent in

---

69 *CO* XL:605. One wonders when and where these conversations took place.
70 *CO* XL:633.
71 E.g., Calvin dismisses Jerome's interpretation of Ezek. 1.26 as "harsh," *CO* XL:53.
72 *CO* XL:491.
73 Parker, *Calvin's Old Testament Commentaries*, ch. 5, "The Exposition of Prophecy"; Richard Muller, "The Hermeneutic of Promise and Fulfillment in Calvin's Exegesis of the Old Testament Prophecies of the Kingdom," in *The Bible in the Sixteenth Century*, ed. D. Steinmetz (Durham, NC: Duke University Press, 1990).

the lectures, for example, are almost entirely absent from the *Institutes*, and are relatively undeveloped even in Calvin's other Bible commentaries. This is especially true of two similar – parallel and overlapping – concepts: "the progress of the Kingdom of Christ" and "the restoration of the Church."[74] What is significant about these concepts as they appear in Calvin's lectures is not simply their depth or prominence, but the way that they function as a framework for the rehearsal of salvation history.

The progress of the kingdom of Christ and salvation history

The characteristic mark of Calvin's exposition of the Prophets is his view that prophecy has a triple reference. He maintains that it refers first to an imminent historical event (such as the return of the people from exile), second to Christ (by which he can mean "the incarnation," or "the ascension," or even "the apostolic era and the preaching of the gospel"), and third to the whole course of history up until the Last Day (on which grounds he applies them to the sixteenth-century church). Thus he construes the history of God's people, at least from the time of the return of the people of Israel from exile, as the history of the kingdom of Christ. Calvin proposes, for example, in a lecture on Ezekiel 17:22 delivered in 1564, that:

When the Kingdom of Christ is under discussion, we must take its beginning to be the building of the temple when the people returned to their homeland after seventy years. Then, we must take its consummation to be, not at the ascension of Christ, nor even in the first or second centuries, but in the whole progress of his Kingdom until he appears at the Last Day.[75]

The comment is typical of the interpretive scheme which Calvin consistently brings to bear on the prophetic books, and illustrates the degree to which he is able to locate Christ's kingdom in history. From the perspective of the sixteenth century he can look back at its beginnings, and forward to its consummation; between these two points, he can chart its inexorable progress. Calvin frequently suggests that a particular prophecy relates "to the whole course of the Kingdom of Christ, from its

---

74 On the progress of the kingdom of Christ, see P. J. Wilcox, "Evangelisation in the Thought and Practice of John Calvin," *Anvil* 12 (1995): 201–217; on the restoration of the Church, see P. J. Wilcox, "The Restoration of the Church in Calvin's Commentaries on Isaiah the Prophet," *Archiv für Reformationsgeschichte* 85 (1994): 68–95.

75 *CO* XL:417.

beginnings right up to its end." Such phrases are repeated so often in these lectures on the Prophets that they acquire the character of a refrain.

The beginnings of the kingdom of Christ

Of course Calvin acknowledged that there were differences between the Old Testament and the New; but his perception of Christ as the substance of the covenants and the scope of the Scriptures led him to emphasize not only the theological continuity between the Old Testament and the New, but their historical continuity too. Calvin saw no neat break at the crucifixion, between the old covenant and the new, viewing the exilic and post-exilic periods of the Old Testament as an era which belonged both to the old covenant and to the new, and yet fully to neither.[76] He considered the deliverance effected by God for Israel at the end of the exile to be an "anagoge" of the deliverance which Christ came to accomplish.[77] Since a course of redemption began at that point which continued right down to the end of the kingdom of Christ, its beginning may be considered to date from the end of the exile.

Yet, on the other hand, Calvin commonly distinguishes between the end of the exile, which was an immediate fulfillment of the prophets' oracles, and the kingdom of Christ (which was their ultimate referent). The end of the exile was only the beginning of Christ's kingdom in the sense of being a prelude to what was to follow.[78] The "proper" inauguration of the kingdom of Christ only took place at the coming of Christ. Calvin does not mean that Christ's kingdom began at his nativity (a "senseless" idea)[79] but when he ascended into heaven.[80] Even this is not to be thought of as a momentary event, since the means by which the ascended Christ established his reign was the promulgation of the gospel. For this reason Calvin also identifies the beginning of Christ's kingdom with the apostolic era, or with "the preaching of the Gospel which was begun under Caligula, Claudius, Nero and their successors."[81]

The consummation of the kingdom of Christ

On occasions, however, Calvin also speaks as if the apostolic era was the period in which the kingdom of Christ attained its consummation. This is the case especially when he expounds prophetic texts which refer to the rule of God over "the nations," and the extension of worship "to the ends

---

76 *CO* XL:241; XLI:87; XLIV:165.   77 *CO* XLIV:107.   78 *CO* XXXVII:566.
79 *CO* XL:606.   80 *CO* XLI:50; XLI:60.
81 *CO* XLI:50; XLIII:348.

of the earth." He interprets these as prophecies of the kingdom of Christ, fulfilled during the lifetimes of the apostles.

For example, the text of Jeremiah 49:6 prompts Calvin to consider the connection between the kingdom of Christ and the calling of the Gentiles. He suggests: "The prophet had respect to the Kingdom of Christ here. There is no doubt that the promise extended right up to his coming, for he is speaking about the calling of the Gentiles, which God deferred until he manifested his Son to the world."[82] For Calvin, the calling of the Gentiles was the means by which the kingdom of Christ was extended to the ends of the earth. He saw the apostolic era as a "Golden Age," in which God suddenly became known everywhere, through the gospel. For although Christ was born about one generation before that time, he only shone out to the world when he became known through the gospel.[83] In an attempt to convey the ultimate significance of Christ's coming, Calvin sometimes creates the impression that his kingdom is already complete.

On the other hand, he also affirms that "the Kingdom of Christ has not yet been completed,"[84] and that its consummation will occur only at the Last Day. "When Christ ascends his judgment seat to judge the world, then that which began to take place at the inauguration of the Gospel . . . shall be fully accomplished."[85] By "the Kingdom of Christ," Calvin means "not only that which is begun here, but that which shall be completed on the Last Day."[86]

The progress of the kingdom of Christ

For Calvin, the character of the present moment, and of the whole of salvation history, is determined by the fact that it falls between the beginning of Christ's kingdom, and its consummation. It is this which gives Calvin's theology its eschatological cast and orientation to the future. He perceives an uninterrupted "course" from the beginning of the kingdom of Christ until its consummation (*ab initio regni Christi usque ad finem*) such that the period between these two moments is essentially one of progress. As it appears in these expositions, then, the notion of the progress of Christ's kingdom functions for Calvin as a framework for the exposition of salvation history. Caught in the interval between Christ's two advents, the church participates in the inexorable

---

82 *CO* xxxix:352.   83 *CO* xli:285.   84 *CO* xxxvii:368.
85 *CO* xxxvii:150.   86 *CO* xliv:73.

progress of his kingdom. Since Calvin considered this progress to have begun at the preaching of the apostles, and to be consummated only at the Last Day, it is no surprise to find him making explicit in his comments what these views imply: that the progress of Christ's kingdom is manifest in the events of the mid-sixteenth century: ("The Kingdom of Christ began in the world when God commanded the Gospel to be proclaimed everywhere, and even today its course has not yet reached completion."[87]) Or again: ("Whenever the prophets speak of fulfillment under the Kingdom of Christ, we should not restrict what they say to one day or a short time. Instead, we ought to include its whole course from beginning to end. For the Lord will carry through to the end what is now making constant progress, until it is completed."[88]) This is the enterprise in which Calvin believed the hearers of his lectures to be engaged.

The Restoration of the church

Closely related to "the progress of the Kingdom of Christ" is a second recurring concept: "the restoration of the Church." In fact, there are two strands in Calvin's understanding of this concept.

In his expositions of the Prophets, the restoration of the church is often its restoration to an "original condition," or to an "integrity,"[89] which has been lost. "Restoration" in this first sense is closely associated in Calvin's thought with the "godly" kings of the pre-exilic Old Testament history, such as Hezekiah and Josiah. "The reformation of the Church" is synonymous with "the restoration of the Church" in only this first sense. However, there is a second concept (or a second strand to the one concept) of restoration, which is ultimately more significant for Calvin. In the expositions of the Prophets, this second strand of thought is closely related to exilic and post-exilic figures such as Cyrus, Zerubbabel, Ezra, and Nehemiah. When Calvin refers to the restoration of the church in this second sense, he is evidently speaking of the inexorable progress of the kingdom of Christ towards its consummation. "Restoration," in this second sense, is a fundamentally eschatological, and therefore forward-looking, concept: Calvin looks to the day when the church and all things will be "fully" and "perfectly"[90] restored.

---

87 *CO* XLIII:348.   88 E.g., *CO* XLIV:390–391.
89 E.g., *CO* XXXVIII:663; XXXVI:276; XLII:323.
90 *CO* XXXVII:248; XXXVIII:647; XLIV:249; XXXVI:442.

Strand 1: The restoration of the church as reformation: the return to original integrity

For Calvin, church history is – at one level – a series of long periods of collapse punctuated by brief seasons of restoration. The church, like humanity, was founded in integrity, purity, and freedom. There was originally a dignity and a splendor about its outward appearance. However, from the beginning the church has been subject to corruption from within. As a result the outward appearance of the church is frequently "corrupted," "defiled," and "reduced to a wretched deformity" by the malice and ingratitude of the ungodly, with the result that it stands in need of restoration. The restoration in question is a restoration of the legitimate form, or order, of the church: it is a reformation.

In fact Calvin seldom employs the word *reformatio* with the church as its object. There are only seventeen instances, in all the expositions of the Prophets put together, in which he speaks of "the reformation of the Church" or refers to the church being "reformed." (There are over 200 references, by contrast, to the restoration – *restitutio* – of the church.) In most of these cases, as one would expect, the context shows that Calvin's concern was with the "outward appearance" or the "form" of the church. In almost every case, these reformations are associated with kings Hezekiah (particularly in the exposition of Isaiah but also in the *Lectures on Jeremiah*) and Josiah (chiefly in the *Lectures on Jeremiah*).[91] Significantly, Calvin also employs the term "restoration" in association with the same two kings, and in connection with the same work. Indeed, it was the particular nature of the restorations undertaken by Hezekiah and Josiah that led Calvin to describe them as "reformations." His use of this language reflects the fact that he understood these restorations to be restorations of the proper form of the church.

A good example is Calvin's comments on Isaiah 28–32, which refer to the restoration of the church undertaken by Hezekiah. According to Calvin, Isaiah was prophesying at a time when "the dispersion of the Church was such that few of the faithful dared hope for its condition to be improved." "The prophet," however, "teaches that the means by which the Church may be reformed afresh is ready at God's hand." The situation facing Isaiah was that some "who wished to be considered pillars of the Church" were in fact "trying, as far as they were able, to raze it to its

---

91 Hezekiah: *CO* XXXVI:542–547; XXXVI:475. Josiah: *CO* XXXVII:552; XXXVII:556.

foundation." At this point in his commentary, Calvin discerns a parallel with the circumstances of his own day:

Although, as a result of a near extinction of the light of faith, and a horrendous corruption of the worship of God, the people were deformed, they nevertheless boasted of their royal priesthood – just as we see the Papists shamelessly bragging in a similar way today, although a deadly confusion cries out that the entire form of the Church has perished among them. For this reason the prophet defines what the reformation of the Church will involve.[92]

In this sorry situation, Isaiah foretells the imminent restoration of the church, proclaiming that

God will still be gracious to his Church so as to restore her to integrity. And the best method of restoring her is when proper government is instituted, and when everything is administered with propriety, and in good order. This prediction undoubtedly relates to Hezekiah and his reign, under which the Church was restored and reformed to its former splendour.[93]

This passage is a comprehensive expression of the first strand in Calvin's understanding of the restoration of the church. Here, the verbs *reformo* and *restituo* are used as synonyms; the church is said to be restored to a former splendor and an original integrity, and the method of restoration is said to consist in the proper government and administration of the church. Later, when Calvin explains the manner in which these prophecies were fulfilled, he says that Hezekiah removed superstitions and cleansed the temple and so restored "the true worship of God" and "the purity of religion."[94] The emphasis is on church order throughout.

Restorations such as these are not accomplished once and for all, however. They must be undertaken again and again, whenever the church is in a state of collapse. Thus, Hezekiah is depicted as an example for all ages, and not least, in Calvin's estimation, for the church of his own day. Indeed, the same is true of all God's past benefits. Calvin's view is that they should always inspire us to entertain high hopes for the future, and should encourage us to believe that God "will equally assist us at the present day, that he may restore the Church to her ancient glory. What he did once and again, he is able to do a third time and a fourth and many times."[95] Of course, Calvin believed that the restoration of the church in the sixteenth century was not only possible, but necessary. This is clear from the way that he constantly draws parallels in these expositions

---

92 *CO* xxxvi:475–476.   93 *CO* xxxvi:542.   94 *CO* xxxvi:600, 601, 605.
95 *CO* xxxvi:246; cf. *CO* xxxvi:291; xxxvii:8; xxxvii:382–383.

between the situation which faced the Prophets, and that which confronted himself and his colleagues. When, for example, he explains the nature of the opposition which Hezekiah provoked by "the restoration of true worship," Calvin shows that he considers his own experience to be analogous. Just as Rabshekah charged Hezekiah with having overturned the worship of God, when what Hezekiah had in fact done was put an end to "superstitious worship," so Calvin says that he himself has had to contend with the complaints of "the Papists." Again, just as Hezekiah undertook nothing except by the Word of God, so Calvin claims that he himself has simply set aside a great heap of ceremonies, and retained only what God has enjoined.[96]

Strand 2: The restoration of the church as redemption: the progress to ultimate consummation
In his expositions of the Prophets, a second strand in Calvin's notion of the restoration of the church is developed chiefly in connection with the return of the people of God from exile. If, at one level, Calvin interprets the history of the church as a series of long periods of collapse punctuated by brief seasons of restoration, it is also true that, at another, he understands all church history after the Babylonian exile to be a single continuous act of redemption. In this sense, the restoration of the church, which was begun under the auspices of Cyrus, has continued uninterrupted ever since, and will continue inexorably until the Last Day, "the day of restoration." This restoration corresponds to the progress of the kingdom of Christ towards its consummation.

Calvin takes the prophetic era, even before the exile, to be dominated by the prospect of the imminent captivity of the people of God, and maintains that their prophecies were intended primarily to console the Jews by looking beyond it to the restoration of the church. Calvin repeatedly interprets such prophecies by saying that "the prophet is speaking about the restoration of the Church."[97]

Calvin's exposition is primarily concerned to establish when this restoration of the church took place. His position is ambiguous. On the one hand, he acknowledges that there is an obvious sense in which the restoration of the church took place when the exile came to an end: "the restoration of the Church began when the people returned from Babylon."[98] At the same time, Calvin is sensitive to those elements for

---

96 *CO* XXXVI:605–606.   97 E.g., *CO* XXXVII:44; *CO* XXXIX:37; *CO* XLIII:198.
98 *CO* XXXVII:376. cf. *CO* XXXVII:566; XXXVI:194.

which he could see no fulfillment in the ministry of Zerubbabel, Ezra, and Nehemiah, such as the calling of the Gentiles.[99] In addition, Calvin considers the message of the Prophets to be couched consistently in language which ultimately transcends the limits of a merely mundane restoration.[100] There is some restraint, therefore, about the way Calvin identifies the end of the captivity as the restoration of the church, and he employs a number of alternative expressions instead, such as "the restoration of the people" – a phrase he uses repeatedly.[101]

When Calvin uses the phrase "the restoration of the Church" in this second sense, it is clear that he has in mind something that goes beyond "the restoration of the people." In several places he alludes to a restoration of the church which took place several centuries after the end of the Babylonian exile,[102] to which the restoration of the people was just "the prelude (*praeludium*)."

For Calvin the restoration of the church ultimately depends upon the promise of God,[103] and therefore finds its final fulfillment only in Christ.[104] In a significant portion of the Isaiah commentaries, he explains his interpretation as follows:

If we wish to ascertain the genuine meaning of this passage, we must again consider, as it has already been stated elsewhere, that the Prophet, when he speaks of bringing back the people from Babylon, does not have a single age in view, but includes all the rest, right up until Christ came and brought the most complete liberty to his people. The deliverance from Babylon was like a prelude to the restoration of the Church, and was intended to last, not just for a few years, but until the Messiah should come: and he would bring true salvation, not only to their bodies but also to their souls. When we have made a little progress in reading Isaiah, we will discover that this was his usual practice.[105]

Whatever Isaiah's usual practice may have been, it was certainly Calvin's usual practice to interpret Isaiah in this way.

When Calvin uses the phrase "the restoration of the Church" in this second sense, it often appears that there are two stages to it: first, the return from exile, when the restoration began; and then, the coming of Christ, when it was fulfilled. "For the first renovation [of the church] took place when liberty was restored to the people . . . and the second occurred at the coming of Christ."[106] However, it is more common for Calvin to

99 *CO* XLIV:142.   100 *CO* XLI:86.

101 *CO* XXXVII:15; XXXVIII:462; XLII:266.   102 *CO* XXXVII:333.

103 Calvin's Christological exposition of such passages as Isa. 7:14 and Isa. 9:6 is intended to establish this point: *CO* XXXVI:154–158, 194–198. Cf. *CO* XXXVIII:636.

104 *CO* XXXVI:412; cf. *CO* XLIII:340.   105 *CO* XXXVI:190.   106 *CO* XLI:121.

speak of the restoration of the church as something which, like the progress of the kingdom of Christ, is still in the process of fulfillment. As with Calvin's exposition of the progress of Christ's kingdom, there are not two, but three, decisive moments in the restoration of the church. Prophecies concerning its future restoration refer, first, to the return of the Jews from exile, second, to the coming of Christ, and, third, to the consummation of the kingdom of Christ. Regarding the future glory of the church, for instance, Calvin advises:

It is right for us always to remember, as I have so often said, that the Prophet is not speaking of a few years or a short period, but embraces the whole course of redemption, from the end of the captivity to the proclamation of the Gospel, and, finally, right up to the end of the reign of Christ.[107]

This triple reference which Calvin discerns in the oracles of the Prophets is the key to the second strand in his concept of the restoration of the church, just as it is to his notion of the progress of Christ's kingdom.

The restoration of the church in this second sense is therefore both an eschatological and an evangelistic concept. It is eschatological in that, although it will not be complete until the Last Day, its progress toward that completion is inexorable.

The prophet is speaking about the restoration of the Church after the return from Babylon. This is certainly true: but that restoration is imperfect, if it is not extended right up to Christ; and even now we are in the progress and course of it – and these things will not be fulfilled until the last resurrection.[108]

This note of inexorable movement is one of the features which unites the restoration of the church with the progress of the kingdom of Christ, and which distinguishes this second strand of restoration in Calvin's thought from the first. Whereas, in the first sense of the phrase, "the restoration of the Church" is something which God accomplishes again and again at intervals throughout history, in this second sense it is something which is effected by God once and for all.[109] For Calvin, the restoration of the world is the ultimate object of God's redeeming act, which is at present evident only in the continuing restoration of the church. The restoration of the church is both the sign and the first fruits of the restoration of all things; indeed, "the restoration of the Church may be regarded as the renovation of the whole world."[110]

---

107 *CO* xxxvii:365; cf. *CO* xxxvii:248.   108 *CO* xxxvii:428–429.
109 *CO* xliv:159; xxxvii:453.   110 *CO* xxxvii:292; cf. *CO* xli:68; xliv:371.

The second strand in Calvin's understanding of the restoration of the church may therefore be summarized as follows: it is the one uninterrupted act of redemption, which began when the captivity of the people of God in Babylon was brought to an end, which was effected when Christ redeemed his people from captivity to the devil, and which is destined to culminate in the restoration of all things. It is a process of restoration which corresponds to the progress of Christ's kingdom toward its consummation, and which thus carries both evangelistic and eschatological overtones.

CONCLUSION

Missionary and eschatological themes are far more prominent in Calvin's expositions of the Prophets than they are in, for example, the *Institutes*, or Calvin's true "commentaries." Possibly this reflects the nature of the texts Calvin was expounding: perhaps Old Testament prophecy itself calls for such treatment. However, the another possibility is that Calvin's own context has found its way into his interpretation of Scripture here: in the last decade of his life Calvin's great project was what he regarded as the evangelization of his homeland. It stretches credibility to suppose that the connections between these expositions and this evangelistic enterprise are entirely coincidental. After all, in the case of the lectures, the expositions were not simply delivered over exactly the period in which the evangelistic enterprise took place, but to the very partners with whom Calvin was engaged in it.

CHAPTER 6

Calvin as commentator on the Synoptic Gospels

Darlene K. Flaming

Beginning this section on Calvin as a commentator on the New Testament with his *Commentary on the Harmony of the Three Evangelists: Matthew, Mark, and Luke*[1] is somewhat ironic because these gospels were the last of the New Testament writings to receive Calvin's attention. Calvin began his New Testament commentaries with Romans, followed by the other letters. He then turned to Acts and the Gospel of John before finally publishing the *Commentary on the Harmony* in 1555. T. H. L. Parker argues that this order is "not only closer to the literary history of the New Testament" and the understanding of Jesus in the early church, but also was in keeping with how Calvin understood "the theological demands of the New Testament."[2] In fact, in the *Argumentum* to the *Commentary on the Gospel of John*, Calvin argued that it was better to begin reading the gospels with John in order to know why Christ "was manifested," because John serves as "a key to open the door into the understanding of the others."[3]

So, what then is the purpose of the other three Evangelists? Calvin began the *Argumentum* to the *Commentary on the Harmony* by defining "Gospel" in the words of Romans 1:2: "promised by God in the Scriptures through the Prophets concerning His Son, who was born of the seed of David, revealed to be the Son of God with power, according to the Spirit of holiness, by the resurrection of the dead."[4] With this definition, Calvin

---

1 *Harmonia ex tribus Euangelistis composita, Matthae, Marco et Luca.*
2 T. H. L. Parker, *Calvin's New Testament Commentaries*, 2nd edn (Louisville: Westminster John Knox Press, 1993), pp. 31–35.
3 *CNTC* iv:6; OE xi/1.8–9. The English translations are drawn from *Calvin's New Testament Commentaries*, ed. D. W. Torrance and T. F. Torrance, vols. i & iii trans. by A. W. Morrison, vols. ii & iv translated by T. H. L. Parker (Grand Rapids: Eerdmans rpt. 1979–1980) with minor revisions as needed. For direct quotations, I will give page numbers in the Latin version and English translation. For more general comments, I will only give the passage on which Calvin was commenting.
4 *CNTC* i:xi; *CO* xlv:i.

claimed that the entire New Testament should rightly be called "Gospel." Although four books are properly named gospels Calvin saw an important but limited role for the Synoptic Gospels in that they display Jesus as the fulfillment of all the promises of God. He writes:

The actual force and effect of His coming are more stressed in other books of the New Testament. In fact John differs in this respect quite considerably from the other three in that he devotes himself very much to describing the character and influence of Christ as it comes from Him to us, while they concentrate more on the one point that our Christ was that Son of God, the Redeemer promised to mankind. They do include teaching on the role He played, to let us understand the nature of His grace, and the reason for its coming upon us, but they deal particularly with what I have said, how in the Person of Christ Jesus were fulfilled the things that God had promised from the beginning.[5]

It is always tempting for scholars to make grand claims for whatever document or doctrine they have studied most recently as absolutely central to understanding Calvin's thought. Realistically, much more modest claims should be made for the *Commentary on the Harmony of The Three Evangelists.*[6] When Calvin turned his attention on the Synoptic Gospels, he brought the fruit of his exegesis of the rest of the New Testament and of Isaiah to his task of understanding the meaning of the life, death, and resurrection of Christ as narrated by the three Evangelists. In this commentary we see Calvin's typical emphasis on "lucid brevity" as he expounds the "genuine and simple sense" of the text. Examination of this commentary does, however, allow us to focus on elements in Calvin's exegesis that might not be so prevalent elsewhere because of the content of the particular biblical texts under consideration. Of particular importance will be his interpretation of parables and miracles, the problem of harmonization, and the relationship to the Old Testament.

COMMENTARY CONTEXTS

The Circumstances of the writing of the commentary

The *Commentary on the Harmony of the Three Evangelists* was published in Geneva in 1555 by Robert Estienne. Calvin did not preach specifically

---

5 *CNTC* 1:xii; *CO* XLV:2–3.

6 Little work has been done on this commentary. So far a critical edition of the *Commentary on the Harmony* has not been released but hopefully this will be remedied soon through the *Opera exegetica* series published by Droz. The only full-length study is Dieter Schellong's *Calvins Auslegung der synoptischen Evangelien* (Munich: Chr. Kaiser Verlag, 1969).

on the Harmony of the Gospels until the second half of 1559 so there is no possibility that the commentary was a reworking of the sermons.[7] However, starting in 1553 the Harmony of the Gospels was the subject of the Friday *congrégations*. Yet it is unlikely that the commentary was based on transcripts of the *congrégations* because Calvin was not the only one to lecture at these meetings.[8]

The commentary was dedicated to "Their Excellencies the Presidents and Council of the noble city of Frankfurt" and is dated August 1, 1555.[9] In this letter, Calvin praised the city not only for its own firm stance in "true belief" but also for having received religious refugees from France and England, so that it is "a fine honor to the Son of God, that His Gospel should be heard in your city in foreign tongues."[10] Calvin made passing reference to the opposition he had faced not only from the Romanists but also from those who had slipped within the evangelical fold. Possibly one of the wolves in evangelical sheep's clothing was Joachim Westphal.

At the time the commentary was written the Hamburg minister Joachim Westphal was attempting to have the English refugees thrown out of Frankfurt. In 1554 Westphal had published a treatise opposing Calvin's view of the Lord's Supper (*Collectanea sententiarum d. Aurelii Augustini de coena Domini*) in Frankfurt, dedicating it to the city council.[11] In the *Commentary on the Harmony*, Westphal is never mentioned by name; however, the passages about the Last Supper are one of the few places where Calvin allows himself an extended disputation. Calvin sees himself as fighting against both the Roman view of transubstantiation and "other literal teachers." He describes these teachers as "others who reject the figurative sense, then immediately like fanatics ask it back."

---

7 T. H. L. Parker, *Calvin's Preaching* (Louisville: Westminster John Knox, 1992), p. 152.

8 Parker, *Calvin's New Testament Commentaries*, p. 28. It would be interesting to know if the passages in the *congrégations* corresponded to Calvin's decisions about parallels.

9 *CNTC* I:vii. In two separate letters, Calvin told Adolph and John Clauburger that they were the primary reason that he dedicated the commentary to the Council of Frankfurt (of which they were a part). These cousins were, according to Poulain, the men who had been most useful in convincing the council to allow the formation of the French refugee church. See letters 400 and 401 (May 1555). An English translation may be found in *Selected Works of John Calvin: Tracts and Letters*, ed. Jules Bonnet, trans. Marcus Robert Gilchrist (Grand Rapids: Baker Books, 1983), VI:182–185 (subsequently abbreviated as *CSW*).

10 *CNTC* I:vii–viii.

11 Wulfert de Greef, *The Writings of John Calvin: An Introductory Guide*, trans. Lyle D. Bierma (Grand Rapids: Baker Books, 1993), p. 101. In 1556 Calvin wrote to the Lutheran ministers in Frankfurt expressing his surprise that Westphal's work had been published in Frankfurt and also protesting that he meant no offense when he had dedicated the *Commentary on the Harmony* to the Council and had not mentioned them (Letter 429 [March 2,1556], *CSW* VI:254–255).

The bread according to them is truly and properly the body, but they do not accept transubstantiation, as lacking all appearance of reason. But when they are asked if Christ be the bread and wine they reply that the reason for the bread being called body is that the body is received under and with it in the Supper.[12]

In refuting these views, Calvin relies on "metonymy" as the way sacramental language always works. He goes further to insist that this figure of speech is no innovation, "but one embraced by all, as handed down by Augustine on ancient authority, that the names of spiritual things are, improperly, ascribed to signs and that in this sense all passages of Scripture where there is mention of Sacraments must be explained."[13] This controversy with the Lutherans over the Lord's Supper also impinged upon ideas of Christology that figure prominently in the *Commentary on the Harmony*.

The other theological controversy in the background of Calvin's writing of this commentary involved the anti-trinitarian views of Servetus. To be sure, Michael Servetus had been executed in Geneva on October 27, 1553, two years before the publication of the commentary. Yet the intervening period had seen Calvin publishing his *Defense of the Orthodox Faith Concerning the Holy Trinity*, in which he both refuted Servetus' views on the Trinity and defended the actions taken against Servetus. In the *Commentary on the Harmony*, Calvin mentions Servetus twice by name (with the epithet "that dog"), refuting his interpretation of particular passages. One of these passages cuts to the heart of the controversy about whether Jesus was the eternal Son of God. In commenting on Luke 1:32 ("He shall be great, and shall be called the Son of the Most High"), Calvin says:

The future tense of the verb is so distorted by that foul dog Servetus as to prove that Christ is not the eternal Son of God, but began to be reckoned so from the time that He assumed our flesh: this is sheer slander. His reasoning is that Christ was not Son of God before He took flesh and came into the world, because the words of the angel were "He shall be called." I take it quite differently; the angel's words precisely mean that the Son of God will be such in the flesh as He had been in eternity, for *be called* refers to the open revelation.[14]

Although Servetus is only mentioned by name twice, the controversy underlies much of the commentary when Calvin deals with the relationship

12 *Comm. Matt.* 26:26 (*CNTC* III:135; *CO* XLV:707).
13 *Comm. Matt.* 26:26 (*CNTC* III:134–135; *CO* XLV:706–707).
14 *CNTC* I:24.; *CO* XLV:27–28. Calvin is surely referring to Servetus a few verses later when he mentions "[t]he heretics who pretend that He was made Son of God only at the time of His human birth" (*Comm. Luke* 1:35, *CNTC* I:28; *CO* XLV:31). The other passage explicitly mentioning Servetus is in the story of the Syro-Phoenician woman (*Comm. Matt.* 15:22).

of Christ to the Father and precisely distinguishes what actions or attributes belong to the divinity of Christ and which ones pertain to the humanity of Christ.

Calvin's humanist background

In addition to the recent theological controversies as background for the *Commentary on the Harmony*, Calvin's humanistic background shines through on almost every page. His exegetical method of philological explication of the words of the text, of sensitivity to rhetoric in the identification of the figures of speech, and of attention to the historical context of the first century all demonstrate his humanist tendencies.[15] The application of his humanist ideas of accommodation, and of true imitation versus aping will also be examined in later sections of this chapter.[16] For now we will focus on some other indications of his humanist training: his citations of classical authors and other humanist authors.

In this commentary, Calvin refers both to the philosophers and to the rhetoricians. He refers generally to the philosophers in the context of seeking the *summum bonum*, the highest good; yet he does not agree with them as to what that good is.[17] Plato is mentioned twice by name, including a vilification of Aristophanes' myth of human origins in Plato's *Symposium*.[18] Calvin's references to the "paradoxical game" and the "empty imaginings" of the Stoics are reminders that Calvin's first commentary was on *De Clementia* by the Roman Stoic Seneca.[19] However, Bouwsma points out the references to philosophy are not necessarily indications of humanist thought because philosophical ideas were often used in theological discourse.[20] Indeed, in this *Commentary on the Harmony* Calvin makes more references to orators, poets, and historians. He cites Cicero and Horace twice each, quotes a line from Ovid, and makes reference to figures from Plutarch's *Lives*.[21] Often these classical references

---

15 William J. Bouwsma, *John Calvin: A Sixteenth Century Portrait* (New York: Oxford University Press, 1988), pp. 117–118 and 122–123.

16 See ibid., pp. 117 and 124–125.

17 See *Comm. Matt.* 5:2; *Comm. Matt.* 5:10; *Comm. Matt.* 5:42; and *Comm. Matt.* 6:21.

18 *Comm. Matt.* 19:5 – "Two shall become one flesh."

19 *Comm. Matt.* 5:2 (*CNTC* 1:169; *CO* XLV:161); and *Comm. Matt.* 5:10 (*CNTC* 1:173; *CO* XLV:164–165).

20 Bouwsma, *John Calvin*, p. 114.

21 Cicero (*Comm. Luke* 2:11 and *Comm. Matt.* 22:2); Horace (*Comm. Luke* 16:14 and *Comm. Matt.* 23:29); Ovid (*Comm. Luke* 8:52 – not cited by name); and Aristides and Fabricius in Plutarch (*Comm. Mark* 10:21).

seem gratuitous ornamentations not central to the argument of the exegesis.

In addition to citing these classical authors loved by the humanists, Calvin also made use of the work of other humanist authors. His own translations of the text are often made in conversation with Erasmus' text although, as will be seen below, Erasmus is generally mentioned by name only when Calvin disagrees with him. Guillaume Budé is mentioned only once by name in the *Commentary on the Harmony*, when Calvin is figuring the value of a denarius using Budé's *De Asse*.[22] Yet Budé's work certainly was an unnamed source for other comments of Calvin on both coinage and philology.[23]

Calvin's dialogue with other interpreters of the gospels

Calvin was certainly not the first exegete to comment on the gospels or even to produce a harmony of the gospels. He approached the text in dialogue with the fathers and with contemporary exegetes. Within these groups, three named commentators had also produced harmonies of the gospels: Augustine, Bucer, and Osiander. Although Calvin had clearly read these harmonies, he did not follow any of them exactly in producing his own arrangement of the text. The church fathers will be dealt with in order of the frequency of Calvin's citation of them in the commentary.

Of course at the head of the list is Augustine, the father whom Calvin respected the most and cited most often in all of his works. In polemical works Calvin most often cited the opinions of the church fathers in support of his own position; but in the exegetical works he cites the fathers mainly to refute their well-known interpretation so that he can establish his own in distinction from theirs.[24] More often than not this holds true even for Augustine in Calvin's commentaries. However, the *Commentary on the Harmony* is an exception to the rule. Augustine is cited by name thirteen times; of these eleven are positive statements with which Calvin agrees without reservation. At least four times Calvin mentions Augustine's wisdom,[25] but he also refers to his "knowledge

---

22 *Comm. Matt.* 14:16.
23 Parker, *Calvin's New Testament Commentaries*, pp. 185–188 and 197.
24 See for example Anthony N. S. Lane, *John Calvin: Student of the Church Fathers* (Edinburgh: T. & T. Clark, 1999), pp. 28–32; and Johannes van Oort, "John Calvin and the Church Fathers," in *The Reception of the Church Fathers in the West: From the Carolingians to the Maurists*, vol. II, ed. Irena Backus (Leiden: E. J. Brill, 1997), p. 677.
25 Letter of Dedication; *Comm. Matt.* 6:13; *Comm. Matt.* 16:19; *Comm. Matt.* 23:3.

and discretion"[26] and says that he was "well-tuned to the mind of Christ."[27] The two times Calvin disagrees with Augustine he never says that Augustine is absolutely wrong. Augustine's argument is "more sophisticated"[28] or is "plausible" but Calvin "would take Luke's words more simply."[29] How does one account for this overwhelmingly positive view of Augustine in the *Commentary on the Harmony of the Gospels?* Augustine's interpretation of the gospels is no less allegorical than his interpretations of other parts of Scripture, yet Calvin does not mention any allegories from Augustine. Perhaps Calvin has made a conscious effort to show Augustine's agreement with him because he is still dealing with Westphal's 1554 publication of a collection of Augustine's writings on the issue of the Lord's Supper. However, Calvin's citations of Augustine are sprinkled throughout the commentary rather than being clustered around the Supper.

On the other church fathers the conventional wisdom holds true, that Calvin cited them to refute their well-known interpretations. After Augustine, Jerome (*Hieronymus*) is the father most frequently cited in the commentary, receiving eight citations. Calvin uses this father, who was a favorite of the humanists, positively only twice, in both instances for geographical information, a very humanistic interest.[30] Calvin most often opposes Jerome because of his "twisting" of scriptures to use them in praise of virginity and against marriage.[31] The longest passage Calvin devotes to Jerome is his refutation of Jerome's solution to what is now referred to as the "synoptic problem." Calvin writes in the *Argumentum,* "But Jerome's comment makes no sense at all, that [Mark] was a shortened form of the Gospel written by Matthew. He does not consistently follow Matthew's order, and from the very start has a different approach in his handling; he relates certain matters omitted by the other, and at times gives a fuller account of the same event."[32] Calvin goes on to argue that the three Evangelists had worked independently with only the Holy Spirit guiding them to produce such a unified account.

---

26 *Comm. Matt.* 5:39 (*CNTC* I:194; *CO* XLV:184).
27 *Comm. Matt.* 23:3 (*CNTC* III:48; *CO* XLV:622–623).
28 *Comm. Luke* 24:28 (*CNTC* III:236; *CO* XLV:807–808).
29 *Comm. Luke* 24:30 (*CNTC* III:237; *CO* XLV:808).
30 *Comm. Luke* 7:11 and *Comm. Matt.* 8:23–27. See van Oort, "John Calvin," pp. 674 and 689 on Jerome.
31 *Comm. Matt.* 13:23; *Comm. Matt.* 19:10–12; and *Comm. Matt.* 25:1.
32 *CNTC* I:xiii; *CO* XLV:3.

The same pattern of Calvin citing a church father in order to disagree with his interpretation also holds true for Chrysostom. Calvin cites Chrysostom seven times in the *Commentary on the Harmony*. Only once does he "willingly subscribe" to Chrysostom's views.[33] In two other cases, Calvin mentions Chrysostom's interpretation as one option but neither accepts nor rejects it.[34] The rest of the time Chrysostom's positions are described as "forced," "baseless," and "unappealing."[35] Concerning the missing prophecy of Jesus as a "Nazarene," Calvin accuses Chrysostom of cutting through the knot he was unable to untie.[36] Clearly Calvin read Chrysostom's *Homilies on St. Matthew*.[37] He distinguishes between Chrysostom, and Pseudo-Chrysostom, referring to "[t]hat ancient writer, whoever he was, whose incomplete commentary on Matthew is inscribed with the name of Chrysostom – and is reckoned among Chrysostom's works."[38] However, Calvin rejected the interpretation, not because it was falsely attributed to Chrysostom, but because there is no textual reason to make the interpretation plausible.

The church historian Eusebius is named three times in this commentary, although in one of these instances the statement in question comes from Jerome's *Latin Chronicle*.[39] Calvin's use of Eusebius is mixed. In one instance, after mentioning "good and experienced interpreters," Calvin uses an opinion of Africanus recorded in Eusebius to support his solution to the differing genealogies in Matthew and Luke, although their solutions are not identical.[40] Calvin's most telling evaluation of Eusebius comes in the *Argumentum*. After saying that Eusebius included an opinion

---

33 *Comm. Matt.* 13:15 (*CNTC* II:136; *CO* XLV:426).

34 *Comm. Matt.* 6:13 and *Comm. Matt.* 9:15.

35 *Comm. Matt.* 7:1 (*CNTC* I:226; *CO* XLV:214–215); *Comm. Luke* 8:19 (*CNTC* II:55; CO XLV:350); and *Comm. Matt.* 2:23 (*CNTC* I:105; *CO* XLV:102).

36 *Comm. Matt.* 2:23 (*CNTC* I:105; *CO* XLV:102).

37 Alexandre Ganoczy and Klaus Müller, *Calvins Handschriftliche Annotationen zu Chrysostomus* (Wiesbaden: Franz Steiner, 1981). Ganoczy and Müller include several texts from the *Homilies on St. Matthew* with Calvin's underlining and marginal notes. Unfortunately none of these marks are on the same passages where Calvin mentions Chrysostom in his *Commentary on the Harmony*.

38 *Comm. Matt.* 2:1 (*CNTC* I:83; *CO* XLV:81–82).

39 *Comm. Luke* 2:1. See Irena Backus, "Calvin's Judgment of Eusebius of Caesarea: An Analysis," *Sixteenth Century Journal* 22:3 (1991):435–436.

40 *Comm. Matt.* 1:1–17 (*CNTC* I:56; *CO* XLV:57). Calvin says Matthew gave the legal genealogy and Luke the natural one, but both genealogies trace Jesus through Joseph. Although Africanus labeled Luke's as legal and Matthew's as natural, Calvin still draws on the agreement that they are both Joseph's genealogy rather than the more typical attempt to have one as Mary's genealogy and the other as Joseph's. See the discussion in Backus, "Calvin's Judgment of Eusebius," pp. 433–435.

"that Paul was the author of the Gospel which bears Luke's name," Calvin says, "It shows us that Eusebius was a man of great industry, but rather lacking in judgment, to string together an indiscriminate lot of dull trifles. I would like readers to take warning from this, in case they should be put off by other ineptitudes of this sort which abound in his work."[41] Perhaps the fault that Calvin sees in Eusebius is amassing a variety of opinions of others without making critical judgments. This is a pattern that Calvin has avoided in his commentaries; relatively speaking Calvin cites few people and is usually clear about whether a cited interpretation is to be accepted or not.

The other church fathers who are cited only once or twice can be dealt with more quickly. Epiphanes, Irenaeus, Ambrose, and Cyril are all cited positively by Calvin.[42] In the comments on Matthew 26:37, Calvin has extended quotations from Ambrose on Jesus' human emotions and from Cyril of Alexandria on whether the suffering of Jesus was voluntary. These long quotations from the fathers are quite unusual in this commentary. However, Calvin is not always positive toward Ambrose. On the other occasion in this commentary when Calvin cites Ambrose, he is lumped together with Chrysostom as falsely accusing Mary of ambition.[43] Calvin also disagrees with other ancient writers. His dislike of Origen's allegorical interpretation is no secret; Origen is mentioned only once, although not in connection with allegory.[44] Helvidius is cited twice for erroneous ideas about Jesus' brothers and his denial of the perpetual virginity of Mary.[45] Calvin seems to know Helvidius mainly from Jerome's refutation of him.[46] Calvin does not mention any medieval interpreters in the commentary.

In addition to Calvin's dialogue with the church fathers on the interpretation of the Synoptic Gospels, two sixteenth-century interpreters are also important dialogue partners: Bucer and Osiander. Both of them produced their own harmonies of the gospels. Calvin had very different opinions of these two exegetes. Andreas Osiander was a Lutheran pastor

---

41 *CNTC* I:xiii; *CO* XLV:4.

42 Epiphanes – *Comm. Matt.* 1:6; Irenaeus: *Comm. Luke* 2:40; Ambrose and Cyril: *Comm. Matt.* 27:36. Van Oort has nice compact statements of the topics on which Calvin agreed and disagreed with each of these fathers, although he does not treat them specifically in relationship to the *Commentary on the Harmony* ("John Calvin," pp. 688–689 and 693).

43 *Comm. Luke* 8:19.

44 *Comm. Luke* 1:26.

45 *Comm. Matt.* 1:25 and *Comm. Matt.* 13:55.

46 *Comm. Matt.* 1:25. In this context, Calvin mentions that Jerome "keenly and copiously" defended the perpetual virginity of Mary (*CNTC* I:70; *CO* XLV:70).

in Nuremberg when he published his *Evangelienharmonie* in 1537. This harmony included all four of the gospels. Later in his life he worked out understandings of justification, the work of Christ, and the image of God which Calvin argued against in the 1559 *Institutes*.[47] Calvin only mentions Osiander by name twice in his *Commentary on the Harmony of the Gospels*. Both times the reference is most likely to Osiander's *Evangelienharmonie*. In the first instance, Calvin does not even bother to give Osiander's opinion. He refutes a number of unnamed interpretations about the timing of the visit of the magi but then adds, "And Osiander's contribution is still more comic, and can be left without refutation."[48] The other instance specifically relates to the harmonization of the gospels. In commenting on the stories of Jesus healing a blind man or men near Jericho, Calvin writes:

Osiander thinks he is very clever to make one blind man into four. In fact, there is nothing sillier than his idea. Because he sees that the Evangelists disagree in a few words, he imagines that sight was restored to one blind man at the entry into the city, and then to a second, and two others were enlightened when Christ went away again. But all the details hang together so well that no sane man can believe that these are different stories.[49]

This particular comment serves to illustrate the underlying assumptions of these two harmonies. Osiander focused on the differences in detail to say that each Evangelist was telling a story of a different healing, rather than telling different stories of the same healing. This way one does not have contradictions among the Evangelists but only different events included. Calvin had the tendency to overlook "minor" differences in the text, such as whether the miracle happened as Jesus was entering or leaving town, or whether one person or two were healed, and to group the similar stories together. In fact, he argued much more often that the stories are about the same event than that two or three events should be distinguished.

Calvin had a much more favorable opinion of Bucer's interpretation of the gospels, although Calvin did not always follow him. In the *Argumentum*, Calvin acknowledged that he was not the first to undertake the task of harmonizing the gospels or even setting similar passages from the Synoptic Gospels together.

---

47 François Wendel, *Calvin: Origins and Development of His Religious Thought*, trans. Philip Mairet (Durham, NC: Labyrinth, 1987), pp. 235–237.
48 *Comm. Matt.* 2:16 (*CNTC* I:102–103, *CO* XLV:100).
49 *Comm. Matt.* 20:29 (*CNTC* II:278; *CO* XLV:560).

There is no question of my seeking the credit for the innovation – I freely confess (in the character of an honest man) that the method derives from imitation of others. I have particularly copied Bucer, that man of holy memory, outstanding doctor in the Church of God, whom I judge to have pursued a line of work in this field which is beyond reproach. As he was aided by the efforts of an older generation who had gone before him in this enterprise, so his industry and research have given me considerable assistance. And should I at times dissent from him (as I have freely allowed myself to do as occasion demanded) he would be the last, if he were still alive on earth, to take it unkindly.[50]

Bucer first published his commentary on the Synoptic Gospels in 1527. In 1530 he released an edition with commentary on all four gospels. In 1536 he revised the commentary on the four gospels.[51] For the commentary on the Synoptic Gospels, Bucer used Matthew as the base gospel and added the material from Mark and Luke.[52] Calvin also gave priority to the order in Matthew although there are occasions where he followed one of the other gospels for a while because he judged that Evangelist had placed the events in a better order. Bucer stood firmly against using allegorical interpretations of the gospels, writing that "[t]he language and speech of Christ in these three Gospels is to be understood in its native sense, neglecting pseudo-allegories and everything which is far from the mind of Christ."[53] Calvin agreed with Bucer on this matter. The format of Calvin's commentary is different because he does not include the long theological discussions or *loci* that Bucer added to the continuous exposition. Apart from the *Argumentum*, Calvin only mentions Bucer by name three times in this commentary. Each time, Bucer is mentioned it is because he has given a "wise"[54] interpretation or even has the "best understanding."[55] However, even in these cases, Calvin does not agree with him entirely. Bucer has the "best understanding" of how the prophecy about

---

50 *CNTC* I.xiv; *CO* XLV:4.

51 Parker, *Calvin's New Testament Commentaries*, p. 78. Parker has a nice concise exploration of Bucer's exegesis on pp. 78–84. He draws on the full study of August Lang, *Der Evangelienkommentar Martin Butzers und die Grundzüge seiner Theologie*, Studien zur Geschichte der Theologie und der Kirche II.2 (Leipzig, 1900, rpt. Aalen: Scientia Verl., 1972), particularly pp. 49–93 on the different editions.

52 Parker, *Calvin's New Testament Commentaries*, p. 79; Lang, *Evangelienkommentar*, p. 379: Immediately after this methodological introduction, "Bucer engages in the battle against *allegoria*. He intends to keep *ad verbum*, to treat the text *verbatim*, and to give the *germanum sensum*, 'so as to place the sure and genuine image of Christ before the reader's eyes.' "

53 Lang, *Evangelienkommentar*, p.383, as quoted in Parker, *Calvin's New Testament Commentaries*, p. 80.

54 *Comm. Matt.* 26:17 (*CNTC* III:126; *CO* XLV:698); and *Comm. Luke* 24:27 (*CNTC* III:236; *CO* XLV:807).

55 *Comm. Matt.* 2:23 (*CNTC* I:105; *CO* XLV:102).

Jesus being a "Nazarene" relates to Samson, but Calvin goes further to say that this interpretive line starts back with Joseph, who was an anti-type of Samson who was an anti-type of Christ.[56] In reference to one "wise conjecture" of Bucer, Calvin does not feel the need to go quite so far on "uncertain ground."[57]

In addition to these named dialogue partners of Calvin in the history of exegesis, he also refers vaguely to others. He always finds fault with the interpretations of the "Papists,"[58] "the Canonists,"[59] and "the Sophists."[60] On rare occasions he mentions Jewish interpreters or the rabbis, mainly in connection with Old Testament prophecies that the Evangelists tie to Jesus. As might be assumed, Calvin is quite negative toward these Jewish interpretations which do not hold out the possibility that the prophet was referring to Christ.[61] Throughout the commentary, Calvin constantly sets his interpretation in the context of other interpreters, but most of the time they go unnamed, indicated only as "some," "many," or "certain interpreters."[62] These designations no doubt include interpretations of church fathers or contemporary exegetes who are mentioned by name elsewhere, in addition to those Calvin does not care to name.

Calvin brought to the text of the gospels his knowledge of how other interpreters had found meaning in it, his humanist training in rhetoric and history, and a polemical setting that brought Christological issues to the foreground.

COMMENTARY CONCERNS

Textual matters

One of Calvin's first tasks was to establish the biblical text on which he would comment. According to T. H. L. Parker's painstaking analysis of

---

56 Ibid.   57 *Comm. Luke* 24:27 (*CNTC* III:236; *CO* XLV:807).

58 There are numerous references to the Papists, both in terms of specific interpretations of the text, and also their practices in general. I have listed only a few passages where Calvin objects to their specific interpretations: *Comm. Luke* 1:6; *Comm. Luke* 1:18; *Comm. Luke* 16:26; *Comm. Matt.* 18:31; *Comm. Matt.* 19:12.

59 *Comm. Matt.* 26:52.

60 *Comm. Matt.* 22:39 and *Comm. Luke* 23:43.

61 He calls the interpretation "mad" and "devious." "[T]he rabbis deprave the genuine teaching of Scripture with their inventions." See *Comm. Matt.* 17:10 (*CNTC* II:204; *CO* XLV:490) and *Comm. Matt.* 22:43 (*CNTC* III:42; *CO* XLV:617).

62 For instance, *Comm. Matt.* 1:19 (*CNTC* I:61–62; *CO* XLV:62); *Comm. Mark* 7:36 (*CNTC* II:174; *CO* XLV:462); and *Comm. Matt.* 24:29–31 (*CNTC* III:93; *CO* XLV:667).

Calvin's Greek text, his early commentaries appear to be based on the 1534 text of Colinaeus. However, by the time Calvin was working on the *Commentary on the Harmony*, he was more critical of the Colinaeus text and was probably working from either the fourth edition of Erasmus (1527) or the first edition of Robert Stephanus (1546).[63] Although Parker thinks that it was more likely the Erasmus text, Calvin made one comment that "Robertus Stephanus cites a Greek codex where the name Jehoiakim is inserted."[64] Parker also refers with approval to the 1840 study of D. G. Escher which argues that for the *Commentary on the Harmony* Calvin was using as a base text, or at least consulting, the Complutensian Polyglot (printed in 1514 but not circulated until 1522).[65]

In establishing the Greek text, Calvin occasionally dealt with textual errors. In Matthew's gospel, he notes that only thirteen kings are listed instead of the fourteen which would keep the correct pattern, conjecturing that this "has probably happened through the fault or error of copyists."[66] Calvin also admits that he does not know how the name of Jeremiah came to be attached to the prophecy about the thirty pieces of silver when obviously it comes from Zechariah.[67] He does not speculate about whether the Evangelist or a later copyist made this error. Calvin is also willing, at least in theory, to remove a phrase which he thinks "is quite out of place."[68] However, he still includes it in his Latin translation of the passage, and in the interpretation that follows he makes several references to "calling," which does not otherwise occur in the text.

Calvin provided his own Latin translation of the Greek New Testament text, yet he was willing to use readings from existing Latin translations.[69] Several times in his *Commentary on the Harmony*, Calvin sets his own translation in the context of either the Erasmus or the Vulgate translations, and sometimes both. Parker notes five times that Calvin refers to Erasmus' Latin translation in this commentary and judges that two are positive, two are negative and one is neutral.[70] Unfortunately Parker provides no notes for this statement and my reading does not bear

63 Parker, *Calvin's New Testament Commentaries*, p. 153.

64 *Comm. Matt.* 1:6 (*CNTC* 1:60; *CO* xlv:61).

65 Parker, *Calvin's New Testament Commentaries*, pp. 127 and 156, citing D. G. Escher, "Disquisitio de Calvino, Librorum Novi Testamenti Historicum Interprete," Dissertation: University of Utrecht, 1840.

66 *Comm. Matt.* 1:6 (*CNTC* 1:60; *CO* xlv:60–61).

67 *Comm. Matt.* 27:9.

68 *Comm. Matt.* 20:16 (*CNTC* ii:266; *CO* xlv:549). The phrase in question is the second occurrence of "many are called, but few chosen."

69 Parker, *Calvin's New Testament Commentaries*, p. 158.   70 Ibid., p. 168.

out this somewhat ambivalent picture. I have found six places where Calvin explicitly mentions Erasmus' word choices.[71] In none of these examples does Calvin adopt Erasmus' translation. In fact, once Calvin explicitly agrees with the Vulgate over Erasmus[72] and in another place Calvin quietly adopts the same word used by the Vulgate.[73] Although my findings on the individual passages disagree with those of Parker, they actually lend more support to Parker's overall argument that Calvin became more critical of Erasmus' translation over time.

Historical issues

Calvin in good humanist form dealt with the historical issues of authorship and the first-century context. In the *Argumentum*, he accepted the traditional designation of the three Evangelists. Matthew, as one of the Twelve, was the only eyewitness; and Luke was a traveling companion of Paul. Calvin is clear, however, that Luke's gospel should not be identified as coming from Paul. He mentions the idea that Mark was writing down what Peter told him, but Calvin does not insist on this connection. It is enough for him that Mark wrote under the direction of the Spirit.[74] Calvin thinks that the three Evangelists wrote independently, inspired, of course, by the Holy Spirit. Apart from introducing the different authors at the beginning, Calvin pays scant attention to the separate personalities,

---

71 I include the citations in question for the convenience of the reader: (a) *Comm. Luke* 1:1 "Erasmus – who borrowed from Virgil for his translation, reckoning it had some bearing – does not take sufficient account of the worth and importance of the calling of God" (*CNTC* 1:3; *CO* XLV:7). (b) *Comm. Matt.* 10:17 "Erasmus added 'those' (men), for he believed that the article had the force of a demonstrative pronoun. But in my opinion, it is quite satisfactory to read it indefinitely, as if Christ had said, one must tread carefully with men, since everything is full of deception and harm" (*CNTC* 1:298; *CO* XLV:282). (c) *Comm. Matt.* 10:24 "Note that in translation, it is preferable not to follow Erasmus, or older interpreters, and for this reason: the participle κατηρτισμένος (Luke 6:40) means perfected, and also trained and well-fitted. Now in the comparison He is making, Christ is not speaking here of perfection, but would rather say that nothing is more appropriate than for the disciple to model himself in the example of his master; hence it is the latter sense that appeared most appropriate" (*CNTC* 1:303; *CO* XLV:285–286). (d) *Comm. Luke* 7:37 "I have translated it literally (*Sic ad verbum habetur, ut transtuli*). Erasmus preferred to put it in the pluperfect, 'which had been a sinner', so that it should not be thought that she still was a sinner. But he is missing the genuine sense (*genuino sensu*)" (*CNTC* II:85; *CO* XLV:378). (e) *Comm. Luke* 11:41 "I take τὰ ἐνόντα to mean the present supply, and not, as the Vulgate (*vetus interpres*) and Erasmus, what is left over" (*CNTC* II:101; *CO* XLV:393). (f) *Comm. Luke* 19:9 "Since the Greek word οἶκος is masculine, this verse has been explained in two ways. The Vulgate (*Vetus interpres*) refers it to Zacchaeus; and this interpretation I prefer. Erasmus would rather translate it that the house itself was the daughter of Abraham" (*CNTC* II:284; *CO* XLV:565).
72 *Comm. Luke* 19:9.   73 *Comm. Luke* 1:1.   74 *CNTC* 1:xii–xiii; *CO* XLV:3.

experiences, or intentions of the Evangelists. Calvin mentions Matthew's unique position as an eyewitness only twice. In the story of the call of Levi the tax collector, Calvin says that Matthew "shows his gratitude . . . in not being ashamed to put down for perpetual memory what kind of man he was, and from whence he was taken, that he might display all the more in his person the grace of Christ."[75] The only other time Calvin alludes to Matthew's eyewitness status is in reconciling the three accounts of blind men healed near Jericho. Luke and Mark both mention one blind man, but Matthew claims two were healed. Calvin thinks that Mark and Luke only mention the more famous one whereas Matthew reports there were two because he was there in person rather than only hearing the stories.[76]

Calvin is also attentive to the world history that serves as a backdrop to the gospels. He intentionally compares materials from Josephus' *Antiquities* and *The War of the Jews* to the accounts in the gospels. If there is a disagreement, then Calvin sees Josephus as lacking and the Evangelists' record of the history as true. However, if Josephus can provide additional information which does not conflict with the gospels, Calvin is quite willing to accept his account. Calvin accuses Josephus of having a lapse of memory on two main points, the dating of the census[77] (which is connected to the birth of Jesus), and the relationships between Herod, Herodias, Salome, and Philip[78] (which are part of the story of John the Baptizer). Calvin also claims Josephus is erroneous in his division of the two tables of the law.[79] More often, however, Calvin is content to use the information provided by Josephus about the magnificence of the temple, the succession of High Priests, the conflict between Jews and Samaritans, and the destruction of Jerusalem.[80] Although he rejects some of the information pertaining to John the Baptizer, he is perfectly willing to use Josephus' statements about where John was imprisoned and the mild-mannered personality of Philip.[81]

Literary and rhetorical dimensions

Calvin clearly uses his knowledge of Greek and Hebrew in this *Commentary on the Harmony*. Throughout the commentary he explicitly refers to

---

75 *Comm. Matt.* 9:9 (*CNTC* 1:262; *CO* XLV:248).   76 *Comm. Matt.* 20:29.
77 *Comm. Luke* 2:1.   78 *Comm. Luke* 3:19 and *Comm. Matt.* 14:3–12.
79 *Comm. Matt.* 19:18.
80 *Comm. Matt.* 24:1; *Comm. Matt.* 26:57; *Comm. Luke* 9:52; and *Comm. Luke* 23:29.
81 *Comm. Matt.* 14:3–12.

the Greek words of the biblical text when he is explaining the translation
he has made, when he is expounding the sense of a passage, and occasionally when he thinks there is special significance in Jesus' word choice. At
times he carefully parses the word, basing his comments on the particular
case or tense. Paying attention to the Greek text and even including Greek
words in the commentary is certainly not uncommon for the reformers,
particularly those in the humanist tradition.

What might be more surprising is how often in a commentary on the
gospels Calvin refers to Hebrew words. He discusses the meaning of the
names of John and Jesus in Hebrew. He recognizes that the Evangelists
were translating Hebrew phrases into Greek, so he is careful about
Hebrew expressions such as "Sons of the Bridechamber" for "wedding
guests."[82] He accuses other interpreters of misunderstanding passages
because they do not take into consideration the Hebrew usage which lies
behind the Greek.[83] Calvin also points out the parallelism and repetition
in the Psalms in his interpretations of the Evangelists' quotations of the
Old Testament.[84] He also makes reference to other Semitic languages in
the text. He attributes "Corban" to the Aramaic (*chaldaicum*).[85] He says
that Jesus' words of forsakenness on the cross are so important that "the
Spirit, to engrave them better in men's minds, chose to record them in the
Syriac language (*syriaca lingua*)."[86]

In addition to Calvin's philological work on the text, he also noted the
use of rhetorical devices and figures of speech in order to arrive at the
"natural sense" of the text. Throughout the *Commentary on the Harmony*,
he points out hyperbole,[87] simile,[88] metaphor,[89] personification,[90] synecdoche, and metonymy. The last two are the most important for his
interpretation, although for different reasons. Metonymy is useful for
Calvin's understanding of the sacraments, particularly the Supper, as
described in the gospels. In this commentary, written in the context of

---

82 *Comm. Matt.* 9:15 (*CNTC* i:268; *CO* xlv:253).
83 See *Comm. Matt.* 10:12, *Comm. Mark* 16:1; *Comm. Mark* 16:14.
84 *Comm. Matt.* 13:35; *Comm. Matt.* 21:2.
85 *Comm. Matt.* 27:5 (*CNTC* iii:177; *CO* xlv:749).
86 *Comm. Matt.* 27:46 (*CNTC* iii:208; *CO* xlv:779).
87 *Comm. Luke* 2:37, *Comm. Matt.* 5:29; *Comm. Matt* 17:19 and *Comm. Matt.* 24:31.
88 A partial list includes: *Comm. Matt.* 6:22; *Comm. Luke* 13:25; *Comm. Matt.* 10:16; and *Comm.
    Matt.* 19:23.
89 *Comm. Luke* 10:20; *Comm. Matt.* 12:28; *Comm Matt.* 12:43; and *Comm. Matt.* 20:22. His
    identification of metaphor can have sweeping theological impact because he sees both the fires of
    hell (*Comm. Matt.* 13:41) and the right hand of God (*Comm. Mark* 16:19) as metaphorical
    expressions.
90 *Comm. Matt.* 2:18; *Comm. Luke* 16:30; and *Comm. Matt.* 20:8.

the controversy over the Supper with Westphal, Calvin strays from his normal brevity to give a long explanation of the Eucharist in the exposition of the words, *This is my Body*. Calvin insists: "No one with a moderate acquaintance of Scripture will deny that sacramental expression must be taken as metonymy. Figurative uses in general I pass by, for they occur often in Scripture. I only say that as often as an outward sign is called the thing it portrays, then by general consent this is taken as an instance of metonymy."[91] Significantly, Calvin understands the figure of speech to be metonymy rather than metaphor because "this form of words is used to indicate the conjunction of the being with the sign," so Calvin's view of the Supper is not "merely" symbolic.[92] While metonymy has a very important but limited use in the commentary, synecdoche is widely used. Synecdoche is helpful in allowing Calvin to draw general lessons from fairly specific teachings; so, for instance, Jesus does not mean a Christian cannot have two coats but rather that a Christian should share whatever he has.[93] Synecdoche also enables Calvin to reconcile differing accounts in the gospels. Thus when Matthew says that the robbers reproached Jesus, but Luke says only that one reproached and the other defended Jesus, Calvin says that Matthew was using synecdoche, mentioning the whole when he only meant part.[94] Calvin identifies synecdoche both as the part mentioned for the whole and the whole mentioned when only a part is intended.

Because of the use of figures of speech, Calvin says often that Jesus was speaking "inexactly" or "imprecisely."[95] He makes this judgment a number of times when Jesus mentions "rewards." To Calvin this seems to smack of merit, so he must distinguish what Jesus intended from the actual words.[96] At other times, though, Calvin understands that Jesus' imprecise language was a way that Jesus accommodated himself to his audience.[97] This understanding would be more in keeping with the

---

91 *Comm. Matt.* 26:26 (*CNTC* III:134; *CO* XLV:706).

92 *Comm Matt.* 3:16 (*CNTC* I:132; *CO* XLV:127).

93 *Comm. Luke* 3:10. See also *Comm. Matt.* 5:6; *Comm. Matt.* 12:7; and *Comm. Matt.* 25:35.

94 *Comm. Matt.* 27:44. Matthew often speaks more widely than he intends the meaning. So Calvin solves the awkward problem that Matthew has Jesus riding on both a colt and an ass, by saying that he said both but by synecdoche meant only one (*Comm. Matt.* 21:2).

95 See *Comm. Matt.* 12:27, 39; *Comm. Matt.* 13:19, 37; and *Comm. Matt.* 15:19.

96 *Comm. Matt.* 6:16–18; *Comm. Matt.* 6:5; *Comm. Luke* 17:7–10.

97 *Comm. Matt.* 12:5 "When He says that the sabbath was profaned by the priests, it was imprecise language (*impropria est loquutio*); Christ was adapting Himself to His hearers (*in qua se Christus auditoribus accommodat*)" (*CNTC* II:29; *CO* XLV:325). See also *Comm. Matt.* 11:21, 23; and *Comm. Luke* 18:7.

humanist understanding of rhetoric. Certainly Calvin also emphasized
that Christ not only accommodated his words to his hearers, but also
accommodated himself to human weakness, as will be discussed under the
theological themes.

Calvin identified figures of speech in all of his commentaries. One
feature, however, which is unique to the Synoptic Gospels is Jesus'
teaching in parables. Calvin wrestles both with why Jesus spoke in
parables and how parables should be interpreted. Matthew 13 provides
the opportunity for Calvin to address at length Jesus' use of parables.

Although similitudes (*similitudines*) usually cast light on the matter in hand, yet
if they consist of one continual metaphor (*perpetuam metaphoram*) they are
enigmatic (*aenigmaticae*). Hence when Christ put forward this similitude
(*similitudinem*), He wanted to wrap up in an allegory (*allegoria*) what He could
have said more clearly and fully without a figure (*figura*). But when the
explanation has been given, the figurative word (*figuratus sermo*) has more power
and effect than the straightforward (*simplex*). That is to say, it is not only more
efficacious in affecting the mind but it is more perspicuous. It is important,
therefore, both to consider how a thing is said and what is said.[98]

As a humanist, Calvin recognized the rhetorical power of figurative
language. Yet as a theologian, he also recognized the twofold nature of
parables: that they are used to enlighten the elect but serve to blind the
reprobate.[99]

The interpretation of parables illustrates a major difference between
Calvin and many medieval interpreters. Although Calvin mentions allegory in the above quotation, he is adamant that usually the details in the
parable are not to be taken allegorically. The first thing that Calvin does
in interpreting a parable is to state the central point Jesus is making in the
parable.[100] The format of the commentary demonstrates this clearly; after
quoting the text, Calvin gives at least a paragraph on the purpose of the
parable, giving the sense of the whole, before starting in on a verse-by-
verse examination. He attempts to lay open the "mind of Christ" or
the "intention of Christ."[101] Calvin's statement in connection with the
parable of the ten virgins explains his method quite clearly:

---

98 *Comm. Matt.* 13:10 (*CNTC* 11:63; *CO* xlv:357).   99 *Comm. Matt.* 13:11–14.

100 *Parabolae finis*: *Comm. Matt.* 22:11; *Comm. Luke* 17:7–10; *Comm. Matt.* 25:1–13. *Summa*: *Comm.*
     Luke 18:1–8.

101 *Christi consilium*: *Comm. Matt.* 13:24–30; *Comm. Luke* 16:1–15; *Comm. Matt.* 20:1–16; and *Comm.*
     Matt. 24:29–31. *Ad Christi mentem*: *Comm. Matt.* 25:1–13; *Comm. Matt.* 25:5.

Once the object of the parable (*parabolae finis*) is understood there is no reason to labor over minute details which are quite beside Christ's intention (*ad Christi mentem*). There is great ingenuity over the lanterns, the vessels, the oil: The plain and natural answer (*simplex et genuina summa est*) is that keen enthusiasm for a short term is not enough unless accompanied by long unwearying effort.[102]

Occasionally even Calvin indulges in some allegorical interpretations,[103] but most of the time he draws the spiritual teaching from the main point of the parable rather than from the details. This focus on the central idea allows him to see certain parables with different details as parallel if the general lesson is the same.

Exegetical emphases and hermeneutical approaches

Calvin's exegetical emphases and hermeneutical principles have been well covered in numerous articles.[104] In this commentary, as in his others, he exhibits a theological understanding of the unity of Scripture under the *"scopus* of Christ,"[105] an emphasis on presenting the "genuine and simple sense" of the passage in opposition to allegorical interpretations,[106] an exegetical style which values "lucid brevity," and a commitment to the edification of the church.[107] Rather than retracing these general principles, this section will address areas pertaining specifically to his exegesis of the Synoptic Gospels. Calvin's emphasis on the unity of Scripture also necessitates a consideration of the relationship of the Synoptics to other parts of the canon. So we start narrowly with issues of harmonizing these three gospels, then move to the relationship between the Gospel of John

---

102 *Comm. Matt.* 25:1–13 (*CNTC* III:109–110; *CO* XLV:683).

103 In the prodigal son parable Calvin admits, "Although (as has often been said) it is foolish to apply all the details in parables, yet it will not twist the literal meaning (*non torquebitur litera*) if we say that our heavenly Father not only so pardons our sins that He buries the memory of them, but He also restores the gifts of which we were stripped" (*Comm. Luke* 15:22; *CNTC* II:224; *CO* XLV:509–510).

104 Calvin's Letter to Grynaeus prefacing the Romans commentary and his preface to an anticipated translation of Chrysostom homilies form the basis for most comments about Calvin's theory of interpretation. The full list of articles would be quite long; two that I found particularly useful in preparing this work are: John L. Thompson, "Calvin as a Biblical Interpreter," pp. 58–73 in *The Cambridge Companion to John Calvin*, ed. Donald K. McKim (Cambridge: Cambridge University Press, 2004); and Hans-Joachim Kraus, "Calvin's Exegetical Principles," *Interpretation* 31 (1977): 8–18.

105 *Comm. Luke* 24:46 (*CNTC* II:246; *CO* XLV:817–818).

106 *Comm. Matt.* 13:41 (*CNTC* II:77–78; *CO* XLV:370–371). See also *Comm. Luke* 10:38 and *Comm. Matt.* 16:28.

107 *Comm. Matt.* 24:35; *Comm. Luke* 22:31; and *Comm. Luke* 23:40.

and Harmony of the Gospels, and then widen the exploration to the relationship between the gospels and the Old Testament.

The first question is why Calvin chose to do a harmony of these gospels rather writing either an individual commentary on each, or a synthesis. In the *Argumentum*, Calvin refers to his method, recognizing that some would object to his rearrangement of the gospels by placing similar passages together. He argues that "one can make no intelligent or apt comment on one of the three Evangelists without comparing the other two."[108] Calvin's *Harmony* is designed for ease in comparing and contrasting the three Evangelists. He wants to allow readers to "see at a glance the points of likeness and difference," so he would not want to do a synthesis which would gloss over the differences.[109]

Calvin is clear that the Evangelists differ, even when they are telling the same story or relaying the same teaching. Yet these are differences in the details rather than in the main sense. He is not interested in arguments about which Evangelist has recorded Jesus' exact words and actions in the correct chronological order. Calvin is much more willing to leave some "breathing room" between the historical reality and any of the texts.[110] Everyone knows "that the Evangelists were not scrupulous in their time sequences, nor even in keeping to details of words and actions."[111] They were interested instead in "bring[ing] the whole pattern together to produce a kind of mirror or screen image (*speculo vel tabula*) of those features most useful for the understanding of Christ."[112] So he can say that they disagree on the details but that they agree on the whole sense of the passage.[113] Calvin tends to bring similar, but not identical, stories together from each gospel, seeing them as "three fingers" which point to the same incident.[114] Once he has established the passages as parallel, then he may

---

108 *CNTC* I:xiii; *CO* xlv:4.

109 *CNTC* I:xiii–xiv; *CO* xlv:4.

110 Richard Burnett, "John Calvin and the *Sensus Literalis*," *Scottish Journal of Theology* 57/1 (2004), p. 5. Burnett is reflecting on the ideas of Hans Frei in relation to Calvin.

111 *Comm. Luke* 8:19 (*CNTC* II:55; *CO* xlv:349). See also *Comm. Matt.* 4:18; and *Comm. Matt.* 21:10–22. Although this understanding of the Evangelists not paying attention to the order of events is useful in reconciling the different gospel accounts, it is difficult whenever Calvin might want to make a point about a particular sequence. For instance, he cannot say for sure whether Judas received the bread and wine at the Last Supper (*Comm. Matt.* 26:21).

112 *Comm. Matt.* 4:5 (*CNTC* I:139; *CO* xlv:133).

113 See for instance *Comm. Matt.* 12:29; *Comm. Matt.* 18:21; *Comm. Matt.* 20:20–23.

114 *Comm. Matt.* 9:18 (*CNTC* I:270; *CO* xlv:255). I can certainly multiply the examples here, but I will only offer a few where Calvin realizes that by combining the accounts he is going against what other interpreters (Osiander for example) do: *Comm. Matt.* 8:5; *Comm. Matt.* 9:18; *Comm. Matt.* 8:23–34; and *Comm. Matt.* 2:2. There are a few times when Calvin insists that the

use the clearer words in one to interpret the problematic words in another.[115] Calvin's method of approaching the parables by looking for the central point rather than analyzing the details seems to be what he thinks the Evangelists were doing throughout the gospels.

The sermons of Jesus are another place where the Evangelists' method of molding disparate sayings of Jesus into a long discourse serves as an example for Calvin's own method in the *Harmony*. Calvin is sure that the so-called Sermon on the Mount and other discourses are compilations of Jesus' teachings which the Evangelists brought together from many different occasions.[116] Since they did not pay special attention to the sequence or occasion, Calvin feels no compulsion to leave sayings or incidents in a particular context.[117] He says, "I have brought into this context what Luke records at another. The Evangelists move Christ's utterances dispersedly as occasion demands, to different places, and we should feel no compunction in setting them together."[118] Although Matthew is his primary text, he feels the freedom to follow Luke's order at times, or Mark's words if they are fuller.[119] This harmonization of the text does call into question one of the ways Calvin typically interprets Scripture. If the goal of the interpreter is to make clear the author's intention, then in the *Harmony* Calvin pays much less attention to the intention of the Evangelists individually.

Although the accounts of the three Evangelists differ, Calvin understands a basic unity brought about both by the direction of the Holy Spirit and by the common subject. Calvin says, "Indeed God's Spirit, who appointed the Evangelists as recorders, deliberately controlled their pen, so that all should write in complete agreement, but in different ways."[120] This agreement is also at work when one narrates an event not mentioned

---

Evangelists are referring to different events, such as when Jesus preaches and is rejected twice in Nazareth (*Comm. Matt.* 13:53). By the way, Augustine sees a single rejection told twice. See Augustine, *The Harmony of the Gospels* 2.42; NPNF VI:144–145.

115   *Comm. Matt.* 8:2. In trying to understand Matthew's statement that the leper "worshiped" Jesus, Calvin says, "the other two Evangelists are our best interpreters" (*CNTC* I:243; *CO* XLV:231). See also *Comm. Matt.* 5:3 and *Comm. Matt.* 13:12.

116   *Comm. Matt.* 5:1 "Both Evangelists had the intention of gathering into one single passage the chief headings of Christ's teaching, that had regard to the rule of godly and holy living" (*CNTC* I:168; *CO* XLV:160). See also *Comm. Matt.* 7:6; *Comm. Matt.* 7:12; and *Comm. Matt.* 7:13 on the Sermon on the Mount. Concerning other discourses, see *Comm. Luke* 22:28; *Comm. Matt.* 20:24; and *Comm. Matt.* 10:16–20.

117   *Comm. Luke* 13:10–17.

118   *Comm. Matt.* 6:24 (*CNTC* I:219; *CO* XLV:208).

119   *Comm. Matt.* 22:1 and *Comm. Mark* 9:14–27.

120   *Comm. Matt.* 2:1 (*CNTC* I:82; *CO* XLV:81), see also *Comm. Matt.* 26:56 and *Comm. Matt.* 28:16.

in another. "I have often noted how the Spirit of God shared out the parts appropriately to each Evangelist, so that what did not strike one or another may be learned from the rest."[121] The *Argumentum* itself is entitled "The Theme of the Gospel of Jesus Christ according to Matthew, Mark and Luke."[122] The three proclaim a singular gospel, which they share also with John and with the other New Testament writings. Calvin sees the three as concentrating "on the one point, that our Christ was that Son of God, the Redeemer promised to mankind."[123]

While the Synoptic Gospels focus more on the facts about the life, death, and resurrection of Jesus, Calvin says that "John differs in this respect quite considerably from the other three in that he devotes himself very much to describing the character and influence of Christ as it comes from Him to us."[124] Calvin, noting that only the Gospel of John gives Jesus' extended discourses at the Last Supper, says that the "aim" of the three Evangelists "was more the narrative of actual events than the doctrine contained in them."[125] The Synoptics indicate what happened, but John tells why. Calvin rarely attempts to bring incidents from John into his harmony of the three Evangelists. The major exceptions are the overlapping ministries of Jesus and John the Baptizer,[126] the cleansing of the temple,[127] and the passion narratives. Within the passion account, Calvin spends the most time in trying to reconcile the days and times given in the different gospels. His solution is that Jesus truly celebrated the Passover meal, on the correct day according to the law, with his disciples before his death, as in the Synoptics, and that John is correct that Jesus was crucified on the publicly observed Day of Preparation for the Passover.[128] Evidently this point is of such crucial importance that Calvin is not willing to reconcile the four by appealing to their lack of concern about the details of the time sequence! Calvin generally gives preference to the Gospel of John, seeing him as having included the things omitted by the other Evangelists.[129] Several times Calvin refers to his own *Commentary on the Gospel of John*, where he has already discussed a story more

---

121 *Comm. Luke* 24:13 (*CNTC* III:231; *CO* XLV:802).   122 *CNTC* I:xi; *CO* XLV:1.

123 *CNTC* I:xii; *CO* XLV:3.   124 *CNTC* I:xii; *CO* XLV:2–3.

125 *Comm. Mark* 14:26 (*CNTC* has this mis-marked as 26:26) (*CNTC* III:139; *CO* XLV:711).

126 *Comm. Matt.* 4:12 – Calvin follows the Gospel of John: the ministries overlapped but the Synoptic Gospels "pass over that short period in silence" (*CNTC* I:144; *CO* XLV:138).

127 *Comm. Matt.* 21:12 – Calvin is convinced that Jesus cleansed the temple twice, once at the beginning of his ministry and once at the end.

128 *Comm. Matt.* 26:17.

129 *Comm. Luke* 24:36. I have found only one place in the *Commentary on the Harmony* where Calvin says that John omitted something because he was trying to be brief (*Comm. Luke* 24:37).

fully and so can be brief in talking about the parallel passage in the *Harmony*.[130]

Connections between the *Harmony* and the rest of the New Testament are evident in the theological discussion below, so we will move on to Calvin's understanding of the three gospel accounts in connection with the Old Testament. First in the *Argumentum*, Calvin is clear about two things: the Old Testament is not the same as the gospel and the gospels do not render the Old Testament superfluous.[131] Calvin sees the Law and the Prophets as setting forth the promises of the Messiah, and the gospel as giving the "glad tidings" that the promised one has come. In commenting on Jesus' interpretation of the law in the Sermon on the Mount, Calvin insists that we must "preserve this connection of Law and Gospel inviolable . . . It has no small effect on consolidating our faith in the Gospel, if we hear that it is no other than the complement of the Law, both in mutual agreement claiming God as their common author."[132]

Although there is a connection between the law and the gospel, the distinction between the two must also be kept. In the *Commentary on the Harmony*, Calvin has several occasions to talk about the ending and beginning points – where the preaching of the law ends and that of the gospel begins. In the *Argumentum*, Calvin locates this juncture in the ministry of John the Baptist.[133] The ministry of Jesus did not bring an end to law, not even to the ceremonies of the law. Based on his reading of Hebrews, Calvin places the abrogation of the practices of the law at the death of Jesus, specifically at the splitting of the veil in the temple.[134] In fact Calvin refutes Luke's ordering of the events at the crucifixion, saying, "It was not appropriate for the veil to be rent, except at the completion of the sacrifice of expiation."[135] This rending of the veil means the end of the observance of the ceremonies of the law which prefigured Jesus (although the significance continues). This whole schema of salvation history is of utmost importance not only for salvation but also for knowing whether one should imitate the actions of Jesus. Jesus' keeping

---

130 See these examples: *Comm. Luke* 4:24 (a prophet is without honor in his own country); *Comm. Matt.* 14:16 (feeding of 5,000); *Comm. Matt.* 14:24 (walking on water); *Comm. Matt.* 27:37 (titles on cross).

131 *CNTC* I:xii; *CO* XLV:2–3.

132 *Comm. Matt.* 5:17 (*CNTC* I:180; *CO* XLV:171–172).

133 However, by quoting both Luke and Mark it is unclear whether the preaching of the gospel began with John or after John. *CNTC* I:xii; *CO* XLV:2.

134 *Comm. Mark* 2:27; *Comm. Luke* 10:22. See Hebrews, chs. 9 and 10.

135 *Comm. Matt.* 27:51 (*CNTC* III:211; *CO* XLV:782).

of the ritual law is not an example for those who live after the splitting of the veil.

In addition to the relationship between the law and the gospel, the *Commentary on the Harmony* focuses attention on how the Evangelists quote Scripture. Calvin sees the Evangelists' main task as revealing Christ as the one who had been promised; perhaps this emphasis is one reason why he chose Matthew as the base text. The Evangelists often quote prophetic passages to interpret the life and death of Jesus. Calvin recognized the fact that often these quotations seem to twist the words, wresting them from their original context and meaning. Calvin's statement on the first of these problematic prophetic quotations is quite enlightening:

> We must always observe the rule, that as often as the Apostles quote a testimony from Scripture, although they do not render it word for word, in fact may move quite a way from it, they adapt it suitably and appropriately to the case in hand. So readers should always take care to note the object of the passages of Scripture that the Evangelists use, not to press single words too exactly, but to be content with the one message which they never take from Scripture to distort into a foreign sense, but suit correctly to its real purpose. Further, as it is their plan to nourish infants and novices in faith with drinks of milk, for as yet they could not digest solid food, so there is no impropriety in the children of God going on to seek diligently and accurately what Scripture contains; thus the appetite which the Apostles encourage may lead them to the source.[136]

Interestingly, the interpretation of the prophetic quotations indicates a method similar to that of the Evangelists overall and to Calvin's interpretation of parables. The reader is not to pay attention to the details or expect the Evangelists to give a verbatim citation; instead the reader should look only for the main point of the quotation. According to Calvin this liberty in citing the meaning of the prophets rather than the words was a practice not only of the Evangelists but also of Jesus.[137]

In the *Commentary on the Harmony*, Calvin treats the Old Testament quotations in three ways. The first is that the Old Testament prophet was referring to Christ and to Christ alone. The only time this is used is in his comments on Matthew's citation of Isaiah 7:14. Calvin adamantly opposes "Jewish interpretations" which apply the statement to Hezekiah, an unknown son of King Ahaz, or the son of the prophet. He will hear of no attempts to tie the prophecy closer to the historical situation of the

---

136 *Comm. Matt.* 2:6 (*CNTC* 1:85–86; *CO* XLV:84).
137 *Comm. Matt.* 13:14 and *Comm. Matt.* 15:9.

crisis facing Ahaz; and certainly will not entertain the possibility that the Hebrew word could be translated "girl" rather than "virgin."[138] This insistence on Jesus as the sole fulfillment of the prophecy is strangely out of keeping with Calvin's more usual way of interpreting the prophetic quotations in the gospels. The second, and more common, way is Calvin's understanding that prophecy rightly refers to more than one situation. "We should take it as unquestioned, that the passage may not be restricted to Christ alone."[139] "Though this passage of Isaiah [40:1], should not be confined to John alone, yet he is included amongst those to whom that speech applies."[140] The prophet's words refer to the restoration, both the restoration after the Babylonian captivity and the restoration brought by Christ.[141] For example, in commenting on Matthew's citation that "the people in darkness saw a great light," Calvin understands that the "true intention of the Prophet" was a "longer view." "The beginning of this light, its dawning as it were, came at the return of the people from Babylon. At length the fulness of its splendor emerged with Christ the Sun of righteousness."[142] The final way that Calvin understood the Old Testament quotations in the gospels was by recognizing that the prophetic statement applied only to the time in which it was given and contained no predictive element for the time of Christ. Yet even these quotations may provide suitable comparisons of the times, so that the Evangelists are not twisting the meaning. For instance, in connection with Matthew's allusion to Isaiah 29:13, Calvin says, "Now although Isaiah was not prophesying for the future but was aiming at his contemporaries, yet Christ says that the prophecy fits the Pharisees and the scribes because they are like the hypocrites of old with whom the prophet was doing battle."[143]

---

138 *Comm. Matt.* 1:22 (*CNTC* I:65–68; *CO* XLV:66–68).
139 *Comm. Matt.* 2:15 (*CNTC* I:101; *CO* XLV:98–99).
140 *Comm. Matt.* 3:3 (*CNTC* I:116; *CO* XLV:113).
141 Richard Muller is quite right "that Calvin consistently understood the 'literal' meaning of Old Testament prophecies of the kingdom to be not only the reestablishment of Israel after the exile but also the establishment of the kingdom in the redemptive work of Christ, the furtherance of the kingdom in the reform of the church in the sixteenth century, and the final victory of the kingdom in Christ's second coming" ("Biblical Interpretation in the Era of the Reformation: The View from the Middle Ages," in *Biblical Interpretation in the Era of the Reformation: Essays Presented to David C. Steinmetz in Honor of His Sixtieth Birthday*, ed. Richard A. Muller and John L. Thompson [Grand Rapids: Eerdmans, 1996], p. 11).
142 *Comm. Matt.* 4:13 (*CNTC* I:153; *CO* XLV:146).
143 *Comm. Matt.* 15:7 (*CNTC* II:160; *CO* XLV:450). See also *Comm. Matt.* 2:18; and *Comm. Matt.* 13:35.

These quotations from the Old Testament are not mere ornamentation in the gospels for Calvin. Indeed, showing that Jesus is the promised Messiah is the main point of the Synoptic Gospels. In addition, a single quotation from the Old Testament becomes Calvin's interpretive key for the whole genre of miracle stories in the gospels. After narrating the healings in Capernaum, Matthew quotes Isaiah: "He took our infirmities and bore our diseases." Calvin recognizes once again that the Evangelist seems to twist the prophet's words by applying to physical miracles what Calvin thinks applies to the grace brought through the death of Christ. Calvin sets the rule he will follow in interpreting all the miracles: "This is the analogy we must follow: whatever benefits Christ bestows on men in their flesh, we must relate to the aim which Matthew sets before us, that He was sent by the Father to relieve us from all our ills and woes."[144] So the raising of the widow's son "is an example of the life of the Spirit to which He has restored us";[145] the exorcisms are reminders that Christ came "as the author of all good, to deliver us from the tyranny of Satan."[146] This analogy runs throughout the commentary, so that Calvin does not focus on the historicity of the miracles so much as on the spiritual lessons taught by them. The miracle stories were included both as proofs of Christ's divinity and lessons about the spiritual benefits of Christ's death.

Theological themes

In the *Commentary on the Harmony*, Calvin interprets Scripture relying on his common theological ideas: the providence of God, original sin, election, predestination, and grace. However, the key theological themes in this commentary are more Christological in nature, focusing on Christ as the mediator, the relationship between the divine and human in Jesus, the self-emptying of Christ, and the benefits of Christ's death. These ideas are already present in early editions of the *Institutes* and in his other biblical commentaries. Although he rarely mentions the controversies with Servetus and Westphal, they may stand behind some of Calvin's fuller Christological statements in the commentary. For the most part, however, he seems to be applying to specific passages of Scripture the doctrine he has already developed.

144 *Comm. Matt.* 8:17 (*CNTC* 1:163; *CO* xlv:155–156).
145 *Comm. Luke* 7:11 (*CNTC* 1:272; *CO* xlv:257).
146 *Comm. Matt.* 10:8 (*CNTC* 1:292; *CO* xlv:275).

Calvin's main understanding of the role of Christ is as the mediator between God and humans.[147] The "proper office" of the mediator is reconciliation, i.e., "to bring back unhappy sinners to favor with God."[148] Calvin understood the Old Testament priests to be a type of mediator to indicate the character of the true mediator.[149] The historical division between the law and the gospel is important here. Calvin saw the Jewish priests of Jesus' day as still serving this typological function. However, the death of Jesus and the rending of the veil put an end to the need for priests because the true mediator had come. Calvin drew on the book of Hebrews and also 1 Timothy 2:5 for the understanding of Christ as the mediator. This mediator is both sacrifice and priest. This true mediator takes what is ours and gives us what is his.

Calvin had a thoroughly Chalcedonian Christology, affirming the union of the divine and the human natures in one person.[150] Yet for Calvin the idea of the mediator was so essential that he had to emphasize Christ's humanity as one of us. Calvin confesses that Christ as the mediator was truly human and truly divine; but holding this classical confession becomes more difficult when interpreting specific accounts from the Synoptic Gospels. Calvin has to decide what is spoken of the human nature, what is spoken of the divine nature, and what is spoken of the unified person. Christ revealed his divinity in performing miracles,[151] and in knowing people's thoughts.[152] Yet Christ also had truly human weaknesses and needs: he was tempted, he was hungry, he needed sleep; he got angry, he was amazed, and he fled from danger.[153] At times the contradiction between divinity and humanity in Christ seems overwhelming. For instance, when Jesus sends the disciples across the sea and goes up on the mountain to pray, Calvin asks why Christ prayed for them instead of divinely guarding them from danger. He answers:

---

147 See *Inst.* II.12–14. See also the helpful discussions in Wilhelm Niesel, *The Theology of Calvin*, trans. Harold Knight (Grand Rapids: Baker Books, 1980), pp. 110–119; and Paul Van Buren, *Christ in Our Place: The Substitutionary Character of Calvin's Doctrine of Reconciliation* (Grand Rapids: Eerdmans, 1957), pp. 11–23.

148 *Comm. Luke* 7:36 (*CNTC* II:85; *CO* XLV:377).

149 *Comm. Luke* 1:23 and *Comm. Matt.* 26:57.

150 *Comm. Matt.* 24:36: "We know that the two natures in Christ were so conformed in one Person that each retained what was proper to it" (*CNTC* III:99; *CO* XLV:672).

151 *Comm. Matt.* 12:16; *Comm. Matt.* 26:18, 64.

152 *Comm. Matt.* 9:3 and *Comm. Matt.* 22:18.

153 The references in order are *Comm. Matt.* 4:1; *Comm. Matt.* 21:18; *Comm. Matt.* 8:23; *Comm. Luke* 6:8; *Comm. Matt.* 8:10; and *Comm. Matt.* 12:14.

But to fulfill both sides of His mediatorial office, He shows Himself to be truly God and man and gives evidence of both natures so far as was necessary. Although He held all things in His power, He showed Himself man by praying, and that not in pretence but with a sincere affection of human love for us. In this respect His divine majesty was in a sense quiescent (*quievit divina eius maiestas*), although at last in its own order it came forth.[154]

Calvin takes this idea of the divine nature resting while the human nature is active from Irenaeus.[155] However, what Irenaeus had applied to Jesus' human body, Calvin extends further to Jesus' human soul. The human emotions, the ignorance, the growth were not God pretending to be human but show the reality of Christ's humanity. Calvin insists that Christ in reality, not merely appearance, grew in wisdom and advanced in understanding.

This assumption of all that is human (except sin) is the self-emptying described in Philippians 2. This passage became Calvin's key for interpreting the life, death, and resurrection of Christ recorded in the Synoptic Gospels. Philippians 2:7 and 9 are cited specifically eight times but the language of self-emptying (*exinanitio*) is infused throughout the commentary. Calvin set the "beginning of the self-emptying" with the genealogy because Christ "might have kept His lineage free and pure of any crime or mark of shame" but instead allowed "one born from incestuous union, to be counted among His ancestors."[156] This self-emptying was also evident in his growth, his subjection to his parents, his temptation, his slipping away secretly. In the passion narratives, the language of self-emptying, of voluntarily accepting human weakness and suffering, becomes even stronger. Calvin uses the second part of the Philippians passage to interpret the resurrection, that after Christ emptied himself, "God exalted him," giving him all authority.[157] Calvin combines this idea of self-emptying with the veiling of divinity, so in the resurrection the veil of the flesh is lifted so that the Godhead may be revealed.[158]

---

154 *Comm. Matt.* 14:23 (*CNTC* II:151; *CO* XLV:440–441). See also this language of divinity resting in *Comm. Luke* 19:41 and *Comm. Matt.* 24:36. Somewhat ironically, when Christ as a human fell asleep, the Godhead kept watch (*Comm. Matt.* 8:23).

155 *Comm. Luke* 2:40 (*CNTC* I:107; *CO* XLV:104). This is a reference to Irenaeus, *Against Heresies*, 3.19.3 "For as He became man in order to undergo temptation, so also was He the Word that He might be glorified; the Word remaining quiescent, that He might be capable of being tempted, dishonoured, crucified, and of suffering death, but the human nature being swallowed up in it (the divine), when it conquered, and endured [without yielding], and performed acts of kindness, and rose again, and was received up [into heaven]."

156 *Comm. Matt.* 1:3 (*CNTC* I:59; *CO* XLV:60).

157 *Comm. Matt.* 28:18 (*CNTC* III:250; *CO* XLV:821).

158 *Comm. Matt.* 17:1–8 (*CNTC* II:198; *CO* XLV:485) and *Comm. Matt.* 17:9 (*CNTC* II:203; *CO* XLV:490).

Calvin's explanation of the benefit of Christ's suffering contains some of the most poetic passages in the commentary. He begins by saying, "First, to remove the scandal of the cross, look at the benefit Christ gives us in His self-emptying: thus will the incomparable goodness of God and the efficacy of grace dispel by their own light whatever is ugly and shameful in the scene."[159] He then goes through all the "ugly" details. This is one of the few places in the *Commentary on the Harmony* where Calvin finds all the details to be significant. Christ was bound to set us free; His face was marred by blows to restore the image of God in us; "Christ kept silence, to be our spokesman now"; "He was reckoned worse than a thief, to bring us into the company of angels"; and He was stripped to clothe us in His righteousness.[160] After this wonderful language of reversal, Calvin finally says that "these are things that ask for secret meditation, not fancy words."[161]

CALVIN AS COMMENTATOR

In looking at the context and the content of the *Commentary on the Harmony*, little attention has been focused on how Calvin applies his exegesis. Calvin was convinced that, like Jesus, every good interpreter of Scripture ought to apply it to the "present occasion."[162] Throughout the commentary, Calvin makes theological applications so that individual Christians may be assured of the benefits of Christ's death, and of Christ's continuing miraculous work, lifting the focus from the physical healing to the spiritual meaning. However, Calvin also makes practical application of his exegesis for the edification of the church as a whole. The process of edification includes tearing down practices inculcated by misinterpretation of Scripture. In the *Commentary on the Harmony*, Calvin addressed a number of practices in the Roman Church: the use of the "Hail Mary," monasticism, auricular confession, the Lenten fast, and anointing with oil.[163] One of Calvin's longest digressions was refuting the justification of the papacy on the grounds that Peter was the foundation of the

159 *Comm. Matt.* 26:57–61 (*CNTC* III:163; *CO* XLV:735).
160 The references in order are *Comm. Matt.* 27:11; *Comm. Matt.* 27:27; *Comm. Matt.* 27:12 (*CNTC* III:180; *CO* XLV:752); *Comm. Matt.* 27:15 (*CNTC* III:183–184; *CO* XLV:755); and *Comm. Matt.* 27:35.
161 *Comm. Matt.* 27:27 (*CNTC* III:189; *CO* XLV:761).
162 *Comm. Luke* 4:21 (*CNTC* I:149; *CO* XLV:142).
163 References in order are *Comm. Luke* 1:28; *Comm. Matt.* 3:4 and *Comm. Luke* 14:33; *Comm. Matt.* 3:6; *Comm. Matt.* 4:1; and *Comm. Mark* 6:12.

church.[164] He also refuted a number of Anabaptist doctrines and practices: refusal to swear an oath, denying the "use of the sword to the church," adult baptism only, and no holding of public office by Christians.[165] At times Calvin sees both the Papists and the Anabaptists as misinterpreting the same passage of Scripture. Take for instance Jesus' refusal to serve as judge to divide the inheritance between two brothers. Calvin rebukes the Papists for not following Jesus closely enough so that the clergy have taken over civil jurisdiction. On the other hand, the Anabaptists have applied this refusal of Jesus too universally so that they say "that it is not lawful for Christian men to receive inheritances, to engage in business affairs, or to undertake any civil office."[166] Calvin instead offers a middle way based on a "true imitation" of Christ, which means recognizing and acting according to one's own calling, doing what is appropriate to one's own office.

Calvin carefully distinguishes between what was a unique action of a single individual, and what may and should be emulated. Christ certainly is to be imitated in certain aspects such as "denial of ourselves and voluntary bearing of the cross,"[167] but things like the cleansing of the temple belonged strictly to Christ's own calling as mediator.[168] Even the actions of other humans in the gospels must be used with care. This careful distinction may be seen in his comments about the woman who anointed Jesus with oil:

Now the reason why the Lord, who was a remarkable pattern (*exemplar*) of thrift and frugality, allowed this expensive ointment to be used was that it was the way in which this poor sinful woman expressed that she owed everything to Him . . . And Luke make this a pattern (*exemplum*) for us to imitate, for her tears were witnesses of sorrow, the beginning of repentance. That she fell to the ground behind Christ's feet and lay there prostrate showed that she offered herself and all she had to Christ as a sacrifice. We should imitate her in all this (but the effusion of ointment was a unique action [*singularis actio*] and it would be wrong to make a rule [*regula*] out of it).[169]

This passage is replete with interesting ideas of imitation and example. Evidently Calvin expects his readers to follow Christ's example of frugality, a pattern which he assumes several times in the commentary, although

164 *Comm. Matt.* 16:19.
165 References in order are *Comm. Matt.* 5:24; *Comm. Matt.* 13:39; *Comm. Matt.* 19:14; and *Comm. Matt.* 20:25.
166 *Comm. Luke* 12:13 (*CNTC* 11:92; *CO* xlv:384).
167 *Comm. Matt.* 16:24 (*CNTC* 11:194; *CO* xlv:481).
168 *Comm. Matt.* 21:12.
169 *Comm. Luke* 7:44 (*CNTC* 11:87; *CO* xlv:379).

he does not point to a scripture demonstrating Jesus' thrift.[170] The woman's extravagance certainly does not receive the same praise. However, by transferring the acts of tears and prostration to a more spiritual level Calvin can and does enjoin on the faithful repentance and self-sacrifice. Calvin does not make the same leap to spiritual meaning for the anointing with oil, so it is relegated to a unique action. In the similar, but not parallel, passage of the woman anointing Jesus before his death, Calvin places this unique action in historical context. Christ could only receive the physical outpouring of the ointment when he had a physical body. After his ascension, attempting to replicate the action is ridiculous.[171]

The idea of "true imitation" rather than the "foolish emulation that has filled the world with apes"[172] is one way that Calvin applied Scripture to the "present occasion." This method relies on making distinctions between unique actions and ones which are always appropriate. Calvin also applied Scripture to the contemporary setting by highlighting an affinity between the situation of the church in the first century and in the sixteenth century.[173] Calvin carefully described the miserable state of religion at the time of Christ even while recognizing that the priests and even the Pharisees had the "ordinary government of the church."[174] This sick state of the church was such a low point that the restoration Christ brought was all the more impressive.[175] Calvin's interpretive key was to relate the horrible state of the church in the first century to his own day by paralleling the first-century priests, Sadducees, and Pharisees with the sixteenth-century papacy, clergy, monks, and theologians. "Truly, if you compare the Pope and his foul clergy with the Sadducees and Pharisees, the kindest thing that you can say is that they should be tossed into the same bundle."[176] Calvin went even further to say "that the corruptions of the Papal hierarchy today are more foul and more disfiguring, than they were under Annas and Caiaphas with the Jews."[177] Of course this interpretive move places Calvin and the other reformers in the

170 *Comm. Luke* 10:38 and *Comm. Matt.* 26:10.

171 *Comm. Matt.* 26:10 (*CNTC* III:121–123; *CO* XLV:695).

172 *Comm. Luke* 2:37 (*CNTC* I:98; *CO* XLV:95–96).

173 Darlene Flaming, "The Appeal to the Apostles: The Use of the Apostolic Church in the Writings of John Calvin," Ph.D. diss., University of Notre Dame, 1998, pp. 318–404. Richard Muller's findings about the prophecies of restoration point out the same tendency ("Biblical Interpretation," p. 11).

174 *Comm. Matt.* 21:42 (*CNTC* III:20; *CO* XLV:596). See also *Comm. Matt.* 16:12.

175 *Comm. Luke* 1:54.

176 *Comm. Matt.* 3:7 (*CNTC* I:121; *CO* XLV:117).

177 *Comm. Luke* 4:16 (*CNTC* I:147; *CO* XLV:140).

position of Jesus and the apostles who stand in opposition to the so-called legitimate leaders of the church. In all of these ways of applying Scripture to the "present occasion," Calvin is acutely aware of the time sequence and the historical context; how his own time does or does not relate to the first century.

What then can we say about Calvin as a commentator on the Synoptic Gospels? Approaching these gospels toward the end of his career, Calvin had already learned from the rest of Scripture what he should find here. The three Evangelists' bare narration of the events of Christ's life, death, and resurrection had meaning only in the context of the unity of Scripture. Calvin's understanding of Christ as mediator, truly human and truly divine, was not born in his reading of the Synoptics, although the controversial context and the struggle to interpret particular passages may have sharpened his Christological articulation. Although Karl Barth placed Calvin's Christology in the trajectory of the Synoptic Gospels (and Nestorius) because of his emphasis on the two natures, Calvin tends to quote the rest of the New Testament more abundantly than Matthew, Mark, and Luke in doctrinal statements on Christology.[178]

In a 1985 article, Richard Gamble looked at the possible sources of Calvin's hermeneutic and ended with the suggestion that Calvin had consciously adopted "what he thought was a biblical hermeneutic."[179] This is a fascinating idea to trace in light of Calvin's *Commentary on the Harmony of the Gospels.* Calvin was not caught up here in any search for the historical Jesus. He was certain that Jesus healed all these people, performed all these miracles, gave all these teachings, but was not under any illusion that the Evangelists were narrating events exactly as they happened. Presumably each of the Evangelists arranged the events as seemed best to him, so Calvin also found the same freedom to rearrange the events and teaching as needed in working out his harmony. He did not feel compelled to follow the Evangelists' order or that of any of the other interpreters of the gospels. With the teaching of Jesus, Calvin most often works with the idea that the Evangelists captured the sense of Jesus' sayings rather than the exact words. According to Calvin, Jesus and the Evangelists referred to the general sense of the prophetic passages rather than analyzing all the words and details in the original context. Calvin

---

178 Karl Barth, *Church Dogmatics,* trans. G. T. Thomson and Harold Knight (Edinburgh: T. & T. Clark, 1956); I/2:24.

179 Richard Gamble, "*Brevitas et Facilitas:* Toward an Understanding of Calvin's Hermeneutic," *Westminster Theological Journal* 47 (1985), p. 17.

turns around and applies the same interpretive method to Jesus' parables, looking for the central point rather than analyzing all the details. Although Calvin followed in many ways the Evangelists' method as he saw it, sometimes his humanist background overshadows it. This is seen particularly in his philological studies and the careful attention to history. It is this discerning of the historical situation which he finds most important in applying Scripture to the present needs of the church.

CHAPTER 7

Calvin as commentator on the Gospel of John

Barbara Pitkin

In his preface to his 1553 commentary on the Gospel of John, Calvin joined a long line of Christian thinkers in expressing high esteem for the Fourth Gospel's unique teaching. Although all four gospels, he claims, aim to make Christ known, the first three exhibit his "body," whereas John exhibits his "soul."[1] Despite this traditional-sounding affirmation of John's special character, Calvin's commentary occupies a singular place in the history of Johannine interpretation. Specifically, it represents the culmination of certain sixteenth-century approaches to the Fourth Gospel, redefining its "spiritual" character and reversing traditional views that this gospel offered more advanced and difficult teaching than Matthew, Mark, and Luke. Moreover, the commentary marks an important stage in Calvin's exegetical activity and his career in Geneva. This was Calvin's first gospel commentary, and it was published in the midst of what was clearly the most turbulent period in his time in the city.[2] He discussed these trials in his dedication to the syndics and town council – a cagey political move, given that the majority of the members of the council were in fact sympathetic to Calvin's opposition. Protesting the charges of excessive severity and reminding these magistrates of their duty to refute the slanders against him, Calvin reasoned that it was important to have a special monument to his teaching – namely, this commentary – inscribed with their name. Echoing Jeremiah, he expressed his hope that this commentary would take a firmer hold of their memory: "I pray to God to inscribe it so deeply with his own finger on your hearts that it may never be obliterated by any stratagem of Satan."[3] Investigation of the

---

1 John Calvin, *In Evangelium Secundum Johannem Commentarius*, *OE* xi/1:8 = *CO* xlvii:vii; CTS xvii:22.
2 W. Naphy, *Calvin and the Consolidation of the Genevan Reformation* (Manchester and New York: Manchester University Press, 1994), pp. 173–178.
3 *OE* xi/1:5 = *CO* xlvii:vi; CTS xvii:18–19.

circumstances surrounding Calvin's commentary, the general trends in the history of the interpretation of the gospel prior to Calvin, and the important methodological and substantive aspects of Calvin's own commentary will demonstrate its singular place both in the history of Johannine interpretation and among Calvin's works.

THE HISTORY OF CALVIN'S COMMENTARY ON JOHN

Calvin had lectured on the Fourth Gospel early in his career, in 1539 at Johann Sturm's humanist academy in Strasbourg.[4] Of these early lectures themselves no record has survived. Nevertheless, that Calvin apparently chose to lecture on John before Matthew, Mark, or Luke, and that he later made this gospel the subject of a written commentary before turning to the Synoptics, fits with his expressed conviction that John's gospel provides the key to understanding the other three.[5] Two years after the appearance of the commentary on John, he published a commentary on Matthew, Mark, and Luke in which he harmonized their respective accounts into a single narrative. From this point on, the two commentaries – on the Harmony of Matthew, Mark, and Luke and on John – were always printed together, and occasionally appeared in French or Dutch along with the commentary on Acts. In the period from its first appearance up to the end of the sixteenth century, Calvin's commentary on John appeared seven times in Latin, twelve times in French, twice in German, once in English, and once in Dutch. All of the French and four of the Latin editions were printed in or before the year of Calvin's death (1564); the Latin version continued to appear once a decade for the rest of the century, and the Dutch, English, and German translations appeared only in the last two decades.[6] The dissemination of the commentary through the end of the century thus reflects the general expansion of Calvinism outside of Geneva, concentrating in the 1560s on France

---

4 J. Ficker, *Die Anfänge der akademischen Studien in Strasbourg* (Strasbourg: Heitz, 1912), p. 41; cf. F. Wendel, *Calvin: Origins and Development of His Religious Thought*, trans. P. Mairet (1963; rpt. Durham, NC: Labyrinth, 1987), p. 61 and T. H. L. Parker, *Calvin's New Testament Commentaries* (Grand Rapids: Eerdmans, 1971), p. 10. For a broader discussion of Calvin's activities in Strasbourg and a list of the most important literature on this period in his career, see C. Augustijn, "Calvin in Strasbourg," in *Calvinus Sacrae Scripturae Professor: Calvin as a Confessor of Holy Scripture*, ed. W. H. Neuser (Grand Rapids: Eerdmans, 1994), pp. 166–177. Details concerning the 1553 commentaries can be found in *BC* I:53/2 and 53/5.

5 *OE* XI/1:8 = *CO* XLVII: vii; CTS XVII:22.

6 See *BC* III:645.

and later in the century on England, the Netherlands, and German territories.[7]

Given Calvin's high esteem for the Fourth Gospel and his view that it provided the key to understanding the other three, it is perhaps no surprise that he chose John as the subject of his first gospel commentary. Moreover, given the theological priority of the Pauline epistles, especially Romans, for Calvin, it is also clear why he completed his commentaries on Paul and Hebrews before turning to other New Testament writings.[8] One can also surmise that having taken over a decade to work his way through the Pauline epistles and Hebrews, Calvin might have made the practical decision to focus in 1549–1550 on the short remaining epistles of the New Testament before tackling the much longer Acts and the gospels, especially since the epistles were conveniently the current topic of the weekly communal Bible studies (*congrégations*).

Beginning in 1550, the topic of the *congrégations* was the Gospel of John.[9] At the same time, Calvin was lecturing on Genesis in the school and trying, without much success, to write the commentary on it.[10]

---

7 From 1561 to 1564, eight French editions appeared from publishers in Geneva, Lyon, and Alençon. All of these were combined with the commentary on the Harmony and the commentary on Acts; moreover, they were often issued with a "companion volume" containing Calvin's commentaries on the New Testament epistles, thus providing a complete set of Calvin's exposition of the New Testament.

8 On the theological priority of Paul in Calvin's theology and exegesis, see B. Girardin, *Rhétorique et théologique: Calvin, le Commentaire de l'Épître aux Romains* (Paris: Éditions Beauchesne, 1979); A. Ganoczy, "Calvin als paulinischer Theologe," in *Calvinus Theologus*, ed. W. H. Neuser (Neukirchen: Neukirchener Verlag, 1976), pp. 39–69; D. Steinmetz, *Calvin in Context* (New York: Oxford University Press, 1995), pp. 23–39, 64–79, and 122–140; B. Pitkin, *What Pure Eyes Could See: Calvin's Doctrine of Faith in Its Exegetical Context* (New York: Oxford University Press, 1999). For a succinct summary of the preparation and publishing of Calvin's commentaries, see J.-F. Gilmont, *Jean Calvin et le livre imprimé* (Geneva: Librairie Droz, 1997), pp. 71–92; cf. Parker, *Calvin's New Testament Commentaries*, ch. 1.

9 The introduction to John presented by Calvin in the *congrégation* was published in 1558 as a kind of a preface to a collection of Calvin's sermons; see *BC* II:58/5. The text can be found in *CO* XLVII:465–484; in English in John Calvin, *Sermons on the Deity of Christ and Other Sermons*, ed. and trans. L. Nixon (1950; rpt. Audubon, NJ: Old Paths Publications, 1997), pp. 13–34. Unfortunately, the English version perpetuates the misunderstanding that this is a sermon. On the *congrégations* in general, see E. A. de Boer, "The Presence and Participation of Laypeople in the *Congrégations* of the Company of Pastors in Geneva," *Sixteenth Century Journal* 35/3 (Fall 2004): 651–670; E. A. de Boer, "The Congrégations: In-Service Theological Training Center of the Preachers to the People of Geneva," in his *Calvin and the Company of Pastors* (Grand Rapids: Calvin Studies Society, 2004), pp. 57–87; E. A. de Boer, "Calvin and Colleagues: Propositions and Disputations in the Context of the Congrégations in Geneva," in *Calvinus Praeceptor Ecclesiae*, Papers of the International Congress on Calvin Research, Princeton, August 20–24, 2002, ed. H. J. Selderhuis (Geneva: Librairie Droz, 2004), pp. 331–342.

10 Already in July 1542 Calvin had written to Farel of his wish to write on Genesis, should God grant him a long life and spare time (*CO* XI:418). Eight years later, Calvin reported that he was

Moreover, he was also working on a commentary on Acts, the book that was the current focus of his Sunday morning sermons.[11] His ecclesiastical duties, of course, were not confined to lecturing, preaching, and participating in the *congrégations*. Energy-consuming also was the fact that the early 1550s witnessed the gradual increase of tension between Calvin and the city council of Geneva, which came to a head in 1553.[12] It is no wonder then that he had no time to write on John. This changed, however, in 1552, or perhaps even earlier, when Calvin interrupted his work on Acts, sent the first half of the commentary to the printer, and devoted himself to writing on the Gospel of John, which appeared in print on January 1, 1553.

Why Calvin shifted his energies at that point in time to the commentary on John is not known exactly. In the introduction to the most recent Latin edition of the commentary, editor Helmut Feld suggests that the immediate impetus may be sought in Servetus' *Christianisimi Restitutio*, a work possibly conceived as an antidote to Calvin's *Institutes*, which defended its Christological and trinitarian doctrine by appealing to passages in the Fourth Gospel. Although Servetus' work was not published until January 1553, the year in which he, in August, made his ill-fated appearance in Geneva, Calvin had a manuscript copy, obtained during a period of correspondence with the author in 1546–1547. Clearly he was certainly troubled by Servetus' heterodoxy and makes reference to him in his interpretation of John 1. However, it is too much to claim that Calvin "seemed to have found it to be necessary to counter Servetus' views . . . as quickly as possible with an orthodox Christology and doctrine of the Trinity based on a correct exegesis of the text of the gospel."[13] As I have suggested above and shall argue below, Calvin does not understand the defense of orthodox doctrines of the Trinity and Christ's person to be the main intention of the Evangelist, and, moreover, he criticizes earlier interpreters who held this to be the case. Criticism of Servetus' interpretation of certain passages would figure in a limited way in Calvin's commentary, but it is hard to see this as the *main* motivation for writing it. Simply put, in 1552, there were more pressing challenges for Calvin to address.

beginning the project, but by November 1550 he complained that he had had to put the project on the shelf for a while (*CO* xii:623, 655). See also *BC* I:54/8. The commentary on Genesis was finally published in 1554.

11 Gilmont, *Jean Calvin*, p. 76. Calvin preached on Acts from August 1549 until the end of 1553.

12 These tensions are chronicled in Naphy, *Genevan Reformation*, pp. 167–199.

13 *OE* xi/1:xi.

One of these has its origins more directly in current debates in Geneva. In October 1551 Jerome Bolsec challenged the Genevan ministers' teaching on predestination during a *congrégation*. The text for the day was John 8, which was expounded by Jean de Saint-André with subsequent comments by William Farel. Bolsec argued in particular against the interpretation of John 8:47 ("He that is of God hears God's words") and was refuted by Calvin's extemporaneous defense of the Genevan doctrine. Bolsec was arrested immediately and a lengthy trial ensued, catching the attention of notables outside of Geneva, such as Philip Melanchthon, Heinrich Bullinger, and Laelius Socinus.[14] Even after Bolsec was banished at the conclusion of the trial in December, the controversy continued to agitate the city. A public debate on the topic was held the following fall between Calvin and Jean Trolliet, who cited from the French translation of Melanchthon's *Loci Communes* to support Bolsec's criticisms.[15] Although Feld notes that the theme of election and reprobation is a major one in Calvin's commentary on John, I think it likely that Calvin's emphasis on this is suggested by certain passages in the gospel themselves. It is not sufficient to attribute his motives in writing on John to a desire to defend his teaching on predestination any more than to a wish to defend orthodox understandings of Christology and the Trinity. Nevertheless, the fact remains that a particular point of interpretation of John had been challenged publicly, and it could be that, with Acts having reached certain proportions, Calvin found himself at a natural breaking point and decided to clarify the interpretation of John.

Despite the contentious climate surrounding the writing of his commentary on John, Calvin rarely alludes in the commentary itself to current ecclesiastical and political difficulties in Geneva.[16] Indeed, the main polemical target he identifies is "papal religion" in general, claiming in his dedicatory epistle that he hopes that this commentary will show papal religion to be a satanic monstrosity. It is thus probably wise to consider Calvin's decision to write on John as a logical next step in the exegetical program he had been carrying forth since the early 1540s. And yet, the dedication envelops the entire commentary in the aura of an apology, in which Calvin pleads the case for his teaching not for the benefit of papal

---

14 For a brief summary, see B. Cottret, *Calvin: A Biography*, trans. M. W. McDonald (Grand Rapids: Eerdmans, 2000), p. 210; and for a full account see P. C. Holtrop, *The Bolsec Controversy on Predestination, from 1551 to 1555*, 2 vols. (Lewiston, NY: Edwin Mellen Press, 1993).

15 For the statements submitted by the disputants, see *CO* xiv:371–385.

16 Explicit political and polemical criticism does appear in his sermons from this time (Naphy, *Genevan Reformation*, pp. 154–162).

opponents but rather before the officials of Geneva. In a certain sense, therefore, this commentary can be viewed as a singular defense of his teaching and pastoral authority.

THEMES IN THE HISTORY OF THE INTERPRETATION OF THE GOSPEL OF JOHN PRIOR TO CALVIN

Since, as we will see in more detail below, past and present interpreters of the Gospel of John figure in Calvin's own commentary as "partners in conversation," I will at this point trace several key themes in traditional attitudes toward and exegesis of the Fourth Gospel. This sketch must remain general and does not – indeed, cannot – attempt to convey all the variety and richness of the conversation concerning John prior to Calvin.[17] Moreover, there can be no question here of identifying precisely *how* these traditional concerns were mediated to him. Rather, my object here is to identify key questions that arose out of the biblical text itself as viewed by some of its most influential interpreters, and to sketch some of their most common responses to these issues. We will then be in a position to examine the ways in which Calvin engages these traditional issues in his own commentary.

The Gospel of John in the early Christian church

A fundamental question addressed by many early interpreters was the relationship of John to the other three gospels.[18] In their responses to this question, early Christian writers reflected on the unique character and purpose of John's account. According to the church historian Eusebius (d. c. 340), John wrote his gospel primarily to supplement the other three (which he had read and approved) with an account of Jesus' earlier

17 For more detailed discussions of the exegesis of the Gospel of John in specific periods or by particular interpreters, see nn. 18, 36, and 49 below. S. P. Kelly provides a sometimes rough and bibliographic catalogue of the history of the interpretation of John that draws on secondary studies (*John's Gospel and the History of Biblical Interpretation*, 2 vols., Mellen Biblical Press Series 60 [Lewiston, NY: Edwin Mellen Press, 2002]). The introduction to the *OE* edition discusses possible sources for Calvin's commentary; see *OE* XI/1:XXII–XXIV.

18 On patristic interpretation of the Gospel of John, see M. Wiles, *The Spiritual Gospel: The Interpretation of the Fourth Gospel in the Early Church* (Cambridge: Cambridge University Press, 1960); S. Brey, "Origen's Commentary on John," Ph.D. dissertation, University of Notre Dame, 2003; L. Koen, *The Saving Passion: Incarnational and Soteriological Thought in Cyril of Alexandria's Commentary on the Gospel according to St. John*, Studia Doctrinae Christianae Upsaliensia 31 (Stockholm: Almqvist and Wiksell, 1991).

ministry.[19] Yet, as he himself points out later in the same work, tradition also held that John complemented the Synoptics not only in the scope of its coverage of Jesus' ministry but also in the nature and content of its teaching about Jesus himself. The long history of viewing the Fourth Gospel as more spiritual than the other three and having as its distinct purpose the conveying and defending of spiritual mysteries has its origins as early as Clement of Alexandria (c. 150–215). According to Clement, John wrote after the other three: "Last of all, aware that the physical facts had been recorded in the Gospels [according to Matthew, Luke, and Mark], encouraged by his pupils and irresistibly moved by the Spirit, John wrote a spiritual Gospel."[20] Soon thereafter Origen (c. 185–254) wrote his commentary on John, which he viewed as the "first fruits" of the gospels – indeed, of all Scripture.[21] These and other early judgments about the unique visionary nature and eminence of John were echoed two centuries later by Jerome (c. 342–420) and found their place in the homilies and commentaries of John Chrysostom (c. 347–407), Augustine (354–430), and Cyril of Alexandria (d. 444).

To varying degrees, patristic writers also endeavored to explain discrepancies between the Fourth Gospel and the Synoptic accounts.[22] In thus comparing the perspectives many suggested or openly proclaimed the superiority of John. Their esteem reflects a popularity that is evident, moreover, in the material culture of the early church. The Fourth Gospel's representation in papyrus finds of the second and third centuries is "unusually strong," and examples of Christian art from the catacomb paintings in Rome "also testify to the popularity of the Johannine presentation of the events of Jesus' life."[23] Popular also, albeit somewhat later, were images of the Evangelist himself, represented as an eagle rising above the others. The basis for this iconography was laid down by Jerome, who revised Irenaeus' (c. 130–200) correlation of the four Evangelists with the

---

19 Eusebius, *The History of the Church from Christ to Constantine*, trans. G. A. Williamson (Penguin Books, 1965; rpt. Dorset Press, 1984), book 3, ch. 24, pp. 132–134.

20 As reported by Eusebius in ibid., book 6, ch. 14, p. 255.

21 "We might dare say, then, that the Gospels are the first fruits of all Scriptures, but the firstfruits of the Gospels is that according to John, whose meaning no one can understand who has not leaned on Jesus' breast nor received Mary from Jesus to be his mother also" (Origen, *Commentary on John*, book 1, section 23, in *Commentary on the Gospel According to John, Books 1–10*, trans. R. E. Heine, Fathers of the Church 80 [Washington: Catholic University of America Press, 1989], p. 38).

22 These efforts are summarized in Wiles, *Spiritual Gospel*, pp. 13–21.

23 C. E. Hill, *The Johannine Corpus in the Early Church* (New York: Oxford University Press, 2004), p. 469.

four-faced heavenly beings of Ezekiel 1:10 or the four living creatures of Revelation 4:6–8. According to Jerome, John becomes the eagle, who "soars aloft, and reaches the Father Himself, and says, 'In the beginning was the Word.'"[24] Interpreters sometimes expanded this comparison by further reflections on eagle behavior. Augustine, for example, relates that parent birds test young eaglets in the following way: "[The fledgling] is suspended, of course, on the claw of the father and held up to the rays of the sun; if it gazes steadily [into the sun], it is acknowledged as a son; if it quivers at the sight, it is dropped from the claw as a bastard."[25] Thus John, as the eagle, is particularly and uniquely qualified to contemplate and proclaim sublime truths. Interpreters found clues into the reasons for the Fourth Evangelist's loftier spiritual insight in the fact that he was the disciple whom Jesus loved; that he reclined at the breast of Jesus and received Jesus' mother as his own at the foot of the cross; and, finally, that he was presumed to be the author not only of the gospel but of three epistles and, significantly, the book of Revelation.[26]

Early interpreters of John also identified a polemical motivation underlying the Evangelist's purpose. Irenaeus argued that John wrote his spiritual gospel particularly to combat the errors planted by Cerinthus and the Nicolaitans.[27] In 392 Jerome repeated this claim and added that John wrote also to refute the Ebionite assertion that Christ did not exist before Mary.[28] Christian writers also found the Fourth Gospel relevant to their own polemical situations; for example, Irenaeus drew on John 1:1–3 to refute Valentinian Gnostics.[29] Johannine passages were particularly influential in fourth-century trinitarian debates, which had only heightened the Evangelist's reputation as the proclaimer and defender of spiritual mysteries, especially concerning the nature of God and the

---

24 Jerome, *Against Jovinianus*, book 1, section 26, in *St. Jerome: Letters and Select Works*, NPNF VI:366. For Irenaeus, see *Against Heresies* in *Early Christian Fathers*, ed. Cyril C. Richardson, Library of Christian Classics 1 (Philadelphia: Westminster Press, 1953), pp. 382–383.

25 Augustine, Tractate 36 [on John 8:15–18], section 5, in *Tractates on the Gospel of John 28–54*, trans. J. W. Rettig, Fathers of the Church 88 (Washington: Catholic University of America Press, 1993), p. 87.

26 Early patristic writers were also concerned to establish the Johannine authorship of the gospel; for a summary of arguments see Wiles, *Spiritual Gospel*, pp. 7–10. For a recent analysis of early views of the relationship of the gospel to the Johannine epistles and Revelation that challenges the position that the Gospel of John was considered problematic in the second and third centuries, see Hill, *Johannine Corpus*.

27 *Against Heresies*, in Richardson, *Early Christian Fathers*, pp. 378–379.

28 *On Illustrious Men*, trans. T. P. Halton, Fathers of the Church 100 (Washington: Catholic University of America Press, 1999), p. 19.

29 *Against Heresies*, in Richardson, *Early Christian Fathers*, pp. 379–381.

Father's relationship to the Son. Both Chrysostom and Augustine expanded the scope of the polemic in their comments on John to criticize pagan philosophy.[30]

The idea that John's gospel proclaimed a deeper spiritual truth than the other three and did so in order to refute supposed perversions of heavenly mysteries invited reflection on the relationship of historical and symbolic meanings in the text. Did the deeper spiritual truth of the Fourth Gospel require a more thorough-going spiritual exegesis? Here interpreters' answers appear to depend more on their general hermeneutical orientations than on their perceptions of the gospel itself. As Wiles notes, Origen, "always on the alert to find deeper meaning in the words of Scripture," believes that "many incidents are recorded for doctrinal purpose, and not as a strict historical account."[31] Theodore of Mopsuestia (c. 350–428), in contrast, insists more consistently on the narrative's historical accuracy, and, with Cyril and Chrysostom, sees the purpose of many of the historical details as being to guarantee "the truly divine character of the events" recorded in the gospel.[32] Regardless of their views on the purpose of historical details, however, all interpreters pursued some deeper spiritual exegesis of many passages. For some, the focus was on uncovering doctrinal truths (a more allegorical interpretation), while others stressed the application of the teachings or events to the Christian life (a more moral or tropological interpretation).[33]

Yet for all their differences in the area of interpretive method, early Christian writers agreed on the main purpose and meaning of the Fourth Gospel. Though they approached it via different hermeneutical paths, interpreters held in common that the central theme of the gospel is Christ's divine nature.[34] The Fourth Evangelist supplements the other three by proclaiming this openly and thus refutes current and future heresies concerning Christ's person. It is the delineation of this particular

---

30 Chrysostom, *Commentary on Saint John the Apostle and Evangelist, Homilies 1–47*, trans. Sr. T. A. Goggin, Fathers of the Church 33 (New York: Fathers of the Church, 1957), pp. 14–19; Augustine, *Tractates on the Gospel of John 1–10*, trans. J. W. Rettig, Fathers of the Church 78 (Washington: Catholic University of America Press, 1988), pp. 63–64.

31 Wiles, *Spiritual Gospel*, p. 22.

32 Ibid., 26.

33 For a comparison of the different approaches of Cyril and Theodore, see ibid., pp. 32–40. Genre might also play a role in the interpretation of symbolism; for example, Chrysostom's homilies generally stress the moral ramifications of the passage for his congregation.

34 As Wiles observes, "Thus there is complete agreement [among Origen, Theodore, and Cyril] that the purpose of the Gospel is so to supplement the other Gospels as to place beyond all reasonable doubt the doctrinal truth of Christ's divinity" (*Spiritual Gospel*, pp. 11–12).

doctrinal truth that makes the Gospel of John more spiritual than the rest and justifies for many interpreters its preeminent status. It also means that the Gospel of John is, for many, seen as a more difficult book to interpret. Yet an understanding of the gospel's main purpose, and the proper exegetical tools, unlock the mysteries and reveal that, in the words of Chrysostom, John's "teachings are clearer than sunbeams."[35]

The Gospel of John in the Middle Ages

Medieval interpreters of John embraced the understanding of the gospel's central purpose advanced in early Christian literature.[36] They accepted the familiar iconography of the eagle for John and the traditional reasons why it applied to him, even when they disagreed over whether Mark or Matthew should be the lion or the man.[37] Patristic opinions on these matters had been enshrined in the *Glossa ordinaria*, a continuous commentary on the Bible that had been compiled in the early twelfth century and served as the foundation for biblical study and scholarship for over two centuries.

Thus, given the traditional and conservative aims of most medieval biblical commentary, interpreters consciously report, seek to synthesize, and, very subtly, build on patristic ideas.[38] For example, in the prologue to his commentary on John, Thomas Aquinas (d. 1274) repeats earlier judgments about John writing after the other three and aiming to refute the Ebionites and Cerinthus. He also claims that the special subject matter of John's gospel is Christ's divinity and discusses in detail John's unique heavenly vision. However, he explicates John's contemplation of

---

35 Chrysostom, *Homilies 1–47*, p. 17.

36 See, e.g., M. Hazard, *The Literal Sense and the Gospel of John in Late Medieval Commentary and Literature* (New York and London: Routledge, 2002); J. A. Weisheipl, "The Johannine Commentary of Friar Thomas," *Church History* 45 (1976): 185–195. On the gospels in general, see B. Smalley, *The Gospels in the Schools c. 1100–c. 1280* (London: Hambledon Press, 1985). The most important medieval commentaries on John were the commentary of the eleventh-century Bulgarian archbishop Theophylact, the *Glossa ordinaria* (early twelfth century), the commentary by Hugh of St. Cher (d. 1236), the commentary of Thomas Aquinas (d. 1274) and his collection of authoritative opinions in his *Catena Aurea*, the *Postilla* of Nicholas of Lyra (d. 1340), and the commentary of Denis the Carthusian (1402/3–1471).

37 K. Madigan, *Olivi and the Interpretation of Matthew in the High Middle Ages* (Notre Dame: University of Notre Dame Press, 2003), p. 17.

38 This character of early medieval exegesis of the gospels is discussed in Smalley, *The Gospels in the Schools*. The secular-mendicant controversy of the thirteenth century had a profound impact on the gospel commentaries by Franciscan interpreters, which began to reveal more contemporary concerns and polemics, e.g., in the John commentaries by Franciscans John of Wales and John of Pecham (see Smalley, ibid., p. 276).

the eternal Word in connection with Isaiah's vision in Isaiah 6:1 and, moreover, outlines the gospel's purpose in terms of its four Aristotelian causes.[39] He also explains that John's full, high, and perfect contemplation surpasses that of the moral and natural sciences, since it contains completely what they have only in a divided way. Similarly, Denis the Carthusian (d. 1471), referring explicitly to Augustine and Bede, affirms the preeminence of John's gospel over other scriptures on the grounds that John wrote more fully, clearly, and profoundly about many things and more sublimely about the Savior's teachings. He refers to the eagle iconography and repeats the standard view that John wrote after the others and wrote against Christological heresies. He adds that, because John's material is so sublime, one must be particularly humble and more earnestly appeal to the teaching of the Holy Spirit.[40]

Medieval interpreters of John continued to be sensitive to resolving discrepancies between the Fourth Gospel and Synoptic accounts, and tended to be more interested than most of their patristic forebears in a more systematic delineation of the relationship between historical and symbolic meanings. In this regard they reflected and deepened the variety of hermeneutical approaches to the gospel taken in the patristic period. In general, medieval interpreters continued to assume that the text has two levels of meaning, a literal-historical and a mystical-spiritual. For example, commenting on John 1:23, where John the Baptist characterizes himself as a "voice crying in the wilderness," Thomas claims that the "wilderness" can be understood literally as the place where John the Baptist lived and says that he lived there in order to remain immune from sin and be more worthy to bear witness to Christ. The wilderness itself also refers symbolically to two things: On the one hand, "wilderness" or "desert" can mean paganism, so it signifies that God's Word would be heard among the Gentiles. Alternatively, "wilderness" can mean Judea, or the Jews whom God has deserted.[41] It should be noted that Thomas does

---

39 See Weisheipl, "Johannine Commentary of Friar Thomas," pp. 191–193.

40 *Enarratio in Evangelium secundum Joannem* in vol. XII of *Opera omnia*, 42 vols. in 44 (Monstrolii: S. M. De Pratis, 1901), pp. 267–268.

41 Thomas Aquinas, *Commentum in Matthaeum et Joannem Evangelistas*, vol. x of *Sancti Thomae Aquinatis Doctoris Angelici Ordinis Praedicatorum opera omnia* (Parma: P. Fiaccadori, 1861; rpt. New York: Musurgia Publishers, 1949), pp. 315–316. Theophylact doesn't talk about the wilderness, but does give the views that the one crying may be either John or Christ and that "voice" is appropriate because the voice precedes the word. Thomas says the voice comes after the word conceived in the heart. Note this is a good example of the interpretive principles that Aquinas outlines in the *Summa Theologica,* 1a 1, art. 9 and 10, especially his claim that the parabolic sense is contained within the literal sense: the "voice" is a figure for John, who came to

not always label the different the levels of meaning, as he does in this instance, but throughout the commentary he nevertheless includes both literal and spiritual explanations similar to this one. Medieval commentators on John also reflected the variety of early interpreters in the weight or importance they assigned to these historical and symbolic meanings, but were becoming more explicit about how they related them to one another. For Thomas, the "spiritual sense is based on the literal sense and presupposes it," and "nothing necessary to faith is contained within the spiritual sense which Scripture does not openly convey elsewhere through the literal sense."[42] Hence Thomas supports each of his interpretations of "wilderness" with cross-references to other scriptures that express literally the ideas symbolized in John 1:23.

The trend among some medieval interpreters, Thomas included, toward seeing the literal sense as foundational for spiritual meaning thus did not diminish, but, in a certain sense, heightened, the prestige of the so-called spiritual gospel.[43] There were two reasons for this. In the first place, the greater appreciation of the literal or historical sense did not necessarily mean a rejection or diminishing of the spiritual senses but rather, according to the original program of Hugh of St. Victor (d. 1142), led to a strengthening of allegory by placing it on a firmer footing.[44] Second, in some cases, this resulted in a blurring of the boundaries between the historical-literal and mystical-spiritual levels, with the literal sense being expanded to contain the meanings formerly contained in the spiritual senses. An example of this can be seen in Nicholas of Lyra's (d. 1340) interpretation of the healing pool of Bethesda (John 5). Traditional exegesis followed Chrysostom's explanation that the waters of the pool presented a typological figure of Christian baptism.[45] Thomas, for example, cited this opinion as one of the mystical meanings of the pool and explained the reasons why the Lord chose water to prefigure the grace

make known God's word. But for Thomas that is the literal, not a mystical, meaning. For an English translation of this excerpt from the *Summa*, see A. J. Minnis and A. B. Scott, *Medieval Literary Theory and Criticism, c. 1100–c. 1375: The Commentary Tradition* (Oxford: Clarendon Press, 1988), pp. 239–243. For Calvin's comments on this passage, see n. 65 below.

42 *Summa Theologica*, 1a 1, art. 10, in Minnis and Scott, *Medieval Literary Theory*, pp. 241–242.

43 This trend in the thirteenth century is outlined in C. Spicq, *Esquisse d'une histoire de l'exégèse latine au moyen âge* (Paris: J. Vrin, 1944), esp. pp. 209–215, 273–278; see also B. Smalley, *The Study of the Bible in the Middle Ages*, 3rd edn (Notre Dame: University of Notre Dame Press, 1978).

44 Hazard, *Literal Sense*, p. 5.

45 Chrysostom, *Homilies 1–47*, p. 352. C. Farmer notes that Tertullian also suggested the baptismal symbolism of the passage (*The Gospel of John in the Sixteenth Century: The Johannine Exegesis of Wolfgang Musculus* [New York: Oxford University Press, 1997], p. 217, n. 39).

of baptism in the sacrament. Lyra made no reference to a "mystical" meaning and instead related the theme of baptism more intrinsically to the literal sense of the passage.[46] Indeed, for Lyra, it was precisely the Gospel of John with its more spiritual character that provided the opportunity to work out more clearly an intrinsic link between the levels of meaning.[47] As Hazard observes, "The Gospel of John's theme, that divine word and sign are intimately related, provided Lyra with important scriptural material and allowed him to base this connection [that the spiritual sense was included in the literal] on Gospel history."[48] Paradoxically, then, the spiritual gospel could be construed according to a certain logic as also the most literal gospel, since, as the fullest, most complete, and perfect expression of the words, deed, and person of Christ, it narrates the fulfillment of sacred history toward which all of the rest of Scripture merely points.

Medieval commentary on the Gospel of John furthered the understanding of the gospel's central purpose, its origins, and its author that were products of the early church. By blending these insights together and formalizing them as aids to the study of Scripture, for example in the *Glossa* accompanying the biblical text or in commentaries for use in the new university context, medieval exegetes crafted a rich interpretive tradition, which guided their reading of Scripture. Their approaches to the spiritual gospel thus differed from those of their patristic forebears in two fundamental ways. First, they consciously read through the lenses of tradition, interpreting the Fourth Gospel not just in relation to the other scriptures but in light of authoritative opinions of the fathers. Second, their engagement with the richness of the exegetical past led them to seek more systematic ways to relate these various levels of meaning one to another.

The Gospel of John in the sixteenth century

Enthusiasm for the Gospel of John and appreciation of its unique qualities spilled over into the sixteenth century.[49] Luther (d. 1546) famously asserted that the Gospel of John, Paul's letters (especially Romans), and

---

46 The differences are discussed in detail in Hazard, *Literal Sense*, pp. 68–69.
47 Ibid., pp. 6–7.
48 Ibid., p. 8.
49 On the interpretation of the Gospel of John in the sixteenth century, see especially Farmer, *The Gospel of John*; A. Rabil, Jr., "Erasmus' Paraphrase of the Gospel of John," *Church History* 48 (1979): 142–155; T. J. Wengert, *Philip Melanchthon's Annotationes in Johannem in Relation to its*

1 Peter were the best and noblest books in the New Testament, and that John was the "one, fine, and true gospel . . . far, far to be preferred to the other three and placed high above them."[50] Erasmus (d. 1536), more reserved with regard to preference, nevertheless held that John's "grand theme" was even more majestic than that of Matthew.[51] These attitudes were reflected in a sudden outpouring of new commentaries on the Fourth Gospel beginning in 1522–1523. Up to that time, interpretations of John by four patristic authors and nine medieval commentators or compilers had become available in print. Erasmus' *Annotationes* also appeared beginning in 1516. However from 1522 to the middle of the century, over thirty living writers published exegetical treatments of the Fourth Gospel. In the same period, the appearance of previously unpublished medieval commentaries paled in comparison and the republication of those previously printed slowed considerably.[52]

If this interest in and esteem for the Gospel of John reflected long-standing attitudes, traditional as well was the variety of hermeneutical approaches these works embodied. Craig Farmer has demonstrated the complexity of early modern interpretations of the Fourth Gospel, which cannot be classified according to simplistic confessional stereotypes. Protestant interpreters, for example, did not uniformly reject traditional exegesis, nor did they all eschew allegorical interpretations. Although Martin Bucer (d. 1551) explicitly rejected allegory in his preface to his commentary on the Synoptic Gospels, other Protestants, such as Melanchthon

Predecessors and Contemporaries (Geneva: Librairie Droz, 1987); U. Gäbler, "Bullingers Vorlesung über das Johannesevangelium aus dem Jahre 1523," in *Heinrich Bullinger, 1504–1575: Gesammelte Aufsätze zum 400. Todestag*, ed. U. Gäbler and E. Herkenrath (Zurich: Theologischer Verlag, 1975), pp. 13–27; E. Ellwein, *Summus Evangelista: Die Botschaft des Johannesevangeliums in der Auslegung Luthers* (Munich: Chr. Kaiser Verlag, 1960); I. Backus, "Church, Communion, and Community in Bucer's Commentary on the Gospel of John," in *Martin Bucer: Reforming Church and Community*, ed. D. F. Wright (Cambridge: Cambridge University Press, 1994), pp. 61–71; B. Pitkin, "Seeing and Believing in the Commentaries on John by Martin Bucer and John Calvin," *Church History* 68/4 (December 1999): 865–885; C. Farmer, "Wolfgang Musculus's Commentary on John: Tradition and Innovation in the Story of the Woman Taken in Adultery," in *Biblical Interpretation in the Era of the Reformation*, ed. R. Muller and J. Thompson (Grand Rapids: Eerdmans, 1996), pp. 216–240; C. Farmer, "Changing Images of the Samaritan Woman in Early Reformed Commentaries on John," *Church History* 65/3 (September 1996): 365–375.

50 This in his preface to the German New Testament of 1522; in English in *Martin Luther's Basic Theological Writings*, ed. Timothy Lull (Minneapolis: Augsburg Fortress, 1989), pp. 116–117.

51 In his dedicatory letter prefacing his 1523 *Paraphrasis in Ioannem*; in English in *Paraphrase on the Gospel of John*, trans. and annotated by J. E. Phillips, vol. XLVI of *Collected Works of Erasmus* (Toronto: University of Toronto Press, 1991), p. 2.

52 These figures are taken from Wengert, *Melanchthon's Annotationes*, pp. 20–21; see also the appendix detailing works printed from 1470 to 1555.

(d. 1560), embraced it or, following the trend exemplified in Nicholas of Lyra, crammed formerly mystical-symbolic or tropological meanings into the literal sense.[53]

Despite this continuity with the antecedent traditions of interpretation, there were significant shifts in approach to the Fourth Gospel in the sixteenth century. In the first place, many interpreters embraced humanistic scholarship and employed critical philological tools to a greater and more systematic degree than medieval interpreters had done. More of them could read the Old and New Testaments in the original languages. Less concerned consciously to synthesize the inherited wisdom of the fathers, early modern exegetes frequently shifted the focus of their comments to the Evangelist's own meaning, often uncovered through philological or rhetorical analysis of the text. Thus Erasmus found *sermo* to be a more accurate translation for *logos* in John 1:1 and 1:14 than the Vulgate's *verbum*, though this substitution in his Latin translation of the New Testament and his *Annotationes* aroused heated controversy.[54] Melanchthon expressed the same humanistic spirit in the way he organized and structured his comments on John according to key "common places" or themes suggested by his reading of the text, even though he used the Vulgate as his base text and frequently ignored or distanced himself from the substantive interpretations in Erasmus' *Annotationes*.[55] It is important to note that interest in textual matters and thematic or topical organization in a commentary was not new but was in certain fundamental ways in continuity with previous commentary traditions. At the same time, the development of these methods in humanistic biblical scholarship, and their self-consciously classical basis, signaled a new direction in biblical interpretation, best characterized perhaps as a shift in emphasis.

This new direction was perhaps most evident in the changing role that the exegetical past played in sixteenth-century commentaries on John. As mentioned earlier, the new printing technology made possible the wider dissemination of the works of ancient commentators. Sixteenth-century interpreters could more easily read the entire commentary of Augustine or

---

53 On Bucer and Melanchthon, see ibid., pp. 110–112; on Musculus, who used allegory occasionally but focused primarily on tropological exegesis, see Farmer, *The Gospel of John*, pp. 50–52. The idea of a literal sense "pregnant with spiritual significance" as a feature of sixteenth-century exegesis comes from D. Steinmetz, "Divided by a Common Past: The Reshaping of the Christian Exegetical Tradition in the Sixteenth Century," *The Journal of Medieval and Early Modern Studies* 27 (1997): 245–264.

54 See C. A. L. Joirrot, "Erasmus' *In Principio Erat Sermo*: A Controversial Translation," *Studies in Philology* 61 (1964): 35–40.

55 Wengert, *Melanchthon's Annotationes*, pp. 132–134.

the homilies of Chrysostom rather than encountering their opinions only as "sound-bites" in biblical glosses, in the commentaries of others, or in anthologies of excerpts. To be sure, the exegetical heritage continued to appear in this excerpted fashion; in the *Annotationes*, Erasmus cited traditional interpretations of passages and used these as guides for unlocking the meaning of difficult passages. Interpreters on both sides of the confessional divide expected that the fathers had important insights into the meaning of Scripture and that this wisdom served as a guide to interpretation, as evident in the popularity of editions of patristic commentary. But whereas in their commentaries most medieval biblical interpreters tended to synthesize and harmonize what were considered authoritative interpretations of the sacred text, many sixteenth-century commentators viewed the tradition with a more critical eye, rejecting some ideas as false or simply bypassing them altogether. Even Erasmus noted in his *Paraphrases* that the ancient interpreters had at times distorted the sense of the text "with some force."[56] Caution is warranted at this point, for recent scholarship has demonstrated the enormous complexity of the reception of the fathers in both the Middle Ages and in the sixteenth century. Nevertheless, one clearly senses in reading the commentaries themselves a distinct difference in the way interpreters engage the inherited tradition and view its authority.

The roots of a final difference lie in the most significant religious event of the sixteenth century, namely, the schism that led to the emergence of different Christian confessional churches. As Steinmetz has argued, Protestants and Catholics did not "disagree in predictable ways over the exegesis of biblical texts, aside, of course, from a few texts on which they had principled and irreconcilable disagreements."[57] Farmer has demonstrated this to be true for the interpretation of the Gospel of John. However, although confessional differences did not influence interpretation in ways one might expect, the issue at the root of the divide – that is, divergent soteriologies – shaped the exegesis of the Fourth Gospel in a profound way. In the first commentary on John by a Protestant writer, Melanchthon exhibited a certain reticence toward the trinitarian and Christological dogmas that figured so prominently in patristic and medieval exegesis of John. Although he discussed and agreed with orthodox

56 Erasmus, *Paraphrase*, p. 12.
57 Steinmetz, "Divided by a Common Past," pp. 245–246.

interpreters on these issues, he shifted the focus from Christological or trinitarian problems to soteriological questions.[58]

He thus unwittingly inaugurated a trend that ran counter to the traditional consensus about John's central purpose. In short, by shifting the focus to soteriology, Melanchthon placed into question the traditional view that John wrote primarily to defend Christ's divinity. His commentary thus promoted a new understanding of John's purpose, one expressed in Luther's contemporaneous judgment about the priority of John. For Luther, it was not John's more complete orthodox Christology, but rather his more clear delineation of "how faith in Christ overcomes sin, death, and hell, and gives life, righteousness, and salvation," that made his gospel superior to the other three. Not all interpreters followed this new trend, but one who did and who can be said to represent its culmination was John Calvin.

CALVIN AS COMMENTATOR ON THE GOSPEL OF JOHN

In both method and substance, Calvin's commentary on John engages both ancient and contemporary trends in interpretation. The remainder of this investigation will focus on the ways in which Calvin's approach to the gospel and his exegesis follow these previously forged paths and where they, on occasion, break off in new directions.

Methodological elements

The mixture of traditional, sixteenth-century, and novel elements can be seen in Calvin's stance on the classic questions of the uniqueness and purpose of the Gospel of John and its relationship to Matthew, Mark, and Luke. As we have seen, Calvin's esteem for the Fourth Gospel was by no means unprecedented. Rather, his attitude represented a judgment about the eminence of John's gospel that was, if not universal, undisputedly longstanding. His understanding of the gospel's central purpose, however, followed the more recent trend inaugurated by Luther and Melanchthon. In the "Argument" prefacing the commentary, his definition of the word "gospel" and his delineation of John's uniqueness clearly echo the sentiments expressed in Luther's Preface to the New Testament. Moreover, this same text also reveals the more critical attitude toward traditional

---

58 Wengert, *Melanchthon's Annotationes*, pp. 93, 113.

authorities that emerged in the sixteenth century. Calvin thus acknowledges that the ancients believed that John wrote chiefly to defend the divinity of Christ against Ebion and Cerinthus, but at the same time he downplays the significance of this opinion. Instead, he argues that God foresaw something much more, namely, that when the witness of all four gospels would be gathered into one body, John's account of the purpose for which Christ was manifested would provide the foundation for reading the other three. Drawing Luther's judgment about the clarity of John's expression of the gospel to its logical conclusion, Calvin urges readers of the gospels to learn from John first, thus reversing the dominant traditional assumption that John's deeper, mystical, teaching was more difficult and his subject matter more advanced.[59]

Similar to Luther as well is the fact that Calvin's understanding of the gospel's subject matter – i.e., not the divinity of Christ but how people are saved by Christ – is profoundly shaped by his interpretation of Paul. Whereas John, for Calvin, provides the key to understanding Matthew, Mark, and Luke, Paul's letter to the Romans unlocks the meaning of the whole of Scripture.[60] This conviction can be seen initially in his appeal to two Pauline passages (Rom. 1:16 and 2 Cor. 5:18–20) to define "gospel" in the "Argument." It also manifests itself throughout the commentary proper as Calvin uses statements or ideas derived from Paul in order to clarify John's meaning or rule out possible misreadings of a passage. One of the most prominent examples of this can be seen in his treatment of the topic of faith. The Gospel of John presents Calvin with a more nuanced portrait of faith and coming to faith than do the Pauline epistles; specifically, it offers a "broader conception of the levels, stages, or types of faith and [a more] complex picture of the role of miracles, signs and external sense perception in arriving at faith."[61] In his comments on passages about faith, Calvin emphasizes that faith ultimately comes from hearing, that it does not rest on carnal sight, and that it is certain knowledge of Jesus as the Christ – all perspectives that reflect his reading of Paul. While giving credit to the development and stages of faith, Calvin nevertheless

---

59 This traditional view is expressed with consummate clarity by Erasmus in the Dedicatory Letter to his *Paraphrase on the Gospel of John*: "No Gospel has given rise to more numerous or more difficult problems concerning the faith, none has been the object of more intense efforts by the greatest intellects of antiquity, none has seen greater disagreement among its interpreters, and this I ascribe not to their stupidity or lack of experience, but either to the obscurity of the language or to the difficulty of the subject-matter" (*Paraphrase*, p. 3).

60 *Comm. Rom.*, Dedicatory Epistle and *Argumentum* (*OE* xiii:4 = *CO* Xb:403 and *OE* xiii:7 = *CO* ii:1; *Comm. Rom.* [CTS xix:xxiv, xxix]).

61 Pitkin, *What Pure Eyes Could See*, p. 95.

harmonizes the Evangelist's meaning with what he takes to be Paul's view. For example, Calvin argues in his comments on John 20 that Thomas does not come to believe merely because he sees, but rather because he remembers "the doctrine that he had nearly forgotten." He continues:

Faith cannot flow from a mere experience of things but must draw its origin from the word of God. Christ therefore rebukes Thomas for rendering less honor to his word than he ought, and for binding faith, which is born from hearing and ought to be completely intent on the word, to the other senses.[62]

Other interpreters are not as concerned as Calvin to identify the ground of Thomas' faith in the word that he had earlier heard or to criticize so sharply his desire to see and touch Jesus' wounds. Many refer to Hebrews 11:1 to stress that the object of faith is unseen, but Calvin alone among the commentators I consulted supplements this commonplace with a reference to a genuinely Pauline passage (2 Cor. 5:7) and, importantly, with a specific mention of the fact that faith depends on the "mouth of God."[63] His attention to these matters offers a particularly striking example of how Paul's perspective, to his mind most fully expressed in Romans, functions for him as the hermeneutical key to the whole of Scripture.

Calvin's treatment of this same incident also provides an example of another hallmark of his exegesis in general and of John in particular, namely, an interest in the moral implications of the narratives for the believers of his day. As in his other commentaries, Calvin focuses primarily on explicating the narrative sense of the text, deviating from this only to offer observations that apply the lessons of the narrative to his contemporaries and their situation. These together make up the literal sense of Scripture for Calvin, which includes both the history or events narrated by the biblical author as well as the spiritual or moral lessons that he, writing under the guidance of the Holy Spirit, sought to inculcate. In a commentary Calvin goes into less detail about how these apply to later generations of the faithful than he does in a sermon.[64] Nevertheless, his

---

62 *OE* XI/2:301 = *CO* XLVII:445; *Comm. John* 20:29 (CTS XVIII:278).

63 *OE* XI/2:302 = *CO* XLVII:445; *Comm. John* 20:29 (CTS XVIII:279).

64 For more detailed discussions about the different emphases in sermons and commentary on the same biblical texts, see M. Engammare, "Le Paradis à Genève: Comment Calvin prêchait-il la chute aux Genevois?" *Études Théologiques et Religieuses* 69 (1994): 329–347; J. Thompson, *Writing the Wrongs: Women of the Old Testament Among Biblical Commentators from Philo through the Reformation* (New York: Oxford University Press, 2001), pp. 86–87; W. de Greef, "Das Verhältnis von Predigt und Kommentar bei Calvin, dargestellet am Deuteronomium-Kommentar und den -Predigten," in *Calvinus Servus Christi*, ed. W. H. Neuser (Budapest: Presseabteilung des Ráday-Kollegiums, 1998), pp. 195–203.

concern with what earlier interpreters designated the tropological sense is evident throughout his exposition of John, even when he views this meaning as not distinct from but an inherent part of the literal meaning.[65]

The figure of Thomas has been subject to a perhaps surprising variety of readings in the Christian exegetical tradition. Rampant diversity characterizes the explanations of the reasons for his absence, the nature of his doubts, whether it was seeing Jesus or touching him that gave rise to his confession, and the overall significance of his story. Common to all interpreters, however, is the conviction – derived largely from John 20:29–31 – that the incident has broader significance and not only was recorded but also actually happened for the benefit of later generations of believers. Some, like Chrysostom, see this in the moral lesson to turn from earthly temptations and vices and fix our eyes on future glory. Others, like Rupert of Deutz (d. *c.* 1130), find a more allegorical meaning: Thomas represents the Jewish people, who did not believe initially but who, in the fullness of time ("after eight days," John 20:26) will believe with the Gentiles. Similarly, the assessments of Thomas' character prior to the encounter with Jesus range from Chrysostom's judgment, that he was obstinate because he scrutinized everything and blameworthy because he considered what the others told him about seeing the Lord to be impossible, to Cyril's more charitable suggestion that "wise Thomas" did not so much discredit what was told to him but rather was distracted by grief that he might not also see the Risen Lord.[66]

---

65 See B. Pitkin, "John Calvin and the Interpretation of the Bible," in *A History of Biblical Interpretation*, ed. A. J. Hauser and D. F. Watson, vol. II (Grand Rapids: Eerdmans, forthcoming). Note that Calvin occasionally acknowledges a figurative meaning, but that even this is tied to (or even stuffed into) this enriched literal-historical sense. For example, in his treatment of the word "wilderness" at John 1:23, Calvin first discusses Isaiah's original meaning, then the sense in which John refers the passage from *Isa.* 40:3 to himself. His main concern is not to lay bare hidden meanings but rather to show that John has not "tortured" the words the prophet spoke concerning a past situation by applying them to his own day. Isaiah, says Calvin, spoke figuratively of the desolation of the church of his own day when he designated it a "wilderness." But inasmuch as the visible wilderness in which John was preaching was "a symbol or an image" of the terrible destitution that took away the hope of liberation (presumably in the world before Christ's advent), the comparison to Isaiah's figurative wilderness is not forced; in fact, God arranged it such that the people would have before their eyes (i.e., in the visible wilderness in which John preached) a mirror of Isaiah's prophetic proclamation (*OE* XI/1:42 = *CO* XLVII:22; *Comm. John* 1:23 [CTS XVII:59]).

66 Chrysostom, *Commentary on Saint John the Apostle and Evangelist: Homilies 48–88*, trans. Sr. T. A. Goggin, Fathers of the Church 41 (New York: Fathers of the Church, 1960), pp. 458–469; Rupert of Deutz, *Commentaria in Evangelium Sancti Iohannis*, ed. R. Haacke, Corpus Christianorum Continuatio Mediaevalis 9 (Turnholt: Brepols, 1969), p. 775; Cyril of Alexandria, *Commentary on the Gospel according to S. John*, 2 vols. (Oxford: James Parker & Co., 1874), II:681.

Calvin follows both Chrysostom's characterization of Thomas as obstinate and his interest in drawing moral lessons from his story. However, he counters against Chrysostom that it is in fact Thomas' slowness and reluctance to believe (and not his scrutiny) that are blameworthy. Moreover, where Chrysostom would have us learn from Thomas to aim for higher things, Calvin articulates in his opening comments on the episode a more negative lesson: "Besides, the obstinacy of Thomas is an example to show us that this wickedness is entirely natural to all, to retard themselves of their own accord, when the entrance to faith is opened up."[67] Thus, in his comments on verses 27–28 Calvin digresses to explain that all believers are like Thomas, obstinate and contemptuous of God's Word until faith – not extinguished but suffocated – suddenly recalls them to their senses. The same thing, he claims, happens to many people now and then. Thomas' example teaches them that they must be on their guard against these errors, but also that ultimately all the elect are protected by God's "secret bridle" by which he "always cherishes miraculously in their hearts some sparks of faith."[68]

Similar sorts of moral digressions run throughout Calvin's commentary on the Fourth Gospel, signaled usually by some phrase such as "this example warns us," or "let us learn from this." Thus, for him the important spiritual and moral truths of the Fourth Gospel are not conveyed in a hidden, mystical, way, but are to be sought through careful attention to the narrative story line. In this regard he stands in continuity with the medieval traditions that laid emphasis on the foundational character of the literal sense and, eventually, blurred the distinctions between the levels of meaning. However, the contemporary significance that Calvin finds in the narrative as often as not diverges from the traditional mystical meanings. For example, in his discussion of the healing at the pool of Bethesda (John 5), Calvin does not mention baptism at all. Departing from the dominant tradition still shaping the interpretations of some sixteenth-century contemporaries,[69] he sees the healing pool first as a sign of God's presence for the Jews of Jesus' day, to foster obedience to the law and inspire hope for the approaching time of redemption. The contemporary significance of the incident is found not

---

67 *OE* xi/2:298 = *CO* xlvii:442; *Comm. John* 20:29 (CTS xviii:274), but note there a different translation of *fere* than I have adopted.

68 *OE* xi/2:300 = *CO* xlvii:444; *Comm. John* 20:29 (CTS xviii:276–277).

69 Farmer, *The Gospel of John*, pp. 117–118. The baptismal symbolism is also mentioned by Melanchthon, but not by Bucer.

in the pool as a type or symbol but in the way Christ forgives the weakness of the diseased man, who limits God's assistance to the capacity of his own mind as, Calvin remarks, "nearly all of us are wont to do."[70]

One further way in which Calvin links the gospel to his own day can be seen in the occasional polemical comments that emerge in his commentary. Given his understanding of the task of biblical commentary to be the lucid and brief exposition of the mind of the writer, Calvin does not wish to make polemic directed at the contemporary situation a central feature of his exposition. However, where he senses alternative explanations of a passage might challenge his own, he addresses them briefly. Thus, for example, at the end of his discussion of the incident with Thomas, he criticizes an alleged papal use of John 20:29 to prove the doctrine of transubstantiation.[71] In his comments on John 1:14, he dismisses in one sentence Servetus and the Anabaptists for supposedly confusing Christ's divine and human natures.[72] By far the vast majority of these polemical asides aim at Roman theology and practice, thereby making good on Calvin's promise in the dedicatory epistle, that this commentary would prove the "satanic" origins of papal religion. In particular, Calvin redirects the gospel's criticism of Jewish opponents of Jesus to the Pope and Roman Catholic practices.[73] Yet here he is neither more nor less polemical than in his other commentaries.

Calvin's criticisms frequently take the form of complaints that those who are the object of his polemic – usually not identified by name – have misread a particular passage of the gospel or drawn inappropriate conclusions from it. Significantly, Calvin does not restrict this charge to his confessional adversaries. Rather, even the interpretations of those whose orthodoxy he acknowledges are occasionally found wanting. For example, Calvin begins his comments on John 3:5, "no one can enter the kingdom of God without being born of water and Spirit," by noting that the passage has been explained in various ways. Some refer water and Spirit to the two parts of regeneration (renunciation of the old man and new life). Others think Christ makes an allegorical contrast between earthly human nature and the purer elements of water and Spirit in order to urge humans to lay aside the mass of the flesh and become more like water and

---

70 *OE* xi/1:155 = *CO* xlvii:107; *Comm. John* 5:7 (CTS xvii:189–190).
71 *OE* xi/2:302–303 = *CO* xlvii:446; *Comm. John* 20:29 (CTS xviii:280).
72 *OE* xi/1:31 = *CO* xlvii:14; *Comm. John* 1:14 (CTS xvii:46).
73 See the fuller discussion of this point in the Introduction to the *OE* edition, *OE* xi/1:xxvii–xxix.

air. Chrysostom (the only interpreter identified by name) refers the water to baptism. According to the notes by Feld, these interpretations can be found in the explanations of this verse by Brenz, Bullinger, and Bucer.[74] Calvin, however, rejects them all as valid or appropriate explanations of what Christ means here. Instead, he argues, Nicodemus labors under the mistaken idea that departed souls enter into other bodies, and, to correct this, Jesus uses "water" as a metaphor for Spirit to say "simply" that spiritual purification and invigoration are necessary for newness of life.[75] Sometimes explicitly and other times implicitly, Calvin thus corrects readings and conclusions he judges to be false when they deviate, in his view, from the sense of the passage and the meaning of the author.

A final aspect of Calvin's approach to the Fourth Gospel thus concerns the role of exegetical tradition in his commentary. As I have already noted, a complete analysis of Calvin's engagement with previous and contemporary commentators in his commentary on John lies beyond the scope of this chapter. And yet this one example from John 3:5 illustrates several features of Calvin's general approach to the exegetical traditions he knows. First, he usually summarizes opinions in a general way and often reports them anonymously. Second, even when he agrees with the view they put forth, such as in the case of the first opinion above that there are two parts to regeneration, he rejects them as valid explanations when they, in his view, do not represent what Christ or the Evangelist means in a particular passage. Finally, Calvin often reports insights from the tradition, even when he disagrees with other aspects of it, without indicating their origin. In this example, his suggestion that Nicodemus believed in the transmigration of souls links Nicodemus to those who in John 1:21 asked John the Baptist if he was Elijah. Calvin's comments on that verse echo an idea found in Thomas Aquinas and Bucer that this idea was current in Jesus' day and accounts for the question put to John.[76]

This general picture culled from Calvin's engagement with the exegetical traditions of the church in his commentary on John confirms that drawn from his other exegetical writings. Steinmetz, for example, concludes from Calvin's exegesis of Romans 8:1–11 that one must attend both to Calvin's explicit as well as his anonymous attributions to patristic writers in order to begin to grasp the role of the fathers in his

---

74 *OE* xi/1:87–88, nn. 13, 14, and 15. Cf. also Melanchthon, *Annotationes, CR* xiv:1080.

75 *OE* xi/1:88–89 = *CO* xlvii:56; *Comm. John* 3:5 (CTS xvii:110–111).

76 *OE* xi/1:40 = *CO* xlvii:21; *Comm. John* 1:21 (CTS xvii:57).

interpretations.[77] The same holds true, as we have seen, for his references to more recent interpreters. In most cases, Calvin refers to the opinions of others only when he disagrees with or wishes to qualify them. Thus, as van Oort has argued, his appeal to the fathers in his commentaries – in contrast to the *Institutes*, for example – is non-polemical in the sense that he does not use them as star witnesses to support or advance his own interpretations.[78] That is certainly true in cases such as that considered, where Calvin identifies different lines of interpretation, all of which he rejects. More subtle, however, are the instances where Calvin incorporates into the explanation of his own view common bits of traditional information – "exegetical lore" – without designating it as such.[79] There Calvin identifies with traditional readings but, importantly, does not refer to the weight of their authority to lend credence to his own reading. He lays out his interpretation in conversation with past and present interpreters, who function not as authorities whose various opinions need to be reconciled but, rather, as exegetical guides who sometimes lead down false paths. This more critical attitude toward the fathers and other interpreters is representative of the new spirit of early modern biblical interpretation that also animates his understanding of the special character of John and his interpretive strategies. More importantly, it allows Calvin to make a distinction that is crucial for his explanation of the substance of the Fourth Gospel.

Substantive aspects of Calvin's interpretation of the Gospel of John

Since Feld has provided an overview of several of the most important theological themes in Calvin's commentary of John, I shall limit this discussion to two areas not addressed in his introduction: most significantly, Calvin's engagement with the Christological implications of the gospel and, in somewhat less detail, the topic of faith in his commentary. Not only are these two topics ones to which the theological contribution of the Fourth Gospel has been enormously significant; they are also, to my mind, the two areas where the distinctiveness of Calvin's interpretation of John vis-à-vis the exegetical tradition becomes most apparent.

---

77 Steinmetz, *Calvin in Context*, pp. 135–136.
78 J. van Oort, "John Calvin and the Church Fathers," in *The Reception of the Church Fathers in the West: From the Carolingians to the Maurists*, ed. I. Backus, 2 vols. (Leiden: E. J. Brill, 1997), II:698; cf. pp. 671, 677.
79 The phrase "exegetical lore" is from Steinmetz, who has rightly pointed to this subtle corporate feature of Calvin's exegesis; see *Calvin in Context*, pp. 73, 210.

Already I have mentioned several times that Calvin does not hold to the traditional view that the central purpose of the Gospel of John was to describe and defend Christ's divinity. One of the most significant aspects of Calvin's commentary on John is how he responds to this traditional theme. Other interpreters who shared the newer orientation, such as Melanchthon and Bucer, merely pass over in silence earlier discussions of this topic in their comments on some of the passages traditionally used to promote or delineate Christ's divine nature. Calvin, in contrast, explicitly rejects these traditional interpretations and, moreover, criticizes the exegesis of those who had proffered them.[80] For example, in his comments on John 6:27, "for it is on him that God the Father has set his seal," Calvin complains:

> The ancient writers have wrongly twisted this [passage] toward Christ's divine essence, as if he is said to be sealed, because he is the imprint and express image of the Father. For he was not speaking plainly here about his eternal essence but [explaining] what he has been commissioned and enjoined to do, what is his office toward us, and what we ought to seek and hope from him.[81]

He voices similar criticisms in his comments on John 5:30; 8:24; 10:30; 14:10–11; 16:15; and 17:21. In his comments on John 5:26; 6:57; 10:38; and 17:1, he does not explicitly criticize earlier interpreters, but nevertheless cautions his readers that the passage does not apply to Christ's divine essence alone. His judgment that the need to combat heresy had led earlier interpreters of the Fourth Gospel to distort the sense of certain passages was not without precedent.[82] But Calvin alone is concerned to point out these failings consistently throughout his commentary.

Before considering why Calvin might have voiced these concerns, it is important to note that he does not think that traditional appeals to verses in John to prove or defend Christ's divine nature were completely off-base. In fact, he begins his commentary by noting that in John 1:1 the Evangelist "asserts the eternal divinity of Christ," and Calvin himself finds this teaching sufficient to refute the calumny of Servetus and the Arians.[83] Similarly, in his comments on John 1:14, ("and the Speech (*sermo*) was made flesh,") he succinctly explains the two-natures doctrine as defined at

80 D. Steinmetz, "The Judaizing Calvin," in *Die Patristik in der Bibelexegese des 16. Jahrhunderts*, ed. D. Steinmetz (Wiesbaden: Harrassowitz Verlag, 1999), p. 142.
81 *OE* XI/1:198 = *CO* XLVII:140; *Comm. John* 6:27 (CTS XVII:242), but note there a different translation of *subtiliter* than I have adopted.
82 Erasmus, *Paraphrase*, p. 12.
83 *OE* XI/1:11–12 = *CO* XLVII:1; *Comm. John* 1:1 (CTS XVII:25–26). See also the *congrégation* on John 1 (*CO* XLVII:469–480; in English, *The Deity of Christ*, pp. 18–30).

Chalcedon and shows how these words of the Evangelist – which are brief but lucid – fittingly refute the "blasphemies" of Nestorius, on the one hand, and Eutyches, Servetus, and the Anabaptists, on the other.[84] Indeed, Calvin views at least part of Christ's message and mission to be to demonstrate his divine origin and nature, even when these cannot be fully grasped until after his resurrection and ascension. For example, he remarks that in the miracle at Cana (John 2:1–11) Christ gave the first proof (*specimen*) of his divinity; that the object of Christ's discourse in John 8:12–19 is to show that all he does and teaches ought to be accounted divine; and that Christ's declaration ["I know whom I have chosen"] (John 13:18), which Calvin understands in terms of eternal election, is a clear testimony to his divinity.[85] The culmination of these scattered observations comes in Calvin's comments on Thomas' confession in John 20:28. He links the two parts of Thomas' cry, [My Lord and my God!] to two stages in knowing Christ. When Thomas calls him [Lord,] he acknowledges Christ as incarnate mediator, but, [having acknowledged him to be Lord, [he] is immediately and justly carried upwards to his eternal divinity."[86] Calvin concludes his comments by remarking that this ["passage is abundantly sufficient for refuting the madness of Arius"] and that it declares [the unity of person in Christ."[87] Clearly the traditional use of passages to infer Christ's divinity was not, for Calvin, entirely without merit. However, he explicitly restricts the number of passages that he thinks can be legitimately interpreted in this way.

The reason for this becomes clearer when one considers what Calvin substitutes in place of the traditional inferences of Christ's divinity. The comments on John 6:27 ("For it is on [the Son of Man] whom the Father has set his seal") are typical in this regard. There Calvin argues that Christ does not refer to his eternal essence but rather to his "office"; in other

---

84 *OE* xi/1:29–31 = *CO* xlvii:13–14; *Comm. John* 1:14 (CTS xvii:44–46). Note that Calvin's designation of the Evangelist's *perspicua . . . brevitas* echoes his own ideal for biblical commentary.

85 *OE* xi/1:69 = *CO* xlvii:41; *Comm. John* 2:11 (CTS xvii:89); *OE* xi/1:268 = *CO* xlvii:194; *Comm. John* 8:16 (CTS xvii:328); *OE* xi/2:122 = *CO* xlvii:311; *Comm. John* 13:18 (CTS xviii:64–65). See also his comments on John 7:29, where he remarks that some (i.e., Augustine) refer "I am from him" to Christ's eternal essence and "he has sent me" to Christ's office; Calvin says he does not reject this view, although he does not know if Christ meant to speak so abstrusely, and, moreover, that this would not be a sufficiently strong proof of his eternal divinity against the Arians (*OE* xi/1:245 = *CO* xlvii:176; *Comm. John* 7:29 [CTS xvii:300]). For Augustine, see Tractate 31 [on John 7:35–36], section 4 (*Tractates on John 28–54*, pp. 32–33).

86 *OE* xi/2:300 = *CO* xlvii:444; *Comm. John* 20:28 (CTS xviii:277).

87 *OE* xi/2:301 = *CO* xlvii:444; *Comm. John* 20:28 (CTS xviii:278).

places Calvin says that Christ does not refer to his "simple divinity" but rather to himself insofar as he was manifested in the flesh. One might say that, for Calvin, the great Christological theme of the Fourth Gospel is not Christ's divinity, but Christ incarnate. Thus traditional views holding that John focused on Christ's divinity while the other Evangelists focused on his humanity underestimate, to Calvin's mind, the fact that it is the "Word made flesh" that is preeminent in John's account. Although believers will, like Thomas, be carried upwards to confess Christ as God, in order for this to happen, faith must begin "with that knowledge that is nearer and more easily acquired."[88] Otherwise they will find themselves like the disciples crossing by boat to Capernaum in John 6:19, filled with terror at the "simple demonstration of his divinity" until Christ calms them by his word.[89]

Thus although Christ's divinity is still a theme for Calvin, this topic cannot be said to constitute the Fourth Gospel's central purpose. Rather, the traditional theme is subordinated to – or perhaps better, included within – the larger, overarching, theme of human salvation. We recall from the "Argument" that the distinguishing feature of John's writing, according to Calvin, was to exhibit more clearly than the other gospels the *purpose* for which Christ was manifested. It is not its deeper grasp of Christ's person that distinguishes John from the other gospels, but rather its more complete portrayal of the "doctrine by which the office of Christ, together with the power of his death and resurrection, is unfolded."[90] This means that the Evangelist's task was not in the first place to describe and defend Christ's divinity but rather to describe and defend how human beings come to full knowledge of Christ as incarnate mediator *and* as eternal Son. As I have suggested, this understanding follows a sixteenth-century interpretive trend; at the same time, Calvin's more explicit rejection of traditional Christological exegesis marks a more definitive development, even a culmination, of this shift in the understanding of the Fourth Gospel's central purpose.

One consequence of this shift of focus can be seen in the way he deals with the theme of Christ's humanity in his commentary. Again, this theme was not new; even interpreters who found the main purpose of John to be to describe and defend Christ's divinity also addressed Christ's human nature, and, ultimately, became more precise in delineating the

---

88 *OE* xi/2:301 = *CO* xlvii:444; *Comm. John* 20:28 (CTS xviii:277).
89 *OE* xi/1:194 [there verse 20] = *CO* xlvii:136; *Comm. John* 1:19 (CTS xvii:236–237).
90 *OE* xi/1:8 = *CO* xlvii:vii; *Comm. John Argumentum* (CTS xvii:21).

relationship between the two. Yet most would likely share Thomas Aquinas' judgment that the other Evangelists treat principally the mysteries of Christ's humanity, while John, without ignoring these, "especially and above all, makes known the divinity of Christ in his Gospel."[91] A slightly different emphasis can be found in Chrysostom, who claims that in his portrayal of Jesus' tears at the tomb of Lazarus, John actually stresses more than the other Evangelists Christ's humanity in his earthly ministry. However, he relates this, says Chrysostom, to make up for the fact the he does not portray Christ's agony on the cross in such humble detail as do the other gospel writers.[92] This view shares with the dominant perspective the assumption that what is most important in passages in which Jesus appears to be ignorant, in which he prays to the Father, and in which he displays human emotions is how they demonstrate that Christ is fully human. For Calvin, however, the demonstration of Christ's true humanity is not necessarily the main point of these passages. This is in part because, in contrast to interpreters of the fourth and fifth centuries, he can simply assume the orthodox interpretation of Christ's two natures. Beyond this, however, his stress on the "office of Christ" more than his person leads him to draw from these passages about Christ's humanity distinctive lessons concerning human nature in general.[93]

The clearest instance of this can be found in Calvin's comments on Jesus' response to the death of Lazarus in John 11:33–35. Most interpreters held that by his display of emotion Jesus proved his truly human nature, even as they disagreed over the reasons why he was so troubled and offered various explanations of the exemplary purpose of his tears.[94] Although early commentators did not treat these latter themes as the main point of the passage, in exploring them, some of them forged a connection between Jesus' humanity and human nature in general, which, as we will see, is prominent in Calvin's interpretation of the passage. For example, Cyril of Alexandria argues that the inclination to tears arises from Jesus'

---

91 Thomas Aquinas, *Comm. Joan.*, p. 280.

92 See Wiles, *Spiritual Gospel*, p. 12. Wiles refers to Chrysostom's Homily 63:2; see *Homilies 48–88*, p. 182.

93 See also B. Pitkin, "The Spiritual Gospel? Christ and Human Nature in Calvin's Commentary on John," in *The Formation of Clerical and Confessional Identities in Early Modern Europe*, ed. W. Janse and B. Pitkin, *Dutch Review of Church History* 85 (2005) (Leiden: E. J. Brill, 2006), pp. 187–204. The following discussion appears in a different context there.

94 Erasmus held to this traditional view in his *Paraphrase on the Gospel of John* (pp. 144–145), and Farmer notes that this "exegetical commonplace" was also expressed by Zwingli, Oecolampadius, and Bullinger (*The Gospel of John*, pp. 163–164). The notes to this passage in Erasmus' *Paraphrase* convey some of the variety of earlier exegetical discussions; see also Wiles, *Spiritual Gospel*, pp. 146–147.

"holy flesh," which in this struggle is reproved by the Holy Spirit. The subjection of Christ's own natural human infirmities to "such feelings only as are pleasing to God" marks a victory and transformation that can be extended to all humans.[95] In the sixteenth century, some interpreters began to argue even more explicitly that the purpose of Jesus' tears was more than a demonstration of his humanity. As Farmer has shown, commentators such as Bullinger, Bucer, and Musculus focus on Jesus' emotion as an example of the character and limits of proper Christian commiseration and grief.[96]

Building on this interest, Calvin seems to take all of this a step further, touching only implicitly on the point of proving Christ's true humanity in his exposition of the passage. Rather, he begins by picking up earlier arguments that Christ's tears give proof of his genuine sympathy with the mourners and sorrow over the whole human condition. He then addresses a traditional concern over how Christ, as the divine Son of God, could be subject to human passions, qualifying a notion he attributes to Augustine (also promulgated in Erasmus) that Christ "brought groaning and grief upon himself by his own accord," that is, at appropriate times by an act of will. Instead, Calvin argues, by virtue of the incarnation, Christ was from the very beginning subject to human infirmities and feelings, sin only excepted. The point of all this is that believers may know that they "have a Mediator, who willingly pardons [their] infirmities, and who is ready to assist those infirmities which he has experienced himself."[97]

At this juncture we see emerging Calvin's focus on what Christ does for humans rather than who he is. His next set of comments leads him to make an important point about the latter; however, this leads him immediately to an extended discussion not of Christ's humanity but rather of human nature itself. Positing an objection that human passions are always sinful, Calvin responds by making an important distinction: "for our affections are sinful (*vitiosi*) because they rush on without restraint, and suffer no limit, but in Christ the affections were adjusted and regulated in obedience to God, and were altogether free from sin."[98]

95 "Surely it is an infirmity of human nature to be abjectly overcome by griefs, but this as well as the rest is brought into subjection, in Christ first, that it may be also in us" (Cyril, *S. John*, II:122; cf. discussion in Wiles, *Spiritual Gospel*, pp. 146–147).

96 Farmer, *The Gospel of John*, pp. 163–167.

97 *OE* XI/2:63 = *CO* XLVII:265; *Comm. John* 11:33 (CTS XVIII:440). The view of Augustine is found in Tractate 49 [on John 11:1–54], section 18, in *Tractates on John 28–54*, pp. 252–253; cf. Erasmus, *Paraphrase*, p. 144. Musculus also alludes to Heb. 4:15 in his comments on the passage (Farmer, *The Gospel of John*, p. 166).

98 *OE* XI/2:63 = *CO* XLVII:265; *Comm. John* 11:33 (CTS XVIII:440).

Human feelings are sinful when they are not regulated by true modesty and when they arise from improper motives. To clarify, Calvin adds that this is the condition of fallen human nature; at the creation, he explains, God implanted affections in the first humans that were obedient and submissive to reason. He does not mention the idea of a Second Adam, but that Pauline notion clearly underlies his argument that it was in this orderly way that Christ experienced human affections: ("Christ was indeed troubled and vehemently agitated, but in such a way as to keep himself in subjection to the will of the Father."[99]) In closing, Calvin echoes a rejection of "the unbending sternness of the Stoics" found also in Bucer and Musculus (but without linking this to Anabaptism, as they do).[100] Rather, he urges his readers to follow Christ as their leader in reining in the passions, ("for even Christ took our affections into himself, so that by his power we may subdue everything in them that is sinful."[101]) Thus the point of the passage, for Calvin, becomes the restoration of human nature. While this conclusion bears similarities to that of Cyril cited earlier, there is an important difference: Cyril focused on a conflict within Christ himself, who extends his victory to others. Calvin, rather, shifts the conflict to human beings, who by the power of Christ dwelling in them are conformed to him and restored to original perfection.

With the mention of the theme of the indwelling of Christ's power we come to the second grand theme in Calvin's commentary on John: faith. Earlier I touched upon Calvin's treatment of this topic in John 20 in order to illustrate the "Pauline lenses" Calvin brings to his interpretation of the Fourth Gospel; to provide an example of his interest in the moral implications of the text; and to clarify how Calvin circumscribes the place that the proofs of Christ's divinity play in the narrative. Since belief and believing are major themes in the gospel in particular, one would expect that faith would naturally be a point of focus in any commentary. Thus, what is distinctive about Calvin's commentary is not its attention to the topic per se, but rather the way in which his concern to delineate the proper character of faith dominates his discussion from beginning to end. Because of this, selecting one or two passages as typical illustrations of his approach is impossible. Instead, I will proceed topically, considering first Calvin's views on how one comes to faith and, second, aspects of faith's character.

---

99 *OE* XI/2:64 = *CO* XLVII:266; *Comm. John* 11:33 (CTS XVIII:441).
100 Farmer, *The Gospel of John*, pp. 165, 167.
101 *OE* XI/2:64 = *CO* XLVII:266; *Comm. John* 11:33 (CTS XVIII:441–442).

Beginning at the end of the first chapter, the Gospel of John presents Calvin with a series of portraits, some more detailed than others, of various persons or groups following or coming to faith in Christ. The first come at the recommendation of John the Baptist (John 1:38); the next in response to Jesus' own command or at the invitation of those called by him (John 1:40–46; 4:39). Some believe in him because of the signs he performs (John 2:23; 7:31; 8:30; 10:42; 11:45); others, like Nathanael (John 1:48) and the Samaritan woman (4:29), because of his penetrating insight. But according to Calvin's Pauline assumptions, faith proper rests on the Word and consists in knowledge of Jesus as the Christ, the Redeemer. Thus throughout the entire commentary, Calvin under-scores that true faith always rests on the Word, as we saw, for example, in his claim that Thomas believed because of the doctrine that he recalled. To this end, Calvin qualifies the Evangelist's use of the word "believe" in cases in which he finds that sufficient grounding in the Word is lacking. For example, he says that in John 4:39, the Evangelist improperly (*improprie*) uses the word "believe" to describe the response of the Samaritans to the initial testimony of the woman whom Jesus met at the well. The Samaritans did not come to full faith in Christ, but only had a beginning of faith, acknowledging him to be a prophet. It is only when they hear Jesus himself (John 4: 41–42) that they believe in him on account of his word and know that he is the Christ. "The word 'believe,'" Calvin remarks, "is now used in a different sense, for it means not only that they were prepared for faith, but that they were imbued with a proper faith (*recta fide*)."[102] Similarly, Calvin argues that, despite the Evangelist's apparent claim to the contrary, people do not truly believe because of Jesus' miracles or signs. Discussing passages such as John 2:11; 2:23; 4:53; 7:31; and 11:45, Calvin stresses that true faith embraces Christ's word and does not rest on his miracles. His view that miracles serve to prepare for faith or confirm already existent faith echoes a traditional definition.[103] But other exegetes are not as concerned as Calvin to point out that the Evangelist's choice of terminology is not quite correct or to caution against assuming too great a continuity between the preparatory stages of faith and full faith in Christ.[104]

---

102 *OE* xi/1:143 = *CO* xlvii:98; *Comm. John* 4:41 (CTS xvii:176–177). For discussion of other examples, see Pitkin, *What Pure Eyes Could See*, pp. 90–95.

103 *OE* xi/2:70 = *CO* xlvii:271; *Comm. John* 11:45 (CTS xvii:448).

104 See Pitkin, "Seeing and Believing."

Another significant feature of the view of coming to faith in Calvin's commentary can be seen in his portrayals of the different people in the gospel who, through an encounter with Christ, either believe in him or, in some cases, draw false ideas about his identity and purpose. When viewed in light of the exegetical tradition, what is most striking about Calvin's discussion of such figures as Nicodemus, the Samaritan woman, Martha, and the disciples in general, is his critical and frequently negative depiction of their character and the quality of their faith. To lift up again the example of Thomas, Calvin argues that he was slow and reluctant to believe – even obstinate, proud, and contemptuous in shamelessly reaching forth his hand to touch Christ's wounds. He compares his abrupt turn around to the way that mentally deranged persons suddenly come to themselves. Similarly, Calvin characterizes Nicodemus in John 3 as proud, ignorant, haughty, and, ultimately, ridiculous; he is loath to admit that Nicodemus has made a whit of progress when he appears before the Pharisees in John 7:50. Only Cyril of Alexandria had approached this level of harshness; most interpreters in contrast saw Nicodemus' weak or imperfect faith as at least serving to derail the Pharisees' discussion. And although Martha's confession of faith in John 11:27 contains "a sum of all blessings," Calvin severely criticizes her excessive timidity and disorderly passions in his comments on John 11:21 and 24.[105]

Calvin's negative depictions are part of an interpretive shift that can be found, as Craig Farmer has demonstrated, among Reformed commentators on John 4. Some sixteenth-century Reformed commentators radically transformed the traditional portrait of the Samaritan woman as a "sweet and courteous soul who allows herself to be led to spiritual illumination."[106] In its stead, Calvin and others presented her as "brash, saucy, and practically insolent in her conversation with Jesus."[107] The reasons for this shift lie in the Reformed emphasis on self-knowledge as the prerequisite for salvation. It is not enough for the woman to know who Jesus is; it is only when, in Calvin's words, she has been informed about her sin that she can proceed to ask (in John 4:20) about proper worship of God.[108] Further, Farmer has suggested that the Reformed emphasis on election helps explain the shift in interpretation. By

---

105 *OE* xi/2:58–61 = *CO* xlvii:261–263; *Comm. John* 11:21, 24, 27 (CTS xvii:434–337).
106 Farmer, "Changing Images," p. 370.
107 Ibid., p. 366.
108 *OE* xi/1:125 = *CO* xlvii:84; *Comm. John* 4:20 (CTS xvii:154). Calvin locates the moment of self-awareness and repentance in John 4:16–19; from that point on, she is eager to listen to the "doctrine of Christ, which she had formerly disdained."

accenting the woman's petulance, they can underscore that her salvation
rests only in God's goodness and mercy, and not in her "pleasing disposition" or "her meritorious response to Jesus."[109] Once again, Calvin can
be seen to represent in a certain sense the culmination of this trend. Not
only is his negative portrayal of characters in John more harsh and more
consistent than, for example, Bucer's, but also this critical depiction of the
biblical faithful is a recurring and dominant feature of Calvin's exegesis in
general.[110]

As Calvin in his commentary on John seeks to delineate precisely the
ways in which and conditions under which individuals come to faith and
progress in faith, he adds nuance to the overall portrait of faith's character.
In the commentary, Calvin explores to a degree not yet evident in his
Institutes different preparatory stages to faith proper as well as the progress
and regress of this full faith. He is reluctant at this point to designate the
preparations for faith – based on miracles, the not yet clear testimony of
others, or teachings of Christ regarded as a prophet – with the term
"faith," since these do not have the certainty and the full grasp of Christ as
Messiah that his Pauline understanding of faith requires. There is no
guarantee these preludes will lead to proper faith. At the same time, he
can recognize their importance, and can even admit that true faith is
sometimes "hidden," as when Thomas forgets the doctrine that he has
heard; it is often ignorant and forgetful; it is in constant need of confirmation. As I have argued elsewhere, these ideas find their echo in expansions
that Calvin makes to the discussion of faith in the *Institutes* in 1559.[111]
Although I have never meant to imply a one-way cause and effect from
commentary to the *Institutes*, the fact remains that it is in fact in his
commentary on John that Calvin first engages fully a more detailed
portrait of faith's developmental character. In fact, in the *Institutes*, Calvin
goes beyond what he is willing to concede in the commentary, openly
confessing a kind of implicit faith, an initial teachableness such as that
exemplified by the court official and the Samaritans in John 4.[112] While he
sharply distinguishes this from what he takes to be the Roman doctrine of
implicit faith, he nevertheless admits that all faith is to some degree

109 Farmer, "Changing Images," p. 375.
110 On Calvin and Bucer, see Pitkin, "Seeing and Believing"; on Calvin's negative images of other
      biblical faithful, see Thompson, *Writing the Wrongs*, pp. 83–87; Steinmetz, *Calvin in Context*,
      pp. 79–94; Pitkin, "John Calvin and the Interpretation of the Bible."
111 Pitkin, *What Pure Eyes Could See*, pp. 134–136.
112 *Institutes* (1559), III.2.5.

implicit (insofar as it is mixed with unbelief) and views the preparatory stages for faith more positively than he had before.

In addition to providing Calvin with the opportunity to explore the developmental character of faith, the Gospel of John also confirms his fundamental understanding of faith as knowledge, a knowledge that is both certain and also goes beyond mere intellectual assent. Again, I must stress that Calvin does not "get" this idea from the Gospel of John alone, but only that the prominence of the theme of faith and the various ways that Calvin finds it depicted by the Evangelist allow for a rich exploration of this important theological theme. This richness can be seen in a comment Calvin makes on John 17:3, "And this is eternal life, that they may know you, the only true God, and Jesus Christ, whom you have sent." Calvin writes:

> Almost every one of the words has its weight. For it is not every kind of knowledge of God that is here described, but that which transforms us into the image of God from faith to faith [Rom. 1:17]. Or, rather, that which is the same as faith, by which, having been ingrafted into the body of Christ, we are made partakers of the divine adoption, and heirs of heaven.[113]

The knowledge that is faith is not a once-and-for-all intellectual insight but a gradual restoration of fallen human nature that begins with an ingrafting into the body of Christ. Calvin concludes his reflections by citing Paul to underscore that renewal to the divine image comes through knowledge of God (Col. 3:10).

While there is clearly much more that could be said about the important theme of faith's character in Calvin's commentary on John, let me conclude by noting that a number of interpreters have found here the primary source for the view of faith as mystical union with Christ, which enjoys increased prominence in the 1559 *Institutes*.[114] In his comments on John 14:20, Calvin says that this sacred and mystical union between Christ and the Father and between Christ and us is known not speculatively but only "when he diffuses his life in us by the secret efficacy of the Spirit." This, he says, is the "experience of faith."[115] Calvin's idea of faith as the work of the Spirit, who both illumines and enlightens and also unites believers with Christ, clearly has its exegetical underpinnings in the Fourth Gospel.

---

113 *OE* XI/2:209 = *CO* XLVII:376; *Comm. John* 17:3 (CTS XVIII:166).
114 See esp. E. A. Dowey, *The Knowledge of God in Calvin's Theology* (1952; 2nd edn Grand Rapids: Eerdmans, 1994), pp. 197–205.
115 *OE* XI/2:150 = *CO* XLVII:333; *Comm. John* 14:20 (CTS XVIII:95).

CONCLUSION

The Fourth Gospel was one of the most important books of the Bible for Calvin, and long before he wrote a formal commentary the dominant theological themes of the gospel had a profound impact on his theology. Undoubtedly one of the most valuable aspects of his 1553 commentary is the insight it provides into the way Calvin addressed these themes, including those explored here, e.g., salvation in Christ and the nature of faith, as an exegete striving to lay bare the mind of the biblical author. Beyond this, the commentary is significant as a "proving ground" for Calvin's exegetical method, revealing little of the contentious domestic climate in which it was written and pressing the depth of his commitment to what he takes to be the Evangelist's proper meaning. That Calvin's explicit rejection of traditional Christological exegesis of certain Johannine passages became itself a source of controversy suggests the singularity of his approach, even among his sixteenth-century contemporaries. For all its perpetuation of traditional attitudes about the special character of the Gospel of John, Calvin's commentary nevertheless offers a genuinely new contribution to the history of Johannine interpretation.

CHAPTER 8

Calvin as commentator on the Acts of the Apostles

Wilhelmus H. Th. Moehn
Translated by Lydia Verburg-Balke

"Was Calvin in seiner Auslegung dem Exegete zu bieten hat, ist noch lange nicht verarbeitet und harrt noch einer Fruchtbarmachung für unsere Zeit."[1]

THE CONTEXT OF THE COMMENTARY

John Calvin worked on Acts both as a commentator as well as a preacher. There is no evidence that Calvin ever lectured on Acts or used this book in the so-called *congrégations* on Friday mornings. Instead, he preached in the Genevan congregation on Acts during the same period that he was writing his commentary. In the scope of his entire exegetical work, this close coincidence between his sermons and his commentary on the same part of Scripture is unique. From Sunday August 25, 1549 until March 1554 Calvin preached in the morning and occasionally in the afternoon on Acts.[2] On November 10, 1550 – when he had been preaching on Acts for more than a year – he wrote to Farel:

Why do you remind me of *Acts* and *Genesis*, embryos hardly yet conceived in the womb? I am ashamed to confess how slowly I am getting on with *Acts*. I have only done a third of it, and what I have written is so long that I foresee it will be a big volume. I have had to give up *Genesis* for the time being.[3]

---

1 W. Bieder, *Die Apostelgeschichte in der Historie. Ein Beitrag zur Auslegungsgeschichte des Missionsbuches der Kirche*, Theologische Studien 61 (Zurich: EVZ-Verlag, 1960), p. 13.

2 See the table in J. Calvin, *Sermons on the Acts of the Apostles*, SC 8, ed. W. Balke and W. H. Th. Moehn (Neukirchen: Neukirchener Verlag, 1994), pp. xv–xix.

3 Calvin to Farel (November 10, 1550), *CO* XIII:655, # 1415; ET in: T. H. L. Parker, *Calvin's New Testament Commentaries*, 2nd edn (Louisville: Westminster John Knox Press, 1993), p. 29. In the dedication to Frederick (dated January 25, 1554), Calvin wrote: "Quum meos commentarios, quibus ante biennium Acta Apostolorum interpretari sum aggressus, in duos libros partitus forem . . .," *OE* 12/1: LXIX. "Two years ago" obviously refers to his beginning to work on the second volume.

From *ex tertia parte,* we may conclude that he had more or less explained the first nine chapters. On November 9, 1550, he delivered the thirty-sixth sermon, on Acts 7:37–38. Therefore, the commentary is to some extent ahead of the sermons, because on Sunday January 11, 1551, he delivered the last surviving sermon, on Acts 7:58–60. However, when he finished his work on Acts, commentary and sermons came close together in time. The dedication of the second part of the commentary is dated January 25, 1554; in March 1554 Calvin finished his *lectio continua* on Acts.

The commentary on Acts was to appear in two parts. The first part appeared in 1552, the second part much later, in 1554.[4] From 1548 onwards, Calvin dedicated many of his commentaries to kings and princes.[5] He decided to dedicate the two parts of the commentary on Acts to members of the royalty as well. The first part is dedicated to Christian III, king of Denmark. In 1554, Calvin wrote a dedicatory letter to Crown Prince Frederick of Denmark, who had been appointed coregent by his father. The second and revised edition was dedicated to Nicolaus Radziwil, count palatine in Vilnius. Calvin wrote a new dedication, because he considered the Danish princes lacking in their support of the Reformed doctrine.

What could be the motivation for a royal dedication and what could a king learn from this book of the Bible? Calvin praised Frederick's father, King Christian, as a defender of true faith among the Danes. "Although many princes see the horribly corrupt state of the Church, yet they do not undertake any reform, because being in ancient and also undisturbed possession, they are hindered and kept back from functioning, by the danger that they fear from newness."[6] In Frederick's position it was especially useful to connect his royal obligations with the story of the beginnings of the Christian church. A close resemblance to the reborn church in Denmark, which the Lord committed to his protection, could encourage him to follow the right course of duty.

In Jerusalem, the church began as a small group, "unarmed and contemptible, relying on the support of the truth and the Spirit alone." Nevertheless, the followers were obedient to Christ's command to proclaim the gospel in the whole world. This meant for Christian kings that

---

4 The commentary is now available in a critical edition in the series *Ioannis Calvini opera omnia recognita* (*OC*): *OE,* vol. xii/1, *Commentariorum in Acta Apostolorum,* Liber Primus, ed. H. Feld (Geneva: Librairie Droz, 2001) and vol. xii/2, *Commentariorum in Acta Apostolorum,* Liber Posterior, ed. H. Feld (Geneva: Librairie Droz, 2001).

5 J.-F. Gilmont, *Jean Calvin et le livre imprimé,* Études de philologie et d'histoire (Cahiers d'Humanisme et Renaissance) 50 (Geneva: Librairie Droz, 1997), pp. 260f.

6 Calvin to Crown Prince Frederick, *CO* xv:16, # 1901, *OE* xii/1:lxix.

they should advance the cause of the Reformation of the church in their countries, "since God has provided them with the sword for the defence of the Kingdom of His Son, being at least just as spirited and faithful in the discharge of such an honourable task."[7]

Together with the Synoptic Gospels, the Acts of the Apostles should be considered as one of the historical books of the Bible. The histories in this book form an important part of the *historia sacra* and are of much more value than the profane *rerum gestarum narratio*. Calvin commences the *Argumentum* with a recommendation for all the godly (*pii omnes*) to read this history. But even the reading of sacred history requires differentiation, which he provides in his commentary on Acts 1:1–2. "Those who simply know the bare history (*nuda historiae notitia*) have not the Gospel, unless there is added a knowledge of the teaching, which reveals the fruit of the acts of Christ." The essence of the gospel is contained both in the teaching of Christ and in his acts:

He not only brought to men the embassy committed to Him by the Father, but also accomplished in deed all that could be required of the Messiah. He inaugurated His Kingdom, He reconciled God by His sacrifice, He expiated the sins of men by His own blood, He subdued death and the devil, He restored us to true liberty, He won for us justice and life. But that all that He did and said might be ratified, He attested Himself by His miracles to be the Son of God.[8]

Reading biblical history can only be fruitful with this lesson in mind. Once more, Calvin refers to Cicero's definition of history – the definition which he quoted earlier, and which he approved of, in his commentaries on Seneca's *De Clementia* and Paul's letter to the Romans:[9]

The highest praise for history by secular writers is to call it an "instructress of life" (*magistra vitae*). If a narrative of events that only gives guidance in connection with men's deeds, as to what ought to be avoided, and what followed, merits such a splendid description, what title will the sacred histories deserve? For not only do they regulate the external life of man so that he may obtain commendation for virtue, but . . . they also show that God has cared for His Church from the beginning, that He always stood by, as a just vindicator, for those who turned to Him for support and protection; that He was gracious to, and easily moved by, miserable sinners.[10]

---

7 Ibid., *CO* xv:17, *OE* xii/1:lxx.   8 *Comm. Acts* 1:1–2, *OE* xii/1:16.
9 *Calvin's Commentary on Seneca's De Clementia*, Renaissance Text Series 3, trans. F. L. Battles and A. M. Hugo (Leiden: E. J. Brill, 1969), pp. 14, 24–27, and *Comm. Rom.* 4:23, *OE* xiii:98.
10 *Comm. Acts Argumentum*, *OE* xii/1:11.

Calvin's interest in history in general and the *historia sacra* in Acts in particular was not induced by a desire to escape from reality or by a fear that the past would distort an intact illusion.[11] Neither was he exclusively looking for an example to be followed. Rather, he perceived such a close connection between events and people in the past and in the present that he therefore considered that the histories described indeed provide us with immediate benefits. When Calvin wrote his commentary on Luke's second book, he often switched from the past to the present (*hodie*). Luke pointed out that Christ continually reigns in His church. However, the Spirit also teaches that the Kingdom of Christ never exalts in itself, for then Satan would arise furiously and try with all his might to overthrow it. This book contains many examples of perseverance in situations of affliction.

For since the Son of God has announced that the Cross will always be associated with His Gospel, there is no cause for us to deceive ourselves with a vain hope, as if the situation of the Church here would always be peaceful and flourishing. Therefore let us also prepare ourselves to put up with similar things. But this tremendous consolation is added, that just as God long ago marvellously saved His Church when it was afflicted and crushed in so many ways, so He will also come to our help today (*ita nobis hodie quoque sit adfuturus*).[12]

When Calvin discovered an analogy between the events described in Acts and the situation in his own time, he presented that as a key with which his readers could understand the text. W. J. Bouwsma mentions in this context Calvin's "talent for discerning analogies between other times and his own."[13]

In the introduction to the commentary, Calvin pays remarkably little attention to the preaching of the apostles and the speeches of other men, of which almost a third of the book consists.[14] The sermons of the apostles (*Apostolorum conciones*) deal with "the mercy of God, the grace of Christ, the hope of blessed immortality, the invocation of God, repentance and the fear of God, and other principal points of the heavenly teaching."

11 Cf. D. Fischer, "L'histoire de l'Eglise dans la pensée de Calvin," *Archiv für Reformationsgeschichte* 77 (1986): 79–125, at pp. 105f.

12 Comm. Acts *Argumentum, OE* XII/1:12f.

13 W. J. Bouwsma, *John Calvin: A Sixteenth Century Portrait* (New York: Oxford University Press, 1988), p. 91.

14 See for a survey E. Plümacher, "Apostelgeschichte," in *Theologische Realenzyklopädie*, III:483–528, at p. 502. Cf. H. O. Old, *The Reading and Preaching of the Scriptures in the Worship of the Christian Church*, vol. 1: *The Biblical Period* (Grand Rapids, MI and Cambridge, UK: Harvard University Press, 1998), pp. 164–180.

CONCERNS SURROUNDING THE COMMENTARY

Textual matters

When Calvin wrote his commentary, he had continually Erasmus' text of the New Testament close at hand. Nevertheless, Helmut Feld, editor of the new critical edition, came to the conclusion that the significance of Erasmus to Calvin was declining: "die Übersetzung ist, im Vergleich mit derjenigen der Paulus-Briefe und des Joh-Evangeliums, viel selbständiger geworden."[15] Calvin also used the fourth volume of the so-called *Biblia Vatabli* with the translation of Theodore Beza and the text of the Vulgate.

Calvin regularly disagreed with Erasmus' translation.[16] At Acts 1:14, he chooses a text that differs from Erasmus' version, but does this without mentioning his name: "Alii 'mulieres' vertunt." In Calvin's eyes, it is impossible to think that "the women" are those who accompanied Christ. "The reason why I think he speaks of wives is that since Paul bears witness that they were later accustomed to take their wives around with them (1 Cor. 9:5), it is hardly likely that they were at that time separate from them." Again, at Acts 3:26 ("God raised up his servant and sent him first to you"[17]), it is clear that Calvin's translation is based on his own interpretation of the text:

I do not like Erasmus' translation; for he says, *when He had raised Him up* [*quum suscitasset* instead of Calvin's *excitavit*] as if he spoke of something done long ago. But Peter means rather that Christ when He was shown to be the Author of the blessing was raised from the dead, and that the fact that this took place recently and suddenly ought to affect them the more . . . Christ was raised up when He performed the duty laid upon Him by the Father, yet this happens daily when through the Gospel He is offered, that He may have first place amongst us."

At Acts 13:42, Calvin disagrees with both Erasmus and the Vulgate. Here he provides his own translation of *eis to metaksu sabbaton*. Carefully reconstructing the chronology of the story, Calvin concludes that Paul and Barnabas left the synagogue when the Jews had not yet finished their meeting. At that very moment, the Gentiles asked them to preach the gospel to them. But at what exact moment did they preach? As opposed to the usual translation "on the next Sabbath" he arrives at *intermedio Sabbatho*, i.e., the days between two Sabbaths. Because the *Gentiles* asked

---

15 *OE* XII/1:XXI.   16 Cf. 1:3, 2:22, 3:26, 7:19, 16:22 and 22:15.

17 The English translation is taken from the NETBible (New English Translation) online at http://netbible.bible.org/.

Paul and Barnabas to deal with them, it was not necessary to choose a Sabbath, which was the fixed day for the Jews. "The Gentiles had as much opportunity on other days. Why therefore should they put off their desire and requests for eight days? And what is more, they wish to hear Paul when he is free and not involved with the Jews." The result of the next Sabbath proved to Calvin that Paul and Barnabas had not been working in vain that week: "the people had been so prepared in their studies that they all desired to have a surer grasp of the whole matter, and they hoped that that would be the case if it were discussed along with the Jews."

Only once does Calvin disagree with Beza openly, referring to him as 'quibusdam magis placet Berrhoeenses conferri Thessalonicensibus'. At Acts 17:11 ('These Jews were more open-minded than those in Thessalonica'), Calvin rejects the comparison between the Jews of Beroea and of Thessalonica and reads: "now these were outstanding in nobility among the Thessalonians."[18] He thinks that the idiom, which sounded rather harsh to Roman ears, was common and familiar to the Greeks. Nevertheless, at the end of the commentary Calvin explicitly calls his colleague "our friend Beza."[19]

Calvin read Luke's quotations of the Old Testament with particular interest. Repeatedly, he observed the instances where Luke departed from the Hebrew text and tried to explain what could be the reason for this change. In Acts 8, Luke recorded the story of the eunuch, who had visited Jerusalem and was returning to Ethiopia. During his journey, he was reading the prophet Isaiah. But which text did he have at his disposal? The surviving text allows for two conclusions: "either the eunuch had a Greek scroll, or Luke has recorded, as he usually does, the reading in use at that time."[20] A decision is left to the reader of the commentary. At verse 33, Calvin has to explain the difficult words of Isaiah 53:8. Being an exegete, he is acutely aware that this verse had been interpreted in different ways.[21] Either Christ was carried by force from prison to the cross, or the verb "to be taken away" means the same as being reduced to nothing. A return to the Hebrew text does not offer any clues for a clear translation, because "the meaning of the Hebrew word לֻקָּח is no less ambiguous than that of the Greek word *airesthai*." Therefore, Calvin

18 *OE* xii/2:103 and n. 11: "*Hi autem nobilitate praestabant inter Thessalonicenses.*"
19 *Comm. Acts* 17:11, *OE* xii/2:291,31: "*Beza noster.*"
20 *Comm. Acts* 8:33.
21 In 1549, Calvin gave an exegesis of Isaiah in his lectures. The first edition of the commentary was published in 1551.

arrives at a conclusion through the context, by pointing out that the intention of the Greek text is the same as the Hebrew words of Isaiah.

More difficult is James' speech to the congregation in Jerusalem. He quotes the prophets of Israel and – as a free quotation of Amos 9:12 – says: "After this I will return, and I will rebuild the fallen tent of David; I will rebuild its ruins and restore it, so that the rest of humanity may seek the Lord" (Acts 15:16–17a). Calvin remarks: "By way of explanation James has added that *seek*, for it is not included in the prophet's statement." However, there is more at stake here than just an explanatory addition, because in the LXX the Hebrew text was not correctly read. Instead of יִירְשׁוּ, יִדְרְשׁוּ was read, which means "to seek"! Secondly, the subject of the Greek verb had been changed to "the residue of men," because the LXX read שְׁאֵרִית אָדָם instead of שְׁאֵרִית אֱדוֹם. This means that the Greek text of the LXX says the opposite of the Hebrew text of the prophet Amos. The question remains how Calvin could still say: "For 'the residue of the nations' which Amos puts, Luke, following the more familiar Greek translation, has substituted *the residue of men*, with the same meaning." Perhaps he did not see a problem, and he even applied the changed text of the LXX and Luke (recounting the speech of James) to his own time: ". . . seeing that the corruption of the world is too bad for the whole of it to yield obedience to Christ, He scatters the refuse and darnel with the fans of various tribulations, so that in the end He may gather to Himself the residue that will remain."[22]

Historical issues

Calvin attempted to interpret the book of Acts within its historical and geographical context, meaning Palestine, Asia Minor, Italy, and Greece in the first century. He was especially interested in Palestinian history. In addition to Luke, his main source was Josephus, whom he read carefully. Regularly, Calvin considered that his duty was to align Luke's account of early church history with the information provided by Josephus. A recurring issue is the chronology of this book. The problems first arise in Acts 4:5–6, where Luke mentions a few of those present in the meeting

---

22 Similar problems can be found in Acts 13:33. Did Luke write the *first* or the *second* Psalm? This question may be asked thanks to a remark of Erasmus that many of the ancient writers had read the first Psalm. The arguments are counterbalanced by the observation that the main issue for us is to realize how Paul suitably adapted the testimony taken from the Psalm to the present situation.

by name: "Annas the High Priest was there, and Caiaphas, John, Alexander, and others who were members of the high priest's family." Josephus is awarded greater authority in matters of the description of history. For that reason, Calvin is amazed that Luke here names Annas as the High Priest, "since it is clear from Josephus that this office was not taken from Caiaphas until Vitellius entered Jerusalem to take command after Pilate had been ordered to Rome."[23] This means that the supposition that the first chapters of Acts describe events taking place shortly after the resurrection can no longer be maintained (*non statim post Christi resurrectionem contigisse*).

At Acts 23:2, a similar problem occurs: "*Non videtur Lucae narratio cum recepta historia congruere*" (*OE* XII/2:229,5f.). Calvin informs his readers exhaustively about the different High Priests and civil authorities in Palestine. He offers a number of conjectures, but in the end does not resolve the problems. Calvin finishes his comment with the remark: "Finally, the things that we have reported from Josephus are to be found, partly in *Antiquities*, book 20, chapters 3 to 8, and partly in *The Wars of the Jews*, book 2."[24]

Another question is the problem of a contradiction between Josephus and the narrative of Acts 5:36f., concerning the chronology of insurrections under Theudas and Judas the Galilean. Gamaliel says to the council: "For some time ago Theudas rose up, claiming to be somebody, and about four hundred men joined him. He was killed, and all who followed him were dispersed and nothing came of it. After him Judas the Galilean arose in the days of the census, and incited people to follow him in revolt." Gamaliel first mentions Theudas and only after him Judas, whose revolt took place during the days of the census. Josephus' statements in *De Bello Judaico* 2.433 and 7.253 are almost identical to Luke's narrative. Here the census of Quirinius in the year 6 is explicitly mentioned. Josephus relates how Judas resisted this and also how he incited the people to refuse their participation. If Josephus' account is correct and Judas acted first, before Theudas, Gamaliel had altered the true course of events. How should one explain Luke's use of *meta* (after)? Calvin comments: "I think that when Luke says, 'after him Judas the Galilean arose', he is not indicating a chronological order, where this man came second, but since Gamaliel brings forward two similar examples, he could substitute the one for the

23 See also E. Schürer, *The History of the Jewish People in the Age of Jesus Christ*, rev. and ed. G. Vermes, et al. 3 vols. (Edinburgh: T. & T. Clark, 1979), II:230.
24 See for full references *OE* XII/2:229, nn. 1–3.

other without respect for time. Therefore the preposition *post* means as much as 'over and above' or 'besides'."[25] Calvin is not just struggling with the correct sequence of these two events, but also draws the obvious conclusion by mentioning these two names regarding the date of the arrest and interrogation of the disciples: "We may deduce from reckoning up the time that at least twelve years had passed from the death of Christ before the beating of the apostles . . . Gamaliel is not recalling the event as if it happened only yesterday or the day before." The way Calvin treated such problems as these offers us an insight into how he integrated lists of periods of government of princes, High Priests, and governors into his explanation, as well as how much authority he attributed to these lists.

The historical problems within the Bible form yet another category. In his speech, Stephen relates the history of Israel. Starting with the patriarchs, he further speaks about Abraham: "The God of glory appeared to our forefather Abraham when he was in Mesopotamia, before he settled in Haran, and said to him, 'Go out from your country and from your relatives, and come to the land I will show you.'" But Moses' narrative appears to differ from Stephen's, because Abraham had left his country (Gen. 11:31), and chapter 12 begins with the remark that God spoke to Abraham.

There is a simple solution, for Moses is not relating, in this latter passage, something that happened after Abraham's departure; but so that no one might suppose that Abraham left home in a rash moment to wander in foreign countries . . . he brings out the reason for his departure, namely that he had been commanded by God to migrate to another place . . . After Moses related that this journey was not undertaken out of human light-heartedness, but by the command of God, he later adds what he had previously omitted, and this is a common Hebrew way of putting things.[26]

---

25 Cf. the comment of C. K. Barrett, "Calvino esegeta degli Atti degli Apostoli," *Protestantesimo* 49 (1994): 312–326, at p. 321: "Non è una via di uscita convincente" (I thank Mrs. I. B. van Veen-Frey, who translated this article for me). Interestingly, this problem is completely neglected in the sermon on these verses. See sermon 21 on Acts 5:33–35, 38–39. When commenting on Acts 21:37–40, Calvin warns that the *Egyptian*, about whom the tribune is asking, is not Theudas, the sorcerer, mentioned by Gamaliel in chapter 5.

26 On Abraham, see also my article "Abraham – 'père de l'église de Dieu'. A comparison of Calvin's commentary and sermons on Acts 7:1–6," in *Calvinus Praeceptor Ecclesiae*, ed. H. J. Selderhuis (Geneva: Librairie Droz, 2004), pp. 287–301. Ward Gasque, *A History of the Criticism of the Acts of the Apostles*, Beiträge zur Geschichte der biblischen Exegese 17 (Tübingen: Mohr, 1975), p. 11, is mistaken when he supposes that Abraham received *two* calls from God, one in Mesopotamia and another in Haran. Instead, Calvin points to the rhetorical figure of *husteron proteron*. On this figure, see also M. Engammare, "D'une forme l'autre: commentaires et sermons de Calvin sur la Genèse," in *Calvinus Praeceptor Ecclesiae*, pp. 107–137, at pp. 115–118.

At Acts 7:16, Calvin does not even hesitate to reproach Luke for making an error. Stephen says that the bones of *all* the patriarchs were carried to Canaan, while Moses only spoke about the bones of Joseph (Exod. 13:19):

I have no definite statement to make, except that either there is synecdoche here, or Luke has reported this not so much from Moses as from ancient tradition (*fama*), as the Jews long ago used to have many things handed down, as it were, from their fathers. But when he goes on to say that they were buried in the sepulchre that Abraham had bought from the sons of Hamor, it is obvious that an error has been made in the name Abraham . . . This verse must be amended (*corrigendus est*) accordingly.[27]

Calvin pays attention to these historical issues in order that the foreign world described in Luke's text may become accessible to readers from an European context. They are informed about the so-called *horae inaequales* (3:1), the Porch of Solomon, but also about many geographical references. After an extensive description of Lydda (9:33), Calvin concludes with the down-to-earth remark: "I gladly accept what Luke's text makes plain to me, viz. that it was a neighbouring town."[28] And immediately after that he puts the value of an amount of historical data into perspective: "But I am not making an issue of this matter, since I am not collecting, for my own self-esteem (*ambitiose*), all the things that could make for an empty show, because it will be enough for godly readers to know the things that suit Luke's meaning."

In the course of his exegetical work, Calvin not only encountered problems related to the history, but even created problems himself. When Damascus became too dangerous, Paul had to leave the city. In the night, a few brethren let him escape by letting a basket down the city wall (Acts 9:25). Calvin asks himself at this point,

---

27 Cf. Sermon 31, Acts 7:15–19, SC VIII:272, 29ff.: "Il est vray que nous ne lisons pas en Moyse que tous les corps des patriarches ayent esté ensepveliz au sepulchre d'Abraham. Mais ce n'est pas aussy l'intention de sainct Estienne. Car il comprend icy une partie pour le tout, d'autant que quand Jacob se feict là ensepvelir, c'estoit pour representer tout son lignage, pour leur monstrer qu'il falloit que tous aspirassent à cest heritage qu'il avoit attendu, combien qu'il n'en eust point eu la jouyssance sa vie durant." See also C. Pellikan, *In sacrosancta quatuor Evangelia et Apostolorum acta . . . commentarij . . .* (Tiguri, 1537) (on Acts 7:16): "Quod vero hic dicitur de patribus translatis in Sichem, et de sepulchro quod emit Abraham a filijs Emor, simpliciter intelligendum est, et sine praecisione, quando Synecdochen novimus totius scripturae locutionem communissimam esse et haberi."

28 See also *Comm. Acts* 21:1: "Readers should consult the geographical writers about the situation of the cities which he lists. It is enough for me to have pointed out Luke's intention"; and *Comm. Acts* 27:3–4: "Let readers find out from geographical works the course of the voyage which Luke records."

whether it was lawful for the disciples to save Paul in this way; and also whether it was right for Paul to avoid danger in this fashion. For the laws pronounce the walls of cities to be sacred (*sanctos*), and the gates inviolable (*sanctas*). He therefore ought to have submitted to death rather than allow public order to be disturbed for his sake.

Do we touch upon a moral issue for Paul here (therefore implicating Luke), or is Calvin showing us how significant a city is to himself as a safe harbor amid many dangers? Calvin refuses to attack Paul for a transgression of a law. By pleading to Cicero[29] he argues that the laws should be applied equally. If Paul had not secretly fled in the night, there would have been a revolt in the city. That would have been dangerous for the city.

Cicero . . . explains correctly that even if the law prevents a stranger from approaching close to a wall, yet a man is not committing an offence, when he mounts a wall for the sake of saving a city, because the laws must always be inclined towards equity. Therefore Paul is free from blame, because he escaped in secret, since that would be possible without an uproar of the people.

Even though Calvin in Geneva was much more aware than we are of the security provided by city walls, we cannot avoid the conclusion that he raises an unreal problem here, which is unconvincingly solved by his plea to Cicero.

Exegetical emphases

The Acts of the Apostles focuses on the transition from the Jewish church of the Old Testament to the church of Christ after His ascension. Helmut Feld has summarized this position as follows: "die Kirche Christi und der Apostel ist keine ganz neue religiöse Gemeinschaft, sondern die legitime Fortsetzung der israelitischen Kirche."[30] Nevertheless, the commentary provides us a with a colorful image of the relation between the Jews and the church. Especially the first chapters of Acts are characterized by an ongoing discussion about authority in the church. The Jewish council did represent the church,[31] but because of its abuse, it should not be obeyed; and Peter and John replied: "Whether it is right before God to obey you rather than God, you decide" (4:19). But the council still remained in function. The church was also represented in the assembly of the elders. "No matter how much the priests at that time stealthily

---

29 Cf. *De oratore* 2,24,100 and also *De natura deorum* 3,40,94: ". . . urbis muris, quos vos, pontifices, sanctos esse dicitis."

30 *OE* XII/1:xxv.

31 *Comm. Acts* 4:19, *OE* XII/1:125,30f.: "Nam consessus quidem ille Ecclesiam repraesentabat."

reached office by fraud, or canvassing, or other evil tricks, or even forced their way to it by bribery and murder of each other, yet the office of the priesthood itself was still continuing in existence, for the Christ had not yet been revealed."[32] The revelation of Christ was the decisive moment. When the truth of God was not sought in the congregation of the elders, the whole outward appearance signified nothing but a mere mask. This point was reached after Christ's resurrection. It was the Sadducees who at that time controlled everything, thereby wrecking the whole government of the church in a terrible devastation. "But God plainly allowed the synagogue to be immersed in this extreme infamy, after He had separated His Church from it (*postquam inde Ecclesiam suam segregaverat*)."[33] How Calvin made differentiations in his statements about the council becomes evident if one considers the several moments when the apostles are summoned to the council. Even though he records in Acts 5:17 that the two groups "had separated," in the next chapters we meet Stephen, who has to justify himself before the council as well. He addresses his judges as "Brothers and fathers." Why would he speak in this manner, as if there were no separation? "Because the orderly government of the people was still in their hands, and they presided over the Church which God had not yet rejected, he does not therefore hesitate, for the sake of propriety, to call them 'fathers'."[34]

An increasingly strong rift between the synagogue and the church manifests itself. In the synagogue at Antioch in Pisidia, Paul makes clear that a compromise is not possible. It is his intention to lead the Jews to the faith of Christ; and the implication of this faith is a breach with the synagogue community: "He calls them the *children of Abraham* not only to honour them, but that they may realize that they are heirs of eternal life. And he urges them so persuasively, that it may not be hard for them to break with the high priest and the scribes, whom they venerated, because of their need to receive Christ."[35]

The relation between the synagogue and the church is important for the structure of the whole book. The rejection of the claim that Jesus is in fact the Christ is closely related to the calling of the Gentiles. Paul's

---

32 *Comm. Acts* 5:21, *OE* xii/1:150, 14–16: ". . . ipsa tamen sacerdotii dignitas adhuc durabat, Christo nondum patefacto. Erat in Seniorum consessu Ecclesiae repraesentatio. Verum ubi non quaeritur Dei veritas, tota externa species nihil est quam mera larva."

33 *Comm. Acts* 5:17, *OE* xii/1:147,24f.

34 *Comm. Acts* 7:2, *OE* xii/1:176,34ff.: ". . . quia tamen adhuc penes eos ordinaria erat populi gubernatio ac praeerant Ecclesiae, quam Deus nondum abiecerat."

35 *Comm. Acts* 13:26, *OE* xii/1:381,21f.: ". . . ne durum sit a Sacerdote et Scribis, quos venerabantur, discessionem facere. Quod necesse erat, ut Christum admitterent."

sermon in the synagogue at Pisidian Antioch marks the turning point in Acts:

Paul is quite right in maintaining that what God promised to the fathers was fulfilled for the Jews. For the promise had been made to them also . . . Yet the worthiness of that nation does not prevent the grace of Christ spreading itself out into the whole world at the same time; because the elder occupies the chief position of honour in such a way that he yet leaves the second place to his brothers. For, seeing that the ancient people were disinherited (*veteri populo abdicato*), and the Church's possession was left vacant for strangers, a new opportunity began for gathering a Church from the Gentiles.[36]

For Calvin, this did not mean that there would have been no calling of the Gentiles if the Jews had accepted this Jesus as their Savior: "Even if that people had continued in the faith (*si ille in fide stetisset*), the Gentiles would have been added to the common fellowship of honour."[37]

The disciples never tired of emphasizing that they were not introducing a new religion. They had a double purpose in mind: first of all to legitimize their position, and secondly to consider the Jews, for whom it was not proper to admit anything that did not agree with the doctrine of the law. Therefore Peter said that he was not bringing a new religion, since that would draw the people away from the Law and the Prophets.[38] After the arrest in Jerusalem, Paul defends himself before the crowd, and wants to show in his speech that he also worships the God of the patriarchs. The possessive pronoun "our" in "the God of our ancestors" underscores the solidarity:

In calling Him *the God of our fathers*, he renews the memory of the promises, so that the Jews may know that Paul's recent call is connected with them; and that those who make the transition to Christ are not abandoning the Law. Therefore by these words Paul confirms what he has previously asserted in person, that he has not deserted the God of Abraham, and the God who had already been worshipped by the Jews in times past, but that he is continuing in the ancient worship of the fathers, which he had learned from the Law.[39]

---

36 *Comm. Acts* 13:33.
37 See also *Comm. Acts* 13:46, *OE* xii/1:402, 25–30: "Si in gradu suo stetissent illi, non sequuta esset talis conversio, sed Iudaeis in gremium receptis continua serie Gentes simul traxisset et pariter utrosque complexus esset. Nunc quum Iudaei tergum obvertant seque subducant ab eius ministerio, non potest uno intuitu eos cum Gentibus respicere."
38 *Comm. Acts* 3:13f. *OE* xii/1:101,4f.: "Negat se religionem novam inducere, ut populum a Lege et Prophetis abstrahat."
39 *Comm. Acts* 22:14, *OE* xii/2:220. See also *Comm. Acts* 2:34, *OE* xii/1:76,6f.: ". . . non debebat novum videri"; *Comm. Acts* 13:17, *OE* xii/1:376,18f.: "Haec praefatio testis erat Paulum minime novitatem aliquam moliri, quae populum a Lege Mosis abduceret."

The continuity between the doctrine of the law and the message of the
disciples was also a hot issue for the Jerusalem council. Promoting peace
and concord between the faithful with a Jewish background on the one
hand and the Gentile Christians on the other hand, James quotes in his
speech the prophet Amos; and he finishes the quotation (Acts 15:18) with
the words of Isaiah 45:21: "says the Lord, who makes these things known
from long ago." According to Calvin, *nota a seculo sunt* is "an anticipation
to remove the odium of newness."

For the sudden change could have been suspect, and was disturbing weak minds
on that occasion. Therefore James counteracts it, pointing out that this was no
new thing for God, even if it did happen suddenly and in a way different from
what men supposed, since God had foreseen before the creation of the world what
He was going to do, and the call of the Gentiles had been hidden in His secret
purpose."

It was not only the message of the apostles that could seem new compared
to the doctrine of the law. The disciples could also be reproached for
having appointed themselves as the new leaders of the church. In the
opening verses of his book, Luke has already mentioned the election of
the disciples as the new rulers of the church, which was at that time in
ruins.[40] This makes clear that we may be assured of their calling, and that
they did not enter lightly into this function.[41] The disciples had to
shoulder the task of organizing the church, beginning with the election
of the successor of Judas.[42] Peter correctly inferred that it was they who
ought to execute this matter. Although the leading role of Peter in the
congregation is evident, Calvin tries to explain in his exegesis that his
position vastly differs from that of the Pope. In chapter 8, Peter and John
were sent to Samaria. Because *the apostles* in Jerusalem sent these brethren,
Calvin especially calls attention to Peter, without mentioning John: "We
can infer from Luke's statement that Peter was sent by the others, that he
did not exercise the supreme power over his colleagues, but was preeminent among them in such a way that he was still subject to and

---

40 *Comm. Acts* 2:17, *OE* xii/1:55,21f.: ". . . non aliter posse instaurari Ecclesiam, quae tunc collapsa
erat, quam si Dei Spiritu renovarentur."

41 See *Comm. Acts* 5:4, *OE* xii/1:140,7ff.: "Homines quidem erant Apostoli, sed non privati homines,
quia Deus illis vices suas mandaverat."

42 On elections, see W. H. Th. Moehn, *"God Calls Us to His Service". The Relation Between God and
His Audience in Calvin's Sermons on Acts*, Travaux d'humanisme et Renaissance 345 (Geneva:
Librairie Droz, 2001), pp. 98–104 and *"Mettre ordre en l'Eglise de Dieu*: The Election of Officers in
Calvin's Sermons on the Acts," in the proceedings of the 7th Congress on Calvin, held in Seoul,
1998 (forthcoming).

obedient to the body." Calvin admits that Peter was the first among the twelve, but that did not automatically make him ruler of the whole world.[43] After meeting with Cornelius, Peter had to explain the matter in Jerusalem; and we see the exceptional restraint of Peter (*raram Petri modestiam*, *OE* XII/1,333,11),

> because he knew that principle was imposed on the whole Church, that each man must be prepared to render an account of his doctrine and life, as often as the situation demands it, and because he remembered that he was one of the flock (*se unum esse ex grege*), not only does he allow himself to be brought to order, but of his own accord (*sponte*) he submits himself to the judgment of the church.

And, applying this observation to his own time, Calvin complains: "Now if the Pope of Rome is Peter's successor, why will he not be bound by the same principle? Although we grant that this was a voluntary sort of submission, yet why does his successor not imitate the example of moderation that is presented to him?"

Hermeneutical approaches

In the *Argumentum*, Calvin had already depicted the theme of this book: "[B]oth the origin and the progress of the Church, from the Ascension of Christ, by which He was declared the supreme King of heaven and earth, are reviewed here for us." Through men of no importance and endowed with no special skills, God brought the whole world to submit to Himself. These *homines nullius pretii* (*OE* XII/1,12,5) have crossed the boundary between Jews and Gentiles. This transgression is essential for Calvin's understanding and interpretation of Acts. The history described is the illustration of Paul's words in Ephesians 2:14: "For he is our peace, the one who made both groups into one and who destroyed the middle wall of partition." This verse is very often quoted in the commentary.[44] Gradually, the disappearance of this boundary is prepared. The Samaritans had the circumcision in common with the Jews. Their conversion was the first fruit of the calling of the Gentiles.[45] The next step is the meeting between

---

43 See also the sarcastic tone in his comment on Acts 1:13f. ("Peter and John, and James, and Andrew, Philip and Thomas . . . were there. . . . together with the women, along with Mary the mother of Jesus, and his brothers"), *OE* XII/1:33,30ff.: "Verum, si ideo Apostolorum est princeps, quia nomen eius in catalogo primum ponitur, ego vicissim inferam Matrem Christi mulierum omnium postremam fuisse, quia in ultimum locum hic reiecta est."

44 See Register I, *Bibelstellen*, *OE* XII/1:419 and *OE* XII/2:323.

45 *Comm. Acts* 8:2, *OE* XII/1:231,21f.: "Samariae enim conversio quasi primitiae fuerunt vocationis Gentium." On the *praeludia vocationis gentium*, see also *Comm. Acts* 8:27.

Peter and Cornelius. Whereas there might have been some doubt whether a boundary truly had been crossed in the case of the Samaritans, this time it is clear that a Jew is meeting a genuine pagan (*alienigenam et incircumcisum*, *OE* 12/1,292,14). On the one hand Calvin maintains the significance of the circumcision, but on the other hand he creates room for the Gentiles to be admitted without circumcision: "At the same time it was a proof of gratuitous adoption to the Jews in this way, that uncircumcision did not prevent God from admitting any of the Gentiles into the fellowship of the same salvation."[46]

Through the service of Paul and his companions the wall is taken down entirely. Because Luke paid such a great deal of attention to Paul's work, it is even more remarkable that Calvin only mentions this apostle implicitly in the *Argumentum* of his commentary, when he writes about the apostles and their speeches in general. Instead, the opening of the commentary on chapter 13 could be read as a general introduction on Paul's missionary work as treated by Luke. Here Calvin shows how he read Acts; he involves the reader of the commentary in the *historia sacra*, which he is reading in Acts. "His calling was, as it were, the key, by which God has opened the Kingdom of Heaven *to us*."[47]

The fact that Christ brought salvation to the world would have been of no advantage to us, unless, with the division removed, an entrance into the Church had been opened for us . . . When Peter was sent to Cornelius it was such a novel and unaccustomed situation that it was looked upon almost like a monstrosity. Again, that could have appeared to be a privilege granted to a few men as an extraordinary thing. But now, when God specifically appoints Paul and Barnabas apostles to the Gentiles, in this way He is making them equal to the Jews, so that the Gospel may begin to be common to both without distinction.

In Lystra, Paul and Barnabas taught that God was hidden, but in such a way that all along He was giving evidence of Himself and His divinity. Nevertheless, according to Calvin, this evidence was insufficient for salvation, because "faith is not conceived by the bare observation of heaven and earth, but by the hearing of the Word."[48] We see here how

---

46 *Comm. Acts* 10:34, *OE* XII/1:317,4ff.: "Interim sic Iudaeis adoptionis gratuitae pignus erat, ut non obstaret Deo praeputium, quin admitteret, si quos vellet ex Gentibus, in societatem eiusdem salutis."

47 *Comm. Acts* 13:1, emphasis added. See also *Comm. Acts* 1:8: "Yet He calls all the nations without distinction, which formerly had been strangers to the hope of salvation. Hereby we learn that the Gospel was preached in every place by the express command of Christ, that it might reach even to us."

48 *Comm. Acts* 14:17, *OE* XII/2:16,1f.: "Atqui fides non ex nudo et caeli et terrae intuitu concipitur, sed ex verbi auditu."

Calvin's exegesis is influenced through his reading of Paul's letters, when he is trying to indicate the relation between personal guilt and the necessity of revelation:

[M]en cannot be brought to the saving knowledge of God except by the direction of the Word. Yet this does not prevent them being rendered inexcusable even without the Word, for even if they are naturally deprived of light, they are nevertheless blind through their own malice, as Paul teaches in the first chapter of his Epistle to the Romans.[49]

It is God's intention to be heard through men. The story of the eunuch shows two ways in which God works with men: reading the written word in the Scripture and hearing the word in sermons. Reading his book many things were concealed to him, but he did not throw the book aside. This attitude is an example for all believers: "we ought to accept eagerly and with a ready mind those things which are clear, and in which God reveals His mind; but it is proper to pass by those things which are still obscure to us, until a clearer light shines. But if we shall not be wearied by reading, the final result will be that constant use will make us familiar with Scripture."[50] Personal reading of the Scripture, however, does not make the explication by ministers of the church superfluous.[51] Calvin does not just accuse Fanatics, but also those who, "relying on their own penetrating insight, do not deign to hear anybody or to read any commentaries."[52]

We did not only receive the Scripture, "but interpreters and teachers are also added to help us." Therefore God summons Philip through the voice of an angel, but the angel himself is not sent directly. "It is certainly no ordinary recommendation of outward preaching, that the voice of God sounds on the lips of men, while the angels keep silence" (*Comm. Acts* 8:31).

This pattern can be observed repeatedly in Acts. Christ showed Himself directly to Paul in a vision, "but . . . left the responsibility of teaching him to Ananias."[53] Also, an angel orders Cornelius to call Peter, but a *man* has

---

49 See also *Comm. Acts* 17:27.   50 *Comm. Acts* 8:28.

51 On the individual reading of the Bible in the sixteenth century, see Moehn, "*God Calls Us*", p. 198, and M. Engammare, "De la chaire au bûcher, la bible dans l'Europe de la Renaissance. Pour rendre compte d'une production récente abondante et lancer quelques pistes de réflexion," *Bibliothèque d'Humanisme et Renaissance* 61 (1999):737–761, esp. pp. 753–761.

52 *Comm. Acts* 8:31, *OE* XII/1:255,6f.: "Alii perspicacia sua freti neminem audire, nullos commentarios legere dignantur."

53 *Comm. Acts* 10:5. Remarkably, Calvin says in his commentary on Acts 9:10, *OE* XII/1:271,18ff.: "Sicuti animat Christus et confirmat Ananiam in visione illi apparens, ita Paulum ad omnia praeparat, ut reverenter Ananiam, non secus atque Angelum e caelo delapsum, excipiat."

to fulfill the actual task of teaching him. The way in which God deals with individuals is normative for the church. Oral messages prevail over revelations and visions.[54] Does this position leave any place for direct guidance of the Spirit? To answer this question, we should survey the miracles in this book. Miracles usually serve as a confirmation of the preceding preaching. Bystanders become eyewitnesses of a miracle, yet in what way the apostles received instructions to perform these miracles remains concealed to them. One should not get the impression when reading about these exceptional deeds that they performed them just as often as they saw fit or as they liked. In their work, they were *ministros divinae virtutis* (*OE* xii/1,95,19f.). God worked through them and they had His Spirit as their guide and director. The healing of Dorcas in Joppa (Acts 9:36–41) and the cripple in Lystra (Acts 14:8–10) may serve as examples.

After Dorcas' death, two brethren were sent to fetch Peter from Lydda. Probably they explicitly asked him to perform a miracle.[55] But did Peter know God's intention at that very moment? For Calvin, it was clear that Peter could follow the brethren without knowing what the Lord would do. He could mitigate their sorrow and strengthen them with godly exhortations. But it should not be forgotten that God is the Guide of His disciples. The general rule is "that as often as the Lord had decided to put forth His power in some miracle through the apostles, He directed them by the secret influence of His Spirit." Calvin considers the gift to perform miracles to be very intimately connected to the secret inspiration of the Spirit.

The primacy of the Word and the hearing of the gospel can also be discerned in Lystra. Because Calvin had given priority to the remission of sins and the newness of life, and the Spirit "is given to us for a better use, that we may believe with the heart unto righteousness, that our tongues may be trained to true confession,"[56] the cripple ought to ask for spiritual healing. To do justice to his demand for physical healing as soon as he had heard Paul, Calvin has to resort to "a unique and extraordinary

---

54 *Comm. Acts* 10:5, *OE* xii/1:299,27ff.: "Et videmus, quam horrendis modis ultus sit Dominus furiosam eorum superbiam, qui contempta praedicatione revelationes e caelo captarunt." On the incidental use of visions in Acts, see also E. A. de Boer, *John Calvin on the Visions of Ezekiel: Historical and hermeneutical studies in John Calvin's* sermons inédits, *especially on Ezek. 36–48,* Kerkhistorische Bijdragen 21 (Leiden, Boston: E. J. Brill, 2004), pp. 127ff.

55 *Comm. Acts* 9:39, *OE* xii/1:289,7f.: "Veri tamen similius est, diserte rogasse, ut veniret ad miraculum edendum."

56 *Comm. Acts* 2:38.

movement of the Spirit in the cripple," and, on the other hand, a special revelation to Paul, "when he recognized the man's faith solely through looking at him." God ensured that the cripple possessed a special kind of faith that allowed for the performance of a miracle. This should not become a general rule, because this kind of faith "is not one that most of God's children have, although they are endowed with the Spirit of adoption all the same."

On one occasion, the Spirit seems to be self-contradictory. In Acts 20:22f. Paul had said: "And now, compelled by the Spirit, I am going to Jerusalem without knowing what will happen to me there, except that the Holy Spirit warns me in town after town that imprisonment and persecutions are waiting for me." But at Tyre some brethren advise – also through the Spirit – not to travel to Jerusalem (Acts 21:4)! Here Calvin provides a somewhat artificial distinction between the different gifts of the Spirit:

I reply that there are different gifts of the Spirit, so that it is no wonder that those who are strong in the gift of prophecy, are sometimes lacking in judgment or courage. The Lord revealed to those brethren, whom Luke mentions, what was to do; but at the same time, they do not know what is expedient, and what Paul's calling demands, because the measure of their gifts does not stretch so far.

Thus, in Calvin's hermeneutical conception there is place for the direct address of the Spirit, but it is clearly defined and reserved for the disciples. It is not possible to derive a general rule from the way in which God treated them. To put it in the words of John Hesselink: "To be governed and guided by the Spirit may mean new insights, deeper understanding, empowerment, and concrete applications or directions for our lives, but no new revelations!"[57]

Theological themes

In his edition of Calvin's commentary on Acts, Helmut Feld provided a valuable survey of *Theologische Leitideen*.[58] This chapter is confined to those issues where Calvin's own theological position is clearly shown and

57 I. J. Hesselink, "Governed and Guided by the Spirit: A Key Issue in Calvin's Doctrine of the Holy Spirit," in *Reformiertes Erbe: Festschrift für Gottfried W. Locher zu seinem 80. Geburtstag*, herausgegeben von Heiko A. Oberman, Ernst Saxer, Alfred Schindler, und Heinzpeter Stucki. Zwingliana, Bd. 19, Teil 1–2 (Zurich: Theologischer Verlag, 1992–1993): 2:161–171, at p. 170.

58 *OE* XII/1:XXIV–LXIII.

also influences the exegesis of the pericope in question. We are searching for Calvin's theological profile as an exegete of Acts.

Between the reader and commentator of Acts and the people who play an important role in this book, Luke is positioned, who collected and arranged the material found during his investigations.[59] Calvin's criticism of Luke's work is one of the keys to his own theological profile. The main point of his criticism focuses on the way in which Luke summarizes the speeches of the apostles. Calvin regards them as brief outlines of what was said, rather than as *verbatim* reports.[60] Already in Peter's speech to the 120 brethren (Acts 1:15–22), Calvin sees Luke at work. Why should Peter have inserted an account of Judas' death? The disciples knew this very well, and "why should he interpret in Greek among Jews a word of their own mother-tongue?" Therefore, the conclusion is justified that "Luke himself inserts this sentence, in case readers ignorant of the events should find Peter's words obscure."[61]

Calvin is well aware of the fact that Peter's sermon on the feast of Pentecost is reported in a condensed form. "Luke has not repeated Peter's words, but only given briefly the main points" (*Comm. Acts* 2:40). The significance of this observation becomes obvious when he explains Peter's answer on the question of the multitude. In Roman Catholic theology, *poenitentiam agite* has been eroded and remains restricted to certain external rites.[62] Further in his analysis, Calvin does not criticize Luke's work; but his remark that he only gave the *capita* provides Calvin with the opportunity to put his own emphasis on matters, because Peter said a lot more than was recorded in Acts. Repentance is explained on the basis of Romans 12:2, "be transformed by the renewing of your mind." Therefore, there can be no doubt that Peter preached at length about the force and nature of repentance.

We have therefore in these few words almost the sum total of Christianity: namely, that a man renouncing himself and the world devotes himself wholly to God; secondly, that he is delivered by the free forgiveness of sins from guilt involving death and adopted into the number of the children of God. And as we can obtain none of these things without price, the name of Christ is placed before us, as the only foundation of faith and repentance. This also we must

---

59 See Luke 1:1–4.

60 Cf. the commentary on 2:38; 7:37; 10:43; 17:26; 17:31 and 13:28.

61 *Comm. Acts* 1:18. In the editions of 1552 and 1554, the Latin text of vv. 18–19 was indeed placed between brackets, "ut a Petri concione separetur," *OE* xii/1:38,36f.

62 *Comm. Acts* 2:38, *OE* xii/1:80,10f.: "Nam poenitentiae nomen fere ad externos nescio quos ritus transtulerunt."

note, that the repentance that has its beginning when first we turn to God must be continued throughout our life.

We can discern some silent criticism of Luke in his comment on baptism. According to Calvin, baptism cannot precede the remission of sins, "because it is nothing else but a sealing of the blessings, which we have through Christ, that they may be established within our consciences." Therefore, he concedes that Peter connected the remission of sins to baptism, which he would not do himself, "for in that we receive Christ's gifts by faith, but baptism is a help for confirming and increasing our faith, the remission of sins, which is a result of faith, is joined to it as to the lesser means."[63]

Peter's important sermon in Cornelius' house consists – like several other sermons in Acts[64] – of two points. "In the first place he recounts a narrative of past events, and then passes on to the effect of the story." Before Calvin provides us with an analysis of this sermon, he first summarizes the main points of Christian doctrine, based on his own reading of the Bible and his theological knowledge. The actual exegesis begins with the trivial remark that Peter maintained this order of teaching (*hunc docendi ordinem servat Petrus*, *OE* xii/1,320,27f.). Calvin's exegesis is biased because of his polemics with the Roman Catholic doctrine of justification. "The angel said to him, 'Your prayers and your acts of charity have gone up as a memorial before God.'" The explanation is placed in a polemical context by the remark that "the papists abuse this verse in two ways."

For, taking the fact that God had regard to the prayers and alms of Cornelius so that He endowed him with the faith of the Gospel, they twist it to be the preparations made by themselves, as if a man acquires faith by his own diligence and virtue, and anticipates the grace of God by the merits of works.

It is impossible that Cornelius' works were acceptable to God before he had been enlightened by faith. Because such works can only be produced by faith, Cornelius must already have had faith at the beginning of the story: "Cornelius obtained fuller knowledge of Christ from his prayers and alms, but his having God well-disposed and favourable to his alms

---

63 *Comm. Acts* 2:38, *OE* xii/1:82,19–22: "Nam quia fide percipimus Christi dona, fidei autem confirmandae et augendae baptismus adminiculum est, illi, tanquam inferiori medio, remissio peccatorum, quae fidei est effectus, annectitur."

64 See the commentary on Acts 15:14; 21:20 and 28:23. The sermon on the Areopagus was divided into five parts; *Comm. Acts* 17:22, *OE* xii/2:114,10f.: "Concionem hanc Pauli in quinque membra partiri licet."

and prayers was already dependent on his faith." Because faith and Christ are indissolubly connected, Cornelius must have had some knowledge of the Mediator; "even if his knowledge was hazy and confused, yet there was some" (*obscura licet fuerit et implicita eius cognitio, aliqua tamen fuit*). According to Calvin, Cornelius has his place among the fathers of old (*veterum Patrum catalogo*), who hoped for salvation by a Redeemer not yet revealed. We see how Calvin explains Luke's story with the aid of Paul's theology of justification. This strategy can also be discerned in the sermon on the Areopagus.

An important issue in that well-known sermon is the knowledge and worship of God among the Gentiles. As usual, Luke gives a summary of the substance of Paul's speech (*concionis Paulinae summam*). Calvin does not openly criticize this, but he does indicate that *brevitas*, otherwise highly valued, is playing false with Luke: "There is no doubt that Paul first of all showed that men are placed here, as in a theatre, to be spectators of the works of God, that he then spoke about the providence of God, that reveals itself in the whole government of the world."[65] When Luke omits an extensive report of the words actually spoken, Calvin seizes the opportunity to put the words of his own doctrine of creation and providence into Paul's mouth:

We gather from Luke's few words that Paul embraced the most momentous subjects. For when he says that the seasons had been previously ordained by Him, he testifies that, before men were brought into existence, He determined what their future circumstance would be like . . . In this verse God testifies through Paul's lips that it was previously fixed by His purpose how long He wished each people to continue in existence, and by what boundaries He intended each one to be contained. But if He appointed a certain time for them, and fixed boundaries of their territories, there is no doubt that He disposed the whole course of their life.

The next question about creation and providence is related to the knowledge of the Creator. The issue concerned is the possibility of coming to "a genuine and clear knowledge of God by nature" (*Comm. Acts* 17:27). The fact that humans do not feel God's presence, Paul attributed to their mental inertia: ". . . that they would search for God and perhaps grope around for him and find him, though he is not far from each one of us." Calvin himself formulates the answer to his own question:

---

65 *Comm. Acts* 17:26.

I reply that such perverseness is mingled with their ignorance and stupidity that, devoid of proper judgement, and with no true understanding, they disregard all the signs of the glory of God that plainly shine out in heaven and on earth. Yes, and since true knowledge of God is a special gift of His, and faith, by which He is properly known, proceeds only from the illumination of the Spirit, it follows that with nature alone as guide our minds cannot penetrate to Him. And of course Paul is not speaking here about the ability of men, but he is only warning that they are inexcusable, when they are blind in such a clear light; as he says in the first chapter of Romans.

As we saw in his exposition of Acts 14:17, Calvin molds Luke's reproduction of Paul's sermon on the basis of Romans 1:19–21. He even takes a step further by exclusively relating the remaining knowledge after the fall to the inexcusability of the blind Gentiles.[66]

In Luke's account, the sermon on the Areopagus finishes with the proclamation of divine judgment: "He has set a day on which he is going to judge the world in righteousness, by a man whom he designated, having provided proof to everyone by raising him from the dead" (v. 31). Calvin seems dissatisfied with this ending of the sermon.

There is no doubt that Paul said a good deal more about Christ, so that the Athenians might know that He is the Son of God, by whom salvation had been brought to the world, and to whom all power in heaven and on earth had been given. Otherwise the speech, such as we read it here [in Luke's version], would have been powerless to persuade.

The supposition that Paul first spoke about grace and salvation, before he spoke about God's judgment, is even more radical. This theory is based on pastoral and homiletical motives. Calvin is certain that a sermon should never fill a hearer with despair, however wicked he or she has been.[67] In Luke's account, Calvin does not recognize the fundamentals of the proclamation of the gospel.

---

66 Cf. H. Feld, "Einleitung," *OE* xii/1:lix: "Man sieht, wie Calvin unter dem Eindruck des Berichtes der Apostelgeschichte die zeitweilige Existenz einer 'natürlichen' Gotteserkenntnis einräumt (man hat den Eindruck: fast notgedrungen)." E. Haenchen, *Die Apostelgeschichte neu übersetzt und erklärt* (Göttingen: Vandenhoeck & Ruprecht, 1965), p. 462: ". . . tatsächlich stecken ja die Hörer des Paulus noch in der Unkenntnis Gottes. Aber damit erklärt der Redner das finden Gottes nicht für unmöglich." See also on *excusabilitas*, S. Scheld, "Die missionarische Verkündigung des Paulus in Calvins Kommentar der Apostelgeschichte," in: *Creatio ex amore: Beiträge zu einer Theologie der Liebe, Festschrift für Alexandre Ganoczy zum 60. Geburtstag*, ed. Th. Franke, M. Knapp, and J. Schmid (Würzburg: Echter, 1989), pp. 312–328, 326f.

67 *Comm. Acts* 3:17, *OE* xii/1:103,2f.: "Sic temperandae sunt nostrae conciones, ut auditoribus prosint. Nisi enim spes veniae relinquitur, terror poenae animos contumacia obdurat." See also Moehn, *"God Calls Us"*, p. 185.

The authority of Christ as Judge is emphasized by His resurrection. The sermon abruptly ends here, because some people laughed at the resurrection of the dead. It remains uncertain how Paul would have proceeded with his sermon. Possibly he would have spoken about Christ as Priest and Redeemer. Calvin is quite determined, stating:

Paul dealt at length with this fundamental principle of doctrine, which Luke briefly mentions with a few words. Not only did he briefly report that Christ rose from the dead, but at the same time he dealt with the power of the resurrection, as was proper. For why did Christ rise again, except that He might be the first fruits of those rising again?

Things only hinted at by Luke are elaborated upon in the commentary, based on a central chapter like 1 Corinthians 15.

Throughout the commentary, we discern Calvin's struggle with Luke and the way in which he told the history of the proclamation progressing from Jerusalem to Rome. After having become acquainted in this commentary with Calvin as a theologian and an exegete, we may finally answer the question of what in fact makes this commentary typical of John Calvin.

CALVIN AS COMMENTATOR

Having investigated Calvin's exegetical strategy, we will now try to perceive something of the man who wrote this commentary. Notwithstanding his famous *dictum* "*de me non libenter loquor*," there is more than one moment when Calvin's persona suddenly seems to drop, and his very humanity to shine through. Calvin was not only a writer of commentaries but also a preacher, who very frequently had to deliver his sermons in Geneva. This personal experience with the church in Geneva and its inhabitants deeply influenced the style of his commentary. Commenting on the deceit of Ananias and Sapphira he says: "it ought not to seem absurd that innumerable hypocrites daily deceive God and the Church just as much as these two, but yet not punished with death" (*Comm. Acts* 5:8). Such people refuse to be admonished:

It is a fault common to all inflexible and stubborn people to admit no admonitions, except when they are compelled to do so by force and authority; yes, and they are like delirious patients who assault their doctors in a fury. That is why we must take more pains to curb our passions, so that we may not similarly rush in a blind fury against those who wish to cure our faults. We are also warned by this example that it is not possible for the servants of God to carry out their duty among men who behave so badly, without constantly suffering many injuries, enduring many affronts, running into dangers, and, above all, hearing evil things about themselves when they do well.[68]

The commentary on the biblical text and his personal experience in Geneva become intertwined. Calvin recognizes himself in the experience of the disciples. We have to fight the same struggle.[69] The "minister of the Gospel" – that is how Calvin shows who he wants to be as commentator and preacher on the Acts of the Apostles: "In a minister of the Gospel it is an excellent virtue, and a most praiseworthy one, if he has been not only diligent and indefatigable in pursuing the task of teaching, but has also been ready to undergo the danger of death for the defence of the doctrine" (*Comm. Acts* 15:25).

---

68 *Comm. Acts* 7:26.
69 *Comm. Acts.* 5:17, *OE* xii/1:147,12f.: "Ergo nos semper ad certamen paratos esse oportet. Neque enim dissimilis est hodie nostra ratio."

CHAPTER 9

Calvin as commentator on the Pauline epistles

R. Ward Holder

The Pauline commentaries are the most significant site, as a series, for grasping John Calvin's biblical work. Certainly, there are other claimants to that accolade – the wonderfully autobiographical preface to the Psalms commentary, the extraordinarily unique approach of the Harmony of the Pentateuch, the general brilliance which is so frequently evident. But the Pauline commentaries stand out, for several reasons. First, they are first! Of all the ways in which Calvin might have address-ed himself to the task of commenting upon the Scripture, he chose to begin with the Pauline epistles, commenting upon them in canonical order.[1] Calvin's health was never very good, and by the time he was deeply into the series he had experienced death in his own family. So, simply by virtue of being the first commentaries Calvin wrote, these were his choice for those books of the Bible that it was most neces-sary for him to comment upon, and, by extension, that it was most necessary to know.[2]

Second, Calvin gave a theological rationale for making these his refer-ence point. In his consideration of the theme of the epistle to the Romans, which was the subject of his very first commentary, he wrote:

I am in doubt whether it would be worth while to spend much time in speaking of the value of this Epistle. My uncertainty is due only to my fear that since my commendation of it falls far short of its grandeur my remarks may merely obscure the Epistle. It is due also to the fact that at the very beginning the Epistle introduces itself better and explains itself in a much better way than any words

---

1 Consider T. H. L. Parker's comment that the reason for this approach may have been a "deliberate theological policy which Calvin believed was demanded by the New Testament itself?" *Calvin's New Testament Commentaries*, 2nd edn (Edinburgh: T. & T. Clark, 1993), p. 31.

2 We will see that as more important if we consider the length of time it took Calvin to move from writing his first to his second commentary. *Romans* was published by Wendelin Rihel in Strasbourg in 1540, the commentary upon 1 Corinthians by the same printer only in 1546!

can describe. It will, therefore, be better for me to come now to the theme itself. This will prove to us beyond any doubt that among many other notable virtues the Epistle has one in particular which is never sufficiently appreciated. It is this – if we have gained a true understanding of this Epistle, we have an open door to all the most profound treasures of Scripture.[3]

For any who wish to find Calvin's canon of the canon, either to admire or to castigate, he himself provides enough evidence in this letter. The epistle to the Romans opens the gates to the whole of Scripture. Since justification by faith is the main subject of the whole epistle,[4] one may with some confidence argue that this is the key to unlocking those profound treasures of Scripture.[5] Whether for good or ill, this concentration presents ample evidence for Calvin's chosen order of commenting upon Scripture.[6] The second reason for concentration upon these commentaries is that Calvin believed that the heart of the theology of the Scripture was found in these epistles.

Third, in reading the Pauline commentaries, we see Calvin learning the craft of being a commentator. He learned to interpret through reading Paul.[7] While that may seem too academic a theme, it is not. One can see the change across these commentaries, which span a period in which

3 *Comm. Rom.*, Theme of the Epistle of Paul to the Romans, *CNTC* VIII:5. *Iohannis Calvini Commentarius in Epistolam Pauli ad Romanos*, ed. T. H. L. Parker (Leiden: E. J. Brill, 1981), *Argumentum in Epistolam ad Romanos*, 5.1–11. "In praedicanda Epistolae huius utilitate, nescio an operaepretium sit diutius immorari, tum quod vereor ne meis elogiis haud dubie infra eius magnitudinem longe subsidentibus, nihil quam obscuretur: tum etiam quod multo magis ipsa primo statim aspectu se proferat, et vera specie melius se explicet, quam ullis verbis enarri queat. Ergo iam ad argumentum ipsum transire satius fuerit: unde citra controversiam protinus constabit, praeter plurimas alias, et eas eximias dotes, hanc ei proprie competere, quae nunquam pro dignitate satis aestimetur: quod siquis veram eius intelligentiam sit assequutus, ad reconditissimos quosque Scripturae thesauros adeundos habeat apertas fores."

4 *Comm. Rom.*, *CNTC* VIII:5, *Ad Romanos* 5.18–19.

5 However, Bernard Cottret simply goes too far in asserting that Calvin chose the epistle to the Romans for "historical [reasons]: the Epistle to the Romans was part of the designated route that led, inevitably it was thought, to the Reformation." This demonstrates a singular lack of engagement with the history of exegesis – Romans had been one of the most commented-upon books of the New Testament for centuries. Bernard Cottret, *Calvin: A Biography*, trans. by M. Wallace McDonald (Edinburgh: T. & T. Clark, 2000), p. 146.

6 Parker points out that Calvin's order of commenting upon the New Testament, beginning with the epistles and proceeding first to John's gospel and only then to the Synoptics, is based on theological hermeneutical concerns, and more closely mirrors what modern historical-critical scholarship has demonstrated to have been the literary history of the New Testament. "We may note that Calvin's method was not only closer to the literary history of the New Testament, in that many of the Epistles pre-dated the Synoptics in their canonical form, but closer also to the history of the early Church, in that its confessions of faith were concentrated on Jesus Christ as Creator and Redeemer and so followed the teaching of St John and the Epistles." *Calvin's New Testament Commentaries*, p. 32.

7 With a very brief detour to the epistle of Jude, published in 1542, by Jean Gerard, in French.

Calvin grew up as a pastor.[8] This change is demonstrable by the kinds
of advice to pastors that he includes in the commentaries. There is far less in
his Romans commentary than in the 1 Corinthians commentary,[9] published six years later, after significant change in Calvin's life and ministry.

The first section of this chapter will begin by considering the history
of the writing of the commentaries, and the record of their editing. This
concerns what Calvin wrote, and when he wrote it – the history of the
publication of the Pauline commentaries. As these were written across more
than a ten-year span, that will take some length. Once that is complete, it is
important to consider both what it meant to Calvin that these commentaries somehow formed a whole, and how the task of commenting upon
Scripture interacted with his writing of the *Institutes*. The next step concerns the historical circumstances Calvin himself faced – did these in any
way interact with the commentaries? From there, we will turn to a consider
the influences, such as humanism, that were directly acting upon Calvin in
his work. Finally, the first section will conclude with a consideration of the
sources he used in writing his commentaries. A second major section,
following the histories of the commentaries, will ask the question, "what
is between the covers of these books?" In other words, enough about the
books, what is in them? Finally, the essay will conclude with a synthetic
effort at gathering together what the Pauline commentaries teach us about
Calvin as commentator, theologian, and teacher.

THE CONTEXTS OF THE PAULINE COMMENTARIES

Publication history

Calvin's first commentary, as is widely known, is the commentary upon
Romans. Wendelin Rihel published it in Strasbourg, in 1540.[10] We can be
certain that Calvin had thought for quite some time about publishing
commentaries, and about the necessary spirit of the commentator. We

---

8 To be blunt, when Calvin began work on the Romans commentary, he was a banished pastor,
   whose inability to navigate the troubled political waters of Geneva had caused his banishment.
   By the publication of the set, he was an accomplished pastor, with both the French congregation
   of Strasbourg and ten years in Geneva to his credit.
9 I have considered this in my article, "Calvin's Exegetical Understanding of the Office of Pastor,"
   in *Calvin and the Company of Pastors*. Papers Presented at the 14th Colloquium of the Calvin Studies
   Society, May 22–24, 2003. Ed. David Foxgrover (Grand Rapids: CRC Product Services, 2004).
10 Parker, *Calvin's New Testament Commentaries*, p. 206. See also Rodolphe Peter, *Bibliotheca
   Calviniana: Les oeuvres de Jean Calvin publiées au xvie siècle*, vol. 1, *Écrits théologiques, littéraires
   et juridiques 1532–1554* (Geneva: Librairie Droz, 1991), pp. 74–75.

know this from the dedicatory epistle to Simon Gryneé (Latinized form Grynaeus), whom Calvin had known in Basel when he lived there in 1535 and 1536.[11] In that letter, Calvin recalled to his friend:

Both of us felt that lucid brevity constituted the particular virtue of an interpreter. Since it is almost his only task to unfold the mind of the writer whom he has undertaken to expound, he misses his mark, or at least strays outside his limits, by the extent to which he leads his readers away from the meaning of the author.[12]

Beyond the interest inherent in what has become a *locus classicus* for those studying Calvin's interpretive work, this letter points out that, from very early in his theological career, Calvin was thinking about commenting upon Scripture, even at a time when the first edition of his *Institutes* was not yet printed. Calvin published his first commentary in 1540, and would follow that commentary with a translation of it in French, in 1550.[13] This would become his general habit, and speaks to his desire to provide instruction in Scripture for more than one audience or public.[14] He wrote the commentaries in Latin to serve the ecclesiastical professional class, but he attempted to supply the needs of the wider faith community by regularly translating his work into French.

Though it is not always possible to date Calvin's writing of the commentaries as precisely as their publication dates, we do have some help from his teaching in that regard as well. Calvin lectured on Romans during his first stay at Geneva.[15] Thus, we are able to guess that the commentary on Romans was written sometime in the period between 1538 and 1539, as the dedication to Romans is dated October 18, 1539.[16]

---

11 Parker, *Calvin's New Testament Commentaries, p.* 10.

12 Calvin, *CNTC* VIII, dedicatory epistle, p. 1. "Sentiebat enim uterque nostrum, praecipuam interpretis virtutem in perspicua brevitate esse positam. Et sane quum hoc sit prope unicum illius officium, mentem scriptoris, quem explicandum sumpsit, patefacere: quantum ab ea lectores abducit, tantundem a scopo suo aberrat, vel certe a suis finibus quodammodo evagatur." *Ad Romanos, Calvinus Grynaeo*, p. 1.

13 Parker, *Calvin's New Testament Commentaries*, pp. 206–207. Actually, Parker notes that as early as 1543 Calvin had published, through Jean Gerard in Geneva, an extract of the Romans commentary in French. But apparently the full version waited until 1550. Peter concurs, noting the publication of the text, but giving its title as *Exposition sur l'Epistre de sainct Paul aux Romains, extraicte des commentaires de M. J. Calvin. Bibliotheca Calviniana*, 1:126.

14 Serene Jones has pointed out the various audiences Calvin considered in her *Calvin and the Rhetoric of Piety*, Columbia Series in Reformed Theology (Louisville: Westminster John Knox Press, 1995), ch. 2.

15 Parker, *Calvin's New Testament Commentaries*, p. 15.

16 *Ad Romanos*, p. 4.

Having written a significant commentary on one of the more difficult books of Scripture in a two-year period, while simultaneously pastoring a church and finishing the second edition of his *Institutes*, Calvin would, we might imagine, have quickly turned out commentaries upon the next installments of the Pauline corpus. That belief would be even stronger when we are supplied with the fact that Calvin was lecturing on 1 Corinthians in 1539 in Strasbourg.[17] However, that assumption would be wrong. It would be 1546 before Rihel would publish the commentary on 1 Corinthians.[18] What happened? Professor Parker's conjecture that Calvin simply was overwhelmed by the workload at Geneva seems the most likely argument. Certainly Calvin himself never seems to have wavered in his commitment to commenting, and his colleagues were universally anxious for him to produce more.[19] As Parker notes, "Ecclesiastical polity, pastoral work in all its branches (especially the burden of frequent preaching), as well as the demands of an extensive correspondence and of controversies demanding polemical replies, left little time for a man in poor health to write what was not immediately necessary."[20] However, the book finally rolled off the press, followed much more quickly by a French translation, published by Jean Gerard in Geneva. This change of publisher was a portent of things to come.

The commentary on 2 Corinthians ended the relationship between Calvin and Rihel. Certainly, the writing was on the wall when Calvin moved back to Geneva, as a distance of over two hundred miles was a significant barrier to simple communication of details between author and printer.[21] But Calvin had maintained the relationship, perhaps because of a debt of gratitude to the printer for helping him earlier.[22] Problems in the printing of *2 Corinthians*, however, proved to be the last straw. Calvin sent the manuscript to Strasbourg, and it never showed up. Calvin was beside himself, for he had no second copy.[23] Only in September could he write to Farel that the manuscript was safe.

The publication history of *2 Corinthians* is unique, suggesting that there are issues for which the historical record is less than complete.

17 Parker, *Calvin's New Testament Commentaries*, p. 17.
18 Ibid., p. 207. Parker notes: "It would seem that Rihel may have intended to publish a uniform set of the Pauline Epistles, for I Corinthians has the same format as Romans." Cf. Peter, *Bibliotheca Calviniana*, 1:214–216.
19 Parker, *Calvin's New Testament Commentaries*, pp. 17–19.
20 Ibid., p. 17.
21 Ibid. It is also safe to assume that Calvin was more than a little put off by the difficulties that surfaced in the publishing of the 2 Corinthians commentary!
22 Ibid., p. 15.   23 Ibid., p. 19.

The commentary was first published by Jean Gerard in Geneva, in French.[24] Because of the problems concerning the loss and subsequent recovery of the manuscript, some of the history of the commentary can be traced. Calvin finished the commentary in July or August of 1546,[25] and sent it off to Strasbourg.[26] In early August, he learned that the manuscript had not arrived. In mid-September he learned that it was safe, but Rihel still did not publish it immediately.[27] By January of the following year the work had been published, in French, by Gerard in Geneva. It was only in 1548 that the Latin edition was printed by Gerard in Geneva.

What can we make of this? First, the frustration of being so far from one's printer at a time when authors were quite involved in the production of books must have been quite significant for Calvin. This would have been especially true when Rihel was not proceeding to press with the manuscript of the commentary which had already been lost once. This factor alone could have influenced Calvin against any further business with Rihel. Second, the Schmalkaldic War stretched from 1546 until 1547. Calvin wrote a letter to de Falais that noted the effect of the war upon the business of publishing.[28] As he was diverted once from Strasbourg to Geneva by a war, may it have been that his commentaries followed that same route? Whatever the final reason may have been, these are some of the factors that could have borne weight for Calvin's decision that, from 1548 on, Gerard would print the Pauline commentaries.

But what reason can be given for the appearance of the French version first, followed by the Latin? This is a singular pattern for the Pauline commentaries, with the possible exception of the very brief commentaries which were only printed in Latin as part of the collected set by Gerard in 1551.[29] But these are possibly explained by the fact that the first collection, that of Gerard in 1551, was never translated into French. Thus, Calvin's ideal of giving tools to the laity for reading the Scripture would have required him to issue these separately. Two explanations appear possible.

---

24 *Ioannis Calvini Opera Exegetica, Commentarii in Secundum Pauli Epistolam ad Corinthios*, ed. Helmut Feld (Geneva: Librairie Droz, 1994), Introduction, p. xi; Parker, *Calvin's New Testament Commentaries*, pp. 20–21.

25 Parker and Peter disagree, Peter supplying August, Parker stating July. In any case, the work was done in the summer of 1546, but not published until 1548.

26 Parker, *Calvin's New Testament Commentaries*, p. 20.

27 Ibid.

28 Feld, Introduction, p. xii.

29 Parker, *Calvin's New Testament Commentaries*, pp. 208–211.

First, Rihel did publish the 2 Corinthians commentary in Latin, some-time in late 1546, and Calvin used that edition to translate his commentary for Gerard's French version which appeared in early 1547.[30] Gerard then published an edition of the Latin, after Calvin had decided to use his press for the rest of the Pauline set. The problem with that scenario is that it requires that all of the copies of Rihel's first edition were lost to history. A second possibility is that Rihel, pressed with other matters, returned to Calvin the Latin manuscript, from which Calvin then trans-lated the French edition. The problem with that seems even worse – why would Gerard not simply immediately print the Latin? The question begs further archival work.

If Calvin had spent much time and considerable anguish bringing forth the two commentaries on the letters to the church at Corinth, the commentaries on the rest of the Pauline corpus fairly flew from his pen. Though the origins of the 2 Corinthians commentary remain obscure, the Galatians group is blissfully simple. Calvin had begun writing the com-mentaries on Galatians, Ephesians, Philippians, and Colossians by the end of 1546.[31] He always treated these four as a group, and they were never published separately. Jean Gerard published these in 1548; Gerard also published the French translation of this group, in the same year. Calvin completed the single commentary on the letters to Timothy in 1548; Gerard brought out the Latin edition in 1548, with the French following in that same year.[32]

The next year, 1549, was as productive for Calvin, with the completion of both the brief commentary on Titus and the commentary on Hebrews.[33] While the *Hebrews* translation was published the same year by Gerard,[34] the *Titus* would wait until 1551 for the Latin version, though Gerard published it in French in 1550. *Philemon* was never published except as a portion of the Pauline set, first published by Gerard in 1551. We may ask why Calvin chose to include Hebrews in his Pauline set. Was this a moment when his good text-critical sense deserted him? No. It is clear from the text of the commentary itself that Calvin was well aware that this book of the Bible could not rest its claim to canonicity on its authorship,

---

30 Peter, *Bibliotheca Calviniana*, 1:242–243.
31 Letter to Farel, quoted in ibid., 1:268.
32 Ibid., 1:266–268; 1:274–275; Parker, *Calvin's New Testament Commentaries*, p. 248.
33 Peter, *Bibliotheca Calviniana*, 1:297–299; Parker, *Calvin's New Testament Commentaries*, pp. 23, 209.
34 *Ioannis Calvini Opera Exegetica, Commentarius in Epistolam ad Hebraeos*, ed. T. H. L. Parker (Geneva: Librairie Droz, 1996), Introduction, p. xxxiv.

but rather upon its doctrine.[35] However, he included it, apparently, so as to meet the traditional division of the church, which did see Paul as the author of this epistle. This was accompanied by the two commentaries on the letters to the Thessalonians, which were published by Gerard in 1551 as part of the Pauline epistle set.[36] The French translations of the commentaries on Thessalonians were published that same year,[37] as a single volume.

By 1549, Calvin had finished commenting upon the Pauline epistles. Yet their publication history does not end there. He would edit the commentaries twice more, first for the collected edition of 1551, and a second, more thorough, reworking for the final collected edition of 1556.[38] While some of the alterations that Calvin made were inconsequential, others were significant additions.

The first set of editorial changes came in the set that Gerard produced in 1551. A second set of changes occured in 1556, for an edition printed by Robert Estienne in Latin, and the following year by Conrad Badius in French. Calvin noted that there were changes in a later edition, but these number only eighteen for the entire set, so are rather inconsequential.[39] But the meaty questions immediately come to our attention. What were the changes, and what was their impact?

When we consider Romans, the suspicion arises that this is a significantly changed book. In 1540, it had been a brief book, of approximately sixty-five thousand words.[40] The revisions of 1551 changed the commentary on Romans to about seventy-seven thousand words; five years later, Calvin again expanded it to reach ninety-six thousand words.[41] Thus, in the course of two revisions, the commentary on Romans mirrored the *Institutes*, in that editing always meant adding. Calvin added almost 50 percent, in terms of words, to his original text, making the question of lucid brevity rather inconsequential.

Clearly the text's length changed. But did the commentary itself? Strangely, such is not always the case. Yes, there are significant additions.

---

35 Calvin, *Comm. Heb. Argumentum, CNTC* XII:1, *Ad Hebraeos*, 12.1–20.
36 Peter, *Bibliotheca Calviniana*, 1:382–383.
37 Though Parker notes that since the volume on the Thessalonians is not dated by month, it is impossible to tell which was published first, the Latin or the French: *Calvin's New Testament Commentaries*, p. 208.
38 Peter, *Bibliotheca Calviniana*, 1:414–419.
39 Parker, *Calvin's New Testament Commentaries*, pp. 36 and 210.
40 Ibid., p. 37. This section is especially dependent upon Prof. Parker's work, as his detail and familiarity with the Romans editions remain the standard.
41 Ibid.

An example comes at chapter 6.17, where Calvin adds almost a paragraph. In the edition of 1540, Calvin had only explained his usage of the word "type (*typum*)," and explained that this meant that believers should not deviate from God's path either to the left or to the right. By 1556, he had commented on Paul's effort at distinguishing between the hidden power of the Spirit and the external letter of the law, Paul's reasons for using such an illustration, and the fact that it was Erasmus who used a different word choice from Calvin's at that point, following the Vulgate. Obviously, an enormous amount has been added.[42] But while this was a great expansion, it does not represent a significant change. Calvin does not deny his earlier ideas, but identifies where he had been too laconic, and remedies the lack.

Further, the Romans commentary remains the one most changed by Calvin's editing pen. The difference between the Romans and Hebrews commentaries, his first and last Pauline efforts, is remarkable. While one has difficulty finding a single page without editing in the Romans commentary, the Hebrews commentary flows almost without interruption, rarely receiving any editing at all.[43] While our space here is too brief to make full comparisons, we may draw the conclusion that Calvin's ongoing study of theology and pastoral tasks did not fundamentally change his grasping of the meaning of the Pauline epistles, hammered out between 1540 and 1551.

The commentaries and the Institutes

For Calvin, the church was in a very real sense the *schola dei*, the school of God. For that school, the true and perfect curriculum was the Scripture. However, that Scripture could not be approached unwarily. To advance into Scripture without a guide would be like going on a journey without a map. For Calvin, part of the map was his *Institutes*. He wrote:

Moreover, it has been my purpose in this labor to prepare and instruct candidates in sacred theology for the reading of the divine Word, in order that they may be able both to have easy access to it and to advance in it without stumbling. For I believe I have so embraced the sum of religion in all its parts, and have arranged it in such an order, that if anyone rightly grasps it, it will not be difficult for him to determine what

---

42 At times, so much so that it is difficult to sustain Parker's belief that the commentary has "been considerably altered in form but remains constant in substance." Ibid., p. 39.

43 For the comparison, I have used the modern critical editions of these commentaries. See *Iohannis Calvini Commentarius in Epistolam Pauli ad Romanos*, ed. T. H. L. Parker (Leiden: E. J. Brill, 1981), and *OE, Commentarius in Epistolam ad Hebraeos*.

he ought especially to seek in Scripture, and to what end he ought to relate its contents. If, after this road has, as it were, been paved, I shall publish any interpretations of Scripture, I shall always condense them, because I shall have no need to undertake long doctrinal discussions, and to digress into commonplaces. In this way the godly reader will be spared great annoyance and boredom, provided he approach Scripture armed with a knowledge of the present work, as a necessary tool.[44]

In order that my readers may better profit from this present work, I should like to indicate briefly the benefit they may derive from it. For, in doing this, I shall show them the purpose to which they ought to bend and direct their intention while reading it. Although Holy Scripture contains a perfect doctrine, to which one can add nothing; since in it our Lord has meant to display the infinite treasures of his wisdom, yet a person who has not much practice in it has good reason for some guidance and direction, to know what he ought to look for in it, in order not to wander hither and thither, but to hold to a sure path, that he may always be pressing toward the end to which the Holy Spirit calls him. Perhaps the duty of those who have received from God fuller light than others is to help simple folk at this point, and as it were to lend them a hand, in order to guide them and help them to find the sum of what God meant to teach us in his Word. Now, that cannot be better done through the Scriptures than to treat the chief and weightiest matters comprised in the Christian philosophy. For he who knows these things will be prepared to profit more in God's school in one day than another in three months – particularly as he knows fairly well to what he must refer each sentence, and has this rule to embrace all that is presented to him.

It is very necessary to help in this way those who desire to be instructed in the doctrine of salvation. Consequently, I was constrained, according to the ability that the Lord gave me, to undertake this task. Such was my purpose in composing the present book.[45]

---

44 *OS* III:6.18–31. *Inst.* 1.4–5, "John Calvin to the Reader": "Porro hoc mihi in isto labore propositum fuit, sacrae Theologiae candidatos ad divini verbi lectionem ita praeparare et instruere, ut et facilem ad eam aditum habere, et inoffenso in ea gradu pergere queant; siquidem religionis summam omnibus partibus sic mihi complexus esse videor, et eo quoque ordine digessisse, ut siquis eam recte tenuerit, ei non sit difficile statuere et quid potissimum quaerere in Scriptura, et quem in scopum quicquid in ea continetur referre debeat. Itaque, hac veluti strata via, siquas posthac Scripturae enarrationes edidero, quia non necesse habebo de dogmatibus longas disputationes instituere, et in locos communes evagari: eas compendio semper astringam. Ea ratione, magna molestia et fastidio pius lector sublevabitur: modo praesentis operis cognitione, quasi necessario instrumento, praemunitus accedat." Hereafter, all citations to the *Institutes* will be as follows, unless otherwise noted. First, the citation to the OS, giving volume, page, and line numbers, followed by *Inst.*, signifying the McNeill/Battles edition, followed by the book, chapter, and paragraph numbers. Further, the Latin text will be given in the body, accompanied by standard translations in the notes, except where otherwise noted. In this way, ease of finding the material is covered in both the standard Latin, English, and occasional French texts.

45 *OS* III:7.15–40. *Inst.*, "Subject Matter of the Present Work," pp. 6–7. "A fin que les Lecteurs puissent mieux faire leur proffit de ce present livre, ie leur veux bien monstrer en brief, l'utilité qu'ilz auront a en prendre. Car, en ce faisant, ie leur monstreray le but, auquel ils devront tendre

Both these passages are prefaces, taken from different versions of
Calvin's *Institutes of the Christian Religion.* The first is the preface entitled
"John Calvin to the Reader." This preface introduced the 1539 edition[46] of
Calvin's *Institutes,* and was appended to all further Latin editions. The
second is the preface to the French edition of 1560.[47] These prefaces act
as bookends to his commenting, the first before he began, and the last after
the great majority of his commentaries had already been published. Given
the length of time between the two prefaces, what is striking is that the
general message has stayed so much the same. In 1539, Calvin stated that he
believed he had "embraced the sum of religion in all its parts, and . . .
arranged it in such an order, that if anyone rightly grasps it, it will not be
difficult for him to determine what he ought especially to seek in Scripture, and to what end he ought to relate its contents."[48] In 1560, Calvin
felt his object in composing the *Institutes* was to guide the simpler
believers by helping them find what God meant to teach, by setting forth
the chief matters of the Christian philosophy.[49]

In the first preface, Calvin makes clear that the *Institutes* was intended
for use in conjunction with commentaries. That he does not place this

---

et diriger leur intention, en le lisant. Combien que la saincte Escriture contienne une doctrine
parfaicte, a laquelle on ne peut rien adiouster: comme en icelle nostre Seigneur a voulu desployer
les Thresors infiniz de sa Sapience: toutesfois une personne, qui n'y sera pas fort exercitée, a bon
mestier de quelque conduicte et addresse, pour sçavoir ce quelle y doibt cercher: a fin de ne
s'esgarer point cà et là, mais de tenir une certaine voye, pour attaindre tousiours a la fin, ou le
Sainct Esprit l'appelle. Pourtant l'office de ceux qui ont receu plus ample lumiere de Dieu que
les autres, est, de subvenir aux simples en cest endroict: et quasi leur prester la main, pour les
conduire et les ayder a trouver la somme de ce que Dieu nous a voulu enseigner en sa parolle. Or
cela ne se peut mieux faire par Escritures, qu'en traictant les matieres principales et de
consequence, lesquelles sont comprinses en la Philosophie Chrestienne. Car celuy qui en aura
l'intelligence, sera preparé a proffiter en l'eschole de Dieu en un iour, plus qu'un autre en trois
mois: d'autant qu'il sçait a peu pres, ou il doibt rapporter un chascune sentence: et ha sa reigle
pour compasser tout ce qui luy est presenté. Voyant donc que cestoit une chose tant necessaire,
que d'ayder en ceste façon ceux qui desirent d'estre instruictz en la doctrine de salut, ie me suis
efforcé, selon la faculté que le Seigneur m'a donnée, de m'employer a ce faire: et a ceste fin i'ay
composé ce present livre.

46 The date of the origin of this preface explains the reference, which seems odd to the modern
reader, that Calvin may publish commentaries on Scripture – he had not at this time seen his
Romans commentary (1540) go to press. An analysis of the function of the prefaces, and the
history of their redaction, can be found in Jones, *Rhetoric of Piety,* pp. 46–58.

47 Richard Muller notes that the history of this was more complicated than the McNeill/Battles
edition demonstrates. See his "Calvin's 'Argument du livre' (1541): An Erratum to the McNeill
and Battles 'Institutes.'" *Sixteenth Century Journal* 29 (1998): 35–38.

48 *Inst.,* "Subject Matter of the Present Work."

49 Having pointed out the necessity of doctrine to guide interpretation of the Scriptures, we should
not go too far in making this an understanding of "Calvin's" doctrine. Richard Muller makes an
excellent point when he states: "What Calvin intended to teach was the church's doctrine, not

piece of advice in the second preface is hardly remarkable: by 1560, every reader of Calvin would know that indeed he had published commentaries. But returning to the 1539 preface, what is the relationship between the *Institutes* and the commentaries to be? Quite clearly, the *Institutes* functions as a hermeneutical guide. Calvin makes it absolutely clear that one must know what one seeks in the Scriptures prior to looking; the alternative is to wander rather fruitlessly. The *Institutes* is a doctrinal hermeneutic, which is a proper propaedeutic to reading the commentaries, which are read to understand the Scripture. Calvin intentionally sets up a circle for the interpretation of Scripture, as a way for both the learned and the novices to progress in the school of the Lord.

Calvin's historical circumstances and the writing of the commentaries

What was the impact upon Calvin's writing of the Pauline commentaries of his own particular historical circumstances? This section of our study easily merits a monograph of its own. Although the traditional view of Calvin's personal history has stressed the imperturbability of his theological output by his own travails,[50] only recently have deep studies of this sort been done, linking the particular historical moments in Calvin's life to their possible influence on his theological output.[51] While Calvin is famously reticent about his personality and life, sometimes it seems that it does come through. Certainly the effort to trace this out could pay rich rewards, and, as certainly, it would expand this essay by a factor of at least ten. But some points are worth making.

his own doctrine. To the extent that he was successful, his originality must be sought more in his manner of presenting Christian doctrine, in the way he received, incorporated, or modified forms and arguments of patristic and medieval theology, in his particular fusion of older theological substance either with his own exegetical results or with Renaissance rhetorical forms, and in the nuances that he gave to the elements of extant tradition." See Muller's *The Unaccommodated Calvin: Studies in the Foundation of a Theological Tradition* (Oxford: Oxford University Press, 2000), pp. 7ff., for expansion on this point.

50 For instance, see, T. H. L. Parker's "Introduction," in *OE Commentarius in Epistolam ad Hebraeos*, p. xi. Parker notes that 1549 was a difficult year for Calvin, with the death of his wife, increasing opposition from the Perrinists, and some sort of ailment on his shoulder. Yet Parker concludes: "It is characteristic, however, that none of the personal sorrow or the civic troubles or his own health is reflected in the commentary."

51 An excellent recent example is Wilhelmus T. H. Moehn's *God Calls Us to His Service: The Relation Between God and His Audience in Calvin's Sermons on Acts* (Geneva: Librairie Droz, 2001). Moehn traces out Calvin's sermons on Acts 4.1–6.7, preached between April 13 and August 24, 1550. He then applies known issues in Calvin's life and ministry to make greater clarity out of the clues in the sermons.

First, it is important to point out the changed confidence Calvin has in his pastoral advice,[52] discernible by the enormous difference in the amount of ministerial counsel he gives in his first two commentaries. In the Romans commentary, he is rather spare in such offerings. He gives only approximately seventeen instances of specific pastoral advice, either by looking at Paul as a pastoral paradigm, or by taking the words of the text as a catalyst to give advice to pastors. By contrast, in the commentary on 1 Corinthians Calvin is generous with his advice, expanding those same types of advice until the tally is well over seventy occurrences.[53]

Here we see the first instance of Calvin's own historical circumstance affecting the commentaries. At the time of his first effort at writing a commentary, though he felt it appropriate to include pastoral advice and encouragement to good ministerial practice, he did not include much. His second commentary did not follow that pattern, instead including rather frequent instances of pastoral advice. Why the difference? Certainly, some of this may have to do with the nature of the two letters and the two churches. Paul does not know the Roman church nearly so well as the Corinthian church. The first letter to Corinth scolds the Corinthians for numerous faults. As Paul acts as a chiding or even accusing pastor, there is more opportunity to consider the pastoral task in the first epistle to the Corinthians. However, that explanation alone is insufficient to account for the whole of the difference. To add to the richness of our consideration, let us reflect on Calvin's own changed circumstances and education in the practical school of ministry. When he was writing the Romans commentary, during the year(s) directly prior to 1540, he was not merely an inexperienced pastor. Rather, he was a pastor whose first call had been a disastrous pastoral ministry, which led to his banishment. By the mid 1540s, Calvin was a changed man. He had pastored a congregation with which he had good success, while following the lead of senior colleagues in a city where he could be in conversation with many respected associates.[54] The very city council that had banished him from Geneva had invited him to return, and he had been more able to place his stamp upon the reforms of that city. In Geneva, by 1546, he had overseen the

---

52 See my articles on this phenomenon, "Calvin's Exegetical Pastor" and "Paul as Calvin's (Ambivalent) Pastoral Model," *Dutch Review of Church History* (Leiden: E. J. Brill, 2004), pp. 284–298.

53 This is even more remarkable considering that the two commentaries are roughly equivalent in length.

54 Cornelis Augustijn notes that our understanding of Calvin in Strasbourg still remains incomplete. Pointing out that, though much basic work on sources has been done, Calvin still escapes our grasp in this period, he writes, "We have at our disposal a great number of bricks, a

establishment of a united Company of Pastors.[55] He had become a theologian and pastor of significant weight; his greater and more successful pastoral experience permitted him the license to speak of pastoral issues more confidently and frequently.

The historical circumstances of the period leading up to the publication of Calvin's second commentary in 1546 and the issue of pastoral advice in the 1 Corinthians commentary are fraught with possibilities. Between 1540 and 1546, Calvin worked on his 1 Corinthians commentary. However, this period coincides almost exactly with his return to Geneva, a time when he was extraordinarily concerned about the quality of pastors. When Calvin returned to Geneva, he was unimpressed with the quality of the pastors. This was both because of their lack of training, and because some had sided against him in a political battle with the city council.[56] He wrote in a letter:

> Our colleagues are rather a hindrance than a help to us: they are rude and self-conceited, have no zeal, and less learning. But what is worst of all, I cannot trust them, even although I very much wish that I could: for by many evidences they show they are estranged from us, and give scarcely any indication of a sincere and trustworthy disposition.[57]

Could it be that some of Calvin's advice to pastors was simply polemic aimed at his recalcitrant colleagues, and awareness of the necessity of a united body of pastors for those who would work effectively in the church? This would certainly explain his insistence on following the example of Paul,[58] or the necessity of ministers avoiding pulling the church apart.[59] While that seems possible, the painstaking work of tying things together is still at too preliminary a stage to make final conclusions. However, this brief survey of the influence of actual pastoral ministry on the content of Calvin's commentaries suggests that this would be a rich source.

Calvin's humanism and other influences

Calvin was trained by humanists, used the tools of humanists, and never left the camp of the humanists.[60] He was a friend of some of the

variety of studies, but the character of the man Calvin remains hidden." See his "Calvin in Strasbourg," in *Calvinus Sacrae Scripturae Professor*, ed. Wilhelm Neuser, International Congress on Calvin Research (Grand Rapids: Eerdmans, 1994), pp. 166–177.

55 William G. Naphy, *Calvin and the Consolidation of the Genevan Reformation*, rpt. (Louisville: Westminster John Knox Press, 2003), p. 84.

56 Ibid., p. 56.   57 Quoted in ibid., p. 54.   58 *CNTC* IX:73; *CO* II:352–353.

59 *Comm. 1 Cor.* 12, *CNTC* IX:28; *CO* II:316.

60 The literature on Calvin and humanism is rather vast. Some significant titles include Ford Lewis Battles, "Calvin's Humanistic Education," in *Interpreting John Calvin*, ed. Robert Benedetto (Grand Rapids: Baker Books, 1996), pp. 47–64; Josef Bohatec, "Calvin et l'Humanisme," *Revue*

most prestigious humanist scholars, such as Mathurin Cordier,[61] had been taught by Cordier and others such as Andreas Alciati, and continued to maintain contact with humanists throughout his career.[62] His early work on Seneca's *De Clementia* was "the epitome of a humanist study of an ancient document."[63] Calvin imbibed deeply at the well of humanist authors, though he was more influenced by Luther than Erasmus or Budé.[64] Having said that, one can wonder about what light this sheds on the complex topic of humanism's influence upon Calvin's interpretation of Scripture in general, and the Pauline epistles in particular. First, it is helpful to grasp what is meant here by "humanism." I take humanism in its sixteenth-century context to be an approach to study and sources, rather than a particular theological stance.[65] In that sense, humanism had a hugely significant impression on Calvin's ideal of handling

Historique 183 (1938): 207–241; 185 (1939): 36–69; William Bouwsma, "Calvinism as *Theologia Rhetorica*," in *Calvinism as* Theologia Rhetorica, ed. Wilhelm Wuellner (Berkeley: Center for Hermeneutical Studies in Hellenistic and Modern Culture, 1986), pp. 1–21; William Bouwsma, "Calvin and the Renaissance Crisis of Knowing," *Calvin Theological Journal* 17 (1982): 190–211; William Bouwsma, "The Two Faces of Humanism: Stoicism and Augustinianism in Renaissance Thought," in *Itinerarium Italicum: The Profile of the Italian Renaissance in the Mirror of Its European Transformations*, ed. Heiko Oberman and Thomas A Brady, Jr. (Leiden: E. J. Brill, 1975); Quirinus Breen, *John Calvin: A Study in French Humanism*, 2nd edn (New York: Archon Books, 1968); Basil Hall, "Calvin and Biblical Humanism," *Proceedings of the Huguenot Society of London* 20 (1960): 195–209; Jones, *Rhetoric of Piety*; Robert D. Linder, "Calvinism and Humanism: The First Generation," *Church History* 44 (1975): 167–181; Olivier Millet, *Calvin et la dynamique de la parole: Etude de rhétorique réformée* (Paris: H. Champion, 1992); Olivier Millet, "*Docere/Movere*: Les catégories rhétoriques et leurs sources humanistes dans la doctrine calvinienne de foi," in *Calvinus Sincerioris Religionis Vindex*, ed. Wilhelm Neuser and Brian Armstrong (Kirksville, MO: Sixteenth Century Journal Publishers, 1997), pp. 35–52; Michael L. Monheit, "Young Calvin, Textual Interpretation and Roman Law," *Bibliothèque d'Humanisme et Renaissance: Travaux et Documents* 59/2 (1997): 263–282; James Payton, "History as Rhetorical Weapon: Christian Humanism in Calvin's Reply to Sadoleto, 1539," in *In Honor of John Calvin, 1509–64*, ed. E. J. Furcha (Montreal: Faculty of Religious Studies, McGill University, 1987), pp. 96–132; Charles Trinkaus, "Renaissance Problems in Calvin's Theology," in his *The Scope of Renaissance Humanism* (Ann Arbor: University of Michigan Press, 1983), pp. 317–339; Charles Trinkaus, "Rhetoric and Responsibility in Calvin's Theology," in *The Context of Contemporary Theology*, ed. Alexander J. McKelway and E. David Willis (Atlanta: John Knox Press, 1974), pp. 43–63.
61 To whom Calvin dedicated his 1 Thessalonians commentary.
62 Ford Lewis Battles lists six humanists who exercised significant impact upon the young Calvin – Guillaume Budé, Mathrin Cordier, Pierre de l'Estoile, Melchior Wolmar, Andrea Alciati and Pierre Danès. See his article, "Calvin's Humanistic Education."
63 Alexandre Ganoczy, *The Young Calvin*, trans. David Foxgrover and Wade Provo (Philadelphia: Westminster Press, 1987), p. 179.
64 Cf. ibid., pp. 180–181.
65 It is well to be careful about how far to carry the question of influence when one considers Calvin's humanism. Clearly, his exegetical methods owe much to the humanist influences, such as that of Andrea Alciati. On the other hand, his theological positions just as clearly can be at

biblical texts. He was not satisfied with dealing with the Vulgate, but worked with the Greek, and in fact at times criticized other scholars for their reliance upon or impression by the Vulgate.[66] He took great pains to set the historical context in the argument of his commentary on an epistle by considering the evidence for its placement in Paul's life, and used that to control his interpretation.[67]

What points are important to consider in evaluating the impact of humanism on Calvin's interpretation of the Pauline epistles? Though this list could be magnified to an extraordinary length, a few points remain so central as to stand out in any consideration. First, we must consider Calvin's use of the Greek text, and his text-critical faculty; second, his historical sensibility, and his emphasis on context; third, his emphasis on rhetoric, both in the text of the Bible and in his own ideal of theological argumentation and formation of the believer. Finally, we will conclude with the significance of Calvin's humanism in tension with his traditionalism.

Calvin, in writing on the Pauline epistles from 1540 to 1550, was an engaged user of the Greek text. By this time in his career, he had overcome the earlier difficulty he had experienced with the Greek language, which marred his Seneca commentary of 1532.[68] He was clearly considering the Greek text, not the Latin, although his habit was to

---

extreme variance with those positions taken by other Renaissance thinkers. In his classic essay, Charles Trinkaus pointed out that, in his doctrines of a closely related set of "Renaissance problems," including epistemology, man and the universe, providence and free will, Calvin completely rejected "any hope for the spiritual or moral regeneration of mankind by its own efforts." From that position, Calvin's issue seems to be that he accepted some of the tools of the scholarship of the Renaissance, without accepting the substance of some of its basic positions. Cf. "Renaissance Problems in Calvin's Theology," esp. pp. 332–333. Donald Williams' work denies Renaissance humanism had a particular definable set of theses or doctrines, and thus he takes on Trinkaus' position. Williams argues that Renaissance humanism is not a set of core doctrines, but instead is marked by a "strong interest in the classical writers from a standpoint of grammar and rhetoric." If this position is taken, then Calvin can be seen as more of a humanist scholar. See Donald T. Williams, "John Calvin: Humanist and Reformer," *Trinity Journal* 5 (1976): 67–78 esp. p. 68.

Williams' position is buttressed by James Michael Weiss' statement that "humanists before and during the Reformation did *not* – this point requires considerable emphasis in the face of perennial misunderstanding – they did *not* share philosophical or theological positions on human nature, revelation, justification, sacraments, free will, or the other questions that generated Reformation controversy." "Humanism," II:264–272 in the *Oxford Encyclopedia of the Reformation*, ed. Hans J. Hillerbrand et al., 4 vols. (Oxford: Oxford University Press, 1996), at 265.

66 Parker, *Calvin's New Testament Commentaries*, pp. 123–157. Calvin chides Erasmus for just such a fault at Rom. 6:17.
67 Especially good examples are his arguments in 1 Corinthians, Galatians, and 2 Thessalonians.
68 Battles, "Calvin's Humanistic Education," p. 57.

quote the Latin.[69] Though it is impossible to say with certainty *which* text Calvin used as his base Greek text,[70] clearly he depended upon it for the consideration of textual points. Thus, frequently when Calvin notes Erasmus, he is arguing with his text.

This leads us to a second point about Calvin's use of the Greek. During the work on the Pauline commentaries, he was quite comfortable presenting his own findings on the correct readings of the Greek text. This establishment as a Greek textual critic[71] happened rather early in his career, and his Pauline commentaries benefited accordingly. Calvin frequently introduces or signals these moments in the text of the commentary by describing himself as seeking the goal of the "fuller meaning." This is the case in his comment on 2 Corinthians 4:4, where he departs from Stephanus' text in order to render the Hebrew idiom more correctly.[72] As well, Calvin was fully aware that translation was a step of interpretation. For instance, when considering Philippians 1:21, he notes that interpreters have failed to render the Greek correctly in their translation, and thus have exposited the material incorrectly.[73] His use of the deponent solves the problem, while demonstrating his skill.

The second gift which Calvin received from his humanistic background was a firm grounding in the lessons of history, and the possibilities for the interpretation of texts and ancient cultures which history grants its students.[74] Calvin eagerly employed historical explanations to consider both the biblical text and the church's exegetical tradition. When commenting upon Paul's "mistake" in confusing the convention of his own day with the order of nature in 1 Corinthians 11:14, Calvin explains

---

69 Parker, "Introduction," in *OE, Commentarius in Epistolam ad Hebraeos*, p. XXIII, states: "Let us therefore lay it down as an irrefragable principle that his commentaries on the New Testament were interpretations and expositions of the Greek text and not of his own or another's Latin version."

70 See ibid., pp. XXIV–XXVIII. Parker notes that Calvin certainly did use Erasmus' and Stephanus' editions.

71 Even the most savage critic of Calvin's language, Richard Simon, only took him to task concerning his Hebrew. See Max Engammare, *"Johannes Calvinus Trium Linguarum Peritus?* La question de L'Hebreu." *Bibliothèque d'Humanisme et Renaissance: Travaux et Documents* 58 (1996): 35–60.

72 *Comm. 2 Cor. 4:4, Ioannis Calvini Opera Exegetica, Commentarii in Secundum Pauli Epistolam ad Corinthios*, ed. Helmut Feld (Geneva: Librairie Droz, 1994), 73.7–10, *CNTC* XI:55.

73 *Comm. Phil. 1:21, Ad Philippenses* 309.18–19, *CNTC* XI:238.

74 Both Battles and Michael Monheit note that Calvin was formed by the historical and linguistic models of Andreas Alciati. See Battles, "Calvin's Humanistic Education," p. 56, and Monheit, "Young Calvin."

through a historical aside.[75] In the same manner, he uses the contexts of the patristic commentators in their comments on 2 Corinthians 4:4 to explain how they arrived at their pious but ultimately incorrect conclusions.[76] Calvin notes that Hilary provided his interpretation in the context of his struggle against the Arians, in which he attempted to maintain the divinity of Christ. Chrysostom was led astray as well, by the exigencies of his doctrinal struggle with Marcionism and Manicheeism. Finally, Augustine, writing in the *Contra Faustum*, was also battling a Manichee, and battling against dualism. Thus, all three fathers were defending orthodoxy, but erred in their overzealousness by incorrectly referring to particular points in the biblical witness.

Even Calvin's failure to complete his exegesis of history in this example is proof of his historical acumen and principles. Calvin also disagreed with a fourth writer, identified in his early modern edition as Ambrose. Later scholarship demonstrates conclusively that it was instead Ambrosiaster.[77] Calvin simply states that it is unclear why Ambrose would have interpreted the verse in the question as he had. But that comment is because Calvin cannot find a historical circumstance for Ambrose that fits the issues!

It is not important to set Calvin out as a paragon of historical practice. In the brief efforts that have been made to consider his abilities as a

---

75 *Comm. 1 Cor.* 11:14, *CNTC* IX:235. "Paul again sets nature before them as the teacher of what is proper. Now, he means by 'natural' what was accepted by common consent and usage at that time, certainly as far as the Greeks were concerned. For long hair was not always regarded as a disgraceful thing in men. Historical works relate that long ago, i.e. in the earliest times, men wore long hair in every country. Thus the poets are in the habit of speaking about the ancients and applying to them the well-worn epithet 'unshorn'. In Rome they did not begin to use barbers until a late period, about the time of Africanus the Elder [b. 235 BC]. When Paul was writing these words, the practice of cutting hair had not yet been adopted in Gaul and Germany. Yes, and more than that, indeed, it would have been a disgraceful thing for men, just as much as women, to have their hair shaved or cut. But since the Greeks did not consider it very manly to have long hair, branding those who had it as effeminate, Paul considers that their custom, accepted in his own day, was in conformity with nature." *CO* II:478. "Iterum naturam illis decori magistram proponit. Quod autem omnium consensu et consuetudine receptum tunc erat, et quidem apud Graecos, vocat naturale: nam viris non semper fuit coma dedecori. Olim ubique viros fuisse comatos, hoc est, primis saeculis, referunt historiae. Unde et poetae vocare solent intonsos veteres trito epitheto. Sero tonsoribus Romae uti coeperunt, circa aetatem Aphricani superioris. Et quo tempore scribebat haec Paulus, nondum in Gallis et Germania invaluerat tondendi usus. Quin potius deforme fuisset non minus viris quam mulieribus, radi aut tonderi: sed quoniam in Graecia parum; virile erat alere comam, ut tales quasi effeminati notarentur: morem iam confirmatum pro natura habet."

76 Cf. *Comm. 2 Cor.* 4:4, *Secundum ad Corinthios*, 70.14–71.15; *CNTC* X:53–54.

77 Feld, *Secundum ad Corinthios*, p. 70, n. 16.

historian, the reviews have been decidedly mixed.[78] However, I do not argue that Calvin reaches the highest excellence of the canons of the modern historian (a highly anachronistic goal!), but that he uses a significant tool of great power in his efforts at coming to knowledge of the Scriptures in their plainest sense, and the church's tradition of interpretation.

This importance of history in the reconstruction of the meaning of the text at hand drove Calvin toward the use of context as one of the deciding factors in grasping a biblical text or author. He would begin to escape the atomistic approach that some of the patristic interpreters used by rising out of the level of the words, to the level of either the argument or the event. This tendency is part of what makes Calvin's interpretations accessible even today: he weaves a strong narrative out of his commentary.

Calvin's final reward from his efforts in the vineyards of humanism was a profound regard for, and consciousness of, rhetoric. Calvin himself was noted as a stylist,[79] and well understood the possibilities inherent in a well-chosen remark.[80] While the requirements of the commentary genre may have kept some of his rhetorical flights rather bereft of ornamentation, his consciousness of the art drew him to consider the very nature of the truth of biblical rhetoric. In this investigation, Calvin points out the starkness of style of the biblical writers, and speculates that this is necessary in order for them to avoid blurring the Holy Spirit's brilliance with their own style. While some have found this the crowning achievement of Calvin's rhetorical investigations,[81] Calvin himself does not make such a claim. Rather, he simply points out again and again the virtue of clarity, while occasionally noting the proper times for either beautiful speech, or the rudeness of the untrained writers used as the amanuenses of the Holy Spirit.

---

78 See Irena Backus, "Calvin's Judgment of Eusebius of Caesarea," *Sixteenth Century Journal* 22 (1991): 419–437; A. N. S. Lane, "Calvin's Use of the Fathers and the Medievals," *Calvin Theological Journal* 16 (1981): 149–200; A. N. S. Lane, *John Calvin: Student of the Church Fathers* (Grand Rapids: Baker Books, 1999); James Payton, "Calvin and the Legitimation of Icons: His Treatment of the Seventh Ecumenical Council," *Archiv für Reformationsgeschichte* 84 (1993): 222–241; James Payton, "History as Rhetorical Weapon: Christian Humanism in Calvin's Reply to Sadoleto, 1539," in *In Honor of John Calvin, 1509–64*, ed. E. J. Furcha (Montreal: Faculty of Religious Studies, McGill University, 1987), pp. 96–132; and James Payton, "Calvin and the Libri Carolini," *Sixteenth Century Journal* 28 (1997): 467–480.

79 Ganoczy, *The Young Calvin*, p. 179. See also Jones, *Rhetoric of Piety*. pp. 25–30.

80 Serene Jones points out that Calvin's ideal of sacred rhetoric would be dispositional as well as pleasing, that it would move the heart's emotions rather than simply the pleasures of the ears.

81 Richard C. Gamble, in his "*Brevitas et Facilitas*: Toward an Understanding of Calvin's Hermeneutic," *Westminster Theological Journal* 47 (1985): 1–17, sees Calvin copying the rhetoric of the Scriptures themselves (p. 15).

Thus, the careful reader finds two sides of Calvin on this issue. First, there is Calvin's own style, brilliantly set forth. Second, there is his determination to avoid Augustine's error,[82] his drive to see only virtue in the rhetorical manner of the Scriptures. Calvin's own style was praised. He is witty, his language is both precise and mellifluous, and his range of expression is enormous. From broad biting satire, to frank discussion of human frailty, to passionate tenderness, Calvin demonstrates himself again and again as an excellent stylist. But the Scripture is different, its skill aims at a separate goal.

For Calvin, the lack of style in Scripture is part and parcel of its elegance. He will consider Paul's rhetoric itself, and sees Paul choosing his style for pastoral reasons. This is true when one looks at the case of the church at Corinth. Calvin gives two reasons for Paul's choice of a "rude" or lowly style. Paul's first reason, in Calvin's reconstruction, is addressed to the Corinthians' particular pastoral need. The Corinthians were afflicted with "itching ears," and were too caught up in empty displays of human eloquence. Because of that weakness on their part, Paul, as a good pastor, gave them the exact opposite of what they wanted; he gave them what they needed. The second reason is of even greater significance for Calvin. This is that "the Cross of Christ is made void, not only by the wisdom of the world, but also by the brilliance of words." Here is the most definitive account of Calvin's stance of anti-eloquence. Any eloquence that obscures the simple intensity of the gospel must be done away with. Calvin writes:

The second question is a little more difficult. For Paul says that the Cross of Christ is made void, if it is mixed up in any way with the wisdom of words. My answer to that is that we must pay attention to those to whom Paul is speaking. For the ears of the Corinthians were itching with a foolish eagerness for high-sounding talk. Therefore they needed to be called back to the humility of the Cross more than other people, so that they might learn to lay hold of Christ alone, and the Gospel in its simplicity, free from any adulteration. However I think that in some measure this viewpoint has a permanent validity, viz., that the Cross of Christ is made void, not only by the wisdom of the world, but also by the brilliance of words. For the preaching of Christ is bare and simple; therefore it ought not to be obscured by an overlying disguise of words. The characteristic work of the Gospel is to bring down the wisdom of the world in such a manner, that, deprived of our own understanding we become completely docile, and do not consider knowing, or even desire to know

---

82 Augustine admits in his *Confessions* to being originally put off from study of the Scriptures by their "rude" style. See Calvin's comment upon Rom. 2:8 on the "inadequate literary style," which offers "spiritual wisdom."

anything but what the Lord Himself teaches. As far as the wisdom of men is concerned, we shall have to give fuller consideration, later on, as to the way it is opposed to Christ. But I shall speak briefly about eloquence here, giving it as much attention as the passage demands.

We realize that from the beginning God has so arranged it, that the Gospel should be handled stripped of any support from eloquence. Could not He who designs the tongues of men for eloquence, be Himself skilful in speech if He wished? While He could be so, He did not choose to be so. I can find two most important reasons for His unwillingness. The *first* is that the majesty of His truth might be all the clearer in the setting of unpolished and unrefined language, and the efficacy of His Spirit might penetrate the minds of men, by itself, without external aids. The *second* reason is that He might put our obedience and teachableness the better to the test, and, at the same time, instruct us in the way of true humility. For the Lord admits only little ones to His school. Therefore the only persons capable of heavenly wisdom are those who are content with the preaching of the Gospel, though it may be worthless in its appearance, and who have no wish that Christ be covered with a disguise. Therefore the teaching of the Gospel had to be made to serve the purpose of drawing believers away from all arrogance and haughtiness.[83]

Calvin balances between rhetorical brilliance and gospel purity. In other places he will argue that rhetorical skill is not to be denigrated, but that it must be kept in its place.[84] He himself will bring all of his rhetorical skills to the service of the Church, but is careful to note that the eloquence and wisdom of the Holy Spirit far exceeds anything which any pastor can add.

---

83 *Comm. 1 Cor.* 1:17, *CO* II:321; *CNTC* IX: 33–34. "Secunda quaestio paulo plus habet difficultatis: dicit enim exinaniri Christi crucem, si qua sermonis sapientia admisceatur. Respondeo, considerandum esse quos alloquatur Paulus. Pruriebant Corinthiorum aures stulta cupiditate magniloquentiae: prae aliis ergo ad crucis humilitatem revocandi erant, ut discerent nudum Christum et simplex evangelium absque fuco ullo amplecti. Quamquam hanc sententiam quodammodo perpetuam esse fateor, Christi crucem eninaniri non tantum mundana sapientia, sed verborum quoque splendore. Christi enim crucifixi praedicatio simplex est ac nuda: obfuscari ergo verborum fuco non debet. Evangelii proprium est, mundi sapientiam sic in ordinem redigere, ut proprio sensu vacui dociles nos tantum praebeamus, nec aliud scire nos putemus, aut etiam appetamus, quam quod Dominus ipse docet. De sapientia carnis fusius mox tractandum erit, qualiter Christo repugnet: de eloquentia paucis hic perstringam quantum locus requirit. Videmus Deum ita ab initio ordinasse, ut evangelium omni eloquentiae subsidio nudum administraretur. Qui linguas hominum format ad facundiam, non posset ipse disertus esse si vellet? Quum posset, noluit. Nur noluerit, duas potissimum rationes invenio: altera est ut in rudi et impolito sermone magis conspicua appareret veritatis suae maiestas, et sola spiritus efficacia absque externis adminiculis in hominum animos penetraret. Altera vero, ut nostram obedientiam ad docilitatem melius experiretur, et simul ad veram humilitatem erudiret. Solos enim parvulos in scholam suam admittit Dominus: ergo illi demum coelestis sapientiae sint capaces, qui praedicatione crucis in speciem abiecta contenti larvatum Christum nequaquam desiderant. Ideo in hunc finem evangelii doctrinam attemperari oportuit, ut ab omni fastu et altitudine abstraherentur fideles."

84 Cf. *Comm. 1 Cor.* 1:17, and especially *Comm. Gal.* 3:1.

Finally, one last point must be made about Calvin and rhetoric. Calvin used French. Not only in his pastoral work, which was necessitated by the language of the audience, but also in his commentaries, Calvin chose to make French his second theological language. He continually provided French translations of his commentaries and *Institutes*. In doing so, Calvin raised French from a vulgar tongue to one of the languages of theology, and of piety.[85] As a Latinist, Calvin was a rhetorician of the first rank. But as an architect of the French language, he contributed to the French *mentalité* about proper speech.[86] Likewise, Calvin's vocabulary introduced a new standard to French of precision and careful choice.[87] This choice showed the determination Calvin gave to fulfilling the goal of making the laity participants in their faith, through the consideration of central doctrinal texts, and most especially of the Bible.[88] While theology might remain a university discipline, it must not remain the province of theologians alone to be edified by knowledge of the Scriptures. This must be offered to all believers, and Calvin's efforts demonstrate his commitment to that end.

Calvin and the church's interpretive tradition

One of the most significant evolutions of the twentieth century's appropriation of the biblical interpretation of the reformers has been the movement away from a simple stance of *sola scriptura*, toward the realization that the reformers read, were formed by, and wrote in conversation with, the prior interpretive tradition of the church, including the medieval tradition. By this point, we have reached the stage where the doyen of the history of exegesis school is able to write, "At any event, it is essential not to overestimate the importance of hermeneutics or underestimate the importance of prior exegesis. In my judgment what has already been

---

85 On this point, see Olivier Millet, *Calvin et la dynamique de la parole.*

86 Francis Higman writes, "Not, of course, that Calvin's sentences are always short. But when his syntax does become more complex, one of its most notable features is the strength of the 'connectives', the syntactic signposts which make clear to the reader which way the sense is going." "The Reformation and the French Language," *Esprit Créateur* 16/4 (Winter 1976), p. 30.

87 Ibid.

88 I have considered this part of Calvin's heritage in the fourteenth chapter of *The Cambridge Companion to John Calvin*, ed. Donald K. McKim (Cambridge: Cambridge University Press, 2004), pp. 245–273. Cottret is incorrect as far as we can tell when he claims, in speaking of the Romans commentary, that "Calvin wrote a commentary, but wrote it in French." Calvin certainly wrote the commentary in Latin, and translated it, much later, into French. Cottret, *Calvin*, p. 143.

written on a passage of Scripture is far more important and exercises more influence on subsequent exegesis than the hermeneutical theory of any would-be interpreter."[89] While I will argue for a position which does not completely agree with that, Calvin certainly does take an enormous amount of insight from the prior tradition.

The first way this is seen is in the frequent mention of, and consideration Calvin gives to, the opinions of the patristic authors as he works through the Pauline epistles. His favorite two patristic authorities are Augustine and Chrysostom. Augustine's interpretations are considered by name thirteen times in *Romans*, and five times in *2 Corinthians*. In those same commentaries, Calvin quotes by name his favorite patristic exegete, Chrysostom, five times in *Romans* and twenty times in *2 Corinthians.*[90] Calvin demonstrates that he has studied the church's tradition deeply,[91] sometimes citing as many as four opinions of the patristic authors, in order to help the understanding of the reader.[92]

As well, Calvin is well versed in the modern commentators. He includes in his introduction to his first commentary mention of and praise for the commentaries of Melanchthon, Bullinger, and Bucer. Throughout his commentaries, he is in constant dialogue with Erasmus about the proper text.[93] The difference here is that the issues overwhelmingly have become textual, rather than interpretive. Though these are mentioned far less frequently, it is clear that Calvin continued to study his contemporaries' efforts at biblical interpretation throughout his career.

---

89 David C. Steinmetz, "Divided by a Common Past: The Reshaping of the Christian Exegetical Tradition in the Sixteenth Century," *Journal of Medieval and Early Modern Studies* 27 (1997), p. 250.

90 Critical editions edited by Parker and Feld note that Calvin is drawing more frequently than he is citing.

91 Further, we must realize that Calvin had continued his studies while a pastor. If Ganoczy's reconstruction of Calvin's educational background and lack of theological training is correct, Calvin did the greatest part of his reading of theology *after* he published the first edition of his *Institutes*. See Ganoczy, *The Young Calvin*, pp. 168–178.

92 Cf. *Comm. 2 Cor.* 4:6. However, David Steinmetz' caveat needs to be taken to heart here. He writes that Calvin "treats the Fathers as partners in conversation rather than as authorities in the medieval sense of the term." *Calvin in Context* (Oxford: Oxford University Press, 1995), p. 137.

93 In the Romans commentary, he mentions Erasmus by name twenty-eight times, in the Hebrews commentary, sixty-two times. To put that in perspective, in each commentary, the dialogue with Erasmus, most frequently about the correct text, dwarfs the conversation with any single patristic author. Cf. *Ad Romanos* and *Ad Hebraeos*.

THE CONCERNS OF THE PAULINE COMMENTARIES

The problem with attempting to describe what Calvin is doing in the Pauline commentaries is obvious – it's simply more satisfying to read the commentaries themselves! But some general trends do appear. So this portion of the essay will consider those. First, we will consider the ways that Calvin in these commentaries deals with issues endemic to biblical commenting. Here, we will review his setting out of textual matters, the importance and use of historical issues, and his sensitivity to literary and rhetorical dimensions. Second, we will consider Calvin's hermeneutical approach. Though this can become overly technical, we will see that it is crucial to understanding Calvin's approach to Scripture. As well, the answer will help to place him correctly in his own context. Finally, we will conclude the chapter by considering some of the themes Calvin adduces from the Pauline commentaries.

Text, history, and literary forms

Because we have considered some of this material at greater length above, it is rather simple to move forward at this point. First, the textual matters. For Calvin, the key to understanding the Pauline epistles was Greek. Although he was steeped in the Vulgate of his youth, Calvin's comments make abundantly clear that he is depending upon the Greek. This is also apparent from the frequent discussions of the work of Erasmus, which rarely focus on his commentaries or paraphrases, focusing far more frequently on his editions of the Greek New Testament.[94] It is also clear that Calvin feels quite at home with Greek, frequently arguing with Erasmus about the proper translation into Latin, or occasionally exposing the less useful textual choice. In short, Calvin began his preparation for biblical interpretation where modern seminaries tell their students they should begin, with a strong grounding in the language.

Second, we consider the historical issues. Although Calvin is not averse to using the tool of history, to consider either the biblical text or a patristic interpretation, he does not do so as frequently as we might wish. Why? The simple answer is that, for Calvin, there is far more in common between the human condition of the sixteenth century and the first than separates them. Karl Barth, in his preface to his commentary on Romans, notes (and lauds) that tendency. He writes:

---

94 See Parker's indices to Romans and Hebrews.

For example, place the work of Jülicher side by side with that of Calvin: how energetically Calvin, having first established what stands in the text, sets himself to re-think the whole material and to wrestle with it, till the walls which separate the sixteenth century from the first become transparent! Paul speaks, and the man of the sixteenth century hears. The conversation between the original record and the reader moves round the subject-matter, until a distinction between yesterday and to-day becomes impossible. If a man persuades himself that Calvin's method can be dismissed with the old-fashioned motto, "The Compulsion of Inspiration," he betrays himself as one who has never worked upon the interpretation of Scripture.[95]

What Barth saw clearly long ago still stands today. Calvin denies, in his interpretation, the general principle of the difference between Paul and the modern Christian situation. Though Calvin can be a sensitive historical thinker, his notion of the unity of human experience precludes some historical avenues.

The literary and rhetorical dimensions do not escape Calvin's grasp in the Pauline epistles. Occasionally he uses analysis of figures of speech to elucidate the text. He will comment upon the hypallage[96] or the mimesis employed by Paul.[97] He will discuss the rhetorical logic of the apostle, directing the reader to think through Paul's strategy, so as to gain insight into the figures of speech.[98] Calvin will discuss at length the proper meaning of allegory, and its relationship to the literal sense of the text, denying the possibility of the Origenistic excess which he believed had led the church astray.[99] But, for all of his insight into the apostle's thought through the tools of classical rhetoric, Calvin's most significant device for understanding remains his dependence upon accommodation.

The term "accommodation" has become enormously important in the modern study of the Genevan reformer's thought.[100] The term links a number of impulses in Calvin's theology. It has been defined as "the process by which God reduces or adjusts to human capacities what he

---

95 Karl Barth, *The Epistle to the Romans*, trans. from the 6th edn by Edwyn C. Hoskyns (Oxford: Oxford University Press, p. 1933), 7.

96 *Comm. Rom.* 1:5, *Ad Romanos* 50.1–4, *CNTC* VIII:17; and *Comm. Rom.* 1:18, Ad Romanos 28.102–103, *CNTC* VIII:30. Hypallage is an interchange of two elements of a proposition, the normal relations of the two being reversed.

97 *Comm. 1 Cor.* 1:12, *CNTC* IX:26; CO II:315. Mimesis is imitation or remembrance.

98 *Comm. Rom.* 1:8, *Ad Romanos* 18.49–54, *CNTC* VIII:20.

99 *Comm. Gal.* 4:22, *Ad Galatas* 105.20–107.21, *CNTC* XI:84–85.

100 See, among others, E. A. Dowey, *The Knowledge of God in Calvin's Theology*, 3rd edn (Grand Rapids: Eerdmans, 1994), pp. 3–7; François Wendel, *Calvin: Origins and Development of His Religious Thought*, trans. Philip Mairet (Durham, NC: Labyrinth, 1987), pp. 229–230; H. Jackson Forstman, *Word and Spirit: Calvin's Doctrine of Biblical Authority* (Stanford, CA: Stanford

wills to reveal of the infinite mysteries of his being, which by their very nature are beyond the powers of the mind of man to grasp."[101] This definition drives toward all forms of God's revelation, and can be considered in all forms of revelation.[102] However, it is particularly relevant to the interpretation of Scripture.

In accommodation, God condescends to the understanding of humans. For Calvin, this is an obvious necessity, and reveals something important about Scripture itself. Scripture does not give humans full understanding of the nature of God,[103] but rather a partial conception appropriate to their ability to comprehend. Calvin believed that God had spoken baby-talk as a baby-sitter might to a baby. The speech gives something to the believers, but cannot be fully revealing, because of the lack of capacity of the hearers. However, it is always clear in Calvin's hands that the fact of accommodation points believers to God's desire to communicate, no matter what barriers must be overcome.

Calvin's hermeneutical and exegetical approach

When Calvin set forth to comment upon the Pauline epistles, he also set out a particular approach to interpretation of the Scriptures. However, frequently, that approach has been obfuscated by the efforts of later generations to understand it. Simply put, there are difficulties involved in categorizing Calvin. Is he a traditionalist? Is he a humanistic innovator? Though both ideas have been proffered, neither seems to satisfy the seemingly contradictory impulses in Calvin's interpretation of the

University Press, 1962), p. 13; Ford Lewis Battles, "God Was Accommodating Himself to Human Capacity," *Interpretation* 31 (1977): 19–38; David F. Wright, "Calvin's Pentateuchal Criticism: Equity, Hardness of Heart, and Divine Accommodation in the Mosaic Harmony Commentary," in *Calvin and Hermeneutics*, ed. Richard J. Gamble, Articles on Calvin and Calvinism 6 (New York: Garland Publishing Co., 1992), pp. 213–230; David F. Wright, "Accommodation and Barbarity in John Calvin's Old Testament Commentaries," in *Understanding Prophets and Poets: Essays in Honor of George Wishart Anderson*, ed. A. Graeme Auld (Sheffield: JSOT Press, 1993), pp. 413–427; and, most recently, David F. Wright, "Calvin's Accommodating God," in Neuser and Armstrong, *Calvinus Sincerioris Religionis Vindex*, pp. 3–20.

101 Dowey, *Knowledge of God*, p. 3.

102 Compare Battles: "Calvin makes this principle a consistent basis for his handling not only of Scripture but of every avenue of relationship between God and man." "God Was Accommodating Himself," p. 20. Thus, the most important moment of revelation, the incarnation, still has some character of accommodation to limited capacity in it, otherwise the fullness of God would obliterate the receiving eyes of the faithful. As well, God's revelation in the created sphere might have been unbearably beautiful, insupportably breathtaking, so as to provide not insight and manifestation, but only tears of pain.

103 See his comments upon Rom. 1:19, *Ad Romanos* 29.19–35, *CNTC* viii:30–31.

Scripture. In this study, I will present a radically different approach to the question, by drawing a theoretical distinction between principles of hermeneutics and practices of exegesis. I will argue that Calvin possesses a doctrinal hermeneutic which is basically traditional and conservative, and dependent on a kind of Augustinian grasp of the Christian message. He interprets Scripture, however, using an exegetical model which is humanistically inspired, contextually considered, and influenced far more by his understanding of the interpretation of Chrysostom. The pairing of these two elements, perhaps not fully harmonized in his interpretation, leads to the modern aporia about what his understanding of Scripture actually was.

This situation has arisen because of the modern interpretation of Calvin.[104] It is fashionable to see him as a man suspended between, or at least facing, two opposing forces.[105] An enormously influential biography of Calvin saw the reformer as a man who "needed to strike a balance between the two sides of himself."[106] That author considered those two forces to be, first, a profoundly traditional impulse, presenting as an effort to build up instruments of cultural and spiritual control, while the second impulse worked against that with stubborn originality, rebelling at the constriction of those very structures![107] On the other hand, one scholar who has examined Calvin's humanism and his biblical commentary argues that Calvin's conscious choice of a different style of rhetoric implicitly critiques the humanistic rhetoric with a biblical rhetoric.[108] Other scholars, in searching for Calvin's hermeneutic choice, have found him "bound by a mindset" that was essentially medieval.[109] In all of these cases, there has been a mistaken impression that by reducing Calvin's interpretive work to a set of impulses, either anticipating the future or remembering the past, one will come to an understanding of him. In fact, the exact opposite is true. What is necessary, unless we adopt the theory of schizophrenia for Calvin, is a heuristic framework that allows Calvin to

---

104 On this point, see Muller, *The Unaccommodated Calvin,* pp. 9–11, where he lists some of the modern difficulties with understanding the Genevan reformer's sixteenth-century thought.

105 Bernard Cottret's recent biography of Calvin proclaimed that Calvin "had one foot in the fifteenth century, the other in the seventeenth." *Calvin,* pp. 345–346.

106 William Bouwsma, *John Calvin: A Sixteenth Century Portrait* (Oxford: Oxford University Press, 1988), p. 48.

107 Ibid.

108 Richard C. Gamble, "Exposition and Method in Calvin," *Westminster Theological Journal* 49 (1987): 153–165.

109 Hans-Joachim Kraus, "Calvin's Exegetical Principles," *Interpretation* 31 (1977): 18.

make sense in the various contexts in which he lived, worked, and worshiped.[110]

I propose that the answer is to divide Calvin's interpretive effort into two layers, those of his principles of hermeneutics, and his rules of exegesis.[111] The two levels interpenetrate each other, but work separately. Hermeneutical principles tend to be below the level of conscious interpretation by the theologian, they are his presuppositions, and as such are rarely questioned.[112] Calvin's own hermeneutical principles can be loosely termed Augustinian, and Augustine is was of his favorite theologians. This can account for the distinctly traditional cast in Calvin's interpretation. However, Augustine was not one of his favorite exegetes! This is because

110 One of the best insights available in Richard Muller's *The Unaccommodated Calvin* is his statement that "[a] reading of Calvin's thought in its sixteenth-century context, in other words, yields the picture of a theology at once intriguing and intractable to twentieth-century concerns" (pp. 14–15).

111 I expound this theory with greater depth in my book, *John Calvin and the Grounding of Interpretation: Calvin's First Commentaries*, forthcoming from Brill Academic Publishers. The distinction between the two levels of interpretation comes from Karlfried Froehlich, who wrote: "Patristic hermeneutics (from the Greek *hermeneuein*, to explain, interpret) concerns itself with the developing principles and rules for a proper understanding of the Bible in the early Christian church. The *principles* reflect the theological framework in which the Biblical writings were interpreted by different groups and individuals at various times; they always included the basic conviction that God's revelation in Jesus Christ was central to God's plan of salvation (*oikonomia*) but they left room for different readings of major themes such as Israel and the church, eschatology, ethics, even Christology, anthropology, and soteriology. The *rules* reflect the methodology by which the language of Biblical revelation was scrutinized so that it would yield insight into God's *oikonomia* and its ramifications for the life of the community; they were often taken over from the literary culture of the surrounding world but were then developed into new, creative paradigms of literary analysis." *Biblical Interpretation in the Early Church*, trans. and ed. Karlfried Froehlich (Philadelphia: Fortress Press, 1984), p. 1.

112 Calvin's hermeneutical principles include hierarchical epistemology, Scripture's authority, divine accommodation, the unity of the Scripture's testimony, the mind of the author, the hermeneutical circle, and the edification of the church. Hierarchical epistemology means simply that. For Calvin, there is a level of things beyond which the unaided intellect cannot go. The authority of Scripture is a related topic, and Calvin finds that authority in God and especially the Holy Spirit, rather than in some textual perfection. Accommodation is a widely used device both in Calvin's thought and in the sixteenth century generally. The unity of the Scripture means that Calvin held that the Old and New Testaments give the same doctrine, and that in fact Scripture does hold a unitive message. The mind of the author is for Calvin that which must be explicated in all interpretation, but the special twist is that for Calvin that is a twofold author. Calvin sets forth a number of hermeneutical circles in his work – understanding a passage within the context of the whole book, understanding a book within the corpus of that author, understanding various authors within the entirety of the Scripture's witness. Beyond those part–whole circles, Calvin holds up the necessity of reading within the church, both in the sense of receiving the church's tradition, and in the gathered community of readers who make up the Genevan congregation. Finally, edification is a canon that argues that all true interpretation of Scripture will build up the church.

of the second level, that of the rules of exegesis.[113] For Calvin, or for any
other interpreter, these are consciously chosen tools, used to make sense of
the text. In Calvin's case, these are directly related to his humanistic
education, and thus are frequently seen by analysts of his interpretive
work as his forward-looking portion. Because of Calvin's exegetical sense,
and his related rejection of (a certain type of) allegory, John Chrysostom
was his favorite patristic biblical interpreter.[114]

Why consider the twofold interpretive scheme? Several answers might
be contrived, not the least being that this allows a certain flexibility in
considering Calvin's interpretation of Scripture. But the only reason with
any weight is that Calvin himself tells the reader that this is the way to
read Scripture. Calvin explained his purpose in his open letter to the
readers of the *Institutes*. As if this were not enough, Calvin's French letter
to the reader of the *Institutes* gives substantially the same ideal.[115] Calvin is
certain that the necessary preparation for the reading of Scripture is true
religion. What I have termed a doctrinal hermeneutical stance, Calvin
calls the "sum of religion in all its parts." Terminology aside, what is
important to note is that Calvin does not merely admit a hermeneutic,
but rather directs that, for those for whom reading Scripture is important,
it is crucial that they arm themselves with knowledge of the Christian
philosophy,[116] so that they know how to read Scripture. The principles of
hermeneutics come as a necessary aid to setting forth the meaning of
Scripture.

One final point must be made about Calvin's hermeneutical/exegetical
stance. He assumes the horizon of the church.[117] All interpretation of

---

113 Calvin's exegetical rules include paraphrase, contextual interpretation, interpretation of Scripture
    by Scripture, the possibilities given by the church's interpretive tradition, a stance of humility
    before the text, preference for the straightforward meaning, and the goal of fuller meaning.
114 Chrysostom is noted far more frequently than Augustine in the Pauline commentaries, and more
    positively.
115 OS, III:7.15–40. "Subject Matter of the Present Work," *Inst.* 1:6–7.
116 Calvin may have found this term in Erasmus. The term "Christian philosophy" is not a phrase
    free from historical baggage. Etienne Gilson wrote an essay entitled "What Is Christian
    Philosophy?" (1941), which surveys the history of the term. Later, in a bibliographical essay at
    the end of his *L'Esprit de la philosophie médiévale*," (2nd revd edn, Paris: Vrin, 1948), Gilson
    considers the history of the notion of a Christian philosophy. Beginning with Augustine,
    and proceeding through figures such as Erasmus, Balzac, and even Feuerbach, Gilson
    completely ignores Calvin's name. In fact, when the index is searched, one finds only three
    mentions of Calvin, each time in a negative context. It may be that Calvin's ideal of Christian
    philosophy – the essence of *pietas* – does not meet Gilson's own definition.
117 See my article, "*Ecclesia, Legenda atque Intelligenda Scriptura*: The Church as Discerning
    Community in Calvin's Hermeneutic," *Calvin Theological Journal* 36 (2001): 270–289.

Scripture must be made for the church, all interpretation of Scripture is placed under the judgment of the church. Calvin quite simply assumes that the home of Scripture is within the church. Though Scripture may make claims about reality outside of the church, its proper sphere is within the church, and members of the church rightly read, consider, obey, and live it. In this way, the church is for Calvin the *schola dei* (school of God), and its permanent curriculum is the Scripture.

Theological themes

In a way, this section of this chapter has already been sketched. Calvin's argument in the commentary on Romans, noted above, lays out some of the characteristic concerns of this group of commentaries. Further, for those who have come to know the general outlines of Calvin's thought, these will not be surprising – rarely do the commentaries hold something completely new and different from the other *loci* in Calvin's work. The main difference lies in the organization of material, which is naturally keyed to the biblical text, rather than being organized topically. Given all these caveats, three themes are important to note.

The first theme, like a permanent undertone that colors the whole of the musical piece upon which it is built, is justification by faith. Calvin writes, "Man's only righteousness is the mercy of God in Christ, when it is offered by the Gospel and received by faith."[118] Setting forth what would come to be known as the Reformed or Calvinist position on justification[119] was a key concern of this set of commentaries. Election for those to whom God is merciful is balanced by the predestination to destruction by God's just decree. Calvin does not harp on the position that came to be called double predestination, but is also not shy about putting it forth. Far more frequently, however, he lauds the benefits that come to the believer from God's gracious mercy, and how consciences can rest easily in the mercy of a loving God.

A second theme that supplements the first theme of justification by faith is the importance of living the Christian life. As firmly as Calvin sees Paul denying any possibility of accepting any merit for human actions in the sphere of salvation, so too, just as firmly, does he assert Paul's emphasis on living lives of holiness. Calvin implores contemporary believers to see

---

118 *Comm. Rom. Argumentum, CNTC* VIII:5, *Ad Romanos* 5.21–22.
119 This is almost indistinguishable from a generic "Lutheran" position on justification, until one considers how justification interacts with God's law.

themselves in the Corinthians or Galatians or Ephesians, and to be instructed by their examples, and heartened to press forward in the Christian life.

The third theme that is important is the way that Calvin sees Paul as building the church. Progress in edification is a frequent theme, which is always attached to the corporate body of Christ. Piety, so central a concern of Calvin's, is regularly set out in the context of the needs of the church.[120] Again and again, Calvin's pleading from the text finally resolves into the life of the church. If believers will avoid the courts, the church will not be imperiled. If pastors will learn the best methods for preaching the Word and for shepherding the congregations, the church will be strengthened. If believers will cultivate a teachable spirit, godly preaching will find a welcome home, and the church will be enlivened. If both laity and clergy will commit themselves to the faithful study of the Scripture under the guidance and inspiration of the Holy Spirit, the living of God's word will inevitably be more sure. All of these are simply specific cases of the emphasis on edification, the building up of the church. For through Scripture, Calvin concludes, the church reforms its image ever more strongly.

CALVIN AS COMMENTATOR ON THE PAULINE EPISTLES

We end with a brief consideration of what Calvin did in commenting upon the Pauline epistles. First, we must note again the importance of his choice to begin with Paul. Certainly Calvin did not know that these texts were some of the first written in the Christian era, that at least a portion of the Pauline corpus predated all other New Testament writings. He never makes that argument. Instead, Calvin sets Romans first as providing the key to Scripture. He then proceeds to finish the Pauline epistles, and the rest of the epistles (excluding 2 & 3 John), before commenting upon the gospels and the Acts of the Apostles. He never comments upon Revelation, and its message seems not to have attracted him.

When we consider what Calvin did, we see him accepting a Pauline approach to the Scripture. One can argue about canons within the canon, but not about the centrality of Paul to Calvin's thought. Calvin believed that Paul's theological masterwork was the most important biblical text to grasp in preparing to read Scripture, and by extension he moved directly into the rest of the apostle's work. While he worked in this particular field

120 On Calvin's understanding of piety, see Sou-Young Lee's "Calvin's Understanding of *Pietas*," in Neuser and Armstrong, *Calvinus Sincerioris Religionis Vindex*, pp. 225–240.

of the Lord, his own development blossomed, moving him from an imprudent prodigy to an established statesman. Calvin has been seen as a Pauline theologian; nothing could be clearer in this regard than his choice to comment upon Paul's complete corpus before turning to any other commentaries.

Calvin had written that the job of the interpreter was to grasp the mind of the author. In his works of interpretation, it seems fair to say that the mind of the author grasped Calvin as well. In Calvin's development as a theologian, while we may say that the original trajectory of his thought was Pauline, commenting upon the Pauline material solidified that character for him.[121] Without rehearsing the summary of this chapter, several important items are apparent. First, Calvin felt that Paul's mind, or Paul's sense of theology, was the correct entry into Scripture. Second, he set this forth from a doctrinal hermeneutic which he called the Christian philosophy, and which I argue is his reception of the Augustinian tradition. The writing of the Pauline commentaries, then, was the movement deeper into the hermeneutical circle of doctrine and Scripture, offered both to other scholars and to the broader church through Calvin's translation of the commentaries into French.

Calvin believed that the church was the body of the elect. But the task of the church was the living out of Scripture, so the curriculum of the *schola dei* was always Scripture. The reformer of Geneva spent his life working through the various tools of explicating Scripture, so that the church of Geneva might be edified. Essentially, that edification was Pauline, mediated through Calvin's reception of the church's tradition, and especially Augustine.

121 Alexandre Ganoczy has argued this in his "Forschungsansatze zur Hermeneutik Calvins: Calvin als paulinischer Theologe." Lecture given at the Europäischer Kongress fur Calvinforschung, Amsterdam, September 16–19, 1974.

APPENDIX A: PUBLICATION OF CALVIN'S PAULINE
COMMENTARIES[122]

Commentary	First published	French translation
Romans	Wendelin Rihel Strasbourg, 1540	Jean Gerard Geneva, 1550
1 Corinthians	Wendelin Rihel Strasbourg, 1546	Jean Gerard Geneva, 1547
2 Corinthians	Jean Gerard Geneva, 1548	Jean Gerard Geneva, 1547
Galatians group (Galatians, Ephesians, Philippians, Colossians)	Jean Gerard Geneva, 1548	Jean Gerard Geneva, 1548
1 & 2 Timothy	Jean Gerard Geneva, 1548	Jean Gerard Geneva, 1548
Hebrews	Jean Gerard Geneva, 1549	Jean Gerard Geneva, 1549
Titus	Jean Gerard Geneva, 1551 (part of set)	Jean Gerard Geneva, 1550 (not part of set)
Philemon	Jean Gerard Geneva, 1551 (part of set)	Jean Gerard Geneva, 1551 (not part of set)
1 & 2 Thessalonians	Jean Gerard Geneva, 1551 (part of set)	Jean Gerard Geneva 1551 (not part of set)
Collected Pauline commentaries	Jean Gerard Geneva, 1551	This edition was not translated
Collected Pauline commentaries (with 1 & 2 Peter, James, John and Jude)	Robert Estienne Geneva, 1556	Conrad Badius Geneva, 1557

122 Collated from Parker, *Calvin's New Testament Commentaries*, and Peter, *Bibliotheca Calviniana*.

CHAPTER 10

Calvin as commentator on Hebrews and the Catholic Epistles

Gary Neal Hansen

COMMENTARY CONTEXTS

Date, circumstances and background issues of the commentary

The commentaries examined in this chapter are varied, covering Calvin's work on all non-Pauline New Testament epistles. In many ways Calvin's work here is much like his work on the rest of the New Testament. The discussion below will focus as much as possible on what is distinctive to these books, saying less on some topics as a result.

Calvin placed these commentaries in separate volumes. The commentary on Hebrews was first published as a freestanding work in 1549. Those on the Catholic Epistles, or rather the "Canonical Epistles" as Calvin termed them in the title and dedicatory epistle,[1] were published in one volume in 1551.

He had done exegetical work on these texts in other contexts prior to or during the publication of the commentaries. Both Hebrews and the Catholic Epistles were studied in the *congrégations* in 1549.[2] T. H. L. Parker notes that a series of Sunday morning sermons on Hebrews was under way in 1549 when data becomes available, possibly having begun in December of 1548, and concluding by August 25 when the sermons on the book of Acts were begun. None of these sermons are extant, as the stenographic work of Denis Raguenier did not begin until September of

---

1 *CO* LV:201–202. For the dedicatory epistle references, *CO* XIV:30 and XIV:37. The Catholic Epistles are scattered among the volumes in the Torrance edition of Calvin's New Testament Commentaries (*CNTC*). The translation of the dedicatory letter is found in the volume surprisingly entitled *The Epistle of Paul the Apostle to the Hebrews and the First and Second Epistles of St Peter*, trans. William B. Johnston, Calvin's Commentaries 12 (Grand Rapids: Wm. B. Eerdmans Publishing Company, 1963; rpt. 1989), pp. 219–226.

2 T. H. L. Parker, ed., *Ioannis Calvini Opera Exegetica; vol.* XIX, *Commentarius in epistolam ad hebraeos* (Geneva: Librairie Droz, 1996), p. x citing *CO* XXI:71. Hereafter *OE* followed by volume and page number.

that year.[3] It is not known whether Calvin preached on the Canonical Epistles.

The Latin commentary on Hebrews was published alone only once, with a dedication date of May 23, 1549.[4] Thereafter it was appended to the Pauline epistles, first in 1551 and again in 1556.[5] Placing Hebrews alongside Paul hints at the theological importance of Hebrews to Calvin, though from first to last he maintained it was not by Paul.

The publication history of the commentaries on the Canonical Epistles is very slightly more complex. An exposition of the letter of Jude, in French, was published in 1542, but this is a different text from that of the Latin commentary of 1549.[6] Only one of the commentaries on the Catholic Epistles was published prior to the one-volume collection. This was a 1550 French translation of the commentary on James, which was published in Geneva by Jean Girard. The complete volume of Latin commentaries on the Canonical Epistles was published by Jean Crespin, with a dedication date of January 24, 1551.[7] The French edition came out the same year from the press of Jean Girard, though with a different translation of the commentary on James than he had previously published.

Calvin presented the Canonical Epistles in non-canonical order: First Peter, First John, James, Second Peter, and Jude. He did not explain the omission of Second and Third John, or the rearrangement of the books. The omissions are puzzling: Calvin was typically thorough, and the books omitted were manageably short. There is nothing in them less amenable to his theology than in the other Catholic Epistles. Perhaps he simply found nothing in these short books that he had not dealt with extensively elsewhere. When he entitled his work on First John "*Ioannis*

---

3 T. H. L. Parker, *Calvin's Preaching* (Louisville: Westminster John Knox Press, 1992), pp. 65, 150, 158. *OE* xix:x.

4 *OE* xix: ix, 9: "X Calend. Iunii M.DXLIX." The French version was also published in 1549, both editions coming from the Geneva press of Jean Girard. Except where noted otherwise, bibliographic information for all these commentaries is from T. H. L. Parker, *Calvin's New Testament Commentaries*, 2nd edn (Louisville: Westminster John Knox Press, 1993), pp. 209–212.

5 Though the Canonicals were not included with the 1551 edition of Paul and Hebrews, there was evidently already some desire to see all the epistle commentaries as a unified work. For example, the copy in the Victoria University Centre for Reformation & Renaissance Studies at the University of Toronto has Girard's 1551 edition of Paul and Hebrews bound with Crispin's 1551 first edition of the Canonicals.

6 Parker, *Calvin's Preaching*, pp. 62, 180. Parker sees this work as possibly having been developed from sermons, and offers this as (admittedly tenuous) evidence that Calvin may have preached through the Catholic Epistles at this time.

7 "Geneva nono Calendas Februarii M.D.LI." *CO* xiv:37. As Parker notes, the colophon date was "sexto Calendas Februarii. M.D.LI." *Calvin's New Testament Commentaries*, p. 212.

Calvini Commentaria in Epistolam Ioannis,"[8] the omission of the number suggests that Second and Third John were superfluous. The rearrangement could have been guided by various concerns: when commenting on Paul's epistles and on the gospels Calvin explicitly dealt with the most important books first. Perhaps he did the same here. He may also have arranged them by size, though Second Peter seems to be placed with Jude also because of the two books' overlapping content.

The 1556 collection of commentaries mentioned above included the Canonical Epistles after those on Paul's letters and the letter to the Hebrews. In this edition he offered the alternate title of "Catholic" Epistles for the Canonicals. The Latin was published by Robert Stephanus, and the French edition followed the next year by Conrad Badius.

The commentaries on Hebrews and the Catholic Epistles were both dedicated to monarchs in an effort to influence reform, but they differ in the relevance of the content of the books to that task. With Hebrews there is a very close relation. In 1526 Johannes Eck had written a treatise on the mass as sacrifice and dedicated it to Sigismund I of Poland, using Old Testament, patristic, and New Testament evidence, including considerable work on Hebrews.[9] When Calvin wrote on Hebrews he dedicated his work to Sigismund II in an explicit attempt to refute Eck's work, "to purify the name of Poland from that rotten filth of Eck" by emphasizing the once-for-all quality, the non-repeatability, of the sacrifice of Christ. He aimed to shore up the Protestant cause in Poland by convincing the king of Reformed perspectives on the contested issues.[10] Calvin would surely have drawn the same conclusions about the meaning of Hebrews regardless of the dedication. However, the treatise by Eck provided a useful catalyst for polemical application of Hebrews, and Hebrews dealt with the points of controversy more clearly than any other book of Scripture.

In dedicating the commentaries on the Catholic Epistles the content of the books was less important. These commentaries were dedicated to Edward VI of England, and Calvin's dedicatory epistle should be read amid the flurry of letters to Edward and the young king's regent Somerset, including dedications of his commentaries on Isaiah and the Pastoral

---

8 Thus as printed in the 1551 copy examined. Corpus Reformatorum lists the title as "*Commentarius in Iohannis apostoli epistola.*" *CO* LV:293–294.

9 Johannes Eck, *De sacrificio missae libri tres (1526)*, ed. Erwin Iserloh, Vinzenz Pfnür, and Peter Fabisch, Corpus Catholicorum 36 (Münster: Aschendorffsch Verlagsbuchhandlung, 1982), pp. 1, 73ff., 122ff.

10 Hebrews Dedication, *CNTC* XII:XII, *OE* XIX:7.

Epistles. Calvin clearly shows his desire to shape the reforms in England.[11] The only explicit connection drawn from the content of the books to their recipient is a rhetorical flourish at the very beginning: They were written to scattered peoples so sending them across the sea to England is not unfamiliar to them. His specific challenge to Edward comes at the very end from other portions of Scripture: Calvin reminds him that Moses required Israel's kings to preserve and read the law of God as a guide for their reigns. The rest of the dedication is primarily a refutation of the Council of Trent, emphasizing the authority of Scripture, lest England be swayed by the fact that reform was opposed by the weighty authority of a council.[12]

Effects of Calvin's background in humanism and other influences

The most distinctive way that Calvin's humanist background shows in these commentaries is in his willingness to question their traditional authorship. The letter to the Hebrews had long been attributed to Paul, but in the Renaissance and Reformation Erasmus, Luther, Bugenhagen, and Cajetan had cast doubts on the possibility of Paul's authorship.[13] After considering evidence from Jerome and Eusebius, from whom he cites a range of possible authors, Calvin firmly states that the author cannot be Paul. This is partly by reason of style, partly from the author's reference to having learned the faith from the apostles – something that Paul would never say – and partly because the letter's references to catechetical practices do not reflect Paul's time.[14]

The issue of Paul's authorship was theologically weighty for some. Cajetan thought that questionable authorship made the book's authority questionable, and so he asserted that it could not be used to settle doctrinal disputes. On the other hand, Jean de Gagny argued that denying Paul's authorship of Hebrews was a dangerous error.[15] Calvin, however, does not question the apostolic authority of these books. He notes patristic evidence of the late acceptance of Hebrews, as he does in

---

11 See Philip Edgcumbe Hughes, "Calvin and the Church of England," in *John Calvin: His Influence in the Western World*, ed. W. Stanford Reid (Grand Rapids: Zondervan Publishing House, 1982), pp. 173–196.

12 Canonical Epistles Dedication, *CO* XIV:30–37.

13 Kenneth Haugen, *Hebrews Commenting from Erasmus to Bèze*, Beiträge zur Geschichte der Biblischen Exegese 23 (Tübingen: J. C. B. Mohr [Paul Siebeck], 1981), pp. 1, 5, 9, 11, 18–24.

14 Hebrews, Argument *OE* XIX:11–12; and 2:3, *OE* XIX:31–32; 6:1, *OE* XIX:11–12.

15 Haugen, *Hebrews Commenting*, pp. 19, 49.

the cases of James, Second Peter, and Jude, again without its making him doubt its authority. In Calvin's understanding, Hebrews is apostolic because it is uniquely clear on important doctrines. This is certainly a different notion of apostolicity than his opponents would use. By this theory one need not know the name of the apostle for the work to be apostolic, though in the end he favors Luke or Clement as the probable author.[16]

He does not question the authorship of First Peter, First John, or Jude, simply claiming in the case of First John that the letter is worthy of that apostle's spirit. In James and Second Peter, however, there is at least some debate about authorship. James' theological differences with Paul are written off to the authors' different purposes. The book's authority is preserved because it contains nothing unworthy of the apostle. The question he does consider is which apostle named James is the author. After considering three options, Calvin says that it is not necessary to answer the question precisely.[17]

A new piece of Calvin's theory of apostolic authority comes into the discussion with Second Peter. Calvin can see from the style that this is not by the author of First Peter, but he is troubled by the presence of Peter's name. If it is canonical, it must be, in fact, by Peter. To put a false name on a book is understood as "a fiction unworthy of a minister of Christ." Calvin extricates the writer by arguing that the teaching is not unworthy of Peter, and speculating that Peter's authentic ideas were put onto paper by one of his disciples in a way that was more interpretation than dictation.[18]

In these discussions Calvin asks a humanist's questions about ancient texts, and bravely so in that the texts were biblical. His efforts to preserve their apostolicity, and therefore their authority, regardless of questions of authorship, show a second stream of influence in his background: his role as a writer in and for the Reformed church.

On questions of authorship and authority, Calvin's backgrounds as humanist and reformer seem to be in tension. When it comes to the place of Peter in the church and the epistles under Peter's name, the reformer predominates. The closing of First Peter cites "Babylon" as the place of his writing. He notes that Babylon has been interpreted as a code word for Rome, supporting Peter's Roman episcopacy and buttressing the

---

16 Hebrews, Argument, *OE* xix:11; 13:23, *OE* xix:247–248.
17 1 John, Argument, *CO* lv:297; James, Argument, *CO* lv:382; Jude, v. 1, *CO* lv:48.
18 2 Peter, Argument, *CNTC* lv:325, *CO* lv:441; 2 Peter 3:15, *CO* lv:478.

authority of the papacy. Calvin argues vigorously that Peter was really in the city of Babylon, evangelizing the Jews as was his calling. His continuing concern with the issue is seen when he notes it in a 1556 addition on Second Peter where Babylon is not actually mentioned.[19] So, Calvin removed Peter from Rome, as well as partially removing him from the authorship of Second Peter. Along the way, he also removed Peter from the role of chief shepherd: He pointedly notes that Peter refers to himself as a fellow elder rather than claiming primacy,[20] and in the commentaries on the epistles of Peter Calvin rarely makes observations that praise the writer as a model of ministry, as he often did with Paul.

He shows a humanist's linguistic and literary awareness in a couple of particular ways here. First is his statement in his comments on First Peter 2:17 that, while the apostles wrote in Greek, their understanding of words and concepts was shaped by their knowledge of the Hebrew. This conviction was clearly already in use in Calvin's interpretation of Hebrews where many Old Testament texts are cited. At times he uses this principle even when no Old Testament text is being discussed, as is the case in Hebrews 13:20 where his argument nevertheless hinges on a Hebrew preposition.[21]

Second, the interpretation of Old Testament citations, especially in Hebrews but elsewhere too, allows Calvin to show his awareness of the multi-layered quality of the texts. This includes attempts to discern where the writers were quoting from the Septuagint instead of working with the actual Hebrew text.[22]

Calvin's humanist background also shows in his frequent use of illustrative material from classical sources. Plato is mentioned seven times, Horace four, Cicero twice, and seven others once each.[23] Other kinds of material are credited more generally to Stoics, grammarians, secular writers, poets, and military law.[24] At least nine times he cites proverbs which may be classical in origin.[25] Beyond this are the many ways in

---

19 1 Peter, Argument, *CO* LV:206; 1 Peter 5:13, *CO* LV:292; 2 Peter 1:14, *CO* LV:452.

20 1 Peter 5:1, *CO* LV:284–285.

21 1 Peter 2:17, *CO* LV:247; Hebrews 13:20, OE XIX:247. See also Hebrews 9:7, OE XIX:137.

22 E.g. Hebrews 10:5, 10, OE XIX:158–159, for two instances.

23 Plato: 1 Peter 1:14, 2:3, 3:13, 2:14; 1 John 2:3; James 1:16, 5:2; and 2 Peter 3:4. Horace: 1 John 2:13; James 3:6, 4:2; and 2 Peter 4:15. Cicero: 1 Peter 4:4 and 1 John 2:16. Also Hebrews 1:17 (Virgil), 1 Peter 3:14 (Cato), 1 Peter 3:21 (Aristotle), 1 John 2:13 (the Lacedaimonian chorus), James 1:26 (Aesop), James 4:3 (Pliny), and 2 Peter 2:18 (Perseus).

24 Stoics: 1 John 3:4 and James 2:10. Grammarians: Hebrews 6:2 and James 3:18. Secular writers and poets: 1 Peter 3:17; James 3:6 and 5:5. Military law: 2 Peter 2:19.

25 Hebrews 10:37; 1 Peter 5:1, 5:5 and 5:7; 1 John 4:1 and 5:3; James 5:2 and 5:10; 2 Peter 3:12.

which patristic literature has added to his understanding of the New Testament era.

A number things in other sections of this chapter could as easily be dealt with as expressions of Calvin's background in humanism, especially his practice of textual criticism, and the prominence of rhetorical analysis. Also, important humanist features such as Calvin's use of biblical languages are seen in all the commentaries.

Sources: Calvin's dialogue with the history of exegesis and other biblical commentaries in his work

Anthony N. S. Lane has shown the difficulty of stating with certainty which sources Calvin used.[26] Parker, in his critical edition of the Hebrews commentary, makes the point as well. Though he provides a wealth of citations documenting the previous occurrence of the interpretations to which Calvin refers, Parker warns the reader not to assume that the reformer found the particular interpretation named in the particular work noted.[27] As is typical, Calvin mentions other interpretations frequently in these commentaries, but he names the interpreters only rarely. Even when he names the sources it is difficult, if not impossible, to determine whether Calvin had encountered the interpretations first hand or through other scholars, and whether he had the texts before him in his study or simply remembered them. Here such analysis awaits further study.

In these commentaries Calvin's discussions of other interpretations are of four main types: named citations, unnamed citations, polemical citations, and wholly vague citations. First are the cases where Calvin names someone in the course of his interpretive work, including the Vulgate, which he often calls the "old interpreter." A summary picture will be followed by specifics arranged by commentary.

Of the approximately sixty-one named citations in Hebrews and the Canonicals, the largest proportion, twenty-five, are discussions of the proper Latin translation, though these are indeed issues of interpretation for Calvin. Six more named citations are about textual criticism. Perhaps fourteen should be considered truly exegetical: these citations are of interpretations of the text at hand, whether in commentaries or as used in other theological works. The remaining sixteen named citations

---

26 Anthony N. S. Lane, *John Calvin: Student of the Church Fathers* (Grand Rapids: Baker Books, 1999), especially his methodological theses, pp. 1–13.

27 *OE* XIX:XXXIII.

do not appear to be from works on the text under consideration. They include commentaries on other biblical texts, useful bits of background, polemical applications of the text, and Augustine's winsome turns of phrase. Chrysostom's homilies on Hebrews would be the only expository work in these commentaries that one could argue Calvin was openly engaged with. Erasmus is nearly always present as a dialogue partner, especially as a translator, through his Latin translation and *Annotationes* on the New Testament.

In the Hebrews commentary Calvin appears to name other interpreters on twenty occasions, but the number is deceptive. Chrysostom is cited six times, always on matters of interpretation. On matters of translation Calvin cites Erasmus three times and the Vulgate twice. The remainder are all citations of other sorts of theological work that may or may not cite the text at hand: Augustine is cited four times, Hilary twice, and Hesychius once. Guillaume Postel and Novatus are both cited by name, but the first of these appears to be polemical hearsay, and the second seems to be information from an unnamed source.[28]

In First Peter, citations of Erasmus are by far the most frequent, with six on translation and one that is more an interpretive issue. The Vulgate is cited once on translation. Augustine is cited once, but not for an interpretation of the text at hand. Eusebius is cited first on an interpretive matter and second, along with Jerome, on historical background. Schwenkfeld is attacked polemically for his interpretation of one text, and another text is applied polemically against Cornelius Agrippa.[29]

The First John commentary is unusual in that Erasmus is not mentioned. The Vulgate is mentioned twice, once relatively positively and once negatively. Augustine is mentioned three times, and though Augustine did write a set of anti-Donatist homilies on First John, two of the three references are explicitly to other works. One, positively, is to anti-Pelagian writings, and another refers negatively to the *City of God* and the letters. Jerome enters the discussion once on a text-critical matter. Servetus is mentioned polemically rather than for an interpretation of this text.[30]

---

28 Chrysostom: Hebrews 2:9, 5:7, 6:2, 9:22, 11:34, 11:39. Erasmus: Hebrews 11:8, 11:35, 12:23. Vulgate: Hebrews 11:8, 12:27. Augustine: Hebrews 1:5, 6:2, 6:10, 11:1. Hilary: Hebrews 1:3, 11:38. Hesychius: Hebrews 8:5. Postel: Hebrews 7:3. Novatus: Hebrews 10:26.

29 Erasmus: 1 Peter 1:3 (interpretation), 1:22, 2:2, 3:4, 4:1, 5:2 (twice). Vulgate: 1 Peter 5:2. Augustine: 1 Peter 2:21. Eusebius: 1 Peter 5:13 (twice). Jerome: 1 Peter 5:13. Schwenkfeld: 1 Peter 3:21. Agrippa: 1 Peter 1:25.

30 Vulgate: 1 John 1:5, 2:16. Augustine: 1 John 1:18, 3:2, 5:1. Jerome: 1 John 5:7. Servetus: 1 John 1:1.

In Calvin's work on James, Erasmus is mentioned six times, once for a text-critical issue, once for interpretation, and the rest for translation. The Vulgate is mentioned three times, twice with approval and once negatively. One saying of Augustine is cited.[31]

In the commentary on Second Peter, Erasmus is mentioned three times on translation. The Vulgate is mentioned twice, once for translation and once for textual criticism. Augustine's *City of God* is mentioned once.[32]

On Jude Calvin mentions Erasmus once on a translation, and the Vulgate twice on text-critical matters. Eusebius is also mentioned once in a discussion of authorship.[33]

The second major group of citations is where Calvin cites one or more other interpretations specifically, but does not name his sources. These are the greatest number of instances. The ability of the scholar to trace them to particular sources depends in part on whether they include apparent quotations of specific phrases, as some do, or whether they instead present the ideas of an interpretation fully digested for Calvin's use. Parker has done a remarkable job of hunting down texts that hold the views Calvin discusses in the Hebrews commentary, but this is where his warning against being too confident that these are Calvin's actual sources is most pertinent. David Steinmetz has pointed out that in cases where Calvin gives his own interpretation without even alluding to sources he frequently gives commonly accepted interpretations.[34] This would seem even more likely in places where Calvin says that a certain interpretation is generally accepted or is held by some unnamed persons. It seems equally possible that some of these instances are, as Parker suggests, the fruit of Calvin's conversations on these texts in the *congrégations*.[35]

Many of these are interpretations with which Calvin disagrees. Many are alternate Latin translations, as was the case in the named citations. Others are issues of interpretation and application, as when he denies that a reference in Hebrews to being called refers to the elect, or where he argues that a passage in First Peter teaches not about eschatology but

---

31 Erasmus: James 1:10, 1:26, 2:1, 2:18 (interpretation), 3:3, 4:7 (textual criticism). Vulgate: James 2:1, 2:18, 5:16. Augustine: James 4:10.
32 Erasmus: 2 Peter 1:16, 2:13, 2:14. Vulgate: 2 Peter 1:3, 1:16. Augustine: 2 Peter 3:6.
33 Erasmus: Jude 22. Vulgate: Jude 1, 22. Eusebius: Jude 1.
34 David Steinmetz, *Calvin in Context* (New York: Oxford University Press, 1995), p. VII.
35 *OE* XIX:XXXIV.

evangelism, and when he says that Hebrews 11:1 does not serve as a definition of faith.[36] The principles by which he refutes the interpretations he discusses are of a piece with his interpretation throughout his work, including the careful reading of context, staying true to the mind of the writer, and avoiding speculative or tortured interpretations.

A subcategory of the unnamed citations is the smaller number of cases where Calvin refers to more than one alternate interpretation of particular texts. The most unusual example is First Peter 3:19, the particularly cryptic text which says that Christ, after death, preached to the spirits in prison. Calvin cites no fewer than five readings in addition to his own, attributing all of them to apparently real but unnamed interpreters.[37]

He often gives the impression of having studied a selection of commentaries, especially when he asserts that "all commentators have been misled" in a particular text.[38] Similarly, but less specifically, in many cases Calvin will cite what he says is the general or common interpretation, that the text is interpreted this way usually or by many exegetes. In other cases Calvin will make his citations more specific by referring to Greek, Latin, western, or ancient commentators. He at least wants the reader to believe that he has really seen a range of views, though Parker's notes show that in some cases the multiplicity of views can be accounted for by Erasmus' *Annotationes* along with Erasmus' translation and the Vulgate.[39] In any case, in this category Calvin's engagement with those who hold other interpretations is relatively peaceable, though he will at times call the other interpreters ignorant.[40]

Calvin is less irenic in the third category of citations where specific interpretations are cited but the purpose is polemical. The opponents are not usually named, with the exceptions of the texts noted in the first category regarding Servetus, Guillaume Postel, and Cornelius Agrippa. Calvin instead typically cites groups in his polemics, most frequently the

---

36 Hebrews 9:15, *OE* XIX:143; 1 Peter 2:12, *CO* LV:243; and Hebrews 11:1, *OE* XIX:180–181, respectively. The last text points out the fact that Calvin divides the chapters of Hebrews differently than is traditional, ending ch. 10 at v. 35 and including 10:36–39 in his discussion of ch. 11. He explains the choice at 11:1, though the Torrance edition does not follow Calvin's arrangement of the text.

37 1 Peter 3:19, *CO* LV:265–266. For similar citations of multiple views see Hebrews 6:7, *OE* XIX:95, where he seems to have the Vulgate and Erasmus' translation in mind, and James 4:5, *CO* LV:416–417. Also see 1 John 5:17, *CO* LV:373, where the alternatives appear more hypothetical.

38 Hebrews 11:3, *CNTC* XII:159, *OE* XIX:183.

39 See Hebrews 5:2, *OE* XIX:75–76, where this is the case. This is not clearly so, however, in such cases as Hebrews 6:4, *OE* XIX:90, and Hebrews 7:9, *OE* XIX:112. See also 1 John 4:7, *CO* LV:352.

40 Cf. Hebrews 9:9, *OE* XIX:138.

overlapping categories of Sophists, Papists, Sorbonnists, and the schools, followed by references to Fanatics and Anabaptists, and finally to the Jews. These passages claim that the named group interpreted a specific text to support a particular problematic doctrine or practice, or, in the case of the Jews especially, that they disagreed with a Christological interpretation of the text. In such cases, while the interpretation Calvin complains about could probably be found, it seems equally possible that he is recording what he has heard as proof texts in the previous decade and a half of controversial activity. The range of issues raised in these polemical interpretations will be discussed below under historical issues.

Fourth are cases in which Calvin's citations are fatally vague. In some cases Calvin seems to raise alternate views as rhetorical devices, putting objections in the mouth of an imagined debating partner.[41] In others, he does not make it clear whether he has actually seen the specific alternate interpretations he describes.[42] In still others he says that specific alternate interpretations exist, but he refuses to say what they are.[43] This points to a potential fifth category, surely legitimate but beyond any proof, consisting of interpretations that Calvin had seen in print but either dismissed or adopted without any explicit reference.

COMMENTARY CONCERNS

Textual matters

Parker notes that, though Calvin probably made much use of Erasmus' 1527 fourth edition of the Greek New Testament for the Hebrews commentary, "it is not possible to identify any one printed Greek text as a basic text for Calvin." He notes with some certainty cases in which Calvin's Greek citation, or more commonly his Latin translation, appears to be dependent on one or another of the Greek editions available to him. As well as that of Erasmus, and Stephanus' first edition of 1546, Parker shows cases where it is possible that Calvin was using the Complutensian Polyglot of 1522 or the 1534 edition of Simon de Colines.[44] There is as yet

---

41 E.g., 1 Peter 1:12, *CO* LV:219.
42 E.g., Hebrews 13:20, *OE* XIX:246. Parker suggests Theophylactus, Pseudo-Oecumenius, and Gorran for the first of Calvin's interpretations here, and Pseudo-Primasius for the second. See also James 2:4, *CO* LV:398, and 2:12, *CO* LV:402.
43 1 Peter 4:6, *CO* LV:274.
44 *OE* XIX:XXIV–XXVIII.

no critical edition of the commentaries on the Catholic Epistles or a similarly detailed study of the Greek and Latin texts Calvin used in their production. However, Parker's evidence suggests that, early on, Calvin made much use of the Greek text of de Colines, but that by the 1550s he favored that of Erasmus and also that of Stephanus.[45]

Parker also shows that Calvin made use of Erasmus' translation from the 1527 edition and the Vulgate.[46] He is not dependent on either one in his own Latin translation, sometimes approving of what he finds there and sometimes disapproving.

There are three issues of interest regarding Calvin's practice of textual criticism in these commentaries. The first is the pattern of frequency. The second is the degree to which he is dependent on Erasmus for manuscript variants. The third is the ways he makes his text-critical decisions.

In the Hebrews commentary he engages in textual criticism surprisingly little: only three times, and one does not actually cite the text in Greek.[47] This is as few as in any of the shorter Canonical Epistles. In First Peter there are four instances, three in First John, eight in James, six in Second Peter, and seven in the one chapter of Jude. If we can assume that the commentaries were written in the order in which they are arranged, it appears that his interest in textual criticism grew over time.

It is as difficult to be sure of the sources of Calvin's knowledge of manuscript evidence as it is to be sure which commentators he read. Parker has found cases in the Pauline epistles where Calvin's statements are so similar to Erasmus' *Annotationes* that he must have had the volume at hand for reference.[48] This is very much the case in his textual criticism here. Calvin's respect for Erasmus in this area is explicit: twice he gives credit to Erasmus for resolving text-critical problems by hypothesizing that they are marginal notes copied into the text by scribes.[49] Of the thirty-one examples of textual criticism, in sixteen cases Erasmus'

---

45 Parker, *Calvin's New Testament Commentaries*, pp. 141–147. In particular Parker was examining the 1535 fourth edition of Erasmus, and the 1550 edition of Stephanus.

46 For Hebrews, *OE* XIX:xxviii–xxx. For broader studies, including some reference to the Catholic Epistles, see Parker, *Calvin's New Testament Commentaries*, pp. 158ff. Parker's collations of references to Erasmus in these books only include nine of the instances from Hebrews, 1 Peter, and James, but the analysis is still useful.

47 Hebrews 9:1, *OE* XIX:134; Hebrews 11:35, *OE* XIX:211; Hebrews 12:27, *OE* XIX:232.

48 Parker, *Calvin's New Testament Commentaries*, pp. 148–150.

49 Hebrews 11:35, *OE* XIX:211, and James 4:[6–]7, *CO* LV:417. Cf. *Erasmus' Annotations on the New Testament: Galatians to the Apocalypse: Facsimile of the Final Latin Text with All Earlier Variants*, ed. Anne Reeve, intro. M. A. Screech (Leiden: E. J. Brill, 1993), pp. 731 and 742. Hereafter cited as *Annotations*.

Annotationes contain the variants and other relevant data that Calvin cites in his discussion.[50] In the others Calvin seems to have additional evidence beyond what is found in Erasmus, or cites issues that Erasmus does not mention at all.[51] Only one case from Hebrews, First Peter or First John appears to be independent of Erasmus, while after the fourth chapter of James Erasmus' evidence seldom plays a part. If we can again assume that Calvin wrote these commentaries sequentially he seems to show an increasing independence from Erasmus over time.

Finding Calvin's manuscript information beyond Erasmus is a task for future research. However, in seven of the cases where Calvin has text-critical discussion, Parker has collated the Greek texts of Erasmus and de Colines.[52] In six of these cases, de Colines's text provides evidence that is taken into account in Calvin's discussion, and three of these cases are among those where Calvin's evidence is clearly not from Erasmus. Further collation of Calvin's text-critical passages with the Greek texts of de Colines, Stephanus, Aldus, and the Complutensian Polyglot could prove fruitful. Since he writes confidently about the "majority" of manuscripts at times, it would be useful to get a sense of what specific evidence is not accounted for in printed editions. This would give a sense of whether he actually examined manuscripts.

Calvin makes his text-critical decisions here in consistent ways, guided by a finite set of assumptions or tacit rules about what makes a good text. The strongest argument in favor of a particular reading is that it fits the

---

50 The text-critical evidence in the following texts overlaps with Erasmus significantly or completely: Hebrews 11:35, *OE* XIX:211, *Annotations*, p. 731; Hebrews 12:27[–28], *OE* XIX:232, *Annotations*, p. 733. 1 Peter 2:18, *CO* LV:248, *Annotations*, pp. 749–750; 1 Peter 3:7, *CO* LV:256, *Annotations*, p. 751; 1 Peter 5:2, *CO* LV:285, *Annotations*, p. 755; 1 Peter 5:10, *CO* LV:290–291, *Annotations*, p. 756. 1 John 2:14, *CO* LV:318, *Annotations*, pp. 765–766; 1 John 2:22[–23], *CO* LV:325–326, *Annotations*, p. 766; 1 John 5:7, *CO* LV:365, *Annotations*, pp. 768–771. James 4:2, *CO* LV:415, *Annotations*, p. 742; James 4:[6–]7, *CO* LV:417, *Annotations*, p. 742; James 5:12, *CO* LV:430 (first of two), *Annotations*, p. 744; James 5:20, *CO* LV:434 (second of two), *Annotations*, p. 744. 2 Peter 2:2, *CO* LV:460, *Annotations*, p. 760. Jude v. 1, *CO* LV:488, *Annotations*, p. 774; Jude v. 4, *CO* LV:490, *Annotations*, p. 774. Some texts are less clear than others, e.g. James 2:18, *CO* LV:404, *Annotations*, p. 740.

51 In the following cases Calvin draws on other unnamed sources:
Hebrews 9:1, *OE* XIX:134, *Annotations*, p. 723. James 5:12, *CO* LV:430 (second of two), *Annotations*, p. 744; James 5:16, *CO* LV:432, *Annotations*, p. 744; James 5:20, *CO* LV:434 (first of two), *Annotations*, p. 744. 2 Peter 1:3, *CO* LV:446, *Annotations*, pp. 757–758; 2 Peter 1:4, *CO* LV:446, *Annotations*, p. 758; 2 Peter 1:10, *CO* LV:449, *Annotations*, p. 758; 2 Peter 1:20, *CO* LV:457–458, *Annotations*, pp. 759–760. Jude v. 3, *CO* LV:489, *Annotations*, p. 774; Jude v. 12, *CO* LV:495, *Annotations*, p. 775; Jude v. 19, *CO* LV:497–498, *Annotations*, p. 776; Jude v. 22, *CO* LV:500, *Annotations*, p. 776; Jude v. 24, *CO* LV:500, *Annotations*, p. 776.

52 Parker, *Calvin's New Testament Commentaries*, pp. 144–145. The texts are 1 Peter 3:7, 1 John 2:23, 1 John 5:7, James 2:18, James 5:12, 2 Peter 1:3, and 2 Peter 1:10. The particular words cited from 1 Peter 3:7 are not used by Calvin for textual criticism.

flow of the author's mind better than the other: he may say that the sense runs better, or it suits best, or it fits the argument, or simply that it is appropriate. Sometimes this judgment is idiosyncratic, as when a reading is preferred because it is energetic.[53] Sometimes he offers alternatives only to say that the sense is basically the same either way, and he may or may not express a preference. His priorities or rules seem objective though, not surprisingly, they seem simplistic relative to the later advances of textual criticism: For instance, he tends to favor the simpler reading, which makes intuitive sense for a commentator convinced that Scripture has a clear and understandable meaning. And he will tend to favor the reading of the majority of manuscripts, or the most broadly accepted reading, unclear as it may be what is being counted, and very clear as it is that he can have little sense of the relation of manuscripts one to the other. He strives, though, to find the oldest reading, and at times this means accepting a variant it appears he cannot find well attested in Greek on the strength of the Vulgate, as at Hebrews 12:27.[54]

Historical issues

Calvin's work in revising his commentaries is a significant aspect of their history, and also can provide windows into Calvin's interests in this period. By Parker's count revisions of the Hebrews commentary in 1551 number only 133, twenty-seven of which were reversed in 1556. The 1556 edition contained an additional 448 revisions. In all only five substantive additions were made, though another thirty changes were significant enough to have been noted in the *Corpus Reformatorum* edition.[55] The great majority of the differences between editions are small editorial changes such as the replacement of one word or phrase with another, or clarification by the addition of one to ten words. Others include the addition of Hebrew script in place of transliteration, numerous new scriptural quotations to begin subsections, and a few corrections of biblical citations.[56]

---

53 James 5:20, *CO* LV:434.

54 Hebrews 12:27, *OE* XIX:232.

55 Cf. *OE* XIX:XIII. The changes of sufficient length for Parker to note are at Hebrews 2:2, 6:17, 7:3, 7:19, and 10:30. Only the change at 7:19 was made in the 1551 edition. *CO* also notes additions or changes at 2:9, 2:10, 2:16, 2:17, 3:5 (two), 3:10, 3:12, 3:16, 4:3, 5:7, 8:13, 9:1, 9:14, 10:38, 12:11, 12:15, 12:23 (two), 12:27, 12:28, 13:1 (two), 13:2, 13:4, 13:9, 13:17, 13:18, and 13:20 (two).

56 Approximately 132 of the small changes add or affect phrases of two or more words. Corrections of biblical citation occur at Hebrews 2:11, *OE* XIX:39; Hebrews 10:1, *OE* XIX:154; and Hebrews 13:10, *OE* XIX:240. Regarding Hebrew script and versification, see *OE* XIX:XIII and XXXIII.

The changes that are more than editorial give some indication of Calvin's thinking in the process of revision and his activity between 1549 and 1556. Most are clarifications, including a number of slight expansions of theological points of interpretation, a few changes of translation and explanations of his translation choices, and occasional additions of biblical examples for illustration. One indicates growing awareness of the Greek manuscript evidence. A small number are polemical references that may indicate matters that were pressing upon him in the intervening period, notably a comment that Guillaume Postel believed himself to be Melchizedek.[57] Some of the additions tempt the reader to suspect changes in the reformer's mood day by day: In 1556 in the last two verses of Hebrews 12 he made two additions to show God as more kindly and faith as more joyful than his earlier text had indicated. By contrast, when he turned to the next chapter, the first two verses received three fairly polemical additions: one on the Jews, one on monks, and one on a perceived lack of hospitality in the current age.[58]

In the absence of a critical edition, a full picture of changes in the commentaries on the Catholic Epistles from 1551 to 1556 awaits further study. The *Corpus Reformatorum* notes forty changes from the 1551 edition in italics and footnotes. They are certainly not all the changes Calvin made. For example, a rearrangement of paragraphs in the discussion of the first verse of First John is not noted. The *Corpus Reformatorum* only indicates notable changes, but these are enough to draw a preliminary picture of the kinds of changes Calvin made. They are distributed as follows: thirteen in First Peter, twelve in First John, seven in James, seven in Second Peter, and one in Jude.[59] Assuming once more that the changes are in the order of production, Calvin was proportionately less concerned with correcting his work as he moved through these books, perhaps because their contents were decreasingly vital or problematic to him.

As in the Hebrews commentary, these changes give some hints as to Calvin's scholarly activity in the years between editions. Two passages

---

57 On manuscript evidence see Calvin at Hebrews 9:1, *OE* XIX:134. There seems to be no evidence in Postel's works for this view, though he did view himself as "Elias" and the "lower Messiah." In this period Postel did feel himself to be under Calvin's scrutiny in the wake of the Servetus affair. See Hebrews 7:3, *OE* XIX:107, and William Bouwsma, *Concordia Mundi: The Career and Thought of Guillaume Postel* (Cambridge, MA: Harvard University Press, 1957), pp. 23, 162.

58 *OE* XIX:232–234.

59 The changes in the *CO* have been verified by comparison with the 1551 edition. They are in the following texts: First Peter 2:6, 2:8 (three), 2:10, 2:25, 3:7, 3:19, 4:17, 5:3 (two), 5:4, and 5:9. First John 1:1 (four), 2:8 (two), 2:19, 2:22, 3:10b, 3:22, 4:14, and 5:16. James 2:17, 2:23, 3:7, 3:9, 5:9, and 5:14 (two). Second Peter 1:3, 1:4, 1:14 (two), 1:20, and 3:18 (two). Jude v. 2.

show Calvin's increasing awareness of the manuscript variants.[60] Two passages add biblical illustrations to his points.[61] Twenty-six of the changes are clarifications, either on theological issues in the interpretation or on translation, though three of these are simply a word or phrase. The longest is ten lines expanding on his interpretation of First Peter 3:19, Christ's preaching to the "spirits in prison," which Calvin says does not refer to Christ's descent into hell. The passage had clearly required more than usual amounts of research in the first edition, and he did not seem entirely happy with his solution even in 1556, since he notes that it conflicts with the grammar of the text. The only other clarifications of significant length are at James 3:7, where he spends almost seven lines applying the apostle's lesson on the danger of the tongue, and James 5:9, where he adds almost six lines on the dangers of taking God's name in vain. A short but significant addition is at First Peter 2:8 where Calvin reverses his earlier position on the sense of the text.[62]

More telling about Calvin's experience in these years and about his personality are the additions of a polemical nature. In 1551 Calvin had applied First John 1:1 polemically against Servetus. In 1556, after Servetus' death, Calvin made no less than four additions to this material. In 1556 James is applied polemically four times against "sophists" and their theology, and against judgmental people. First Peter is applied against the use of the term "clergy" for ministers, and Second Peter is used to continue an argument against Peter's death having taken place in Rome.[63]

The issue of polemics, then, is a major way that historical issues are reflected in the commentaries. Calvin takes nearly every imaginable opportunity to apply the text against his opponents, primarily Catholics but also Libertines and Anabaptists, and occasionally Jews and Turks. As well as finding cases where the plain sense of the text serves to contradict known points of his opponents' theology or practice, Calvin will wade in where his opponents have used the text at hand to support their own views. This, and the range of issues in his polemics, can be illustrated conveniently by the occasions in the commentary on James where Calvin cites specific interpretations of his opponents, since James seems at times the most useful of books for the Catholics. Issues include the sacraments (as when James seems to support both confession and extreme unction),

---

60 1 Peter 3:7, *CO* LV:256; 2 Peter 1:20, *CO* LV:457.

61 1 Peter 2:6, *CO* LV:236; James 5:14, *CO* LV:431.

62 1 Peter 3:19, *CO* LV:266. James 3:7, *CO* LV:411. James 5:9, *CO* LV:431. 1 Peter 2:8, *CO* LV:239.

63 1 John 1:1, *CO* LV:300–301. James 2:17, *CO* LV:404; 2:23, *CO* LV:406; 5:14, *CO* LV:431; 3:9, *CO* LV:411. 1 Peter 5:3, *CO* LV:286. 2 Peter 5:14, *CO* LV:431.

the distinction between formed and unformed faith (since James teaches that faith without works is useless), the need for merits and works in justification (since James cites Old Testament cases to this effect), the need for preparation for grace, and the limitation of mortal sin to acts rather than desires. Calvin must also counter the Anabaptists when James appears to support their opposition to oaths.[64] Examining all the cases of Calvin's polemical applications of the text would yield a rich picture of his current concerns, though these commentaries are by no means unusual in this.

Though it would be difficult to prove, there appear to be a number of cases where Calvin's frustrations over reforming his church and city are expressed in these pages. In the Hebrews commentary these would include references to the current lack of hospitality for refugees, and encouragement to Christians to be obedient to their pastors lest ministers be depressed and worn down.[65] In these and many other cases Calvin stays close to the text but seems to speak of things he has experienced.

Literary and rhetorical dimensions

In form and style these commentaries are much like the other New Testament commentaries. Calvin continues to hold his priority of clear brevity, though it is not restated here. As well as that famous principle one should also note in passing that a literary characteristic of Calvin's work here is the interconnection of these commentaries with his other commentaries and the *Institutes*. He himself is conscious of this as he writes, and he will refer the reader at times to topics treated more fully in these other works.

These commentaries also show Calvin's explicit engagement with the rhetorical tradition. Parker has noted that Calvin's interpretation of Hebrews included discerning the structure of the work by the terms of rhetoric. In the Argument Calvin states the *status causae*, the *caput*, and the *cardo*. He finds the exordium, followed by a discernment of the main argument, digressions, and exhortations, and an epilogue. Parker also notes the frequent use of the rhetorical techniques of raising a question and giving a response, or raising a difficulty and offering a solution.[66]

Calvin also used his knowledge of rhetoric as an interpretive tool on smaller portions of the text. He viewed language as a very direct

---

64 Sacraments: James 5:16 and 5:14, *CO* LV:432 and 431. Faith: James 2:14, 2:21, and 2:17, *CO* LV:403, 406, and 404. Merit: James 2:20 and 2:25, *CO* LV:405 and 407. Preparation: James 4:8, *CO* LV:418. Desire: 1:15, *CO* LV:391. Oaths: James 5:12, *CO* LV:429.

65 Hebrews 13:2 and 13:17, *OE* XIX:234 and 244.

66 *OE* XIX:XV–XVII.

expression of the mind of the author, and appears to assume that the
devices of rhetoric are inherent to language, whether the writer was
formally trained as an orator or as a Galilean fisherman. He expected all
these authors to use rhetorical devices, either consciously or naturally in
the ordinary process of speaking and writing. With these assumptions in
place, the search for rhetorical devices was a very useful means of finding
the author's intended meaning.

This is extremely typical for Calvin, so a set of examples from Hebrews
will suffice. The rhetorical devices Calvin discerns are of two general
types. First are tropes, or figures of speech such as metaphor, synecdoche,
metonymy, simile, hypallage, and paraphrase.[67] The second is forms of
argument such as an implied comparison, or argument from opposites,
proof from the nature of something, argument from the less to the
greater, reasoning from connections between things, anticipation of objections, comparison of greater and lesser things, differentiation of genus
and species, argument from sign to thing signified, syllogisms, and
reasoning from a principle to a particular case.[68] For many of these types
of devices and arguments multiple instances could be cited within the
Hebrews commentary or that on the Canonicals. They are, if not all
directly cited from the rhetorical manuals of Cicero and Quintilian, at
least recognizable adaptations of those classical writers' models.[69]

Exegetical emphases

Calvin's exegetical work here is quite typical of the New Testament
commentaries. Though it would be an illusion to think that he worked
through a predictable set of steps, he does regularly emphasize a number

---

67 Metaphor: Hebrews 3:3, *OE* xix:49. Synecdoche: Hebrews 3:17, *OE* xix:59. Metonymy: Hebrews
    4:14, *OE* xix:70. Simile: Hebrews 6:1, *OE* xix:87. Hypallage: Hebrews 6:12, *OE* xix:99.
    Paraphrase: Hebrews 7:25, *OE* xix:119.

68 Implied comparison: Hebrews 3:16, *OE* xix:16. Opposites: Hebrews 4:3, *OE* xix:62. Nature:
    Hebrews 4:13, *OE* xix:69. Less to greater: Hebrews 6:16, *OE* xix:100. Connections: Hebrews 7:26,
    OE xix:120. Anticipation: Hebrews 8:5, *OE* xix:125. Whole to part: Hebrews 8:8, *OE* xix:129.
    Greater and less: Hebrews 8:10, *OE* xix:131. Genus and species: Hebrews 9:9, *OE* xix:137. Sign to
    thing: Hebrews 9:13, *OE* xix:141. Syllogism: Hebrews 11:1, *OE* xix:180. Principle to case: Hebrews
    13:9, *OE* xix:239.

69 Cf. *The Institutio Oratoria of Quintilian*, with trans. by H. E. Butler, Loeb Classical Library
    (Cambridge, MA: Harvard University Press, 1921) viii.vi for tropes, and v.x for arguments. See
    also Cicero's *Topica* in *Cicero: de Inventione, de Optimo Genere Oratorum, Topica*, with trans. by
    H. M. Hubbell, Loeb Classical Library (Cambridge, MA: Harvard University Press, 1949), esp.
    chs. i–iv. Readers interested in more on this topic should consult Olivier Millet, *Calvin et la
    dynamique de la parole: Etude de rhétorique réformée*, Bibliothèque Littéraire de la Renaissance
    série 3 (Geneva: Editions Slatkine, 1992), esp. pp. 351–376.

of distinct things. These include work to establish the Greek text, and to make a linguistically accurate translation, as well as discussion of what the words mean in the context of the writer's work, and what the words or sentences mean in the context of the unfolding argument of the book, and indeed in light of the whole of Scripture.

Examination of a short passage in First Peter will illustrate a few exegetical emphases somewhat more distinctive to these books. First, as Calvin prepares to discuss First Peter 1:10–12, he makes an unusual declaration: "In order that each particular may be more evident, the passage must be arranged under certain propositions." He then lays out five propositions on the work of the prophets in a paragraph. These are drawn quite directly from the text, and so it is hard to fault him on the points he makes. However, his language and organization illustrate more plainly than usual Calvin's way of finding meaning in Scripture. The Bible is about doctrine, and doctrine can be summarized in propositions.[70]

Second, as he comments on the text's affirmation that the prophets searched out the time of the coming of Christ, he surprisingly adds, "Moreover, to seek particular time in prophecies seems to me unprofitable."[71] Calvin seems to oppose what Peter affirms, but the more significant thing is the priority that is reflected in the opposition: Calvin opposes speculation into eschatological matters. Admittedly, Peter was not here discussing eschatology, but Calvin's statement seems to flow from the opinon he expresses on the specifically eschatological texts in these books. Thus, on the portrayal of the violent dissolution of the world in Second Peter 3:10 Calvin dismisses exposition of the details, arguing that the author was actually only concerned with the exhortation that comes after. He condemns those who speculate on such matters as too focused on earthly things, and calls believers to focus on holy living. He softens what appear to be other predictions, as when in the third verse of the same chapter Calvin interprets a reference to the "last days" as the present age, based on a comparison with a passage in Paul.[72] Calvin does have an eschatological hope here, but it is firmly grounded in the doctrine of justification rather than in apocalyptic imagery.[73]

---

70 1 Peter 1:pre-10, *CNTC* XII:.238, *CO* LV:216. Somewhat similar attempts to organize his interpretation by enumerated points occur at Hebrews 5:1–4, *OE* XIX:74–78; 7:1–6, *OE* XIX:105–110; 8:5, *OE* XIX:125–127; 8:10, *OE* XIX:129; 11:7, *OE* XIX:189–191; and 11:27, *OE* XIX:205.

71 1 Peter 1:10, *CNTC* XII:239, *CO* LV:217.

72 2 Peter 3:10, *CO* LV:476. 2 Peter 3:3, *CO* LV:472–473. See also 1 Peter 2:12, *CO* LV:243; 1 John 2:18, *CO* LV:320–321; 2 Peter 2:1, *CO* LV:459.

73 See Jude v. 21, *CO* LV:499.

A third significant feature illustrated in these verses is Calvin's urgency to find a meaning that applies to his readers. In verse 11 the writer refers to the content of the prophets' predictions as Christ's sufferings. Calvin relates this immediately to the readers' afflictions, drawing out general truths about the cross, death, and suffering as the way to victory, life, and glory. "In short," says Calvin, "Peter does not speak of what is peculiar to Christ, but is describing the universal state of the Church," buttressing the transition by reference to the church as Christ's body and the Christian's union with him, and cross-references to Colossians three and First Timothy four. This illustrates two things generally true about Calvin's interpretation: First, the meaning he seeks is richly grounded in the rest of Scripture, particularly Paul. Second, as well as seeking a doctrinal meaning, he seeks to relate the meaning of the text to the current living of the Christian life. This may be in the form of advice for individual and corporate piety. Or it may be guidance for pastoral ministry, church reform, and polemical defense of the faith.[74]

Hermeneutical approaches

Calvin's hermeneutical views are shaped by his theological convictions about Scripture and God's work through salvation history. These convictions remain consistent throughout his commentaries, but particular commentaries can exemplify them in ways that stand out. This is the case in the First John and Hebrews commentaries.

The commentary on First John provides a particularly good example of Calvin's conviction that the meaning of any one biblical text must and will be harmonious with the rest of Scripture. Calvin understands that human authors differ in particular points and emphases, but he is guided by the theological conviction that behind or through all the human authors the clear consistent voice of God is speaking. This functions as a lively hermeneutical approach rather than a static doctrine of inspiration.

The classic description is that Calvin interpreted Scripture with Scripture, but it is somewhat more complex than that. He began with the interpretation of Romans, arguing explicitly that it would guide the interpreter to the whole of Scripture. Romans, and Paul's works in general, were taken to be clearest on the most important theological

---

74 1 Peter 1:11, *CNTC* xii:240–241, *CO* lv:217–218.

issues, especially justification by grace through faith. In significant ways Calvin then proceeded to interpret the rest of Scripture in a Pauline way, and that is seen quite clearly in the case of First John. It can also be said that Calvin's theology, as synthesized in the *Institutes*, is an attempt to organize and summarize the teachings of all of Scripture, through this Pauline lens. Therefore, when he interprets problematic passages of First John by positions argued in the *Institutes*, he was actually trying to interpret Scripture with Scripture.

The most striking example is the treatment of faith in this commentary. The text of First John is dominated by ideas of love and obedience to God's command, a call to a confident and seemingly sinless discipleship. Faith does not enter the discussion explicitly until the end of the third chapter. Faith in this letter is focused on the factual issues of the coming and identity of Jesus, and results in victory over the world. The tone and content are quite distinct from Paul's treatments of justification by faith. Nevertheless, through Calvin's eyes, this letter is about faith from its first verse. Faith is treated as the subject matter in the preface to the comments on the first verse, and again in the third, and the seventh. The text does not mention faith, but according to Calvin "the apostle here tells us to rely on faith alone."[75] In chapter 2 the "old commandment" is interpreted as the gospel by which the readers were first converted, leading to faith in Christ. Then, when the writer mentions forgiveness, Calvin emphasizes that this comes only by the free grace of Christ, noting that he "drives home the doctrine which is peculiar to faith, that this foundation may always be retained . . . we must always beware lest the doctrine of faith be smothered . . ." The call to holiness should be moderated "that faith may always retain its primacy."[76] Calvin is, in part, reading backward from the statement at 3:23 that the command is to believe. However, the emphasis on faith alone justifying by grace in Christ alone comes by reading the text of First John through Paul alone.

The text of First John presents views counter to Calvin's own, and his response can range from nuance to contradiction. Thus in the first verses of chapter two, John seems to assert two theologically problematic ideas: the possibility of sinless perfection and the universal effect of the atonement. Calvin's response to the first issue includes the assertions that sinlessness is only as much as human ability allows, and that the text's "if" anyone sins should be read as "when" anyone sins.[77] On the second issue

---

75 1 John 1:pre-1, *CO* LV:299; 1:3, *CO* LV:302; and 1:7, *CNTC* V:240, *CO* LV:306.
76 1 John 2:7, *CO* LV:313; 2:12, *CNTC* V:250, *CO* LV:316.
77 1 John 2:1, *CO* LV:308.

Calvin asserts that when the text says the atonement was for the sins of all it means only all who believe.[78] These points are true to other portions of Scripture and to his *Institutes*. When he contradicts the text, he is interpreting in light of his synthesis of biblical teaching found there. This hermeneutical approach can be seen elsewhere, but First John provides an unusual number of instances.

The letter to the Hebrews prominently shows a second hermeneutical approach rooted in Calvin's theology. His conviction that the testaments are related typologically, as shadow and reality, shapes several aspects of this work. First, his understanding of typological relationships allows him to make sense of the many citations of Old Testament texts. Taken at face value they tend to appear out of context or contorted. With the vocabulary of typology, Calvin can say that the Old Testament writer describes something that is true in exactly the way the New Testament writer uses it.[79] Second, typological relations give him a frame within which to interpret the work of Christ and the Christian sacraments in light of Old Testament roles and rites said to have foreshadowed them.[80] The text of the letter provides him a wealth of vocabulary and images for typology in relation to Christ and the sacraments, and a rich opportunity to practice typological interpretation and develop the related concepts. Though he uses this approach to Scripture in many passages throughout the commentaries, it is most clearly explored, explained, and given New Testament authority through the commentary on Hebrews.

Theological themes

The theological themes within these commentaries are as varied as the books, and so they will best be described briefly and individually, focusing first on Calvin's statements in the Arguments. In his commentary on the letter to the Hebrews, Calvin states that the book's subject matter is the office of Christ, especially his sole priesthood and sacrifice, and the great change he brought by abrogating the Old Testament ceremonial law.[81] In the commentary itself he also carries out a major program of

---

78 1 John 2:2, *CO* LV:310.
79 E.g. Hebrews 1:5, *OE* XIX:21–23.
80 E.g. Hebrews 7:1–6, *OE* XIX:105–110; 9:24, *OE* XIX:149–150.
81 Hebrews, Argument, *OE* XIX:11–13. See T. H. L. Parker, "Calvin's Commentary on Hebrews," in *Church, Word, and Spirit: Historical and Theological Essays in Honor of Geoffrey W. Bromiley* (Grand Rapids: William B. Eerdmans Publishing Company, 1987), pp. 135–140 for a study of the twofold office of Christ in the commentary.

applying these points polemically against the Roman Catholic priesthood, the mass as sacrifice, and the whole structure of ceremonies which he so abhorred.

First Peter, Calvin says, is primarily intended to move its readers to deny the world and seek the heavenly kingdom, equipping them to fight temptation. In the text of the commentary the emphasis shifts slightly to endurance in suffering and persecution. The call to look up to heaven rather than to the world, familiar from his Eucharistic theology, here seems almost a kind of refrain pointing to the essence of the Christian's spiritual life.[82]

Calvin says that First John contains teaching about the grace and benefits of Christ, especially adoption, and exhortation to holiness and love. As described above, Calvin treats these things in the context of Paul's understanding of faith, but all these themes are of value in his theology. The emphasis on love, eventually linked with faith, allows Calvin to emphasize issues of sanctification and holy living in important ways.[83]

James is not really summarized in the Argument, but cited as "a rich source of varied instruction" on Christian living. No epistle of straw to Calvin, the commentary seems to hold together around the theme of the Christian life. He seems to work at presenting a unified text, as when he interprets "teachers" as censorious critics and maintains the position throughout the third chapter.[84] Further unity comes through the process of ticking off points against Roman use of the text, and harmonization of James with Paul.

In Second Peter the focus is on calling Christians to persevere in and prove their calling by holy living, and the dangers of false teachers while waiting for Christ. In addition to the clear emphasis on Christians' need to put effort into perseverance and progress, there is a good deal of emphasis on God as the initiator of this calling.[85]

Jude is intended to keep the faithful from being corrupted by deceivers, a message Calvin says is particularly relevant to his own era. As well as doing a surprising amount of textual criticism on this little letter, Calvin attributes a great deal to Satan and shows himself impressed by the author's use of metaphor.[86]

---

82 1 Peter, Argument, *CO* LV:205. Cf. 1 Peter 1:3, *CO* LV:209; 1:7, *CO* LV:213; 1:9, *CO* LV:214; 1:13, *CO* LV:221; 2:11, *CO* LV:242; 5:4, *CO* LV:286.

83 1 John, Argument, *CO* LV:297–298. Cf. 1 John 3:23, *CO* LV:344–345; 4:7, *CO* LV:352.

84 James, Argument, *CO* LV:381–382; 3:1, *CO* LV:407–408.

85 2 Peter, Argument, *CO* LV:441–442; 1:3–4, *CO* LV:444–446, 1:9–10, *CO* LV:448–451.

86 Jude, Argument, *CO* LV:485–486; v. 1, *CO* LV:488; v. 4, *CO* LV:489–490; v. 9, *CO* LV:494; v. 20, *CO* LV:498.

Further discussion and analysis of Calvin as biblical commentator

Overall Calvin's work on these texts is similar to the rest of his New Testament commentaries. He remains clear and brief, at least by his own standards, avoiding lengthy excursuses on doctrinal topics and even occasionally referring the reader to the *Institutes*. The overwhelming feature of Calvin's exegetical work is that it is fully integrated with his theology. Indeed, interpretation of Scripture is so deeply rooted in his theology that it is difficult, perhaps anachronistic, to separate his hermeneutics and his exegesis. Both are guided by his theology, which is self-consciously drawn from Scripture itself.

Throughout he shows himself both humanist and reformer. He interprets the text with a humanist's training in languages and rhetoric, able to explore grammar and argumentation, and with a humanist's questions about the authorship and manuscript variants. At the same time his commentaries constantly show a reformer's concern for the welfare and increase of the church, as he uses all his tools for the sake of establishing true doctrine, encouraging piety, and confronting error.

Summary and conclusion

These books are, in a sense, in Paul's shadow. Calvin wrote commentaries on Paul's letters first because he was convinced that Paul's theology is clearest on the most important topics. With the important exception of the letter to the Hebrews, these letters are less important to Calvin's theology.

Hebrews is a very important book for Calvin's theology, both for its clarity on Christ's priesthood and sacrifice, and for its usefulness in undercutting Roman Catholic theology and practice. The Canonical Epistles, on the other hand, are far less crucial to him. They present many theological points that are in tension with Calvin's positions, and he must expend a good deal of energy softening, contextualizing, or contradicting such things as the emphasis on works in First John and James, and the eschatology of Second Peter and Jude. Doctrine is still important here, in multiple senses. Calvin interprets the text for a doctrinal meaning and he interprets the text in light of Christian doctrine, especially as discerned through Paul's letters.

These letters also provided a wide range of opportunities for Calvin to engage polemically with the ideas of his opponents, both when the text had been used by them and when the text could be used against them. In this these commentaries provide an interesting window into his historical moment. As is typical, his written sources are hard to discern precisely, though it seems clear that he consulted Chrysostom's homilies on Hebrews and worked with Erasmus' *Annotationes* throughout. The latter work appears to account for a good number of the instances where Calvin notes other interpreters without naming them. As a result, at times Calvin gives the impression that he has studied more works than he actually has, whether in interpretation or text-critical discussions. Perhaps he hoped to do so.

John Calvin as an interpreter of the Bible

David C. Steinmetz

When John Calvin published in 1540 his first commentary on the Bible, an interpretation of St. Paul's letter to the Romans, he joined a lively conversation that had been taking place in the Christian church ever since its inception. Paul's letter was itself a kind of commentary, a reinterpretation of stories and songs from the Old Testament, especially from Genesis and the book of Psalms. Paul was convinced that these ancient Hebrew writings had taken on a new meaning as a result of the death and resurrection of Jesus Christ.

His reinterpretation of older biblical traditions was itself reinterpreted by such stalwarts of the early church as Origen, Augustine, and John Chrysostom. Medieval interpreters repeated and revised these early insights and added their own, many of which were preserved in such standard exegetical works as the *Glossa ordinaria* and the *Postilla* of Nicholas of Lyra. By 1540 there was a substantial body of literature on Romans, including several recent works by Calvin's contemporaries. Aspiring commentators, confronted by this body of exegetical literature, might well have been forgiven if they had wondered whether there was anything fresh to say about Romans. Calvin concluded there was, but not before he had read a generous sample of the exegetical tradition, including the impressive commentaries by Philip Melanchthon, Heinrich Bullinger, and Martin Bucer.

APPROACHES CALVIN DOES NOT USE

Letter and spirit

In order to understand Calvin's place in the history of the Christian interpretation of the Bible, it may be useful to begin by describing the approaches to the Bible that Calvin did not use or that he greatly modified.[1]

For example, Calvin did not devote much, if any, attention to the traditional distinction between letter and spirit. He did, of course, distinguish what he called the "simple" or "natural" sense of the text from allegorical readings, almost all of which he regarded as inadequate. But he did not normally use the language of "letter" and "spirit" to describe the distinction between the "natural" story line of the text and a deeper "spiritual" meaning hidden beneath it.

Origen had first used the distinction of letter and spirit in order to account for what he regarded as absurdities in the biblical text. Origen found several such "absurdities" in the creation account in Genesis 1–2. He could not credit the notion that there was light and darkness before there were sun and moon and stars or that the invisible and transcendent God took an evening stroll in the Garden of Eden like a squire surveying his estate. He also resisted the suggestion that Adam and Eve were successful, however, briefly, in their almost laughable attempt to hide themselves from God. Origen did not reject the stories that contained such details as worthless but admitted they were unhistorical. The story of the creation of the world, like the parable of the good Samaritan, makes a point that is separable from the question of whether it actually happened as described. What matters for Origen in the creation story is its spiritual point, revealed by God for the benefit of the church, not its doubtful historicity. In Origen's view, God sometimes teaches the church what it needs to know through stories that are historical, while at other times he uses stories that bear only a "semblance" of history.

An absurdity in the text was an indicator to Origen that the text should be read allegorically. Allegory could be used to uncover the spiritual point in the most unpromising text, but it could not be employed successfully by the spiritually immature. Origen believed that discerning the spiritual

---

1 The observations in this concluding chapter are based in part on the excellent essays in this book and in part on my own research, especially in *Calvin in Context* (New York: Oxford University Press, 1995); "Calvin and the Irrepressible Spirit," *Ex Auditu* 12 (1996): 94–107; "Calvin as an Interpreter of Genesis," in *Calvinus Sincerioris Religionis Vindex: Calvin as the Protector of the Purer Religion*, ed. Wilhelm H. Neuser and Brian G. Armstrong, Sixteenth Century Essays & Studies 36 (Kirksville, MO: Sixteenth Century Journal Publishers, 1997), pp. 53–66; "The Judaizing Calvin," in *Die Patristik in der Bibelexegese des 16.Jahrhunderts*, Wolfenbütteler Abhandlungen zur Renaissanceforschung (Wiesbaden, Otto Harrassowitz, 1999); "The Scholastic Calvin," in *Protestant Scholasticism: Essays in Reassessment*, ed. Carl R. Trueman and R. Scott Clark (Carlisle: Paternoster Publishing, 1999); and "The Theology of John Calvin," in *The Cambridge Companion to Reformation Theology*, ed. David Bagchi and David C. Steinmetz (Cambridge: Cambridge University Press, 2004), pp. 113–129.

meaning hidden in an otherwise unedifying text was an activity that could only by pursued by interpreters who were advanced in holiness and formed by a life of prayer. Allegory was not a tool that could be safely used by a mere beginner.

Augustine's line of argument went in a somewhat different direction. Like Origen, Augustine believed that Scripture had been given to the church in order to edify it. But, unlike Origen, he was less worried about absurdities than with the failure of some quite unremarkable texts to edify, especially to edify in the three theological virtues of faith, hope, and love. When the text as letter failed to edify, Augustine believed that Christian interpreters were authorized to look underneath or beyond the "letter that kills" for the spiritual meaning that "makes alive."

The medieval church elaborated Augustine's rudimentary hermeneutical framework into an elaborate structure known as the Quadriga or fourfold sense of Scripture. In addition to the literal sense there were three spiritual senses corresponding to the three theological virtues of faith, hope, and love. The allegorical sense corresponded to the virtue of faith and told the church what it should believe; the tropological sense corresponded to the virtue of love and told the church what it should do; and the anagogical sense corresponded to the virtue of hope and told the church what it should anticipate. On this reading Jerusalem was not only a city in ancient Israel, but also allegorically the church, tropologically the faithful soul, and anagogically the heavenly city "not made with hands" that will appear at the end of time.

Theologians made a further distinction concerning the literal sense, dividing it into the literal-historical sense, which referred to events in the past, and the literal-prophetic sense, which pointed through past events to events still to come. On the literal-historical plane Isaiah 53 refers to Israel as a suffering servant, while on the literal-prophetic plane it points to Jesus Christ, whose innocent suffering redeemed the sins of the world. Both meanings were regarded as literal by interpreters like Nicholas of Lyra. Neither was considered spiritual. Both events, the suffering of Israel and the suffering of Christ, occurred in history at a specific place and time and were related to each other as type and antitype.

Calvin accepted some of the elements of this traditional approach to biblical interpretation. Like Origen and Augustine. he believed that anyone who attempted to interpret Scripture should have attained some degree of spiritual maturity and be participating in the reality to which the Bible witnesses. Although Calvin would not have put it quite this way, he agreed in general with the sentiment of Athanasius that no one could understand the mind of the saints who did not imitate their lives. Neither Calvin nor Athanasius prized distance from the text as a source of insight, much less alienation from its teaching. Just as a tone-deaf critic should not attempt to interpret the fugues of Bach, so a spiritually deaf commentator should not try to interpret the letters of Paul.

Calvin also accepted a typological reading of some passages of Scripture, which sounds, on the face of it, very much like what medieval commentators had in mind when they spoke of a double-literal sense. Calvin had no difficulty with a messianic reading of Isaiah 53 or with typological comparisons between the offering of Isaac by Abraham and the later, and far more important, offering of Jesus Christ by God the Father.

What Calvin was not keen to embrace were allegorical readings of the Bible – by which he had in mind the fourfold sense of Scripture accepted as a commonplace by medieval theologians. Calvin preferred what he called the "plain" or "natural" sense of the text. However, on closer inspection it becomes clear that Calvin's understanding of the "plain" sense was not woodenly literal. Indeed, many of the meanings that earlier commentators had ascribed to one or another of the so-called spiritual senses seemed to Calvin to be in fact the plain and natural sense of the letter itself. In his interpretation of Genesis 49, for example, Calvin identified as the plain or natural sense some readings that both Denis the Carthusian and Martin Luther had previously identified as spiritual. Perhaps it would therefore be more accurate to say that Calvin stood for a principled reduction of "spiritual" readings of the text rather than a total and unconditional rejection of them. Indeed, by modern standards, Calvin adhered to what can only be regarded as a generous reading of the "plain sense" of the text.

Sharp distinction between the testaments

Calvin was also not enamored of any interpretation that drew too sharp a line between the Old Testament and the New. The ancient heretic, Marcion, had drawn the sharpest line of all, when he insisted that the Redeemer God revealed in the New Testament had nothing whatever to do with the Creator God revealed in the Old. Orthodox churches rejected the heretical view of Marcion, while nevertheless drawing fairly sharp lines of their own. Medieval Catholic theology distinguished sacraments of the Old Testament from sacraments of the New. Sacraments of the "old law" like circumcision and Passover were only effective on the basis of the pious disposition of the participants, while sacraments of the "new law" like Baptism and Eucharist were effective on the basis of the proper performance of the rite. It was an ineradicable advantage the new covenant had over the old.

In Calvin's day Anabaptist theologians like Pilgram Marpeck described the difference between the Old Testament and the New as the difference between "yesterday" and "today." "Yesterday" ancient Jews were allowed to practice polygamy and engage in warfare. "Today" Christians are bound to strict monogamy and forbidden to engage in violence of any sort. From this perspective a "Christian soldier" was an oxymoron and the use of coercive force a lapse from the gracious world of today into the obsolete world of yesterday.

Luther tended to level the playing field between the two testaments, since in his view every generation was more or less equidistant from God. It was true, of course, that the Old Testament contained more law than the New and the New Testament more gospel than the Old, but law and gospel were found throughout the Bible. Indeed, law and gospel stood in a dialectical relationship to each other. The law was God's law just as the gospel was God's gospel. Ironically, if one should believe the judgment of God in the law without grasping the promise of God in the gospel, one could find that the last obstacle on the road to God was God himself. Luther knew therefore that one must overcome the law with the gospel and grasp from underneath God's "no" his deeply hidden "yes."

Calvin thought less dialectically than Luther. He was willing to accept the notion that there were some ineradicable differences between the Old Testament and the New but saw the transition from the old to the new more as a gentle slope than as a sharp disjuncture. For Calvin there was one covenant and one people of God in both testaments. The Old Testament differed from the New in its administration but not in its substance. That being the case, it was appropriate for the Christian interpreter to see analogies between the Old Testament and the New – such as the analogy between circumcision and infant baptism – and to find typological correspondences between events in the Old Testament and events in the New. While Anabaptists could accept typological readings of the Old Testament, they rejected any analogy between circumcision and infant baptism. Calvin embraced both.

Use of a glossed text

Medieval theologians did not lecture on the original Greek and Hebrew text of the Bible. Instead they lectured on a standard, if not yet standardized, Latin translation known as the Vulgate. This translation had been enhanced in the twelfth century with a series of glosses or running comments on the text. Glosses were of two types: interlinear, so named because they were written between the lines of a biblical text; and marginal, so described because they dominated the sides and bottom of the folio sheet on which a small portion of text was written. The vast majority of glosses were brief quotations from the writings of the early Christian fathers or carefully worded summaries of their teaching. The overall effect was to present a Latin text illuminated by comments from the leading teachers of the Christian past. The Dominican, Hugh of St. Cher, continued the trajectory of the *Glossa Ordinaria* in his commentaries, while Nicholas of Lyra, Paul of Burgos, and Matthias Döring added comments from the Jewish exegetical tradition. Denis the Carthusian in the fifteenth century presented the results of medieval reflection on the Bible in a literary form that seems more early modern than medieval.

The glossed texts were not immediately laid aside by all Protestants. Luther in particular relied heavily in his lectures on Genesis on the *Postilla* of Nicholas of Lyra. At times his lectures seem to be a running argument with Lyra or, at the very least, with the rabbinical commentators Lyra cited. Luther also wrote a preface for all the books of the Bible in his German translation, summarizing the main argument of each as a guide to the reader. The Geneva Bible, an English translation completed by Marian exiles in 1560, provided its own brief gloss in the form of marginal notes.

Probably the most ambitious attempt to provide a new glossed Bible for Protestants was the multivolume commentary, never completed, of Augustin Marlorat, a French pastor martyred in Rouen. Marlorat's commentaries consisted of quotations taken from the writings of such prominent Protestant commentators as Bucer, Melanchthon, and Calvin. To their comments, clearly identified by author, he added some of his own. Although Calvin was aware of Marlorat's project, he does not seem to have approved of it. Even the annotations in the Geneva Bible were added after Calvin's death.

CALVIN'S ALTERNATIVE PROPOSAL

Humanism and biblical interpretation

Calvin accepted without hesitation the humanist belief that the understanding of an ancient text depended in the first instance on the mastery

of the language in which it was written. Calvin therefore preferred to read
the Bible in its Greek and Hebrew originals, going so far as to take the
Hebrew and Greek text into the pulpit with him. Which is not to say that
Calvin was opposed to translation. On the contrary, he supported and
encouraged fresh and reliable translations into Latin, French, and English.
But Calvin believed that advanced interpreters, who want to understand
the mind of St. Paul and interpret him accurately to others, must first
inhabit the linguistic world in which Paul lived and thought. Translations
are, after all, rudimentary commentaries that stand between the reader
and the original text. They are useful tools but no substitute for the actual
words of the author.

Calvin's critical interests extended to questions of authorship, historical
background, philology, and rhetoric. Yet he never allowed such questions
to dominate his exegesis, which had as its constant goal the edification
of the church. The story of the migration of ancient Semites was interesting to Calvin, less out of historical curiosity than out of a sense of its place
in the unfolding of God's plan for the redemption of the world.

Calvin accepted the medieval notion that the early Christian writers
serve as important, though not inerrant, guides into the meaning of Scripture. But he agreed with humanist scholars who argued that these early
writers should, whenever possible, be read in their entirety – preferably
in new critical editions – rather than in brief quotations removed from
their original context and organized by topic. Topical anthologies had
their legitimate place – as a lawyer Calvin was only too aware of their
value for beginning students. But no one can gain a proper understanding
of an ancient writer without paying close attention to context. The same
assertion in different contexts can mean very different things.

Ancient writers provided insight into Scripture through their learning
and holiness, but their opinions, however worthy of consideration, were
no better than the exegesis on which they rested. The opinions of the early
fathers, like the opinions of Calvin and his contemporaries, were always
subject to correction by better exegesis. In the end, what was normative
for Calvin was the teaching of Scripture, correctly understood, and not
the teaching of any father, however venerable. In spite of this disclaimer,
Calvin remained serenely confident that the consensus of the fathers, or at
least of the "sounder" fathers, supported the teaching of the Protestant
reformers.

Catholic teaching during the Middle Ages represented to Calvin
a departure on many issues from the consensus of the best teachers of
the early church. The task of the Protestant reformers was to rescue the

church from medieval innovations and restore the ancient consensus which such innovations obscured. Whatever failings Protestants might have had, they had at least, in Calvin's view, avoided such innovations.

Universalizing the scholastic classroom

There were some medieval innovations, however, of which Calvin approved. While he found unsatisfactory the tendency of later medieval theologians to lecture on the glossed Latin text rather than the unglossed Hebrew and Greek originals, he did approve of their decision to treat the Bible as a textbook that should be explained in the classroom chapter by chapter, verse by verse, line by line, and word by word. Medieval preachers might comment on pericopal lessons or single texts or on texts strung together thematically. But a scholastic interpreter facing a classroom of young students liked to begin at the beginning of a biblical book, follow the order of its unfolding argument, and only declare his work of exposition done when he had reached the final words of the last chapter, however long that process might take.

Some lecture series were legendary in their length. Even Martin Luther lectured for a decade on the book of Genesis, by no means the longest series on record, Calvin did not admire long-windedness and even complained in print about Martin Bucer's tendency to be prolix. But he admired an exegetical method that followed the twists and turns of the text, attending to details and omitting no passage, however difficult. It was a method he took with him from the classroom into the pulpit, preaching through entire books of the Bible in series that stretched over weeks.

Lucid brevity

Calvin agreed with the Roman statesman Cicero that brevity was a great charm of eloquence, and thought that interpreters should combine the painstaking thoroughness of university lecturers with the no-nonsense brevity of people eager to get to the point. Of course, one could go too far in the search for brevity and get to the main point in the discussion of a text too soon by omitting consideration of its sometimes puzzling details, an error Calvin thought Philip Melanchthon had committed in his 1532 commentary on Romans.

Brevity was not a fixed measure for Calvin, an invariable quantity of words, to be used in the discussion of any subject, no matter how difficult.

Brevity varied according to the difficulty of the subject matter. One could discuss at some length a complex passage of Scripture without violating the ideal of "lucid brevity." The brevity Calvin sought was fitted to the requirements of the text, no longer than it need be, but no shorter either. Above all, the explanation should be clear, since brevity was never more than a tool to that end.

The principle of accommodation

Central to Calvin's understanding of the self-revelation of God was the principle of accommodation. By accommodation Calvin referred to God's adjustment to human limitations. Some limitations were fixed and belonged to the permanent condition of finite humankind. Others were variable, subject to historical circumstance and cultural differences. John Duns Scotus made much the same point when he distinguished *theologia in se* (God's knowledge of God) from *theologia in nobis* (human knowledge of God). "Unaccommodated man" (to borrow Shakespeare's phrase from *King Lear*) can never know God as God knows God, but can only grasp something much less. Calvin suggested that when God spoke to the prophets and apostles, he lisped.

The Bible illustrated God's accommodation to changing cultures. God did not deal with ancient Israel in exactly the same way he deals with the church. Circumcision and Passover were replaced by Baptism and Eucharist, even though all four rites were signs of what was substantially the same covenant. God meets human beings on their level and does not require them to rise to his. Revelation takes place in space and time and under the conditions of sin and finitude. The interpreter of Scripture needs to bear in mind the necessary and wonderful accommodation of God to human limitations and to realize that behind such accommodation there remains an inexhaustible and impenetrable mystery.

The hermeneutical circle

In the preface to his *Institutes of the Christian Religion* Calvin laid out the exegetical procedure he was to follow throughout his career. Because of his ideal of "lucid brevity" he was unwilling to include in his commentaries extended discussions of theological topics. Bucer had mixed both together in his commentaries. But extended discussions seemed to Calvin to deflect readers from their first task, which was to understand the plain sense of the text itself. Calvin therefore shifted all such topical discussions to the pages of the *Institutes*, where lengthy discussions would not be experienced as interruptions in the flow of exposition. As Calvin continued to write commentaries, sermons, and tracts, his biblical work contributed to a steady enrichment of his topical discussions in the *Institutes*. The *Institutes*, first published in 1536, were revised again and again in 1539, 1543, and 1550, until the final Latin edition of 1559 and the last French edition of 1560.

But just as the commentaries enriched the succeeding editions of the *Institutes*, so, too, did the *Institutes* enhance the work of exposition by providing a broad frame of reference within which to understand individual texts. The point had been made repeatedly in the early church – by Irenaeus and Tertullian, among others – that individual texts in the Bible could only be understood correctly if they were properly situated within the theological structure of Scripture as a whole. Individual texts were like stones in a mosaic. The same stones that were used by one artist to portray a lion might be rearranged by another to portray a fish. What mattered was the underlying plan.

The *Institutes* provided the underlying plan of Scripture as Calvin understood it. The *Institutes* was not merely a "sum of Christian doctrine" or, as Calvin also put it, "a sum of religion in all its parts," though it was certainly intended to be both. It was also written as a guide to Scripture so that beginners could read the Bible without becoming lost in its sometimes confusing detail. The *Institutes* uncovered the architectonic structure of the Bible, the underlying plan of the whole, that placed the details in their proper context.

All of which created what Alexandre Ganoczy has called Calvin's hermeneutical circle. As an interpreter of the Bible, Calvin moved from his commentaries and sermons on particular texts to the *Institutes* and from the *Institutes* back again to the interpretation of particular texts. Good exegesis required both attention to detail and a knowledge of the larger context in which those texts were fully intelligible.

In the end, however, the significance of Calvin's exegetical work lies less in its methodology than in its execution. Calvin's commentaries were read in his own day because they were regarded as sources of genuine insight into the meaning of Scripture. Since then fresh generations of readers have admired his work for much the same reason. In a century that produced more than its fair share of interesting and original commentators on Scripture, both Catholic and Protestant, Calvin stands out as one of the best. He was judged worth reading then. He is still worth reading now.

Index